SELVA CENTRAL

Selva Central

History, Economy, and Land Use in Peruvian Amazonia

Fernando Santos-Granero
Frederica Barclay

Translated by Elisabeth King

SMITHSONIAN INSTITUTION PRESS
Washington and London

Originally published in Spanish as *Ordenes y desórdenes en la Selva Central: Historia y economía de un espacio regional* (Instituto Francés de Estudios Andinos/Instituto de Estudios Peruanos/Facultad Latinoamericana de Ciencias Sociales—Sede Ecuador, Lima, 1995).

COPY EDITOR: Susan F. Fansler
PRODUCTION EDITOR: Deborah L. Sanders
DESIGNER: Janice Wheeler

Library of Congress Cataloging-in-Publication Data
Santos-Granero, Fernando, 1955–
[Ordenes y desórdenes en la Selva Central. English]
Selva Central : history, economy, and land use in Peruvian Amazonia / Fernando Santos-Granero, Frederica Barclay ; translated by Elisabeth King.
    p. cm.
Includes bibliographical references and index.
ISBN 1-56098-761-8 (cloth : alk. paper)
1. Peru—Economic conditions.   2. Land tenure—Peru—History.   3. Peasantry—Peru—History.
4. Indians of South America—Peru—History.   5. Agriculture—Economic aspects—Peru—
History.   I. Barclay, Frederica.   II. Title.
HC227.S3313   1998
330.985′2—dc21   98-10480

British Library Cataloguing-in-Publication Data is available

Manufactured in the United States of America
05 04 03 02 01 00 99 98   5 4 3 2 1

CONTENTS

ACKNOWLEDGMENTS

The English edition of this book owes much to Ira Rubinoff, director of the Smithsonian Tropical Research Institute, who encouraged us to have the original, Spanish edition translated. The Atherton Seidell Grant Program for the Dissemination of Previously Published Scientific Research of the Smithsonian Institution financed the translation. For this we are most grateful. We are also very thankful to Elisabeth King, who gave her best to the translation of a rather difficult text and in the process became a friend. We are deeply indebted to Susan F. Fansler for her substantial improvement of the translated version and her creative editing of the entire manuscript. We hope that through this edition the book will be available to a wider audience and that it will contribute to a better understanding of the development opportunities and the environmental risks implied in the colonization of tropical forest lands.

Numerous individuals and institutions made this book possible. First we thank Yves Saint-Geours, director of the Instituto Francés de Estudios Andinos (IFEA) until 1989, who provided us with the institutional resources and the support necessary to initiate this study. We also thank Christian de Muizon, director of the IFEA until 1995, for the invaluable personal and institutional support that he gave the project, which enabled us to secure additional funding from the Bernard Lelong Fund of France's Centre National de Recherche Scientifique.

The Asociación Interétnica de Desarrollo de la Selva Peruana, through its president at the time, Miqueas Mishari, welcomed the idea of a study of this type and made the necessary arrangements for support from the Central de Comunidades Nativas de la Selva Central (CECONSEC). We extend our profound thanks to him, to Wilfredo Gutiérrez, and to Martha Salazar—president and treasurer, respectively, of CECONSEC—for having helped us to better understand the difficult economic and political challenges that the indigenous peoples of the Selva Central confront today. Because of the scope of our investigation, we had to turn to various public and private institutions to collect the information that we required. Mario La Rosa, former mayor of La Merced, helped us to make many contacts and always offered us his warm friendship, making our stay in Chanchamayo very pleasant.

We owe our thanks to numerous institutions and individuals for their collaboration on this project. We especially thank Moisés Chávez and the personnel of the Unidad de Catastro y Titulación del Programa de Desarrollo Rural Chanchamayo-Satipo, based in San Ramón, for making us aware of the existence of, and facilitating our access to, the computerized information that they collected between 1984 and 1988. We also extend our gratitude to Roberto Koc, former chief of the Programa Nacional de Catastro in the Ministry of Agriculture, who offered us the support of the program in systematizing the information according to the combinations of variables we designated.

In the Satipo branch of the Banco Agrario, the manager, Luciano Bravo, and the chief of information, Joaquín Medina, were especially helpful. The interim manager of the Chanchamayo office of the Proyecto Especial Pichis-Palcazu (PEPP), Víctor Rivadeneira, put the documentation center of the PEPP at our disposal and constantly helped us to resolve our doubts regarding the information we were reviewing. The personnel of the Centro de Documentación en Selva Alta of the Instituto Nacional de Desarrollo, and of the libraries of the San Ramón office of the Instituto Nacional de Información e Investigación Agraria and of the Centro Amazónico de Antropología y Aplicación Práctica in Lima, offered us ample assistance in our literature search. Likewise, the directors and unit heads of the Rural Development Centers of San Ramón, Satipo, and Oxapampa were always willing to provide us with information and to respond to our queries. We offer our sincere thanks to all of them.

We are also grateful to the Servicio Aerofotográfico Nacional for permitting us to obtain and reproduce the aerial photographs of the Kivinaki area (Perené River) that are presented in Chapter 6.

We thank the Sede Ecuador de la Facultad Latinoamericana de Ciencias Sociales for giving us the time and space to get the manuscript ready for publication in book form.

Last, but not least, we thank Carlos Iván Degregori for the interest that he showed in incorporating the Amazonian question into the research agenda of the Instituto de Estudios Peruanos with the first publication of this book in 1995.

INTRODUCTION

Every book has a long history. The history of this one began in 1979 when Mario La Rosa, then mayor of La Merced, suggested through Alberto Chirif that we present the town council with a research project treating the processes of pioneer occupation of the Chanchamayo Valley. The project that we subsequently designed focused on the economic activities developed by the Peruvian Corporation Limited in their Perene Colony, based on our assumption that, since 1891, this British company had played a fundamental role in the shaping of the current economic profile of the region. Although the original project was never pursued, the idea of a study of the economic organization of the Perene Colony and its influence on the process of internal and external articulation of the Chanchamayo Valley was reconsidered and amplified by Frederica Barclay several years later, resulting in the publication of the book *The Perene Colony: British Capital and Coffee Economy in the Configuration of the Chanchamayo Region* (1989).

This interest in understanding the complex process of colonization of the Selva Central region—the "central jungle," "central *montaña*," or central portion of the Peruvian *selva alta* or high jungle—coincided with an earlier interest in the mechanisms and modes of integration of the local indigenous peoples into the regional economy. Our first approach to this phenomenon began in 1977 and took the form of an extensive field study in the Yanesha communities of the province of Oxapampa. At the time, our interest centered on the two most generalized mechanisms of their integration into the regional economy—cattle production in the communities of the Palcazu River basin and coffee production in the communities of Villa Rica—as well as on the symbiotic relationship be-

1

tween producers in both types of community (Barclay, Basurto, and Santos-Granero 1977).

The research project that we presented to the French Institute for Andean Studies and to the Bernard Lelong Fund in 1988 was shaped by these two interests. Insofar as the emphasis of the study was placed on the modes of economic integration of the region's indigenous peoples, as well as on their productive strategies and their contribution to the regional economy, it was necessary to attempt to understand the character and function of the latter. Thus, the emphasis gradually shifted from the indigenous economy to the agrarian economy of the Selva Central and the spaces that constitute it: the provinces of Chanchamayo, Satipo, and Oxapampa (see Map I.1).

This shift was facilitated by the wealth of computerized information on land use and tenure collected by the Office of Land Registration and Titling of the Chanchamayo–Satipo Rural Development Program, which had not yet been processed and analyzed. Once systematized, this information allowed us to identify the patterns of production and type of agrarian structure that had crystallized in this region, as well as to define more precisely the context in which the productive activities of the local indigenous peoples are carried out.

Finally, the analysis of the land-tenure structure and the contrast between the indigenous peoples' and colonists' patterns of production and land use led us to reflect upon the effects that the process of extensive colonization and the development of certain productive models have had on the regional environment and landscape.

It was thus that this book acquired its present structure. In the first two chapters, which constitute the first part of the book, we analyze the processes of occupation and articulation of the Selva Central as a "regional space" from the perspective of the expansion and contraction of economic fronts and frontiers that began in the 17th century and continued through to the present. Rather than providing a linear account of the important highlights of these processes, we have attempted to construct an economic history that illustrates the multiple advances and retreats, and the periods of order and disorder, experienced throughout a process that would culminate in the present configuration of the Selva Central regional space. In this first part of the analysis, emphasis is placed on (1) the struggle among the elite groups of the highland cities of Tarma, Jauja, and Huánuco to obtain the monopoly on access to the resources of the Selva Central, which were critical for the 17th-, 18th-, and 19th-century Andean economies; (2) the differences in the processes of occupation of the diverse areas that compose the region and its gradual internal articulation; and (3) the transformation of the economic connections that linked the Selva Central with the adjacent Andean regions and with national and international markets, a process by which

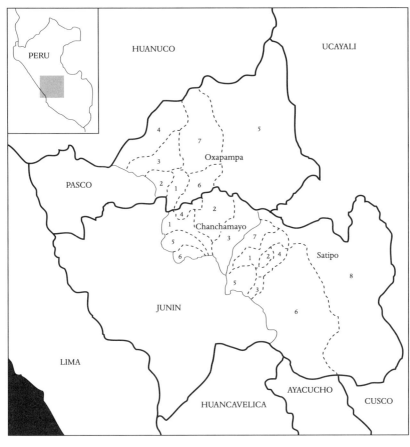

Districts of Oxapampa Province:
1. Oxapampa
2. Chontabamba
3. Huancabamba
4. Pozuzo
5. Puerto Bermúdez
6. Villa Rica
7. Palcazu

Districts of Chanchamayo Province:
1. Chanchamayo
2. Perené
3. Pichanaki
4. San Luis de Shuaro
5. San Ramón
6. Vitoc

Districts of Satipo Province:
1. Satipo
2. Coviriali
3. Llaylla
4. Mazamari
5. Pampa Hermosa
6. Pangoa
7. Río Negro
8. Río Tambo

Map I.1. Districts and provinces of the Selva Central region, 1991.

the Selva Central was transformed from being the "hinterland" of the highland town of Tarma to being a regional space with its own dynamic.

The second part of the book, composed of four chapters, is dedicated to an analysis of the characteristics of the colonist economy. Throughout the process of occupation of the Selva Central, certain patterns of production have crystallized, which have provided the region with a distinctive economic profile and have become models to be copied by the newly arrived colonists. These patterns of production — synthesized in the coffee-fruit-timber triad — are analyzed in the third chapter, both in terms of the dynamic generated by each of these activities as well as in terms of their strict interdependence. As a result, we conclude that coffee and fruit production have a simultaneously antithetical and complementary relationship with respect to timber extraction. Both types of activities lead, each in their own way, to an expansion of economic frontiers, and although their contribution to the stability of these frontiers is different, both generate local economic dynamics that deepen the levels of economic density and agglomeration of the region as a whole.

In the fourth chapter we undertake the study of the present regional order through an analysis of the land-tenure structure of the colonist sector. We have utilized unpublished land-registry information covering approximately 30 percent of the agricultural units in Chanchamayo and Satipo provinces, as well as complementary information from Oxapampa Province. The systematization and analysis of this information demonstrated the existence of an intense process of demographic pressure on the land, particularly on those that we have termed "lands with economic value." A systematic analysis of the studies that attempt to define the size of *"minifundios"* (small landholdings) in the *selva alta* (high-jungle region also known as the *montaña*) led us to define a *minifundio* as any holding of 10 hectares or less. This, in turn, allowed us to conclude that more than 50 percent of the agropastoral units in these provinces can be classified as *minifundios* and that more than 30 percent of these holdings are extremely small. This situation constitutes the framework that is necessary for understanding current land-use patterns and the negative effects that colonization has had on local ecosystems — themes that are addressed in subsequent chapters.

The fifth chapter is dedicated to the analysis of land-use patterns in a context of expanding agropastoral frontiers, highlighting the characteristics associated with the economic profile of the Selva Central. The analysis of the land-use patterns of the diverse types of agricultural units, in a context of intense pressure upon this resource, has allowed us to unveil the production constraints that the majority of agricultural units in the region are subject to. This led us to an analysis of land-use intensification in the *selva alta*, a task that involved some methodological problems that we have attempted to illustrate and solve. The contrast between results obtained in the Selva Central and those recorded for other areas of the high jungle brings into question some of the suppositions about Amazonian agropastoral development that are taken for granted by the majority of agrarian researchers in this region.

In Chapter 6, we analyze the effects that the expansion of economic frontiers has had on the regional environment. First, we present an overview of the diverse ecosystems that compose the region and the use capacity of its soils. We then analyze how severe demographic pressure on the land and the increasing number of *minifundios* have contributed to the progressive destruction of the environment because producers have had to use soils unsuitable for agropastoral activities, that is, soils appropriate only for logging (type F soils) or for conservation (type X). This phenomenon is, in turn, stimulated by the dialectical relationship between timber extraction and agricultural production, which makes forest roads the bridgeheads for the establishment of new colonists and for the initiation of agricultural activity on soils that are only suitable for forestry. Despite the fact that the negative effects of these processes are attenuated by the predominant production pattern in the region—which favors perennial over annual crops and thus more intensive land use—forest and soil degradation in the region has arrived at a point at which huge extensions of "fallow land" have, in reality, lost all of their capacity for agropastoral production. To illustrate the extent of the severe environmental degradation experienced in the Selva Central, we present a detailed study of one area in particular, Kivinaki, based on an analysis of aerial photos taken between 1957 and 1983.

A holistic analysis of the agrarian economy of the Selva Central cannot ignore the contribution of the indigenous sector, which represents approximately 20 percent of the rural population in the region. The third part of this book, consisting of three chapters, is dedicated to an investigation of this theme. Thus, in Chapter 7, we analyze the problem of the despoiling and colonization of indigenous territories in order to understand the diverse processes that have led to the formation of the present "native communities." As in the case of the colonist sector, we also analyze land availability as well as land-use patterns, which allows a comparison of the two groups. To understand the accelerated processes of economic change undergone by the native communities, we have used data corresponding to various points in time over the last 30 years. These processes form the backdrop that permits us to identify the different ways in which indigenous peoples participate in the regional economy. The analysis of these modes (in Chapter 8) has allowed us to establish that the integration of the indigenous population into the regional economy does not respond to external pressures only but also to its own economic and political strategies, which paradoxically count on economic integration to ensure a certain degree of ethnic autonomy. This phenomenon is analyzed in the last chapter through a reconstruction of the organizational process followed by the indigenous peoples of the Selva Central and a discussion of the nature and workings of contemporary indigenous movements.

The present research may appear to be somewhat untimely in that it concentrates on the study of a regional economy that is currently strongly convulsed and distorted by armed violence. If we were to undertake an investigation of the Selva Central today, it would surely be in response to different concerns and therefore would have a different focus and different goals. When we began this study in 1988, looking for answers to questions that stemmed from our initial fieldwork in the area, the terrorist violence of Sendero Luminoso (Shining Path) and the Movimiento Revolucionario Túpac Amaru (Túpac Amaru Revolutionary Movement) was limited to the peripheral areas of the region and still exerted only a weak influence over those areas that were more consolidated and stable both in demographic and economic terms. At that time, everything led us to believe that the interest of these groups in the region lay only in its strategic location, which allowed the insurrectionists to use it as a safe zone and a center of operations for attacks on targets in the Andean region.

Later events proved that these groups established themselves in the zone not only because of its strategic location but also in order to create bases for support and recruitment for their activities, with a clear objective of turning it into a "liberated area." The intensification of armed actions by these groups, both against military objectives and basic infrastructure and against the civilian population, resulted in the spread of the climate of violence from the periphery toward the more consolidated areas, introducing a new element to be considered in any study of the region. By then, however, data collection in the zone itself and from the archives had been completed and the structure of the investigation defined. Thus, although this study was not planned as an analysis of this sociopolitical juncture, it has not been able to escape it. However, although the phenomenon of violence has been touched upon in Chapters 2, 3, and 9, as well as in the conclusions, it does not have as central a role in this book as it does at present in the Selva Central. This does not invalidate the results of the investigation, but it leaves many unanswered questions regarding the type of economy and regional society that will emerge from the current period of disorder.

* * *

From our point of view, the principal contribution of this book is to fill a gap in the brief series of studies—initiated in the 1970s—that deal with the economic history and the agrarian analysis of a given region. In effect, although the importance of regional studies in poorly integrated countries like Peru have been emphasized in the past 20 years, there are still relatively few studies of this type, and of these, none are dedicated to the study of a tropical forest region. From the pioneer studies of Klaren (1970) and Burga (1976) on the *haciendas* of the northern coast to the studies of Flores Galindo (1977) and Burga and Reátegui (1981) on the economy of the southern Andes, and to the work of Montoya (1980) and Manrique (1987) on the Puquio area and the Sierra Central (central highlands), respectively, the Amazonian region has remained at the margin of efforts to reconstruct and understand the history of the country from a regional standpoint. Except for the early work of Fioravanti (1974), which, although centered on the phenomenon of agrarian unions in the La Convención and Lares valleys, presents a synthesis of the evolution of the agrarian structure of this region, and of the more recent study of Maskrey, Rojas, and Pinedo (1991), which deals with the area of San Martín, the Amazonian region seems not to have attracted the attention of researchers interested in studying Peruvian regional economies. Maybe this reflects the commonly held belief that the Amazonian region is a space without a history. The present work intends to demonstrate the opposite.

Far from lacking history, the Amazonian region has been involved in the dynamics that have shaped the country since early colonial days. Although not always systematic or successful, the efforts on the part of various economic agents from the coast and from the Andean highlands to exploit the resources of this geographic area for their own benefit contributed to the gradual incorporation of diverse Amazonian spaces that, today, are considered among the most dynamic in the country. This process has taken the form of a constant expansion of the economic frontiers toward the east, which has accelerated since the 1940s. Insofar as the concept of "economic frontier," as well as other related concepts, have already been discussed by Santos-Granero (1991a), here we limit ourselves to a presentation of its central elements. Thus, we understand economic frontier to mean the limits that separate the areas governed by the logic of the marketplace from those in which other economic forms take precedence. Understood this way, the phenomenon of economic frontiers in Peru is not restricted to the Amazonian region but is rather a reflection of a larger process that involves other geographic areas and that, because of its nature, tends toward the unification of national territory and to its articulation on the basis of the generalization of capitalist forms of production, distribution, and consumption.

In the Amazonian region, this process assumes particular characteristics, since the expansion of economic frontiers goes hand in hand with important waves of immigration and takes place through the constant opening of new economic fronts. By economic fronts we mean "a more or less well-defined vanguard space that is barely or loosely linked to that portion of the national territory where the laws of the marketplace predominate and that has limited links to other, similar areas, where a variety of agents from outside of the zone establish themselves, temporarily or permanently, with the goal of promoting or carrying out mercantile activities" (Santos-Granero 1991a: 229). However, the process of the opening of new fronts and expansion of economic frontiers is not always identical in its rhythms or constant in time. Not all Amazonian spaces have been affected in the same way by this process, and the latter has been marked by important advances and setbacks. The history of Amazonian spaces is, therefore, the history of the advances and setbacks of the market agents and market forces in their effort to incorporate the former into their own dynamic.

As a result of this process, which, in some areas, goes back to the 16th century, several regional orderings have taken place. Each of these has its own characteristics, in terms of relations of production and forms of property, type of resources exploited and modes of exploitation, structures of economic and political power, and forms of social stratification and segmented identities that have arisen. However, as a result of their marginal status, and the weakness of their institutional foundations, and because, until recently, the State has not always managed to establish itself effectively in these spaces, these orderings have been characterized by their fragility and instability. Thus, the history of these spaces seems to be marked by an alternation of periods of order and periods of disorder—hence the title of the original, Spanish version of this work.

In the case of the Selva Central, these orders and disorders, which are part of the structuring of Amazonian spaces, have led to the progressive articulation and configuration of this zone as a regional space. This term refers to a space where the articulation or interconnection of old economic fronts and the advance of economic frontiers have made possible the existence of a stabilized spatial nucleus, with a high degree of economic density, defined in terms of the intensity of economic transactions in a given space, in which market relationships predominate and where, to various extents, the markets for land, labor, goods, services, and capital have become generalized. The concept of a regional space is situated at an intermediate point between that which Gonzales de Olarte (1982) has defined as a "mercantile space" and that which he has defined as a "region." In this sense, the Selva Central would be more than a mercantile space, which already participates to a certain extent in the market dynamic but which assumes the form of a hinterland of an already developed region, and less than a region, or space fully incorporated into a capitalist dynamic with particular internal and external articulations that distinguish it from other similar spaces. Having defined the concept of regional space, it is fitting to note, however, that throughout the text we will occasionally employ the term region either in a geographic sense or as an abbreviated form of "regional space."

The second contribution of this book is related to the level of detail of the information used, as well as the constant evaluation of its origin, quality, and reliability. Given the deficiencies in the agrarian statistics provided by official sources, the limitations of the information that results from small-scale studies, the flagrant contradictions between the data furnished by different sources, and the inappropriate ways in which these are frequently put to use, we have been extremely cautious in indicating the limitations and scope of the information we use. For this same reason, we have placed special emphasis on quoting in detail all sources that we have employed, as well as explaining the methodological procedures that we have used to assemble the tables and statistics presented here.

On the other hand, the computerized information on land tenure and land use collected by the Chanchamayo-Satipo Rural Development Program has allowed us to access detailed information about these subjects not only at the provincial level but also at the district level. This, in turn, has allowed us to make important distinctions among the various districts that compose these provinces, as well as to refine the conclusions at which we arrived. Furthermore, access to this type of information has allowed us to make interesting correlations, such as those between degree of minifundization and demographic pressure on "lands with economic value," and those between length of occupation and the processes of intensification and deintensification of land use. Finally, this sort of detailed information has allowed us to question some of the assumptions and generalizations frequently encountered in previous studies on the Amazonian basin. In this sense, we hope that the conceptual and methodological contributions of this work stimulate not only a discussion about the more adequate approaches needed to understand the processes of regional configuration in the Amazonian basin but also the undertaking of new regional studies from the perspective of economic history and agrarian analysis.

PART ONE

GENESIS OF A REGIONAL SPACE

In the last several decades, various works that deal with the post-Hispanic history of the Selva Central have been written. Apart from the classical sources—chiefly Franciscan accounts that chronicle the events that marked the rise and fall of the missions (Córdoba y Salinas 1957; Rodríguez Tena 1780; Biedma 1981; Amich 1975; Izaguirre 1922-1929)—a number of other general and specific regional histories have been produced. Among the more general works are the historical accounts of the region written by Father Dionisio Ortiz (1961, 1967, 1969, 1978, 1979), as well as the historico-ethnographic studies by Varese (1973), Lehnertz (1970), Santos-Granero (1980), and Renard-Casevitz, Taylor, and Saignes (1988). Among the more specific studies are those by Tibesar (1950, 1952), Smith (1976), Santos-Granero (1985, 1986, 1987, 1988, 1991b), and Zarzar (1989), which treat the colonial period, and studies of the republican period by Bodley (1976), Barclay and Santos-Granero (1980), Shoemaker (1981), Manrique (n.d.), Fernández (1986), and Barclay (1989). All of these works have contributed to a broad reconstruction of the history of the region from both a historical and an anthropological perspective.

In Part One we will not attempt to synthesize this literature but rather to present the data in a systematic way that will permit us to visualize the processes both of occupation and configuration of the Selva Central. We differentiate between these two processes, insofar as not every area that undergoes a process of occupation becomes a "region" or a "regional space." Although, in general terms, both processes take place concurrently, a given area may be occupied gradually over an extended period of time before it becomes internally and externally articulated as a distinct regional space. In the case of the Selva Central, this latter phenomenon did not crystallize until the 1970s, more than 300 years after the arrival of the first Franciscan missionaries. Until then, this geographic space had been occupied in a piecemeal fashion, and only Chanchamayo, one of the areas that forms it, took the character of an "articulated" regional space, at the same time that it showed signs of becoming the "articulating" space of what we define, in this study, as the "Selva Central."

By "occupation" we mean the appropriation of any given space. In the case of the Selva Central, this turns out to be a complex issue because the space was already inhabited by indigenous populations when colonial expansion to the east began. Therefore, when we speak of occupation, we refer not only to the standard dictionary definition—"possession, settlement, or use of land or property" —but also to how the responses of the indigenous population have affected these modes of appropriation. Appropriation has both a physiogeographic dimension and a juridico-ideological one. The concrete manifestation of these dimensions in any particular case will determine whether a given regional space will or will not become configured as such, as well as the characteristics that it assumes once it is configured.

The history of occupation of the Selva Central may be divided into two extended periods: colonial and republican. The colonial period may be subdivided in turn into two stages: missionary settlement (1635-1742) and indigenous reconquest (1742-1847). The republican period is also composed of two major stages: pioneer settlement (1847-1947) and mass settlement (1947-1990). In analyzing these stages, which culminate in the complex and still-unresolved current situation, we will take into consideration the behavior of the variables that form the two dimensions of the process of occupation that we have already mentioned. For the moment, we will limit ourselves to the presentation of these variables as well as to the discussion of their interrelationship.

The physiogeographic dimension of any given process of occupation is often treated in a more detailed fashion than are others because its effects are more visible and easier to evaluate. There are three important variables related to this dimension. The first is human occupation itself, which we will consider in terms of demographic analysis and the crystallization of specific social landscapes. Thus we will not only quantify absolute population growth but also consider specific indexes that will allow us to understand the nature of population fluxes and settlement patterns. The second variable is production, which refers to the activities carried out by this population in relation to its environment. It is thus important to determine the development of the different modes of use of the space and its resources, which in turn defines the regional economic landscape. If these first two variables allow us to determine the cumulative rhythm of the appropriation of a given space, the last variable, which refers to the expansion of communication networks, allows us in contrast to establish the rhythm of internal articulation between zones that form a given space and their external articulation with the markets and spheres of power that encompass it. It should be borne in mind, nevertheless, that occupation and communications are phenomena that, although they go hand in hand, are independent. In some cases, as we will see, the establishment of an important population center results in the establishment of the means of communication that will make its articulation possible, whereas, in other cases, the establishment of such means of communication drives the occupation process.

Not often considered, perhaps because of the difficulty in disentangling its complexities, is the juridico-ideological dimension of appropriation. Once again, we encounter three variables to evaluate. The first is related to the ideological discourse that upholds the actions of the diverse agents of occupation over time. A complete understanding of these arguments inevitably leads to an analysis of the political, economic, and social structures—both global and local—in which these agents are involved: in this case, the colonial and republican states, as well as the spheres of regional power linked to the neighboring Andean cities of Tarma, Huánuco, and Jauja.

Ideological appropriation is inseparable from physical appropriation, insofar as it provides the elements to legitimize the right to occupy a given space that a certain population exercises and the mechanisms it employs. This dimension is even more crucial in the case of the Selva Central because it was previously occupied. As we will see, the terms in which the diverse agents or centers of power legitimized their claims did not always coincide. The ideology of occupation is not and has never been monolithic and has given rise to contradictions whose resolution has gradually shaped the face of the region.

The second variable that we are interested in examining is the "verbal" appropriation of the space, a subtle process by means of which the agents of occupation claim a territory by naming geographic features (such as rivers, hills, lakes, and settlements) that were previously named. In the same way that the landscape is "domesticated" when its land and resources are used for new forms of production, it is domesticated in this case through the imposition of new names. The reverse of this practice, which occurs more frequently when the occupation of a space has already been consolidated, is to appropriate indigenous names in order to name features, entities, or things that are the exclusive creation of the occupying agents (such as restaurants, stores, transport companies, and trademarks). In most cultures, the act of naming constitutes a sacred creative act that gives shape and existence to a given reality. In contrast, in the context of previously occupied and therefore "named" areas, the act of naming, or more specifically, renaming, appears as an act of despoliation and alienation.

The last variable that we will take into consideration is the juridical. In the realm of law, this variable gives shape to an act of physical or ideological appropriation that has already taken place or that will take place and thus reinforces both the domestication of a given space by means of its actual occupation as well as its domestication through verbal acts. Expression of physical appropriation is the profuse legislation on tropical lands that, in some cases, provides legal instruments for the occupation of supposedly "unoccupied" lands and territories and, in other cases, sanctions, regulates, and structures this process. Expressions of ideological appropriation are the internal political and administrative divisions that are gradually imposed and that constitute a sign of the complete incorporation of the region. Finally, as we will see, both aspects converge in the creation of legal terminology such as "native community" *(comunidad nativa)*. The analysis of the evolution of the process of territorial demarcation will allow us to understand changes in power relationships within the region and between it and neighboring regions.

The simultaneous analysis of these variables for each historical stage will allow us to identify not only advances and retreats in the process of configuration of the regional space in the terms in which we defined it in the introduction but also the periods of "order" and "disorder" that this regional space has experienced. In effect, this process has not been linear, insofar as the occupation attempts in each period were not motivated by the same objectives, and therefore their effects were not always cumulative. Furthermore, the often successful indigenous response created interruptions in the process, some of which lasted for quite some time and allowed the indigenous peoples to retake control of their territories. To its lack of linearity one should add the conflictual character of the process of configuration of the Selva Central, which has given rise to times of order, in which a certain stability and climate of peace have prevailed, and times of disorder, when the region has become unstable and violent.

In spite of these characteristics, it is possible to discover some sort of thread that runs through the process of occupation of the Selva Central. This appears as a kind of leitmotiv and is expressed in recurring actions and discourses, some of which have objective bases and others of which are merely ideological. Among these we can mention the supposed emptiness of the Amazonian region and the need to occupy it, its inexhaustible riches and the necessity to exploit its potential, the isolation of the Selva Central and the necessity to ensure sovereignty over it, and finally the supposed savageness of its inhabitants and the need to "civilize" them. But apart from these recurring themes, the analysis of the process of configuration of this regional space reveals that the elements that were to determine its current extent and boundaries were already present in the first stage of occupation.

1

CONQUEST AND INCORPORATION IN
THE COLONIAL PERIOD

The Selva Central, traditional homeland of the Yanesha and Ashaninka indigenous peoples, was not affected by the military and political events that resulted
in the destruction and subjugation of the Inca empire and remained unexplored
by the Spaniards until well into the 17th century. It is difficult to establish why
this area, the tropical forest space closest to the capital of the viceroyalty of Peru,
did not attract the attention of the conquistadors until such a late date. When
the first Franciscan missionaries arrived in 1635 at the Cerro de la Sal, a hill cut
through by a large salt vein located in the boundaries of the Yanesha and Ashaninka territories, there were already old Spanish settlements in several other
regions of Peruvian Amazonia: to the north, Jaén de Bracamoros, which was
initially founded in 1536, and Santiago de los Ocho Valles de Moyobamba,
founded in 1540; and to the south, San Juan de Oro, founded sometime between
1540 and 1553 (Santos-Granero 1992: 81–104).

Various factors could explain their lack of interest. First, although there is
evidence of a long tradition of contact between the highland and lowland populations of the central Andes, there is no evidence that the Andean peoples were
ever able to conquer their Amazonian neighbors or establish colonies or trading
outposts in their territory. That none of these occurred in the Selva Central, in
contrast to what took place in the northern and southern Amazonian regions,
seems to be related to the lack of important pre-Inca population centers in the
neighboring Andean highlands (see Maps 1.1 and 1.2).

This brings us to the second factor. Although in the Inca period there were
often successful attempts to conquer the Amazonian lands that constituted the
natural areas of expansion of large Andean population centers, in the Selva

15

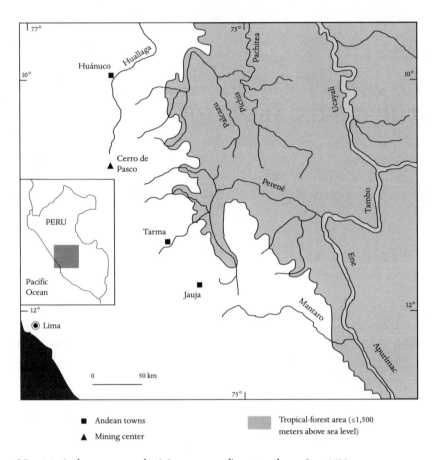

Map 1.1. Andean towns and mining centers adjacent to the region, 1630.

Central the situation was different. The area of expansion of the Inca town of Huánuco was the Huallaga Valley, north of our study area; Tarma was an Inca storage center of little importance; and the prosperity of the larger center of Jauja was based, for the most part, on the control it exerted over the rich Mantaro Valley in which it was located. During the first century after the conquest this situation remained unchanged, and none of these Andean centers seem to have had the interest or the capacity to incorporate the neighboring tropical valleys of Chontabamba, Paucartambo, Chanchamayo, Perené, or Satipo. Last but not least is the fact that almost all the initial Spanish settlements in the Peruvian Amazonian region were in areas that were rich, or supposedly rich, in gold deposits. In contrast, the Selva Central was never known as a region rich in precious metals.

How do we explain, therefore, the sudden interest sparked by the Selva Central in the middle of the 17th century? An important part of the answer lies in the opening of silver mines in the neighboring Andean area of Cerro de Pasco (see Map 1.1). According to Fisher (1977: 26), these mines "that were to become the most important in South America following those in Potosí, began to operate in 1630"—that is, five years before the arrival of the missionaries. The exploitation of the mines at Cerro de Pasco had an immediate effect on the volume of silver production of the viceroyalty. According to records of silver shipments from the port of Callao, in the period between 1620 and 1630 an annual average of 1,321,620 *pesos* were sent to Spain. Immediately after the opening of the Pasco mines (1632–1642), this rose to an annual average of 2,282,000 *pesos,* an increase of roughly 72 percent (Fisher 1972: Table 2). Although these data should be regarded with caution, insofar as the volume of silver shipped fluctuated according to the quantity that was deducted from the total to cover government expenses, they seem to indicate that the contribution of these mines to the total production of the viceroyalty was substantial from the very start of their operations. Moreover, their relative importance seems to have been maintained throughout the 17th and 18th centuries. In 1776, the Pasco mines continued to compete with those in Oruro for second place in silver production after those in Potosí (Fisher 1977: Table 3). This fact, as we will see, had a significant effect on the orientation of the production of the Selva Central region during colonial times.

The opening of the Cerro de Pasco mines and the speed with which they acquired prominence resulted in a major population influx into what until then had been a sparsely inhabited highland area, while simultaneously seizing the attention of the inhabitants of the city of Huánuco, under whose jurisdiction the mines operated. Since the beginning of the 17th century, the *encomenderos* (Spaniards who had received in custody an *encomienda,* or group of Indians as a reward for services rendered to the Crown) from Huánuco had already manifested their interest in the zone, from which they could control the natural entrances to the tropical valleys of Huancabamba, Chontabamba, and Paucartambo. Thus, Don Fernando Tello de Sotomayor, an important gentleman from Huánuco and *encomendero* of the Chinchaicocha area since at least 1616, owned an important *obraje,* or wool mill, in the town of Paucartambo, located at the headwaters of the river of the same name, which directly connects the Pasco range with the Cerro de la Sal (Varallanos 1959: 268). The economic growth that resulted from the exploitation of the silver mines, and the prosperity that this brought to the elite of the *corregimiento* (area under the jurisdiction of a *corregidor,* who was in charge of collecting tributes for the Crown) of Huánuco, stimulated expansion toward the neighboring tropical areas. It is not, therefore, a mere coincidence that the first missionaries who explored the Selva Central came from the Franciscan convent located in the city of Huánuco.

But to attribute these initial missionary expeditions solely to the mining development in Pasco and to the economic interests of the Huánuco elite is not entirely correct. One hundred years after the conquest of the Inca empire, the surviving indigenous population had already been evangelized and Christianized. The clergy who accompanied the conquistadors from the outset—as well as missionaries of the Dominican, Franciscan, Augustinian, and Jesuit orders (since 1567 the only orders permitted by royal mandate to operate in the New World)— were instrumental agents in this process.

As a result of this regulation and the establishment of *reducciones* (the concentration of indigenous populations in small towns) by Viceroy Toledo beginning in 1570, the Crown managed to impose order in both the secular and religious administration of the coastal and highland indigenous populations. Sixty years later this process had culminated, and it seems that a consensus was achieved between the religious orders—principally the Jesuits and the Franciscans—to undertake the task of converting the indigenous inhabitants of the marginal areas of the viceroyalty.

MISSIONARY SETTLEMENT AND EARLY ARTICULATION: 1635–1742

The first step in this direction was taken by the archbishop of Lima, who, in his visit to the city of Huánuco in 1626, managed to baptize the chief of the Panatahua, an indigenous group that occupied the tropical lands of the upper Huallaga Valley (Santos-Granero 1985: 25). The landmark events of this missionary advance toward the Amazonian frontier occurred in rapid succession. In 1631, the Franciscans assumed the task of converting the Panatahua and the other indigenous peoples of the Huallaga basin. In 1635, the first Franciscans entered the Selva Central by way of the Pozuzo River, giving rise to the future *conversiones*, or mission territories, of Huánuco, Tarma, and Jauja. In 1636, the first Jesuits arrived in the city of Borja, on the upper Marañón River, in order to take charge of what would become the famous Maynas missions.

In the short space of 10 years, the Crown and the Church put the evangelical machinery into motion, this time directing its efforts toward the Amazonian region. The alliance between secular and ecclesiastical power that resulted from a series of concessions that Rome made to the Spanish Crown had culminated, in 1508, in the dispatch of the papal bull *Universalis ecclesiae*, which explicitly conceded the Right of Patronage to the kings of Spain and their successors (Trujillo Mena 1981). However, this alliance was not always harmonious. The abuses that the Spanish committed against the indigenous population set off various calls of alarm in religious communities in America. Allegations in defense of indigenous rights and in opposition to the *encomienda* system by Father Bartolomé de las Casas, made public in 1539, were to have a great influence on the Leyes Nuevas (New Laws) promulgated by Carlos V in 1542 (Santos-Granero 1992: 108-109). They limited the power of the *encomenderos* and established less onerous forms of tribute. In the following years, the dictum of Las Casas—that "the only method to call all peoples to the true religion is that of Christ: the preaching of the Gospel by missionaries escorted by unarmed soldiers, sent 'like sheep among wolves'"—was gradually accepted (Bataillon 1976). This was expressed in two royal decrees issued in 1550, through which all new exploration and conquests were suspended until further notice (Santos-Granero 1992: 120). In 1573, the Las Casas ideal triumphed, as Philip II issued the *Ordenanzas sobre nuevos descubrimientos y poblaciones* (Statute on New Discoveries and Settlements), which established peaceful expeditions by missionaries as the most efficient means for the conversion of indigenous populations and the colonization of new territories (Santos-Granero 1992: 118-120). It is in this legal and ideological context that the incorporation of the Amazonian region into the colonial domain was undertaken.

In the Selva Central, the first stage of this process—which lasted until the end of the 17th century—had very irregular results, due, in large part, to indigenous resistance but also to the conflicts that arose among missionaries of various orders, between missionaries and soldiers of fortune, and among the elites from Tarma, Jauja, and Huánuco who disputed their hegemony over the region. Local confrontation between Franciscans and Dominicans arose because the Crown did not specify which of these orders ought to take charge of the new *conversiones*. When the Dominicans arrived in Chanchamayo in 1646, the Franciscans had already made two unsuccessful attempts to establish themselves in the valley: in 1635-1637 and in 1640-1644 (Amich 1975: 45; Biedma 1981: 71). The competition between the two orders was accentuated by the rivalry between Huánuco and Tarma. The Franciscans established their headquarters in Huánuco and controlled the *doctrina* (parish of newly converted Indians) of Huancabamba as their primary religious outpost in the Selva Central, while the Dominicans had their headquarters in Tarma and controlled the *doctrina* of Acobamba (Santos-Granero 1986: 128-129). In terms of the politico-administrative hierarchy, the Franciscans were in a better position, since Huánuco, as a city and a Spanish *corregimiento,* had jurisdiction over Tarma, which was categorized as a town and an Indian *corregimiento.* In terms of administrative and evangelical efficiency, however, the Dominicans had the upper hand. They were the first to establish a combined system of Andean and tropical *haciendas* (large landholdings) in order to support their missions (Santos-Granero 1986: 126-129); and they invested large sums in the construction of two roads that linked the Chanchamayo Valley with the towns of Tarma by way of Yanamayo, and Jauja by way of Monobamba. Thus, the triad of Andean cities that would vie for control of the Selva Central was complete. The influence of Jauja was to expand, beginning in 1673 with the successive expeditions that Father Manuel Biedma undertook from this town by way of Comas to convert the indigenous peoples of the Satipo Valley (Biedma 1981: 28).

But the missionaries were not the only colonial agents who were interested in the Selva Central during this century. In spite of the triumph of the Las Casas doctrine with respect to new conquests, the 17th century was a century of transition, during which the colonial administration still oscillated between offering its support to evangelical missions and providing it to military expeditions. The incursions of Martín de la Riba Herrera into the lower Huallaga and the upper Marañon River valleys and those of Pedro Bohórquez into Chanchamayo and Cerro de la Sal—both around 1650—constitute a manifestation of the old, and by then already anachronistic, spirit of adventure shared by the first conquistadors who were attracted by American gold. Bohórquez's main expedition took place a few years after the establishment of the Dominican missionaries in the Chanchamayo Valley. Exhibiting the license granted to him by Viceroy Salvatierra, the conquistador initially obtained the support of the missionaries. But his continual abuses of the indigenous converts living on the missions and his authoritarianism won him their enmity. The protests of the Dominican order before the viceroy resulted in Bohórquez's arrest and exile to the fort at Valdivia in Chile (Santos-Granero 1986: 132). With this, the era of military conquest during the colonial period was put to an end. In the future, the missionaries resorted to armed force only to put down uprisings or to inspire fear among the indigenous peoples, but the troops employed were always subject to the religious authority of the *comisario de misiones* (the head of the missionary territory).

In spite of the fact that the Dominicans persisted in their evangelical work after Bohórquez's incursion, his presence had generated so much unrest that the missionaries were forced to withdraw in 1669 (Santos-Granero 1986: 129). In the following years, the Franciscans retook the initiative, but not until the beginning of the 18th century did they achieve their goal of firmly establishing themselves in the region.

Aguardiente, Coca, and Textiles: Pillars of the Missionary Economy

During the 17th century, none of the attempts of Franciscan and Dominican missionaries to subdue the indigenous population were successful. The intense resistance of the Yanesha and Ashaninka, vacillation on the part of colonial authorities (who just as readily supported evangelical projects as military expeditions), and disputes among religious orders combined to cause these failures. Only in 1709, with the arrival of Father Francisco de San Joseph in Peru, was the evangelization of the Selva Central undertaken, this time successfully. It was San Joseph who established the guidelines for the organization of the mission towns, as well as the internal administrative structure that the new mission territories were to assume. Perhaps in order to reduce the conflicts of interest between the elites of the three Andean cities that were attempting to monopolize control of the region, San Joseph made incursions from each of them. In 1709, he set out from Tarma to found the Ashaninka mission of Quimirí in the Chanchamayo Valley and the Yanesha Mission of Cerro de la Sal in the Paucartambo Valley. In 1712, he entered the Pozuzo Valley from Huánuco, reducing the Yanesha population in the mission towns of Pozuzo and Cuchero. Finally, in 1713, he entered the Pangoa and Satipo valleys from Jauja, founding the Sonomoro Mission with Ashaninka and Nomatsiguenga peoples (Amich 1975: 118–120).

The establishment of these missions gave rise to three *conversiones:* Huánuco, Tarma, and Jauja. These mission territories were dependent on the *corregidores* of each of these cities for administration and on the *comisario de misiones,* who had jurisdiction over all of them, for religious authority. With the creation of the hospice and convent of Santa Rosa de Ocopa in 1725, all of the evangelical activity in the region was directed from there. By 1730 the three *conversiones* had almost acquired their final configuration. The Huánuco *conversión,* which, in what corresponds to the Selva Central, was entirely populated by Yanesha, included four mission towns in addition to the parish of Huancabamba. The Tarma *conversión,* which included parts of the Yanesha and the Ashaninka territories, had six missions, among which Cerro de la Sal was the most noteworthy. Finally, the Jauja *conversión,* located in Ashaninka and Nomatsiguenga territories, comprised three missions (Amich 1975: 123–124) (Map 1.2). In subsequent years, the total number of missions increased, in particular because of the evangelization of the Ashaninka from the Gran Pajonal beginning in 1733. In 1739, there were already 10 small mission towns in this area that was under the jurisdiction of the Tarma *conversión* (Amich 1975: 141).

In contrast to the ephemeral occupation attempts of the 17th century, in the first half of the 18th century the process of missionary occupation was accompanied by the establishment of large and medium-sized *haciendas* and the arrival of numerous Andean peasants. The largest number of estates was concentrated in the Vitoc and Chanchamayo valleys, which belonged to the Tarma *conversión.* According to a report by Intendente Juan Ramón Urrutia y Las Casas (1808: 446), who was the supreme authority of Tarma in the declining years of Spanish colonial rule, during the first half of the 18th century there were seven large *haciendas* in the Vitoc Valley, all belonging to citizens of Tarma, except for Colpa,

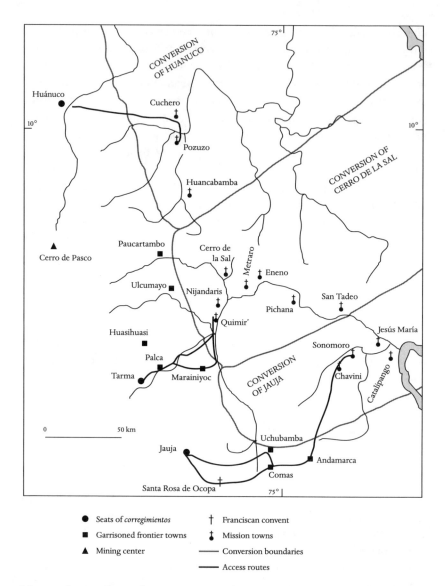

CONVERSION OF HUANUCO

Huánuco
10°
Cuchero
†
Pozuzo
†

Huancabamba
†

CONVERSION OF CERRO DE LA SAL
10°

Paucartambo
Cerro de la Sal
Metraro
▲
Cerro de Pasco

Ulcumayo
Nijandaris
†
Eneno
†
San Tadeo
†

Pichana
†

Quimir′
†

Huasihuasi
■

Jesús María
†

Sonomoro
Catalipango

Palca
■
Chavini
†

Tarma
Marainiyoc
■

CONVERSION OF JAUJA

0   50 km

Uchubamba
■
Jauja
Andamarca
■

Comas
Santa Rosa de Ocopa
†
75°

75°

● Seats of *corregimientos*   † Franciscan convent

■ Garrisoned frontier towns   ╪ Mission towns

▲ Mining center   ·········· Conversion boundaries

                              ——— Access routes

Map 1.2. Access routes and mission towns in the Franciscan conversions, 1730.

which was owned by the Ordoños family from Jauja. In the upper fringes of the Chanchamayo Valley there were four *haciendas:* Chanchamayo, which belonged to the Dominican college of Santo Tomás de Lima and was dedicated to coca and sugarcane cultivation; the tobacco *hacienda* of Juan Baos y Trujillo; a *hacienda* by the name of Ocsabamba; and the *hacienda* of José Arnedo, the lieutenant governor of frontiers (Urrutia 1808: 445; Loayza 1942: 90). In addition to these holdings, there were numerous *chacras* (small farm plots) belonging to the inhabitants of the small Andean village of Sayria. In the lower part of the Chanchamayo Valley there were two large estates, one near the Nijandaris Mission and dedicated to the production of cocoa, coffee, coca, and annato, as well as several nearby smaller holdings that produced sugarcane and were close to the Quimirí Mission (Urrutia 1808: 445–446).

In the Huánuco *conversión,* there were at least two large *haciendas:* a coca-producing holding that belonged to a local mine owner by the name of Sandoval and was located in the Huancabamba Valley (Ortiz 1967: vol. 1, 169), and the one belonging to the Count of Las Lagunas, which comprised all the area north of the Cerro de la Sal and the Chorobamba Valley, Parara, and Lucén (Urrutia 1808: 446). The Count of Las Lagunas, descendant from an old line of Huanucan *encomenderos,* also owned a wool mill in the Andean town of Paucartambo and had mining interests in the Cerro de Pasco area (Varallanos 1959: 230, 259, 268, 346). In addition to these *haciendas,* there were numerous smaller *fundos,* or medium-sized farms, in the Pozuzo area dedicated to coca cultivation. The volume of the coca production of this area must have been quite significant, for the chronicles of the period report that a road was opened with great effort "in order to be able to enter on horseback so as to facilitate the sale of coca, which the neighbors from Huánuco come to buy" (Amich 1975: 119).

The Franciscan missions of the period were also dedicated to the cultivation of coca and to the cultivation of sugarcane for the production of sugar, molasses, and *aguardiente* (an unrefined liquor). Several sources mention that the Franciscans had extensive cane fields in the Quimirí Mission, and an inventory of the mission records the existence of a "bronze sugar cane mill with two heads, all new" (Rodríguez Tena 1780: 836). These sources also mention the existence of another cane mill at the Eneno Mission near the Cerro de la Sal. Production of commercial crops, such as coca and sugarcane, as well as of subsistence crops took place on "mission lands," where new converts were required to work for three days per week (Santos-Granero 1980: 107). It is difficult to estimate the volume of coca and *aguardiente* production on the missions. However, in a document from the second half of the 18th century (after the Franciscans had already lost most of their missions as a result of the 1742 rebellion led by Juan Santos Atahuallpa and maintained only those at Pozuzo and Sonomoro), the head of the Ocopa convent petitioned the government to exempt the missions from a new tax on the sale of *aguardiente* (Santos-Granero 1980: 109), indicating that, even at that time, this production was still important for the economy of the Franciscan missions.

Apart from these commercial crops, the missionaries appear to have encouraged textile production among indigenous women of the missions, as becomes apparent in the *Reglamento de Misiones,* the mission bylaws, which stated that women should work two hours per day in mission textile workshops (Amich 1975: 540). Coca, textile, and *aguardiente* production seem to have been necessary to cover the expenses of the *conversiones* (which included the maintenance of missionaries, the financing of evangelical expeditions, the construction and ornamentation of convents and churches, and the purchase of gifts for the indigenous peoples). It is important to remember that, in contrast to other orders, the Franciscan was a mendicant order that could not own land or real estate and that nominally depended on alms and donations. In the case of the Amazonian missions, the Spanish Crown had agreed to pay their expenses from the Royal Treasury. However, although the Crown issued numerous royal decrees ordering the payment of the sums allotted to the missions, these rarely arrived in the hands of the missionaries (Santos-Granero 1980: 110). Thus the commercial production of the missions was necessary to provide funds for their operation.

The primary market for the products of both the missions and private landholdings was the mining center of Cerro de Pasco. Because of its geographic location, which impeded the development of its own agricultural production, Cerro de Pasco depended entirely on trade with the more temperate inter-Andean and tropical valleys (Fisher 1977: 35). There is little information on the mining production of Pasco for the period considered here (1709–1742), but everything indicates that, although production levels fluctuated because of flooding in the mines and the lack of adequate technology to overcome this problem, Cerro de Pasco continued to be the most important mining center after Potosí. During this period, Cerro de Pasco became an important commercial center for the products from the valleys of Conchucos, Huaylas, Tarma, Jauja, Cajatambo, Yauyos, and Chancay (Varallanos 1959: 261), having a permanent population of 5,000, which was augmented by a floating population that gathered when silver production experienced a rise (Fisher 1977: 38).

Andean mines and tropical *haciendas* made up the essential binomial equation on which the economy of the Selva Central was based. It should be pointed out that in the viceroyalty of Peru, only Potosí and Huancavelica enjoyed the benefit of the mining *mita,* the compulsory tribute in labor that the Andean indigenous communities owed the Crown. In contrast, the Cerro de Pasco mines functioned on the basis of wage labor. This favored the formation of a free market and of a wealthy merchant class, which in many cases financed the miners by offering them high-interest loans (Fisher 1977: 46–47). Coca and *aguardiente* were strategic products as a result of their high demand among mine workers. Their sale fueled the economy of the Selva Central during all of this period. For this reason, the citizens of Pasco vied with those of Huánuco to ensure control of the nearby lowlands (Ortiz 1967: vol. 1, 168–169). In some cases, the miners themselves attempted to control both terms of the binomial (the Andean mines and the tropical *haciendas*) as a way to avoid middlemen and to increase their profit margins. We have already seen that the Count of Las Lagunas, owner of a large holding in the Chorobamba Valley, also had interests in the Pasco mines. The case of Juan Esteban Durán, a mine owner in Pasco, is even more illustrative. In order to justify his request for land in the tropical region, he stated to the authorities that "he owned mines, and that in order to feed his workers he needed provisions, and that jungle lands are suitable to grow corn, sugar cane, and fruit and to raise cattle. . . . He also speaks of growing sugar cane to produce *aguardiente* and to maintain the energy and spirit of his workers" (Ortiz 1967: vol. 1, 168–169). It was thus that in 1776, in an era in which most of the Selva Central was under control of Juan Santos's followers, Durán established the Chilache *hacienda* in the Huancabamba Valley.

Andean wool mills and tropical *haciendas* formed an equally important economic binomial. Since at least 1681 there is evidence that wool-mill owners were quite interested in access to the *montaña* valleys. On this date the owner of the Hualahoyo wool mill in the Jauja Valley, who was simultaneously a *hacienda* owner and treasurer of the missions, put up capital to finance the Franciscan initiative to open a road from Andamarca to the Pangoa Valley (Amich 1975: 88–89). The Count of Las Lagunas, owner of the wool mill in Paucartambo, also owned a large estate in the Huánuco *conversión,* in addition to numerous properties in the area of Chinchaicocha. Clothes and textiles were in great demand in the mines (Fisher 1977: 35). By controlling the production of coca and *aguardiente* in the tropical lowlands and that of textiles in the highlands, the elites of Huánuco, Tarma, and Jauja controlled the three most valuable consumer goods in the colonial economy.

That control of tropical products was essential to maintaining the commercial circuits that linked the Selva Central with the mining center of Cerro de Pasco by way of Tarma, Huánuco, and Jauja is proven by the fact that, at the most critical moment in the indigenous hostilities begun in 1742, the *corregidor* of Tarma provided troops to guard *mestizo* peasants from the highlands who went to the *montaña* "to harvest coca leaves" (Loayza 1942: 229). In this context, the case of the Count of Las Lagunas is exceptional in that he controlled all of the factors in the triad of mines, wool mills, and highland and lowland *haciendas,* and thus all of the key economic activities in the central Andes. The economic integration of the Selva Central and the neighboring highland areas was to be disrupted, however, with the expansion of coffee as the major tropical product at the end of the 19th century.

Missionary Geopolitical Strategies

In the occupation of a previously inhabited space, the main tasks of occupying agents are to subjugate and exercise control over the local population in order to neutralize their resistance and to clear out the space in order to colonize it. In the Selva Central, Franciscan missionaries exercised four types of control over the Yanesha, Ashaninka, and Nomatsiguenga populations: social, economic, cultural, and military. The ultimate objective of these geopolitical strategies was to extend the domain of the Crown through the conquest of new land and vassals, as well as that of the Church through the conquest of new believers and souls for the Catholic faith. An analysis of these methods of control not only provides the key to understanding the characteristics of the process of occupation at this early stage but also allows us to establish the origin of various forms of control that recur again and again in later stages of occupation.

The primary means of social control was the concentration of the indigenous population in mission towns. In pre-Hispanic times, the population was organized in what the missionaries called *parcialidades,* localized units composed of extensive family groups linked by kinship bonds and headed by a given leader. These *parcialidades* were local and extremely fluid social units: their composition varied over time, their membership growing or shrinking according to the degree of respect or influence generated by the performance of their leaders. In the Franciscan chronicles, each *parcialidad* was generally identified by the name of the river or valley that its members inhabited or by the name of its leader.

In most of these cases, the strategy of the missionaries consisted of attracting the leaders of the *parcialidades* with gifts of iron tools and other objects highly valued by the Indians. If their response was positive, a cross was erected near the house of the leader and a small chapel was constructed where the missionaries offered Mass when they visited the *parcialidad.* Throughout a variable period of time during which religious instruction was given, the missionaries invited the members of the *parcialidad* to move to the closest mission post. In a first stage these moves seem to have been voluntary, for the indigenous population saw them as opportunities to have permanent access to iron tools, which significantly reduced the energy investment and the number of hours of work required by their agricultural activities. But later, when the indigenous population began to resist these moves, missionaries resorted to armed escorts to recruit converts or to capture those who had fled from the missions.

For peoples with dispersed settlement patterns, the semi-forced concentration in mission posts, which sometimes brought together more than 600 people, constituted such a violent change that it soon provoked many people to flee. The strict regimentation of mission life also created discontent. Converts were obliged to work on mission lands and in workshops, and to provide various services to support the missionaries and maintain the missions (e.g., the construction of living quarters, cleaning, and the provision of wild game). All of these tasks were done in shifts, and together with daily religious instruction and attendance at Mass they implied a strict control over the new converts' schedule of activities.

But the most serious and unexpected effect of concentrating the indigenous population was the recurrent spread of epidemics of European origin, to which the new converts lacked the proper antibodies. Measles, smallpox, and various types of influenza affected the mission populations of the Selva Central in 1709, 1711, 1713, 1715, 1718, 1721–1724, and 1736–1737 (Santos-Granero 1987: 34). The refusal of missionaries to let new converts abandon the missions and to disperse themselves in order to break the chain of transmission made the situation worse. As a consequence of the epidemics, in five Yanesha missions of the Tarma *conversión* the average number of family members declined from 5.48 in 1718 to 3.75 in 1739. In the same period, the average number of surviving children in each family unit fell from 2.25 to 1.19, and the percentage of the population in the age group of 0–14 years declined from 52 percent to 32 percent (Santos-Granero 1987: 44–45). Although epidemics decimated the whole population, these demographic indicators show that the juvenile population was the most affected. Shamans and indigenous religious leaders insisted that plagues had been brought by the missionaries in order to eliminate them. Therefore, it is not surprising that epidemic outbreaks were followed by local rebellions and that the resentment created by the effects of the epidemics became one of the most important factors to explain the massive following of the rebel Juan Santos in 1742 (Santos-Granero 1987: 44–45).

When new converts showed the first signs of resistance, the missionaries organized forays to capture the dissidents. But when these proved to be less than effective, they designed a strategy that combined economic control and physical coercion to ensure the definitive subjugation of the indigenous population. Monopoly over tool supplies and distribution became the first of these mechanisms of control. In the beginning, Franciscan missionaries brought tools from the highland region. These were only distributed to *indios principales* (indigenous leaders), who in turn redistributed them among their followers to establish or cement ties of political allegiance. In these early years, the missionaries established forges at several mission posts to repair the tools and firearms used to keep

Indians at bay. But when demand grew, the missionaries began to import iron in bulk so they could manufacture the required tools at the missions themselves (Santos-Granero 1988: 6-7). The monopoly on tool production, along with certain coercive measures, seems to have achieved the desired effect, as might be inferred from the words of the conversor of the Sonomoro Mission: "The forge and the stocks make these children very diligent and obedient, and have produced two very opposite effects in them: fear and greed, or interest; which are very becoming to their temperament" (Fernando de San Joseph 1723).

The second mechanism of economic control is related to the exploitation of the Cerro de la Sal. This hill is located near the mouth of the Paucartambo River at the limits of the traditional territories of the Yanesha and Ashaninka. As one of the most important salt deposits in the region, the Cerro de la Sal attracted countless numbers of indigenous people annually, who came from areas as far away as the Ucayali or the Urubamba watersheds, arriving by land and water to supply themselves with this product. Although salt extraction was carried out on a consensual basis and the Cerro de la Sal constituted a sort of interethnic enclave, the Yanesha and Ashaninka, who lived nearby, profited by cutting blocks of salt and exchanging them *in situ* for products brought by the people who came to the Cerro from distant areas. Thus it might be asserted that, in pre-Hispanic times, the Cerro de la Sal constituted the economic node that articulated indigenous commerce in the Selva Central (Varese 1973; Santos-Granero 1980; Renard-Casevitz, Taylor, and Saignes 1988). The importance of the Cerro de la Sal, however, went beyond its economic value, insofar as its exploitation promoted contact and exchange between peoples with different languages, cultures, and social organizations. Moreover, because access to the Cerro de la Sal was open and consensual, as a result of the widespread indigenous belief that salt was a divine gift to be used by all, this space assumed an almost sacred character.

The Franciscans were aware of the strategic importance of the Cerro de la Sal, and beginning with their first incursions, they attempted to establish a mission post nearby. In time, and in view of indigenous resistance, the missionaries came to the conclusion that only by controlling and restricting access to the Cerro de la Sal could they control already converted indigenous people, as well as expand their sphere of influence. One of the first to expound on this strategy in detail was Father Biedma of the Jauja *conversión,* who in 1686 asserted, "The easiest way to gather not only the souls that we have identified in those places, but also many more, and that will ensure their conversion, maintaining the preachers and our holy law, is to take possession of the Cerro de la Sal on behalf of the king, or to ensure that it is given to an individual for conquest or as an *encomienda* . . . and then occupying it with Spaniards, who will not give salt to the infidels, nor allow them to extract it, unless they carry written permission from us, the missionaries" (1981: 177). Although it was never possible to implement this scheme fully, at various moments of the missionary period different types of restrictions on the exploitation of salt were imposed, some of which inspired bloody rebellions, such as that of chief Mangoré in 1674 (Biedma 1981: 33). It was only with the advent of the republican era in 1897, when it was placed under the jurisdiction of the *Estanco de la Sal,* the State agency that held a monopoly on salt production and distribution, that outsiders were effectively able to control the Cerro de la Sal (Varese 1973: 256). In a bizarre historical recurrence of geopolitical strategies, colonial and republican authorities, separated by more than two centuries, resorted to similar mechanisms to achieve the same goal: the neutralization of indigenous resistance.

More subtle, but no less effective, were the mechanisms of cultural control. In contrast to the colonization policies of the 19th century, which considered indigenous peoples an obstacle to be eliminated, to the missionaries of the 17th and 18th centuries they constituted the reason itself for their existence and their efforts. Moreover, to the missionaries the indigenous peoples were human capital, both spiritual (souls rescued from the shadows) and physical (future contributors to the Crown), that could not be squandered. But for the potential of this human capital to be realized, the indigenous population had to assimilate Spanish norms, customs, and beliefs. In other words, to be effectively dominated, the indigenous peoples had to accept the idea of domination, which was totally foreign to their culture. Intense religious instruction, prohibition of traditional forms of social interaction, intentional weakening of local links of political loyalty, imposition of a new system of authority, establishment of new economic activities, and continual attempts to discredit political and religious leaders were among the most common mechanisms used to achieve acculturation. In the end, this strategy had the opposite effect, since in contrast to Andean indigenous peoples, who were familiar with hierarchical social structures, the indigenous peoples of the Selva Central rejected them completely.

Although, in general, the Franciscan missionaries preferred to use nonviolent means of subjugation, persistent indigenous opposition led them to resort to armed force early on. Since the beginning of the 18th century, both the Quimirí and Sonomoro missions, gateways to the Tarma and Jauja *conversiones,* respectively, were fortified. After the Eneno uprising in 1712, this mission port was also fortified and provided with cannons to control the boat traffic that plied the Perené River in search of salt (Francisco de San Joseph 1732). Moreover, each of the Selva Central missions had a small military garrison to protect the mission as well as to organize forays to recruit new converts.

For the same reason, the missionaries had armed black slaves who acted as foremen. In the beginning they were brought as mission servants, but, seeing the fear that they inspired among the indigenous population, the missionaries gradually armed them, as might be inferred from the following request by the *comisario de misiones:* "If the Viceroy could accomplish the miracle of providing some aid in order to assist in the enterprise I refer to [the subjugation of the Piro], I have already informed him to use it for the purchase of recently captured negroes, for thus, we will have peons and soldiers" (Francisco de San Joseph 1723). Some of these slaves, such as Onofre and Antonio Gatica, ended up holding trusted positions in the missions. When the Juan Santos uprising began, however, they quickly joined the rebel forces.

In spite of all of these precautions, from early times the missionaries were aware of the limitations of military control. Thus in 1686 Biedma commented that, although one way to deal with the problem of indigenous resistance was to send troops to their settlements to capture them and burn down their houses so that they could not return, maintenance of these troops proved to be too onerous. As an alternative, he proposed that "it would be more effective to attempt to populate these frontier lands with some Spaniards who want to found sugar cane, cocoa or tobacco *haciendas;* who, in taking root, would do their best to defend themselves, and who, from their estates, without living with priests or infidels, would become the terror of the latter and the defense of the former" (Biedma 1981: 177). This proposal was put into practice with great success in the Tarma *conversión,* and with lesser success in the Huánuco and Jauja *conversiones.*

The combination of all these mechanisms of control reinforced the Spanish presence and conferred to the 18th-century *conversiones* a stability that they had not enjoyed in the previous century. As a result, Spanish dominion could be extended over the Vitoc, Chanchamayo, Paucartambo, and upper Perené valleys in the Tarma *conversión;* over the Chorobamba, Huancabamba, and Pozuzo valleys in the Huánuco *conversión;* and over the Pangoa, Satipo, and lower Perené valleys in the Jauja *conversión.* With the establishment of mission posts in the Gran Pajonal toward the end of this stage, the missionaries had explored, subjugated, and to a lesser extent occupied nearly all of the areas that were to constitute the most important colonization spaces in the 19th and 20th centuries. The Christianization of the indigenous population went hand in hand with the Christianization of the space that they inhabited. The erection of large crosses in strategic locations and the use of the names of saints combined with indigenous names to designate the missions were some of the forms of ideological appropriation of the space at this stage. Thus, in the mid-18th century the future Selva Central region and the spaces that composed it were already outlined. However, the numerous controls imposed by the missionaries, in addition to the levies and abuses of the colonial authorities and local power groups, constituted a time bomb that would explode in 1742 with the arrival of Juan Santos Atahuallpa in the Gran Pajonal.

RECOVERY OF INDIGENOUS TERRITORY AND RETRACTION OF FRONTIERS: 1742–1847

When, in May 1742, Juan Santos proclaimed himself "true Inca, descendent of Atahuallpa," initiating the general uprising of the indigenous population of the missions, the Selva Central was one of the key components of a commercial network whose centers of power were located in the central Andes. At that moment everything indicated that the Selva Central was to become part of an integrated Andean–Amazonian region dominated by *hacienda* owners, wool-mill owners, miners, and traders from Tarma, Huánuco, and Jauja, whose economy would revolve around the Yauli and Cerro de Pasco silver mines. The Juan Santos rebellion put an end to this process of regional integration, dealing a severe blow to the highland economic groups. It is not surprising, then, that these groups did everything possible to smother the rebellion and reconquer the region.

In spite of the conflicts that often arose between the missionaries and the local *corregidores, hacienda* owners, and wool-mill owners, this time they joined forces to combat Juan Santos. Members of the Tarma elite were the most interested in achieving this objective because they were most affected by the uprising. And although putting down the rebellion became a priority of the most powerful authorities of the viceroyalty, the measures taken demonstrate the enormous weight of local economic interests.

In a first phase of the conflict, Spanish troops were under the joint command of the *corregidores* of Tarma, Huánuco, and Jauja and of their respective frontier governors. In this phase, several Andean indigenous leaders voluntarily played an active part. One such leader was Joseph Calderón Conchaya, headman of the indigenous population of Tarma Province, who, following the old pattern of vertical control of a maximum of ecological zones, was interested in having access to land in the Selva Central (Villagarcía 1742). Nevertheless, given the lack of coordination among *corregidores* and the successive defeats that they suffered as a result, the new viceroy, Manso de Velasco, appointed José Llamas, general of the Callao troops, as supreme commander of the Spanish forces (Amich 1975: 165).

Under Llamas, the Spanish troops undertook various large-scale punitive expeditions. But Juan Santos's forces, far from being crushed, became increasingly audacious in their attacks. In 1747, Manso de Velasco ordered Llamas to step down and gave captain Alfonso Santa y Ortega, already acting *corregidor* of Tarma and superintendent of mines since March 1742 (Villagarcía 1746), command of the military government in the region. Thus, civilian and military command of the area were unified. Santa y Ortega not only had important personal economic interests in the region but also represented the interests of the Tarma elite, as is evident from the following statement: "The five punitive expeditions that have been undertaken . . . have been useless, and did grave damage to these Provinces; especially to this one [Tarma], which has been completely ruined; I myself have been ruined, having lost more than two thousand mules during the last two years, which were really necessary for the transport of metal and whose loss has affected us all" (Santa y Ortega 1747). Mules were of vital importance in the exploitation of the Pasco silver mines, since the raw ore had to be transported by pack animals to the mills, which were usually some distance from the mines (Chocano 1983: 3). According to Santa y Ortega (1747), this was not the only hardship suffered in the area: "Because of the continuous incursions and expeditions that have recently occupied all of the people of the region, diverting them from the usual tasks and duties related to the trade in which they are engaged, and on the basis of which they pay tax to the Corregidor, the Province is in desolation."

During the first years of the rebellion, the tropical land estates in the Chanchamayo Valley were seized and destroyed, and many *hacienda* owners died at the hands of the rebels while defending their property (Urrutia 1808: 445–446). In spite of the fact that the *corregidor* of Tarma provided troops to escort the small groups of Andean peasants who went to the lowlands to harvest their coca plots (Loayza 1942: 229), the demand of the mines for coca and *aguardiente* could not be satisfied as it had been in the past. Not even the reinforcement of the Quimirí fort, which was equipped with "four Artillery cannons and a stone throwing mortar," could keep Juan Santos from destroying the *haciendas* of the Chanchamayo Valley. The Quimirí fort fell into rebel hands in 1743 (Villagarcía 1744). The *haciendas* in the Huancabamba Valley and the mission at Huancabamba suffered similar fates at nearly the same time as the fall of Quimirí (Villagarcía 1744).

Had Juan Santos limited his military actions to the lowland mission territories, it is possible that the Spaniards would have continued harassing him from the highlands until his troops tired, as they were not accustomed to prolonged wars. But instead of defending what he had conquered, the indigenous leader continued to take the offensive. In 1746, a few years after taking the fort at Quimirí, Juan Santos attacked the highland settlement of Monobamba (Amich 1975: 166); and in 1752, one year after having taken the fort at Sonomoro, he attacked the Andean town of Andamarca (Amich 1975: 173). In the interim (the date is still uncertain), the rebels attacked and burned the San Juan de Colpas wool mill located in the foothills of the province of Tarma (Silva Santisteban 1964: 161). The fact that these military actions took place in areas so far from the frontier where the rebellion originated severely alarmed the viceroyal authorities.

Even more alarming was the continual support that Juan Santos received not only from the highland indigenous population but also from many *mestizos* and poor Spaniards, tired of the heavy burden they had to bear in wool mills, mines, *haciendas,* sugar mills, and cane fields (San Antonio 1750). The rebellion threatened to extend into the neighboring highland provinces and to engage the whole central Andes. Spanish authorities were not going to allow this to happen. After the attack on Andamarca – the last large-scale indigenous military action – the authorities decided to close the borders that divided the tropical lowlands from highland areas.

One factor that drove them to make this decision was the burden to the royal treasury resulting from the maintenance of troops and the provisioning of fortified missions and punitive expeditions. These expenses were covered by the revenues of the Pasco and Jauja royal treasuries. An analysis of their accounts for the period from May 1745 until April 1752 shows that expenditures for the military campaigns to defeat the rebellion represented 73 percent of the total income of the Pasco treasury and 99 percent of the Jauja treasury (Table 1.1).

In the case of Jauja, for four years the amount of military spending exceeded the treasury's total income, which meant not only that the Crown was not receiving any income but that, on the contrary, it had to provide additional funds to cover the deficits. On the one hand, the considerable sums invested by the Crown in military efforts demonstrate the economic importance that was attributed to the Selva Central and the Crown's interest in reconquering it. On the other hand, it also demonstrates the authorities' fear that the rebellion would spread to the highlands.

To keep Juan Santos out of the Andes and isolate him in the lowlands, the Spanish established small military outposts at virtually all of the routes of access into the Selva Central. By 1746 the Chanchamayo and Ocsabamba fortresses had been established (Amich 1975: 167). In the years following 1752, the forts at Monobamba and Andamarca were reinforced, and new outposts were erected in the frontier towns of Utcubamba, Quiparacra, Palca, and Huasi-huasi (Santos-Granero 1988: 8).

Beginning in 1752, the border closings took effect. Although the rebel forces continued to harass small highland property owners, they no longer made important advances into the Andes. And although the missionaries and local authorities continued to contrive new ways to defeat Juan Santos (including the idea of poisoning him), they no longer mounted military expeditions into the Selva Central. The Juan Santos rebellion resulted in the retraction of the colonial

Table 1.1. Revenues and Military Expenditures of the Pasco and Jauja Royal Treasuries

Royal treasury and year[a]	Total revenue (pesos)	Military expenditures	
		Amount (pesos)	% of total revenue
Pasco Treasury			
1745–1746	39,803	26,768	67.2
1746–1747	42,164	37,540	89.0
1747–1748	35,589	32,306	90.7
1748–1749	41,475	29,988	72.3
1749–1750	36,935	28,200	76.3
1750–1751	35,721	28,163	78.8
1751–1752	61,043	31,199	51.1
1745–1752, overall	292,730	214,164	73.1
Jauja Treasury			
1745–1746	28,572	15,156	53.0
1746–1747	22,884	23,445	102.4
1747–1748	22,009	21,024	95.5
1748–1749	21,230	23,738	111.8
1749–1750	13,660	25,032	183.2
1750–1751	20,253	24,505	120.9
1751–1752	24,043	18,651	77.5
1745–1752, overall	152,651	151,551	99.2

Sources: Caja de Pasco 1745–1752; Caja de Jauja 1745–1752.

[a]Revenues and expenditures are tallied from May 1 of the first year in each range to April 30 of the second year in the range.

frontiers in the Amazonian region and the establishment of a new frontier. In effect, the fortification of the adjacent Andean towns and the prohibition against dealing with the rebels interrupted the demographic, economic, and cultural flows between the highlands and the lowlands, acting as a physical barrier that was to have repercussions in the attitudes of the pioneer colonists of the 19th century.

Cultural Innovations and Development of New Forms of Intraregional Articulation

Recovery of their former territories did not signify a simple return to traditional ways of life for the indigenous peoples of the region. Thirty-three years of mission life left its mark on the Yanesha, Ashaninka, and Nomatsiguenga, not only in economic terms but also in ideological terms. Certainly the expulsion of the Spaniards allowed the resumption of a series of practices and lifestyles that were previously repressed, but by the middle of the 18th century the indigenous peoples of the Selva Central had acquired a series of needs that could be satisfied only by Western technologies. In the following 100 years, the Yanesha and Ashaninka appropriated and recreated these technologies, adapting them to their needs and patterns of social organization.

The foremost of their new needs was iron tools. As we have said, the Franciscans encouraged this need and monopolized the means of satisfying it, establishing forges at the most important missions: Quimirí, Cerro de la Sal, and Pichana in the Tarma *conversión* and Sonomoro in the Jauja *conversión* (Santos-Granero 1980: 92, 1988: 6–7). As a result of the chaos that reigned in the years of the Juan Santos uprising, tool production was completely interrupted. This situation was remedied, in part, by trade between the rebels and the highland indigenous population. But as early as 1744, the authorities placed a ban on all trade with the rebels, and especially on trade in axes and knives (Loayza 1942: 64). This partially explains the attacks made on frontier towns to steal cattle and tools in subsequent years.

The closing of the frontier that took place after 1752 forced the rebels to design their own production strategies that were adapted to their economic needs and cultural patterns. Likewise, they maintained certain crops brought by the missionaries, such as citrus and sugarcane. Cattle production continued, and the old mission forges were rehabilitated. In the case of the forges, historical accounts mention that in the colonial period new converts were trained as assistants to Spanish or *mestizo* blacksmiths. After the Juan Santos uprising, this trade was incorporated into the complex of priests *(cornesha')* and ceremonial centers prevalent among the Yanesha as well as, through cultural loan, the Ashaninka of neighboring areas. In time, many *cornesha'* assumed the double role of politico-religious leader and blacksmith. In other cases, they had groups of blacksmiths under their authority, who resided with them in their ceremonial centers (Santos-Granero 1988: 16–17).

The association between temples and forges had a profound effect on the social organization of the Yanesha and on the articulation of indigenous territories. On the one hand, the combination of the roles of priest and blacksmith reinforced the authority that religious leaders had traditionally held among their followers. On the other, the fact that most iron ore deposits were located near the confluence of the Paucartambo and Chanchamayo rivers, near the Cerro de la Sal, reinforced the role of this latter site as an axis for the articulation of the regional economy. Now the Cerro de la Sal not only attracted innumerable people from all over the Selva Central who came to extract and trade salt, as it did formerly, but it also attracted anyone who needed new tools or to repair their old ones (Santos-Granero 1988: 17).

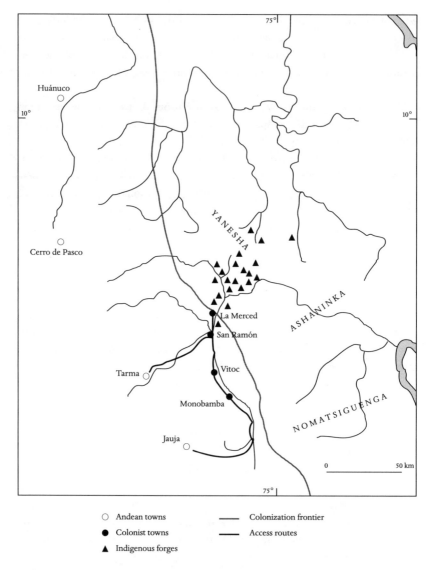

Map 1.3. Colonist towns, indigenous forges, and ethnic territories, 1847. *Source:* Santos-Granero 1991b.

After the reconquest of the Selva Central in 1847, military expeditions reported the existence of 12 of these temple-forges, of which 10 were in operation and 2 were abandoned. Indigenous oral tradition mentions another 9 centers of tool production (Santos-Granero 1988: 10-14) (Map 1.3). Explorers of this period also report the existence of large herds of feral cattle on the borders of the Perené River, as well as orchards of fruit species introduced by the Europeans near small indigenous settlements. All of these data suggest that, far from rejecting European material contributions outright, the indigenous economy strengthened itself through the adoption and development of some of these technologies. If the salt trade in the Cerro de la Sal region brought Yanesha, Ashaninka, Nomatsiguenga, Piro, Shipibo, Conibo, and Machiguenga ethnic groups together, tool trading must have further stimulated these old exchange networks. Nevertheless, this autonomous development of the ethnic groups of the Selva Central was to be abruptly interrupted by the postcolonial advance into the region beginning in 1847.

2

RECONQUEST AND OCCUPATION IN THE REPUBLICAN PERIOD

In 1808, more than 60 years after the Spanish lost control over the Selva Central, the *intendente* of Tarma, Juan Ramón Urrutia, wrote a report in which he expounded vehemently and at length on the benefits that could result from the reconquest of this tropical region. The document, addressed to Viceroy de la Croix, examines in detail the achievements of the Franciscans before the Juan Santos uprising, making reference to the Christianization and pacification of the Indians and the trade that was established with them, which gave the Franciscans access to products of "their collection and industry" (quinine, vanilla, cinnamon, resins, balsams, wax, and fine woods) for the benefit of the viceroyalty. Likewise, it enumerates the prosperous tropical *haciendas* that produced sugarcane, coca, cocoa, annato, cotton, coffee, fruit, and corn, and allowed Tarma to expand its scarce farming lands and thereby to realize substantial profits (Ortiz 1978: 425, 460). In spite of the strength of Urrutia's arguments, the Crown did not undertake the reconquest of the Selva Central, and it was not until the mid-19th century, after Peru achieved independence, that new attempts at colonizing the region were made. As we will see, this was, to a large extent, a consequence of the rivalry between the adjacent Andean cities to attain exclusive control over the lands and resources of the Selva Central.

PIONEER COLONIZATION AND THE *HACIENDA* ECONOMY: 1847-1947

After the final expedition against the forces of Juan Santos, and more so after they had learned of the rebel's death, the Franciscans urged the authorities over and over again to move the highland garrisons that protected the frontier further down into the lowlands. The idea of converting defense posts into advance positions was aimed at inducing the authorities to lift the prohibition against making expeditions into the lowlands and at providing better protection to colonists and missionaries so that they could begin to reoccupy the region. In spite of two royal decrees, issued in 1757 and in 1767, that ordered the reconquest of the missions at Cerro de la Sal, the Franciscans were not granted military support or effective authorization until 1778.

In that year, missionaries from the Franciscan convent of Ocopa financed a military expedition that culminated in the construction of Fort Santa Cruz de Chanchamayo, 35 kilometers downriver of the highland settlement of Palca. Nevertheless, in 1784 the authorities ordered that it be destroyed, forcing the colonists and missionaries to abandon the area. Ten years later, Fort San Carlos was established in the Tulumayo Valley, allowing settlers from Tarma to repopulate the Vitoc uplands (see Map 1.3). Simultaneously, the Jaujinos sponsored the construction of a road through Monobamba as an alternative, though longer, route to reach the old mission of Quimirí. Except for the construction of the Andamarca road to Jesús María—begun many years afterward in 1815 to provide access to the mission of Sarayacu on the Ucayali River—no other advance into the Selva Central was made from its southern frontiers (see Map 1.2).

The Royal Army repeatedly stated that it was not convenient to withdraw its garrisons from the highland outposts in view of the risk that indigenous troops could reinstate their attacks against the people and *haciendas* located at the entries of the *montaña* region. Since the end of the 1770s, moreover, we can assume that the colonial authorities did not consider it wise to disperse their forces because of the effects that the massive anticolonial uprising of Túpac Amaru centered in Cusco could have in the Tarma and Jauja highlands.

The increase in the mining activities at Cerro de Pasco put more pressure on the authorities to reconquer the Selva Central. Beginning in 1786, silver production at Cerro de Pasco soared as a result of the introduction of steam-powered pumps and tunnels for drainage of water, an element that in the past had impeded mineral extraction at a certain depth. The value of silver production increased from an annual average of 63,000 *marcos* during the 1776-1785 period to an annual average of 226,500 *marcos* during the 1786-1811 period (Fisher 1977: Appendix) (Figure 2.1).

The growth in silver production in Pasco not only stimulated trade in the region but also generated an increase in the demand for coca and *aguardiente,* products that had traditionally been supplied by the *haciendas* of the Selva Central. According to Chocano (1983: 24), in 1792, 1793, 1796, and 1798 *aguardiente* represented an average of 23.5 percent of the total goods that passed through

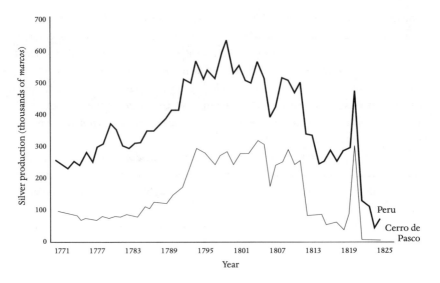

Figure 2.1. Silver production in Cerro de Pasco and Peru, 1771-1824. *Source:* Fisher 1977: appendix.

customs in Cerro de Pasco. By then, most of it was produced on the coast, as the Selva Central was closed to the Spaniards. The reopening of this region would allow local *aguardiente* production to replace that from the coast, since transport costs were lower. It is not surprising then that it was at this particular time that Intendente Urrutia sent his report to the viceroy insisting that he support the reconquest of the region.

With such a glorious past as that depicted by Urrutia, and such interesting economic prospects, how do we interpret the indecision of the Crown? The answer is found in what Antonio Raimondi elegantly called "the jealousy and incomprehensible rivalry" of the provinces (1879: 32). Rivalry among the three neighboring upland cities, and particularly between Huánuco and Tarma, pervades Urrutia's report, which is in essence a plea in favor of access by way of Palca that would favor Tarma. The town that controlled access to the *montaña* would be in a better position not only to acquire tropical land and produce highly valued tropical products but also to reap the benefits of the increase in commerce and the right to impose taxes.

As we have seen, Huánuco, which had the official status of city and was the seat of a Spanish *corregimiento,* had jurisdiction over Tarma. In an attempt to maintain their privileges, during the second half of the 18th century Huánuco's elite did its best to prevent the Franciscans from obtaining the Crown's authorization and backing to construct a road from Tarma to Palca and establish themselves in Cerro de la Sal. In 1753, the Huanucans had reestablished communications with the Pozuzo and Mayro areas through the activities of some Franciscan missionaries. After the Yanesha population of the Pozuzo Mission was moved into the highlands (where many of them died), some families from the neighboring Andean town of Muña established their coca plots near the old mission (Ortiz 1967: vol. 1, 135). In addition, the road to Pozuzo was improved in an attempt to allow Huánuco to recover its previous standing in the production of coca and *aguardiente* in the Selva Central (Varallanos 1959: 275). This would permit Huánuco's elite to attain control over two of the most wealthy *selva alta* regions of the viceroyalty: the upper Huallaga basin, which was already under its jurisdiction, and the territories of the Cerro de la Sal.

However, in spite of these early efforts, Huánuco's elite was never able to settle the Pozuzo Valley and incorporate it into its area of economic influence. This was partially because the route from Huánuco to Pozuzo offered greater difficulties than that from Pasco to Huancabamba. For this reason, some important members of Huánuco's elite applied for land along this latter route. One example was Juan Esteban Durán, an important mine owner and later subdelegate of the province of Panataguas, who in 1776 applied for land in the Huancabamba Valley (Varallanos 1959: 196; Ortiz 1969: vol. 1, 169). The epidemics that ravaged Pozuzo and Huancabamba in 1806 further affected the possibility of settling and exploiting the resources of these two valleys. For this reason, the mule trail from Huánuco to Pozuzo and Mayro, where in 1768 the Franciscans had established the mission of San Bernardino del Mayro, became important as a way through which to reach and supply the Franciscan missions located in the Ucayali basin, rather than as a colonization route.

Meanwhile, at the height of the conflict of interest between Tarma and Huánuco, Jauja, with its rich interandean valley, was able to control access to the *montaña* region through Monobamba and Andamarca. Thus, at the beginning of the 19th century, Tarma was the only one of the three cities whose access to the Selva Central was still blocked.

This situation was to change with the establishment of the *intendencias,* the politico-administrative units that replaced the old *corregimientos.* In this context, Tarma, raised to the status of *villa,* was established as the head of the *intendencia* of the same name in 1784. This curtailed the privileges of Huánuco, which now became a province of the Tarma *intendencia,* and reversed the previous administrative order. Furthermore, under the new political and administrative plan, the Cerro de Pasco silver mines came under the jurisdiction of Tarma. This change, nevertheless, did not immediately resolve the conflict. In 1785, Huánuco won one last battle with Tarma when it was given control of the province of Panataguas, which included the Cerro de la Sal area and could only be entered from

Huánuco. At that time there was some speculation as to the possibility of connecting Pozuzo with the Cerro de la Sal through a road along the Palcazu Valley. This, however, proved to be an impractical project.

The wars of independence in the 1820s were to delay the resolution of this conflict of interest until the middle of the 19th century, when a series of internal and external factors prompted the government to support Tarma's attempts to reconquer the Chanchamayo Valley.

Fiona Wilson's study of the Tarma oligarchy (1979) allows us to better understand the regional socioeconomic context in which the final conquest of Chanchamayo took place. Tarma's elite, whose economic and political power was based on landownership and control of labor in the highlands, had nevertheless maintained its ties with the mining industry in Pasco and Yauli. Wilson asserts that by the middle of the 19th century each of the families that formed this power group owned at least one mine. Beginning in 1830, silver mining began to recover after the collapse resulting from the wars of independence (Fisher 1977: 237). As a result, the demand for *aguardiente* increased. Once again, this acted as an incentive for the establishment of *haciendas* in the neighboring *montaña* region, prompting Tarma's elite to exert pressure over the government to undertake the reconquest of the Selva Central. Adducing that because of its geographic position, Tarma offered more advantages for the achievement of this objective than Jauja or Huánuco, and promising its financial support to the military enterprise, Tarma's elite persuaded President Ramón Castilla to reopen the area. This was finally achieved in 1847 with the foundation of Fort San Ramón at the confluence of the Tulumayo and Palca rivers.

With the reopening of the Selva Central, landowners from Tarma had an opportunity to seize again the Cerro de Pasco market, which until then had been supplied by the coastal production of *aguardiente* from Pisco and Ica (Ortiz 1978: 446-447; Wilson 1979: 48). They were not disappointed. When, in the 1860s, as a result of the U.S. Civil War, agricultural production on the coast shifted from sugarcane to cotton, the price of *aguardiente* rose by 33 percent (Wilson 1979: 46). The abolition of slavery in Peru also contributed to the increase in the price of alcohol by increasing the cost of sugarcane production on the coast (Raimondi 1942: 46). All of these factors favored *aguardiente* production in Chanchamayo. In 1869 it was estimated that Chanchamayo produced 100,000 *arrobas* of *aguardiente* per year (Ortiz 1969: vol. 1, 253). Wilson (1979: 48) estimated that a year later *aguardiente* production in the area increased to 120,000 *arrobas*. This was shipped through Tarma to the Cerro de Pasco, Yauli, and Huarochiri mines.

The oligarchy in Tarma was in an optimal position to take advantage of the reopening of the Selva Central. Not only was Tarma the shortest export route, but the prefect of Junín, who resided in this city, was in charge of allocating land to participants in the 1847 military expedition and to people who collaborated in the reopening of the road to Chanchamayo—primarily the *hacienda* owners from Tarma. Moreover, because it had access to highland labor, Tarma's elite was in a position to put the new lands into immediate production of sugarcane, coca, and other foodstuffs.

The reopening of the Selva Central and its occupation differed from the conquest of the lowlands during the colonial missionary period in that it was an essentially military enterprise. Fort San Ramón had a military contingent equivalent to that assigned to the upland outposts during the Juan Santos uprising. The new colonies were under the direction of army officials until 1876. To the government and to colonists from Tarma, the Juan Santos uprising—which had taken place 100 years earlier—was an event still fresh in their memories. It reminded them that indigenous resistance could threaten the new opportunities for the economic expansion of Tarma. Hence, they initially chose to exclude the Franciscan missionaries, who had so strongly advocated the reopening of the region, from the colonization enterprise and instead tried to subjugate the indigenous population through the use of military force. The local Ashaninka population was driven violently out of the area chosen for the establishment of the first colonist settlement. Their houses and fields were burned. Having Fort San Ramón as their center of operations, colonists and military forces made continual armed raids on indigenous settlements to "take some boys into their service" (Santos-Granero 1988). From the opposite bank of the Tulumayo River, the Ashaninka tenaciously opposed the advances of the colonists.

References to confrontations between colonists backed by military forces and the indigenous population are frequent during the first 30 years of the reconquest and are not infrequent even later, when the authorities invited the Franciscans to collaborate in the pacification of the region. The prior of the mission convent in Ocopa warned that there was "no spiritual benefit to expect" on the part of the indigenous peoples from "such a form of conquest" (Ortiz 1969: vol. 1, 240) and ordered the missionaries to retreat. Although the missionaries eventually returned, they subsequently had a very restricted role and managed to establish only a few missions. Only after the pioneer colonists became established and the scarcity of labor became evident was the proposal by the Franciscans to incorporate the indigenous population into "civilized life" taken seriously.

The attempts to subdue the local indigenous population not only met with their stubborn armed resistance but were thwarted by the fact that they continued to produce tools in their own forges, even during the first few decades of the colonists' presence. Indigenous tool production limited the applicability and effectiveness of the primary form of conquest used during the colonial era: subjugation by means of a monopoly on the supply of axes and machetes. Since the indigenous peoples were self-sufficient, nothing could limit their freedom of movement or challenge their refusal to work for the colonists. This drove various expeditionary forces to destroy the indigenous forges and their tools (Santos-Granero 1988: 19).

For the Yanesha, control of tool production also became a key element in their resistance. According to mythic tradition, in ancient times Yachor Aserr—"Our Mother Iron"—spoke to the Yanesha, saying that it had been created by the supreme divinity for their benefit and that they should not allow it to fall under the control of the whites (Santos-Granero 1988: 19). In the face of the colonial advance, both the Yanesha and the Ashaninka did everything possible to prevent the forges from falling into the hands of their adversaries, choosing to destroy and despoil their anvils and other utensils. Paradoxically, the indigenous response coincided with the strategic objectives of the colonists, producing the same result: the destruction of the temple-forge complex that had originated after the Juan Santos rebellion. As the indigenous forges ceased to operate, the traditional sociopolitical system that revolved around them collapsed, and with it, armed resistance (Santos-Granero 1988: 20). The successive epidemics that plagued the region throughout this period, which were still interpreted by the indigenous peoples as a magic weapon of the whites before which they had no way of defending themselves, also paved the way for colonization.

From contemporary reports it becomes apparent that the colonists saw indigenous peoples as simply a potential threat to be eliminated or a potential source of slave labor; they did not distinguish one ethnic group from the other and at most would classify them as *mansos* (tame) or *bravos* (fierce). Indigenous resistance to working for the colonists was invariably interpreted as a negative character trait—namely, laziness. It was the military nature of the occupation and the lack of interest in the native population that characterized the style of colonization during this period. Whereas in the missionary era the redemption and civilization of the indigenous peoples was a central element in the legitimation of the conquest of their territories, in this period the indigenous population appeared as an "obstacle" that should be eliminated by military means or absorbed by the new economic dynamic in the region.

Evolution of Land Legislation and Colonization Policies

Land legislation and colonization policies formulated after 1847 to promote the incorporation of the Amazonian region had a particular impact on the Selva Central, attracting an important flow of national and foreign colonists. These policies left their mark on both the structure of land tenure and the socioeconomic structure of Chanchamayo in the period preceding the massive occupation of the Selva Central.

Whereas the establishment of the San Ramón Colony in 1847 resulted from the political and economic pressures exerted by Tarma's elite, the founding of the La Merced Colony in 1869 was a State initiative, which expressed a radical change in the way the government perceived the Amazonian region. As a result of the enormous success of the sugarcane *haciendas* owned by prominent members of Tarma's elite, the occupation of the Selva Central shifted from being a regional endeavor to being a national enterprise for ensuring the "future of the Republic." This shift was very much associated with the fact that the ruling class was becoming aware of the convenience of connecting Lima with the Atlantic through one of the navigable rivers that flow from the Selva Central into the Amazon. The exploration of these rivers by the Franciscan missionaries, and the increasing prosperity of the lowland region of Loreto as a result of the opening of the Amazon River to international steamship navigation, reinforced this perception.

The legislation to encourage foreign immigration, initially conceived to solve the labor problem on coastal and Andean *haciendas,* did not exclude the Amazonian region. The frontier nature of this region made it attractive to European and Asian immigrants, both because the new laws provided free access to land and because local social structures were not as closed and stratified as those encountered on the coast and in the highlands, thus providing them with better opportunities for economic growth and upward mobility. These laws offered future colonists a variety of schemes to choose from. Thus, whereas the immigration and colonization laws of 1849, 1853, 1868, and 1893 issued by Presidents Ramón Castilla, Rufino Echenique, José Balta, and Remigio Morales Bermúdez, respectively, offered colonists land at no cost, paid their passage, and offered them assistance for a period of six to eight months (the latter does not apply to the law of 1849), the laws of 1898 and 1909, which are proper land legislation, established various means of access to land in the Amazonian region: land could be bought, received as a temporary or permanent concession, appropriated at no cost, or granted under a colonization contract (Chirif 1975: 270–276). Some of these laws emphasized colonization by foreign immigrants, whereas others also benefited Peruvian colonists. Nevertheless, all of them were equally imprecise when it came to the size of the awards. Only the size of the free awards (up to 2 hectares in the law of 1898) and that of the grants that had to be approved by the Congress (law of 1909) were explicitly established.

This lack of precision stemmed from the ambiguity in the models of immigration and colonization of this period, that is, the lack of definition regarding what the goal of attracting colonists should be. Whereas, on the one hand, a greater number of independent farmers, capable of making the country prosperous, was desirable, on the other, and in the face of the chronic scarcity of labor, they sought to attract agricultural workers for coastal, highland, and tropical *haciendas.*

This contradiction became apparent early on in Chanchamayo and must have fueled the tensions between the objectives of the government and those of the local power groups. From then on, *hacienda* owners from Tarma tried to restrict the size of the properties awarded to European immigrants who had settled in the La Merced Colony. This was possible because land grants were made by the prefect of Tarma and later by the director of the La Merced Colony with the previous approval of the prefect of Tarma. This practice generated numerous complaints by foreign colonists (Giordano 1875; La Rosa 1969: 50).

The scarcity of labor, a constant theme in the descriptions of Peruvian agriculture of the period, was a serious drawback for Tarmenians who owned *haciendas* in Chanchamayo and a factor that limited the expansion of their sugarcane plantations (Raimondi 1942: 2; Barclay 1989: 62-71). To avoid having to work as paid laborers for the *hacienda* owners, most La Merced immigrants, especially those of Italian origin, resorted to forming mutual-aid associations and merging their lands. Others managed to acquire small plots by working on a temporary basis for their fellow countrymen who alloted land to them. In turn, the Chinese immigrants were not even granted legal rights to land under the existing legislation, and those who did not have enough capital to enter into commerce ended up working as paid laborers.

In Chanchamayo, as in other frontier areas, land tenure was characterized from the very beginning by extreme inequality. In 1876, after visiting the area, a jounalist from the *El Comercio* newspaper in Lima reported that, from a sample of 98 property owners, 87 percent owned up to 50 hectares, while 13 percent owned up to 600 hectares, among them some of the large Tarmenian landowners of the San Ramón Colony. It should be noted that, in this period, some colonists already owned extremely small landholdings (up to 1.2 hectares), whereas the average area of Chanchamayo's landholdings (excluding the seven largest *haciendas*) was 32.4 hectares (La Rosa 1969: 50-67).

However, land-tenure structure in Chanchamayo was not static. As we will see, some Italian immigrants, originally attracted by increased trade in this area, were able to accumulate capital and to acquire some of the best *haciendas* in the Chanchamayo Valley (Wilson 1979). This, in turn, allowed them to mechanize sugarcane harvesting and *aguardiente* processing, as well as to control the regional *aguardiente* trading networks.

The conflicts that arose from the decision of the provincial council of Tarma to impose a new tax on the *aguardiente* produced in Chanchamayo reveal the changing relationship between this town and its tropical hinterland. This change, in turn, stems from the processes leading to the gradual conformation of Chanchamayo as a distinctive and autonomous regional space. Beginning in 1873, the provincial council that governed the district of Chanchamayo started to levy a tax that significantly affected *aguardiente* export from Chanchamayo to the highlands (Wilson 1979: 50). The colonists in Chanchamayo appealed to the central government and eventually arranged for tax revenues to be appropriated for the improvement of the road between Tarma and La Merced. In this conflict, *hacienda* owners from the Tarma Valley opposed the tax and their own peer group and aligned themselves with pioneer colonists from Chanchamayo. To avoid the customs post established on the Palca road, landowners began to repair older mule trails that connected their tropical estates with the Andean highlands. This challenge to the authority of Tarma did not mean, however, that Chanchamayo was no longer its hinterland, as confirmed by the fact that it did not acquire the status of a separate province until 1978. In time, the expansion of coffee cultivation, as well as several other factors that we will analyze in the following section, contributed even more significantly to the conformation of the Selva Central as a differentiated regional space.

Existing land-use and colonization policies were oriented to encourage the complete use of the lands that were conceded over the short term. Therefore, the laws stipulated the rights of the new colonists to receive a stipend for a limited period, after which their land was expected to be under production. Labor limitations, difficulties in transporting their produce, taxes, and lack of capital caused the area that was actually cultivated to be much smaller than the area granted. The figures provided by del Valle indicate that of the 36,359 hectares conceded in Chanchamayo in 1876, only 3 percent were under cultivation (La Rosa 1969: 50–67).

Another source of tension with respect to land tenure resulted from the introduction of the formula of temporary or permanent grants and concessions in the land legislation of 1898 and 1909. As a result of this formula, some corporate entities and individuals obtained large areas of land. In general, their owners barely worked them and did not comply with the tax on unused land. The most well-known but not unique case is that of the Peruvian Corporation and its Perene Colony, conceded in 1891 as part of a State payment to external, primarily British, creditors (Manrique n.d; Barclay 1989). These land grants were primarily speculative ventures on the part of their owners. Nevertheless, the existence of concessions in the Perené, Satipo, Mayro, Palcazu, and Pichis areas did not generate greater tensions until they became the target of new flows of migrant colonists. In some cases this took place as early as 1930, and in others, more recently. The revocation of the 1909 law in 1974 did not eliminate all of the conflicts that resulted from the existence of these previous concessions.

Different population flows into the Selva Central gave rise to a complex socioeconomic structure, in which not only were the size of the holding and the volume of capital accumulated by different types of colonists important but so were racial considerations. The combination of these factors determined the opportunities that each of the socioracial sectors extant in the region had to establish links or alliances with the local, regional, and national power groups. Paradoxically, the discriminatory structures prevailing at the national level were reproduced in the Selva Central, the region that was represented as the promised land, full of opportunities for those who possessed initiative and pioneer spirit.

Until the 1930s, European migrants were the most dynamic colonist sector, even if in demographic terms their supremacy was exceeded in 1895 by Peruvian colonists who were attracted by the rise in coffee prices. The majority of these European colonists arrived in the area under the auspices of the Sociedad de Inmigración Europea created in 1872 by President Manuel Pardo. Others arrived on their own or under immigration agreements signed between the State and private organizations, as was the case of the colonists of Tyrol origin who settled in the Pozuzo Valley in 1853. Often these colonists arrived in the area after having attempted some kind of job on the coast or in the highlands. Seven years after the foundation of the La Merced Colony, only 28 percent of the colonists were Peruvian. The rest were immigrants of various nationalities, among whom the Italian group, representing 54 percent of the total, was clearly preponderant (La Rosa 1969). It was not only its large size that determined that this group would become the nucleus of traders and landowners who were to represent the interests of the region. As we shall see, its increasing power was also a result of changes that occurred within Tarma's elite. Thus, the Italians, the few Tarmenians who managed to keep their *haciendas,* and the rest of the European immigrants, who differed according to the size of the landholdings and the volume of capital that they controlled, became the local power group. The racial factor also played an important role in the consolidation of this group.

The group of immigrants from central Europe (Prussia and the Tyrol) who settled in the Pozuzo River valley in the mid-19th century did not achieve an equivalent position until the end of the century, since their arrival to the region was radically different. The 170 families of German descent who formed the Pozuzo Colony were located in an area that was quite isolated from the nearby highlands. Therefore, although the choice of this area for colonization reflects the influence of Pasco mining interests (Ortiz 1967: vol. 1, 250), their involvement in regional commerce ran up against major limitations. Germans succeeded in establishing a small coca-processing industry in the Pozuzo Valley, exporting shipments of cocaine—for pharmaceutical purposes—and *aguardiente* and tobacco to the Pasco and Huánuco highlands. However, most of their output was for their own consumption and for local exchange.

The triumph of Tarma's interests, resulting from the choice of the Tarma-Palca-Chanchamayo route as the main access into the Selva Central, led Huánuco's elite to favor the occupation of the upper Huallaga Valley. Their interests in the Pozuzo Valley were rooted only in the opportunities that this area offered as a connection to a larger navigable river, the Ucayali, that provided them with a connection to the Amazon River and the Atlantic. As a result of the absence of the members of Huánuco's elite in the area, German colonists remained isolated and were prevented from linking themselves with other regional groups. In contrast to the Italians from Chanchamayo, who managed to establish links with Tarma's elite, the Germans in the Pozuzo Valley remained a basically closed group. In time, this group expanded their activities toward the Oxapampa, Palcazu, and Villa Rica valleys and, by 1940, controlled the most aggressive timber industry in the region.

Along with these two groups of European colonists there was a third immigrant group: the Chinese, who settled in Chanchamayo. Chinese immigrants did not constitute a homogeneous group. By 1860, groups of *chinos comprados* (literally, "bought Chinese") were reported to be working on the sugarcane *haciendas*. We are not told by what means this slave labor force was acquired. At the time, another group of Chinese immigrants were working as free laborers or as *mejoreros* (literally, "improvers"), laborers who were hired on various *haciendas* and farms of the valley to establish and maintain plantations until they began to yield. Two of the most prosperous San Ramón estates, Naranjal and Auvernia, depended heavily on Asian laborers when they were first established. A third, less significant group managed their own landholdings, always small in size and principally dedicated to the production of foodstuffs. However, these Chinese families, who also played an important role in the initial phases of the region's occupation, did not succeed in becoming part of the emerging power group formed by the Italian immigrants and the *hacienda* owners from Tarma.

Chinese families that were involved in commerce were more fortunate. They established stores in San Ramón, La Merced, and eventually in Tarma itself. As we will see, this group controlled most of the commercial activity in the valley until 1930, when commercial capital related to coffee trading was restructured. The extent of their importance can be inferred from tax records. In 1908, 59 percent of the traders who paid commercial taxes in Chanchamayo were of Chinese origin, and their payments represented 70 percent of the total revenue (Ministerio de Hacienda 1910: 34). Because of their marginal position in the regional society, the families of Chinese origin living in Chanchamayo retained their own identity, forming a basically independent group.

The bulk of the work force providing field labor came from the highlands, but it was always scarce. In the tropical *haciendas* belonging to members of the Tarma elite, most laborers came from the *haciendas* they owned in the highlands or were provided under formal agreements by relatives who owned highland

estates (Wilson 1979: 47). As immigrant colonists gradually expanded their cultivated lands, they also required labor from the highlands, which they obtained
primarily by advancing some money in order to recruit workers under the *enganche* system (a system whereby laborers are engaged by means of advance
payments of goods or cash). With the progressive expansion of the coffee economy since the 1890s, this system became very widespread and involved large
contingents of Andean laborers each year. Beginning in the 1930s, these migrant
laborers started invading the uncultivated lands of large concessions.

In this hierarchical social context, the local indigenous population constituted
a distinctive group, whose primary feature was its resistance to participation in
the nascent mercantile economy of the area. The relationship between colonists
and the indigenous population was, in principle, based exclusively on the exercise
of military power of the former over the latter. Contemporary legislation provided indigenous peoples with almost no protection against being driven from
their lands, and the few laws that existed were not enforced. An 1847 resolution
declared that "the ownership rights of pacified Indians must be protected" (Ortiz
1969: 237), and another, dated 1853, which was originally formulated in reference
to Loreto but was later extended to Chanchamayo, stated that "Indian lands . . .
may not be taken away by any person or any power if the Indians do not
spontaneously and freely want to sell or cede them" (Chirif 1975: 271). Although
these provisions referred only to areas that were effectively under cultivation and
did not include additional land that groups of indigenous families considered to
be theirs, these norms were never respected. Thus, for instance, when three
French colonists applied to the prefect of Junín for land near the left margin of
Chanchamayo that was "currently under control of the savages," he did not
hesitate to grant it to them (Ortiz 1969: vol. 1, 288).

In 1885, policies referring to the indigenous population were modified when
the Franciscans—Father Gabriel Sala, in particular—once again proposed the establishment of a mission system. The idea of establishing stable settlements for
the indigenous population was intended to satisfy three needs. The first was to
clear out certain areas of interest for colonist occupation by pacifying and concentrating the scattered indigenous families who were opposed to the presence of the
colonists. The second was to place the indigenous population under the care of
the missionaries so as to protect them against the abuses and the armed violence
exercised against them, and, at the same time, to offer them "the advantage of an
isolated home, according to their liking." Finally, the new mission towns were
supposed to make the indigenous population "useful to the country" and to help
them to find "paid jobs" (Izaguirre 1922-1929: vol. 12, 32-33).

The new mission system was tested in San Luis de Shuaro and Sogormo (near
the Paucartambo River) and in Quillazú (near the town of Oxapampa), in areas

that were subsequently occupied by colonists (Barclay and Santos-Granero 1980) (Map 2.1). Hence, whereas from the colonists' point of view the missions achieved their goal, from the missionary viewpoint they were only a partial success. In effect, in at least the first two cases nearly all of the Yanesha who had been gathered left "so as not to become servants and laborers for the European colonists who had settled there" (Izaguirre 1922–1929: vol. 12, 32–33).

Since the end of the century, however, the strategy of retreating no longer allowed the indigenous population to isolate itself from the processes unleashed by colonization. Increased material needs and the debt-peonage system gradually led a growing number of indigenous families to work for the colonists in exchange for payment in manufactured goods (such as cloth, machetes, and shotguns), which they valued highly. With the expansion of coffee cultivation, this process was to have an impact beyond the colonization areas, in that, each year during the harvest season, numerous indigenous families who lived in areas that had not been colonized were attracted to the region. Without any form of effective legal protection, without the knowledge necessary for the development of commercial productive activities, and trapped in the market system by their need for manufactured goods, the Yanesha and Ashaninka finally became involved in the regional economic structure as a cheap labor force.

By the end of this period, colonization and land-tenure policies had become obsolete instruments, inadequate as a response not only to the dynamic acquired by the region but also to the goals that the State originally had envisioned for the Selva Central.

Transition from a Sugarcane Economy to a Coffee Economy

The stimulus that coffee cultivation provided to the occupation of Chanchamayo implied not only substantial changes in the regional economic profile but also, as a result, profound changes in the nature of its articulation with the highland economy and with the national economy. In time, coffee cultivation became the region's primary productive activity, and the coffee economy came to articulate the different colonized areas of the Selva Central in economic, social, and physical terms.

Coffee cultivation was not unheard of in the Selva Central when, in 1887, a sudden increase in coffee prices attracted hundreds of colonists to Chanchamayo (see Figure 2.2). Colonial reports mention coffee on *haciendas* established before the Juan Santos uprising, and, by 1850, it was a crop of some importance on several Vitoc and Monobamba landholdings (Raimondi 1942: vol. 1, 9). In 1870, as a consequence of a severe frost that affected Brazilian coffee production and resulted in a period of high coffee prices between 1870 and 1877, coffee cultivation was introduced, although still in experimental form, in the colonies of San

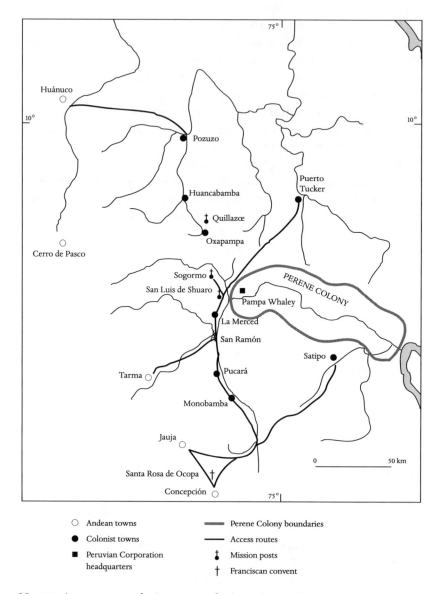

Huánuco ○

10° —

Pozuzo ●

Puerto
Tucker ●

Huancabamba ●

Quillazœ ‡

Oxapampa ●

Cerro de Pasco ○

Sogormo ‡
San Luis de Shuaro ‡

Pampa Whaley ■

PERENE COLONY

La Merced ●

San Ramón

Satipo ●

Tarma ○

Pucará ●

Monobamba ●

Jauja ○

0   50 km

Santa Rosa de Ocopa †

Concepción ○

○   Andean towns

●   Colonist towns

■   Peruvian Corporation
     headquarters

▬▬▬ Perene Colony boundaries

─── Access routes

‡   Mission posts

†   Franciscan convent

Map 2.1. Access routes, colonist towns, and mission posts, 1930.

Figure 2.2. International coffee prices, 1880–1980. *Source:* Raymond 1977: 20.

Ramón and La Merced. Nevertheless, until the price hike of 1887, which stemmed from the suppression of slavery and the establishment of the republic in Brazil, coffee continued to be basically secondary, grown in association with other crops (Barclay 1989: 85). Sugarcane was clearly the most important crop in terms of the area it occupied, and *aguardiente* not only was the product with the highest market value but also constituted the connection between the Chanchamayo and the upland mining economies. To understand the rapid expansion of coffee cultivation at the end of the 19th century, we must take into consideration not only the price increase itself but also the internal and external factors that encouraged this productive reorientation.

After a rebound at the end of the previous century, silver production had stagnated (Fisher 1977: 233). Although in 1820 the combined yield of the Pasco and Yauli mines rose to 312,931 silver *marcos,* representing 66 percent of Peru's total silver production (Fisher 1977: appendix), by 1874 it had dropped to 288,750 *marcos,* representing only 38 percent of the national yield (Dirección de Administración 1874: 15).

Also in 1874, only 90 mines were in operation in Cerro de Pasco, whereas 3,000 had been abandoned (Dirección de Administración 1874: 15). War with Chile in 1879 affected mining production even more, because of the difficulty of shipping ore to the coast by rail. Finally, at the beginning of the 20th century, North American interests began to acquire the Yauli and Cerro de Pasco mines, emphasizing copper rather than silver extraction. This led to the redefinition of the way that these mining centers were connected with the regional, national, and international economies. These transformations profoundly affected the traditional mechanisms of articulation between the upland mining economy and sugarcane production in Chanchamayo.

Up until the end of the 19th century, demand for *aguardiente* by the mining economy in Pasco continued to make sugarcane production on Chanchamayo estates profitable. Thus, in 1888, the Pasco revenue from taxes levied on alcohol consumption rose to 6,000 *soles* (the Peruvian monetary unit after independence) —double that collected in taxes on alcohol in the province of Tarma and five times that collected in Jauja (Memoria Administrativa 1888: 24). The profitability of sugarcane production to the mining economy is further demonstrated by the fact that, in about 1880, the largest sugarcane-producing *haciendas* were mechanized. Steam-powered mills were installed and the cane began to be transported in cable cars. However, the interests of the owners of tropical *haciendas* began to differ from those of land and mine owners in the highlands because of changes in the land ownership system (Wilson 1979: 44, 50–53).

War with Chile ruined the country's economy and affected most regional elites. Tarma's elite was no exception. Ruined by the war and heavily in debt, many Tarmenian landowners were forced to sell their properties, including those in the lowlands. Many of these ended up in the hands of European immigrants who had prospered through their trading activities in Tarma and Chanchamayo. Wilson (1979: 44, 51) contends that by 1860, each of the nine families of Tarma's oligarchy owned at least one property in the lowlands but that, by the end of the century, seven families had lost their holdings. The diminishing economic power of Tarma's elite is reflected in the rural property tax records of Chanchamayo. By 1908, 66 percent of the taxpayers were European immigrants who paid 69 percent of the tax collected (Ministerio de Hacienda 1910).

The displacement of Tarma as the center of control over tropical lands was also a result of the fact that the Europeans and Asians took over commerce in the valley, operating both in Chanchamayo and in Tarma. As one infers from Table 2.1, on the basis of the Chanchamayo taxes registered for "industrial contributions" (which, in 1908, listed only traders), 35 percent of the taxpayers were Europeans, who paid 28 percent of the total taxes collected. Chinese traders accounted for the bulk of the taxes paid, as well as being the largest group of taxpayers in this category (Ministerio de Hacienda 1910: 34). In the district of Cercado de Tarma, 16 percent of the taxpayers were European immigrants (including both traders and industrialists), who paid 31 percent of the taxes

Table 2.1. Industrial Taxpayers and Their Contributions, 1908

National origin	Chanchamayo		Tarma	
	% of all taxpayers	% of total revenue	% of all taxpayers	% of total revenue
Peruvian	5.9	1.6	66.7	35.6
European	35.3	28.1	16.0	31.7
Asian	58.8	70.3	17.3	32.7

Source: Ministerio de Hacienda 1910: 34.

collected. Peruvian nationals, who constituted the numerical majority (67 percent), paid a sum roughly equivalent to that paid by their foreign rivals (36 percent) (Ministerio de Hacienda 1910: 13-14). The strong influence of the Asians (who contributed 33 percent) on trading activity in Tarma did not have a counterpart in the sphere of productive activities. This may be because Chinese immigrants were marginalized in the land-allocation process in the Chanchamayo Valley. It might also have resulted from a consciously elected strategy on the part of the members of the Chinese community. Be that as it may, what is certain is that the Chinese traders did not take advantage of their economic position to acquire large tracts of land in lowland areas, as their Italian counterparts did.

Even after war with Chile, the model of sugarcane cultivation for *aguardiente* production was still viable and attractive to the European immigrants who displaced the Tarma *hacienda* owners of Chanchamayo. Thus, some of these immigrants (such as Juan A. Monier, Pedro Buraschi, and Pablo Kohler) continued to produce *aguardiente* on their sugarcane estates until well into the 20th century. Nonetheless, for Peruvians and for most immigrant colonists, this model was clearly limited. They could not afford to mechanize because of their lack of capital. In addition, the tax on *aguardiente* sales that was established in 1873 greatly reduced their opportunities to accumulate capital and would eventually make sugarcane production untenable. Nor did these colonists have the option to avoid the customs house at Puntayacu by taking the alternate routes that, as we have seen, were constructed or repaired by the large *hacienda* owners. That sugarcane was not a very attractive crop to this group of agriculturalists is reflected by the fact that, in 1876, the existence of cane fields was reported on only 3 percent of the small and mid-sized farms in the valley (La Rosa 1969: 55-65).

In contrast, it was precisely among this group of colonists that coffee production quickly spread. Thus, in 1894 Carranza found that, on the 120 farms located

Table 2.2. Early Coffee Cultivation in the Chanchamayo Valley

	1876			1894
Producer[a]	Nurseries (No. of seedlings)	Plots (No. of plants)	Area in coffee (hectares)[b]	Area in coffee (hectares)[b]
Carranza	_[c]	_[c]	_[c]	5.0
Guillén	_[c]	_[c]	_[c]	2.0
Monier	150,000	0	0.00	50.0
Colombo	5,000	375	0.30	4.0
Maritón	0	1,000	0.80	10.0
Lambert	0	5,550	0.00	15.0
Vergani	285	0	0.00	8.0
Dogo	0	5,550	0.00	30.0
Ghiberti	0	5,550	0.00	20.0
Pirola	0	5,550	0.00	4.0
Gianella	0	2,500	2.10	554.0
Pizzorno	0	5,550	0.00	10.0
Tamagno	0	5,550	0.00	2.0
Strada	0	5,550	0.00	20.0
Curletti	0	5,550	0.00	2.0
Rippamonti	_[d]	1,500	1.25	13.0
Barlagino	_[d]	1,500	1.25	9.0
Pianna	6,000	1,000	0.80	4.0
Sottocorno	0	5,550	0.00	4.0
All 19 producers	161,285	7,875	6.50	216.0

Sources: La Rosa 1969: 55–65; Ortiz 1969: vol. 1, 33-34.

Note: Dashes denote no data.

[a]These producers represent a sample of the producers in the Chanchamayo Valley.

[b]Area is calculated on the basis of an average density of 1,200 coffee plants per hectare.

[c]Coffee plants were still immature.

[d]It is reported that they planted 6 pounds of coffee seeds in nurseries.

between Utcuyacu and San Luis de Shuaro, there were 835 hectares cultivated in coffee (Ortiz 1969: vol. 1, 33). Table 2.2 presents the data from del Valle (La Rosa 1969) and from Carranza (1894), taking only colonists who are listed in both sources into account. This allows us to evaluate the sudden impact that coffee production had on the economy of small and mid-sized producers in Chanchamayo. According to this sample of 19 farmers, the area under coffee cultivation increased by some 3,223 percent in a period of 18 years. From the data provided by del Valle and Carranza, it is also possible to infer that, in 1894, the area under coffee cultivation alone represented eight times the total area under cultivation in 1876. This indicates not only a rapid increase in the number of colonists in the area but also the predominant position that coffee was acquiring in the agricultural production of the valley at the end of the 19th century.

In 1894 there were a total of 2,618 hectares planted in sugarcane in the Chanchamayo and Vitoc valleys (860 and 1,758 hectares, respectively), whereas the area planted in coffee in the two valleys amounted to 1,400 hectares, slightly more than half of the area planted in sugarcane (Ortiz 1969: vol. 1, 423). Nevertheless, the export value of coffee far exceeded that of *aguardiente:* coffee sales from these two valleys produced an income of 330,000 *soles* per year, while revenue from the export of *aguardiente* was reported to be only 161,000 *soles* (Ortiz 1969: vol. 1, 424). By 1903, Chanchamayo and Vitoc already produced the bulk of the total volume of coffee exported by Peru.

Colonists with small and mid-sized holdings adopted coffee cultivation most rapidly, while continuing to grow certain food crops for their own consumption and for the local market. Judging from the observations of the commissions sent by the Peruvian Corporation in 1890 and 1891, coffee cultivation and processing were not highly systematized (Barclay 1989: 86–87). Meanwhile, older estates retained their cane fields and continued to produce *aguardiente,* while some introduced coffee cultivation as well. This combination allowed them to survive the fall in coffee prices that occurred in the first decade of this century, which forced many immigrants, in contrast, including most of those who had been drawn by the rise in coffee prices, to leave, abandoning their coffee farms.

The expansion of coffee cultivation in Chanchamayo had a two-fold effect: on the one hand, the highlands (and mines in particular) were no longer the primary market for Chanchamayo; on the other, the bulk of production in the valley began to be directed toward Lima, principally for export. This accelerated the rate of occupation of the Selva Central and changed the type of relationship that had traditionally linked it with surrounding highland areas. Paradoxically, whereas coffee production forced a reorientation of the commercial network of the Selva Central, severing its connection with the highlands as a consumer market, coffee production strengthened its relationship with these areas in that it depended heavily on them as a source of seasonal labor for coffee harvest. Additionally, along with coffee cultivation, a new form of commercial capital from both the coast (Lima) and from the highlands (Tarma) appeared in the valley: foreign investment. This capital facilitated the expansion of coffee cultivation by outfitting the colonists through the *habilitación* or debt-bondage system. This permitted new colonists to contract labor and to buy depulping machines through advances on their coffee harvest income. Commercial capital that came into circulation through this system of advances took the form of usury capital. In some cases, loans were made at 5 percent monthly interest, and coffee was purchased at market prices. In other cases, interest was not charged, but the coffee was purchased at half the market price (Barclay 1989: 81).

The Tealdo family provides one of the clearest examples of the early connection between commercial capital and coffee production. Santiago Tealdo, the first of the Italian brothers to arrive in Peru, became a trader, establishing a store in Chorillos, close to Lima. War with Chile bankrupted his business and forced Tealdo to peddle his wares in the provinces. In the 1880s, he visited Tarma and La Merced and, realizing the opportunities of the nascent coffee industry, transported the first shipments of Chanchamayan coffee to Lima (Ortiz 1969: vol. 1, 347). In 1886, he established a shop in La Merced and, a short time later, a branch for coffee sales in Lima in partnership with his brother-in-law Tito Praeli (Ortiz 1969: vol. 1, 347). Three years later Tealdo returned to Italy. The firm Tealdo Brothers became N. B. Tealdo and Company, with Nicolas and Miguel Tealdo (brother and son of the former, respectively) as partners of the Italian immigrants Juan Praeli and Luis Peri.

In 1892, the firm, which sold to the national coffee market, inaugurated its own building in Tarma and, in 1896, a new building in La Merced (Ortiz 1969: vol. 1, 347). In 1897, this firm was among one of the major taxpaying businesses in Tarma. In the same year, N. B. Tealdo and Company paid 40 *soles* for two local shops that they had established in Tarma (Matrícula 1897: 81), and they paid 200 *soles* in industrial tax, which represented 29 percent of the total collected, making it the principal taxpayer in the city (Matrícula 1897: 75). Around the same time, the company established the *hacienda* La Romilda for coffee cultivation.

After the sudden fall in coffee prices in 1903, the firm made its first attempts to export to Europe, which became their primary activity in subsequent decades. In 1908, already in competition with other commercial firms, the company (which had by then become N. B. Tealdo, Peri, and Company) paid industrial taxes in Tarma and in La Merced (15 percent and 8 percent, respectively) (Ministerio de Hacienda 1910). Even then, Casa Tealdo continued to be the principal taxpayer in Tarma.

One of the most important consequences of rising coffee prices at the end of the 19th century was that the Peruvian Corporation adopted coffee as the primary product of the Perene Colony. This company, which was composed of British investors holding Peruvian government bonds, had obtained, among various concessions (such as railways and duty collection rights), an area of 500,000 hectares that included both banks of the Perené River. In 1891, it established the Perene Colony at the confluence of the Chanchamayo and Paucartambo rivers. It made major investments both in the preparation of land for cultivation and in bringing European colonists to Peru. From the start, the Perene Colony established coffee plantations. On the basis of the systematization of coffee production and processing, it succeeded in introducing substantial improvements in the operation of its plantations (Barclay 1989: 111–115). When the fall in coffee prices suddenly occurred in 1903, the Peruvian Corporation lost the majority of its immigrant colonists but opted to absorb their lands. Thanks to the financial backing of the British parent company of which it was a subsidiary, the Perene Colony survived the crisis. By then, it was owner of various coffee plantations totaling 400 hectares in area, it had an impressive infrastructure at its disposal, and it had sufficient capital to invest in the recovery of its estates.

Although the organizational systems developed by the Perene Colony were never completely adopted on the other *haciendas* in the valley, the Peruvian Corporation was clearly responsible for the establishment of the technical and production standards for the coffee producers of the Selva Central, as well as for coffee producers in the rest of the country. Furthermore, it was the persistence of the colony, despite labile coffee prices, that, in the long run, provided continuity for the standards adopted in Chanchamayo. This was largely possible not only because the Perene Colony had the backing of British capital but also because, until 1945, the colony controlled a significant proportion of the coffee production of the valley and therefore of the country. The production of select, high-quality coffee placed the company among the most modern and efficient production units of the valley. The extensive use of seasonal labor, as well as the system of *mejoreros* and contractors, led to the spread of the techniques employed by the company on a small scale. This turned out to be against the interests of the company, because of the increased demand for land for the development of independent agricultural production that followed.

In spite of the fact that coffee prices remained unstable throughout this period (with price increases between 1910 and 1920 and between 1925 and 1935, and with a prolonged upturn beginning in 1945) (see Figure 2.2), the region continued to attract colonists who produced coffee on a small scale. From the mid-1920s on, the Perene Colony began to divide into lots and sell the land located north of its coffee plantations, which formed part of the traditional Yanesha territory (Entás, Palomar, and Puñizás). This area was later invaded by the incoming immigrants. In addition, to the northeast of the British-owned *haciendas,* a group of colonists from Oxapampa settled in Villa Rica, establishing their own coffee farms. By 1940, as a result of this expansion, the coffee-growing region of Chanchamayo stretched beyond the geographic limits of the valley. This gradual occupation process, closely linked to the coffee economy, had a homogenizing effect on the interior of the Selva Central. Also, as a result of the increase in activity in the region, the State attempted to restructure land tenure in Chanchamayo. On the basis of 1929 legislation, the government attempted to establish which lands were not cultivated and where they were located so as to be able to collect taxes on uncultivated lands. This law had little effect but fueled protests against the Peruvian Corporation, which owned most of the available land.

The development of the coffee economy in the Selva Central was not uniform. In Oxapampa and Pozuzo, for instance, the transition to a coffee economy was gradual, and although at certain times coffee production predominated, it never completely displaced cattle and sugarcane production in these valleys. Satipo, to the east of Chanchamayo, was a latecomer in the expansion of the coffee econ-omy. Nevertheless, coffee production became the dominant agricultural activity after a few years. As a result of missionary activity, some *haciendas* and a few farms were established along the Ipoki River at the beginning of the century. The area was colonized again at the end of the 1920s, this time under the auspices of President Augusto B. Leguía, who declared all of the lands of the valley freely available (Shoemaker 1981: 79, 81). The first 200 families to enter the area re-ceived an average of 30 hectares each, in a territory that had traditionally been occupied by Ashaninka and Nomatsiguenga. However, these small farms did not prosper until 1940, when the road to Huancayo was built. This road, which was built to transport the expanding barbasco crop (*Lonchocarpus nicou,* the roots of which are used in the manufacturing of insecticides), drew a large number of migrants in search of free land. Soon afterward, coffee prices began to rise again. As major investors and farmers became established, Satipo developed into a coffee-growing region.

During most of this period, the Palcazu and Pichis basins remained on the periphery of the new activity. In both valleys the government had granted large concessions for rubber exploitation, but this activity did not have a significant effect on the structure of the area's economy. At the end of this period, cattle-ranching estates began to appear in both valleys, and in the Pichis basin, the State-run Corporación Peruana del Amazonas (Peruvian Amazon Corporation) successfully encouraged rubber collection between 1942 and 1950.

The evolution of loans granted by the Banco Agrícola (Agricultural Bank) was closely tied to the expansion of coffee production (Table 2.3). Loans in the Selva Central were dedicated to coffee production from the start, although in several years (1940-1944) long-term loans were also given for tea, barbasco, and fruit cultivation. In Satipo, loans were given for rice cultivation between 1944 and 1946. During these years, the credit was mainly allocated to large landowners, primarily on the basis of long-term loans. This situation was to be radically altered in the following years (Banco Agrícola 1931-1950).

The expansion of the coffee economy had two major effects on the social and economic situation of the indigenous peoples in the Selva Central. First, the

Table 2.3. Loans Granted by the Banco Agrícola in the Selva Central

Year	Chanchamayo No.	% of total no.	% of total amount	Oxapampa No.	% of total no.	% of total amount	Satipo No.	% of total no.	% of total amount	Selva Central No.	% of total no.	% of total amount
1936–1937	7	0.8	0.43	0	0.0	0.00	0	0.0	0.00	7	0.8	0.43
1937–1938	59	3.8	0.89	0	0.0	0.00	0	0.0	0.00	59	3.8	0.89
1938–1939	87	4.3	1.53	0	0.0	0.00	0	0.0	0.00	87	4.3	1.53
1939–1940	124	5.2	1.94	9	0.4	0.02	0	0.0	0.00	133	5.6	1.96
1940–1941[a]	38	1.6	0.88	0	0.0	0.00	0	0.0	0.00	38	1.6	0.88
1941–1942	79	2.5	1.30	0	0.0	0.00	0	0.0	0.00	79	2.5	1.30
1942–1943[b]	97	2.8	1.30	0	0.0	0.00	0	0.0	0.00	97	2.8	1.30
1943–1944	76	2.1	1.09	18	0.5	0.04	66	1.9	0.10	160	4.5	1.31
1944–1945	80	2.1	1.39	16	0.4	0.03	56[c]	1.5	0.00	152	4.0	1.53
1945–1946	77	1.7	1.45	13	0.3	0.03	19	0.4	0.00	109	2.4	1.54
1946–1947	70	1.4	1.22	16	0.3	0.06	33	0.6	0.00	119	2.3	1.51
1947–1948	66	1.3	0.73	8	0.1	0.03	15	0.3	0.19	89	1.7	0.95
1948–1949	48	0.8	0.58	5	0.1	0.03	0[d]	0.0	0.00	53	0.9	0.61
1949–1950	65	0.9	1.40	8	0.1	0.03	2	0.0	0.10	73	1.0	1.58

Sources: Banco Agrícola 1936-1950; data elaborated by the authors.

Notes: "% of total no." denotes the percentage in relation to the total number of loans granted in the country. "% of total amount" denotes the percentage in relation to the total amount of loan money granted in the country. 1936 was the first year in which loans were given for the Selva Central by the Banco Agrícola. Until 1939-1940, all loans were for coffee; because of the fall in prices of this product, beginning in 1940 the cultivation of barbasco and tea were encouraged through the granting of long-term loans.

[a] In 1940-1941 and the following two periods, loans to Chanchamayo and Oxapampa were registered jointly.

[b] In 1942-1943, it was reported that an indeterminate number of loans were given in Satipo, Tingo María, and Huánuco.

[c] In 1944-1945, all of the loans authorized in Satipo were for rice cultivation.

[d] In 1948-1949, loans were not given in Satipo because of the 1947 earthquake.

gradual occupation of space was achieved not only by taking over their territory but also through the physical displacement of indigenous families settled in the major areas of interest for coffee cultivation. Second, hundreds of indigenous families eventually became involved as temporary laborers for coffee harvest. Indigenous laborers received lower daily wages than did the rest of the harvesters. Furthermore, as they were not offered lodging, nor did they require the payment of travel expenses from the highlands, as was the case with seasonal Andean laborers, the so-called *chunchos* became a valued labor force. *Hacienda* owners not only employed the indigenous people living immediately adjacent to their lands but also drew up contracts with the headmen of local indigenous groups located within several days' journey by giving them pay advances.

Following this procedure, Yanesha harvesters from Oxapampa, Palcazu, and Cacazú and Ashaninka from mid- and lower Perené, the Pichis, and from the Ene and Tambo rivers went to work at the Chanchamayo and Villa Rica *haciendas,* particularly to the Perene Colony and to Cedropamapa. Their numbers never exceeded that of the highland workers who arrived annually in the Selva Central. In 1939, Máximo Kuczynski-Godard estimated that, in the Perene Colony, the indigenous laborers represented 5 percent to 10 percent of the total work force, on average, but in some years this rose to 39 percent (Barclay 1989: 122). At the end of this transitional period, some of the indigenous families established in the upper Perené Valley began to grow coffee on small plots that ranged in size from 0.25 to 3.25 hectares (Barclay 1989: 225). By then, the Selva Central had become one of the most important colonization frontiers in the country, while it developed an economic profile based on coffee production and established the foundations for its internal articulation.

Road Construction and the Process of Internal Articulation in the Selva Central

It was during this stage that the various areas that were to form the Selva Central region were progressively occupied. However, these areas did not become articulated during this period because each preserved its own routes of access to the highlands and to the coast. The few roads that linked one tropical area to another were still basically mule trails.

Tarma's victory in the dispute for control of access to the Selva Central in the mid-19th century did not translate into control over all of the occupied areas in the region during this period. During the second half of the 19th century, schemes that were designed to enlarge the sphere of influence of Tarma and of the State were based on the construction of a road network that linked the highlands with the Amazonian region, crossing the newly colonized areas. Tarma successfully persuaded the government to abandon the idea of building a central railway line that would extend from the Pasco highlands to a navigable Amazonian river in favor of the construction of the Via Central del Pichis (Central Pichis Route), which would serve as the continuation of the Tarma–La Merced–San Luis de Shuaro road (see Map 2.1). In this campaign, Tarma's elite once again had the support of Franciscan missionaries and of Father Gabriel Sala in particular, who played an important role in the exploration of the region and later in the process of its occupation. Equally important was the fact that the Peruvian Corporation, originally in charge of the design and construction of the railway, established the Perene Colony precisely in the area where the road from Tarma to Chanchamayo connected with the Via Central del Pichis.

Although the Via Central, which linked Tarma with Puerto Tucker on the Pichis River, was completed in 1898, it was never a great magnet to colonists.

Only the initial stretches of this road, which extended along the banks of the Paucartambo River, were settled. Because of the hardships of travel on this road, the long distances to consumer and trading areas, and constant fluctuations in the price of coffee, this route did not attract large numbers of colonists.

Because the interests of the local power group were directly related to the *haciendas* of the Chanchamayo Valley, and because commercial capital associated with this area had not extended its radius of influence toward the other colonized areas, the road-building efforts pushed by *hacienda* owners tended to concentrate on the maintenance and improvement of the road to Tarma. This road allowed them to export their products to Lima, taking advantage of the expansion of the central railroad from this town to the mining center of La Oroya. Thus, the most powerful landowners and traders in the valley gathered to form the Junta de Vigilancia de Obras Viales (Transportation Oversight Group), which was to become the most important association in the area.

Through the Junta, the local power group monopolized control over funds for maintenance of this road—which gave vehicles access up to the entrance of the Perene Colony—as well as for the construction of new roads. This effectively meant that the local power group had absolute control over the direction that the process of occupation of the region should take and could include or marginalize certain geographical areas according to their economic interests. That control of the Junta was of fundamental importance to this group is reflected by the fact that between 1920 and 1929 its president, Victor Valle Riestra, was director of the Perene Colony, and its other two members were the owner of the Naranjal and Auvernia coffee *haciendas* and a representative of the Casa Tealdo, the most important coffee trader in the valley together with the British Perene Colony. Support given by President Leguía to the continuation of this road construction project was crucial during this period.

Only since the mid-1930s, when the logging industry developed in Oxapampa and when one of the first sawmills signed a contract for the sale of railway ties for the central railroad (which, by then, belonged to the Peruvian Corporation), did the Junta push for the expansion of the road network into this new area. Previously, the agriculturalists in Oxapampa had managed to construct, through their own efforts, half of the route to La Merced, while the authorities and the Chanchamayo power group did nothing to finish this section. The decision to complete it was also influenced by the fact that Villa Rica was becoming another important coffee-producing center, which awoke the interest of investors in Chanchamayo. It was for these reasons that during most of this early stage Oxapampa maintained its connection and means of communication with Huánuco and Pasco.

Satipo continued to be linked to the Andean town of Huancayo (which, at the end of the period, had replaced Jauja as the commercial center of the central Andes) by way of the small town of Concepción, until the road was completely destroyed by an earthquake in 1947. At this point, Tarma began to make efforts to block reconstruction of the route. It should be noted that, whereas it is true that Tarma's elite lost influence in Chanchamayo, this area remained administratively attached to the province of Tarma, which continued to reap benefits from local colonists through tax collection.

For this reason, as we will see later, it was not in Tarma's best interest to rebuild the Satipo-Concepción road. During this entire period, therefore, Satipo remained totally independent of Chanchaymayo, while the Perené Valley — the area between the two, which was owned by the Peruvian Corporation — was only partially occupied at its two extremes.

Finally, the Palcazu and Pichis areas, associated with the German colonies of Oxapampa and Pozuzo, were economically oriented toward the town of Pucallpa on the Ucayali River. By 1943, trading activities in Pucallpa were fueled by the opening of the road that connected it to Lima. Cattle, the principal product of these areas, were carried downriver by raft, since air transport between these valleys and San Ramón had not yet been established.

A few observations on the lack of internal articulation of the Selva Central during this period are necessary at this point. First, from road-building schemes in the first decades after the reconquest (1847), which sought access into or attempted to connect the coast and the highlands with the Amazon River by way of the Selva Central, there was a shift to a scheme that emphasized road construction to facilitate the export of products to coastal markets. Thus, during this stage, the idea of building roads in order to stimulate and direct the flow of colonization had not developed, and that of linking various colonized areas of eastern Peru even less so. These concepts arose as a response to problems created by the rigid agrarian structure of the highlands and increased migration toward the coast, phenomena that were to become more evident in the 1940s.

Second, the lack of connection between the various colonization areas within the Selva Central reflects the fact that, in economic, political, and social terms, the forces that were to lead to its integration had still not developed. The independent economic dynamics of these areas were translated into distinctly different cultural profiles.

Finally, it should be noted that when these different areas were finally linked by roads, it was La Merced, and not Tarma, that became the gateway for export. As a consequence, it is not surprising that commercial interests expanded from this central area into the rest of the region. In spite of the fact that Tarma

Table 2.4. Major Towns in the Selva Central

Town	Year of foundation	Population in 1940
San Ramón	1847	1,275
Pozuzo	1857	1,340
La Merced	1869	831
San Luis de Shuaro	1886	8
Oxapampa	1891	796
Puerto Bermúdez[a]	1892	119
Villa Rica	1925	139
Satipo	1927	232

Source: República del Perú n.d.

[a]Originally Puerto Tucker.

continued to be the provincial seat, its commercial role was reduced to being a way station for products that were being transported to the coast.

As we will see, the rate of demographic growth of the Selva Central during the period of pioneer colonization was basically a function of periodic increases in coffee prices. The population was mainly concentrated on *haciendas*. Thus, San Ramón and La Merced, declared district capitals at the turn of the century, continued to be sparsely populated in spite of their commercial dynamism. By 1894, the total population of the Chanchamayo Valley was 4,500, of which only 11 percent lived in the settlements of San Ramón (140 inhabitants), La Merced (250 inhabitants), and San Luis de Shuaro (100 inhabitants) (Ortiz 1969: vol. 1, 420). All of the major towns extant in the region today were founded at the end of this period, except for Pichanaki, Santa Ana, and Iscozacín. In fact, most of them were founded very early in the colonization process (Table 2.4).

Their fates varied widely, however. Whereas, beginning in the 20th century, some towns, like La Merced and Satipo, grew quickly, others, like Pozuzo and San Luis de Shuaro, which began with great dynamism, are only small villages today. This unequal development, both of rural areas as well as of more populous towns and villages, is explained by the differential evolution of the road system that connected the areas with the rest of the country and shaped the direction of their trade flows. Thus, for instance, San Luis de Shuaro maintained its importance while it served as an intermediate supply point in the Via Central del Pichis. As this route was gradually abandoned during the first half of the 20th century, and communication systems were modernized, San Luis entered a period of decline which it never managed to reverse. The earthquake that destroyed the Satipo-Concepción road, as we will see, had even more far-reaching consequences with respect to the external and internal articulation of the region.

MASS OCCUPATION AND CONSOLIDATION OF THE REGIONAL SPACE: 1947-1990

The sustained rise in coffee prices in the period from 1949 to 1959, with a peak price of US$0.70 per pound—which represented an increase of 174 percent with respect to the 1947 price—attracted new waves of Andean colonists to the Selva Central. This marked the beginning of a period of accelerated migration into the region. By that time, the best land in the Chanchamayo and Oxapampa valleys was already allotted. Pozuzo, which did not have a road connecting it with Chanchamayo and facilitating the export of its products to the market in Lima, remained in relative geographic isolation and at the periphery of the massive colonization processes that were unleashed at this stage. Thus, the flow of migrants was oriented toward the vast lands of the Perené and Satipo valleys and, to a lesser extent, toward the mountainous area around Villa Rica. Demographic pressure on the land, along with other political, economic, and even natural factors, led to the decomposition of the *hacienda* system that had dominated the previous period. In order to evaluate the significance of these processes, we will analyze three different cases in the following section: the Perene Colony, the agricultural conglomerates of Chanchamayo, and the speculative holdings of Satipo.

The Case of the Perene Colony

The Perene Colony, with its concession that spanned both shores of the Perené River, was an obstacle to the achievement of the goals of the Andean colonists who in the 1940s entered the area through Chanchamayo and Satipo looking for land. Until 1940, the colony's coffee plantations occupied only about 1,000 hectares of the 500,000-hectare concession, which also included some 250 hectares of orchards, natural and planted pastures, and food crops (Barclay 1989: 155). The enormous discrepancy between the total area granted and the area that was actually under production prompted colonists to question the legitimacy of the concession. The Peruvian Corporation had failed to comply with the terms under which the concession was originally granted. These terms stipulated that the area should be colonized within a period of no more than three years after it was granted and that the concessionaires should complete colonization of the area within a maximum of nine years. In the case that they did not, they would lose a third of the lands granted for each year that they delayed (Manrique n.d.: 18). In addition, under the 1909 Ley de Tierras de Montaña, the Perene Colony would be required to pay an annual tax of one cent per hectare of uncultivated land (Barclay 1989: 137).

At the beginning of this stage, the Perene Colony had achieved its maximal level of technical advancement and had standardized its coffee-exploitation model. Since 1940 the company had begun to make a profit, obtaining the highest profit margins in its history in 1950. However, the overall output of the colony dropped during this period, partly because of the abandonment of the oldest *haciendas* but also because, beginning in 1948, the colony stopped outfitting small property owners located within the original concession and therefore lost access to their output (Barclay 1989: 156). Nevertheless, high coffee prices led the business to consider the expansion of its best plantations and the establishment of new *haciendas*. Thus, in 1950, it began to expand the San Juan *hacienda,* its most productive unit. In 1965, the Perene Colony had 1,672 hectares of coffee, 168 hectares of pastureland, and 126 hectares of fruit crops.

The favorable situation for coffee production had, therefore, contradictory effects: on the one hand, it attracted numerous colonists who were willing to establish themselves in the lands that were not being exploited within the colony; on the other, it awoke in the directors of the colony a renewed interest in preserving their lands, which were rapidly becoming more valuable. Conditions were ripe, therefore, for a confrontation between the Peruvian Corporation and the invading Andean peasants. This took place beginning in 1954 with the arrival and establishment of 70 colonist families on the right bank of the upper Perené Valley and the foundation of Villa Amoretti, a town across from Pampa Whaley, the administrative headquarters of the Perene Colony.

In the preceding period, the colony had begun to feel the effects of pressure from colonists along its northern frontier. The first land sales to individual colonists were made in the 1920s and 1930s. The explicit intention of the company was to award only small plots that would allow colonists to produce enough coffee to guarantee the permanence of their families in the neighborhood of the colony but little enough so that the same colonists could be employed as seasonal laborers when necessary (Barclay 1989: 132-133). Beginning in 1946, as a result of pressure from new colonists as well as from the government, the colony was required to sell off land in the north and east (Manrique n.d.: 51-52). Thus the areas of El Palomar, Alto Yurinaki, Paucartambo, San Juan, and Río Vayós were divided into several plots. Two areas were set apart especially for the Yanesha and Ashaninka (Manrique n.d.: 53-57). In all of these cases, the Perene Colony made arrangements with individual colonists to pay for their lands, thus preserving its rights of ownership of the concession.

In contrast, the occupation of lands by colonists that took place after 1954 on the right bank of the Perené River, in the southern part of the colony, was principally by means of invasion. In spite of its influence on Peruvian politics, the right of the British company to continue to occupy the lands of the Perené Valley was, by that time, often questioned in Congress. Taking advantage of this political uncertainty, several waves of migrant colonists entered from both Satipo and Chanchamayo, invading the colony at its two extremes. This process was not free of violence. In the face of the refusal of the colonists to pay for the land they occupied, the colony resorted to the public police force and its own armed personnel to remove them. Economic pressure was added to the use of force, since to take out their produce the colonists had to make use of the ferry and the roads on the left bank of the Perené River, an area under the strict control of the colony. The requirement that colonists be able to show a land title in order to use these facilities, as well as to obtain loans from the Banco de Fomento Agropecuario (Agricultural Development Bank), forced many colonists to agree to the company's conditions.

But the growing number of invading colonists, as well as the scandals that the situation in the colony provoked in national forums, resulted in a weakening of the control that the Peruvian Corporation exercised over its lands. In the beginning, the firm tried to use various legal subterfuges to preserve its rights. In 1958, it transferred its property to two subsidiary firms: the Compañía Agrícola Pampa Whaley, which, with 61,307 hectares, conserved the original *haciendas* as well as an area of expansion, and the Negociación Perené, which, with 391,989 hectares, was dedicated to land sales (Manrique n.d.: 69). But because of the public outcry, the government nullified these arrangements in 1965, as well as all rights to the concession granted in 1891.

Beginning in 1965, the government started to distribute land on both banks of the Perené River under the agrarian reform of 1964. However, it was only in 1970, under the 1969 Agrarian Reform Law of the military government, that the old *haciendas* of the colony were affected. These became the Cooperativa Agraria de Producción Juan Velasco Alvarado, with a total of 2,278 hectares for 276 families of former colony workers. By that time, Andean colonists had occupied most of the bottom of the Perené Valley. They were grouped in several colonies: Anashironi-Pichanaki, Río Ipoki, and Margen Derecha del Río Ipoki (all on the right bank of the Perené River); and Santos Atahuallpa, Ubiriki, Sutziki-Perené, and Miratirini-Cascadas (on the left bank). Some of these groups of colonists were organized into 13 agricultural cooperatives for coffee marketing, which took off with the inauguration of the La Merced-Satipo road in 1973.

The Case of Chanchamayo *Haciendas* and Agricultural Conglomerates

High coffee prices, which resulted in the invasion and subsequent partition of the Peruvian Corporation's concession, led to a different set of processes in Chanchamayo. Whereas, beginning in 1947, the Perene Colony was forced to divide its efforts between driving out invading colonists and implementing investment and expansion projects, the Chanchamayo *haciendas* modernized and increased the efficiency of their production system. At the beginning of the century, the districts of Chanchamayo and Vitoc registered 61 *haciendas,* each with a population that ranged from 80 to 400 inhabitants (Ortiz 1969: vol. 1, 480). These estates were never as extensive as the highland and coastal *haciendas,* most of them ranging in size from 500 to 5,000 hectares.

In 1940, in the San Ramón district alone, where the oldest *haciendas* of the valley were concentrated, 21 large and mid-sized landholdings were registered. Their population exceeded 1,673, representing 47 percent of the total population of the district and 73 percent of its rural population (República del Perú n.d.). In the district of Chanchamayo, where there were also numerous farms, there were 37 *haciendas* registered in 1940, whose 2,324 inhabitants represented 26 percent of the rural population. Thus, a high percentage of the rural population in these districts was composed of permanent *hacienda* peons and their families. In spite of the ups and downs experienced by the *hacienda* system, *haciendas* continued to be the predominant units of production in the Chanchamayo Valley for most of this period.

With the upturn in coffee prices, the *hacienda* system underwent a restructuring process that was expressed, on the one hand, in the transfer and concentration of property, and, on the other, in the increased investment of commercial capital in coffee production and management. An examination of several examples will allow us to see how both changes led to the capitalization and modernization of the *haciendas* in the valley. The Perene Colony, although under a different administrative structure, was the first to set out in this direction, and, as we have seen, for a long time it was the undisputed leader in the application of new technologies and modern forms of management in Chanchamayo. When it transferred its estates to the Compañía Agrícola Pampa Whaley, in 1958, it assured its association with commercial export capital by placing a large portion of Peruvian shares (which made up 40 percent of the total) in the hands of Jorge Harten (Barclay 1989: 208). Harten owned three companies related to the coffee industry: J. and G. Harten and Company, a coffee-warehousing business; Mokafé, which roasted coffee for the national market; and Productos Peruanos, a coffee-export company. In subsequent years, this last firm was to become the principal coffee-export house in the country. Harten also became the administrator of the Perene Colony from 1958 until its liquidation in 1967.

The changes that took place on the traditional Génova *hacienda* beginning in 1947, when it was acquired by Víctor M. Zanabria, are representative of some of the trends that predominated in the Chanchamayo Valley during this period. The new owner of the *hacienda* — which encompassed a total of 1,000 hectares — also owned a commercial firm based in Lima, V. M. Zanabria e Hijos, devoted to coffee trading (Ortiz 1969: vol. 2, 634). To modernize the *hacienda*, its new owner diversified production, combining coffee cultivation with the cultivation of fruit crops (citrus, avocado, papaya, pineapple, and banana). In addition, there were food crops to feed the *hacienda* personnel—more than 500 people in 1956, including workers and their families (Ortiz 1969: vol. 2, 635). The *hacienda* had a modern plant for coffee processing and selection, as well as agricultural machinery and repair workshops. In 1959, Génova was in the process of expanding its coffee area, with a nursery of more than half a million coffee plants of the standard variety. Likewise, it was building a coloring chamber for fruit crops, in order to improve their appearance and increase their price on the national market (Ortiz 1969: vol. 2, 643).

The Génova case is an example of a single *hacienda* that was modernized with the aid of commercial capital. In other cases, however, modernization and mechanization were tightly linked to a process of property concentration. The phenomenon of agricultural conglomerates was not new to the region. At the beginning of the century, Pedro Buraschi already owned three *haciendas* (Chalhuapuquio, Cañaveral, and San Miguel). Francisco Santamaría had two large properties (Huacará and Santo Domingo de Palmapata), and Carlos Galleres owned two other important *haciendas* (San Jacinto and La Victoria) (Ortiz 1969: vol. 1, 480). The new element at this stage was the organization of the so-called *sociedades agrícolas* (agricultural societies) or *negociaciones agrícolas* (agribusinesses): conglomerates of *haciendas* managed as corporations. This structure allowed access to commercial capital for the development of large-scale agricultural and pastoral activities based on the modernization and technological development of groups of traditional *haciendas*.

In some cases the modernization process developed within previously existing organizational structures, such as those of the Naranjal, Auvernia, and Chincana *haciendas*. In 1942, these three estates, with a total of 14,845 hectares, were in the hands of Leoncio Lanfranco, owner of one of the most important coffee-export firms in the country. In 1924, Lanfranco had already invested considerable capital in upgrading the production and processing technology of his coffee estates (Ortiz 1969: vol. 1, 517). His *haciendas* also produced *aguardiente*, fruit, cotton, and fine timber (Ortiz 1969: vol. 2, 632). When coffee prices peaked in the 1940s, Naranjal became the most modern coffee *hacienda* after the Perene Colony and provided a reference point with regard to productivity levels, salaries, and wholesale coffee prices for the Perene Colony to measure its success against (Barclay 1989: 153, 158). In 1970, these *haciendas* had 2,803 hectares under cultivation and 100 hectares of pastureland (Reforma Agraria n.d.).

The clearest example of property concentration and modernization related to the investment of commercial capital is represented by Sociedad Agrícola

Chalhuapuquio, formed in the 1940s. This society belonged to the Casa Tealdo and Company economic group, which, in this period, was the largest coffee exporter in the country. It was composed of the old Chalhuapuquio, Cañaveral, San Miguel, and Amable María *haciendas*. As has been mentioned, the first three were already associated at the beginning of the century, under another owner. With the addition of the Amable María estate and the formation of Sociedad Agrícola Chalhuapuquio, the Tealdo group set a new economic model in motion that revolutionized the production schemes that prevailed on these *haciendas* in the past.

The principal change was the final abandonment of large-scale sugarcane cultivation. On the San Miguel *hacienda,* extensive cane fields were replaced by corn, banana, and avocado plantings, whereas, on other *haciendas,* they were replaced by tropical forages brought from Costa Rica (Ortiz 1969: vol. 2, 640). Also imported from Costa Rica were new varieties of coffee, which had become the preferred crop. Furthermore, former coffee fields were abandoned and new areas were developed to increase productivity. The second most important crop was fruit, primarily citrus and avocado. Sociedad Agrícola Chalhupuquio produced 20,000 crates of avocado in 1958, which represented approximately 16 percent of the avocado production registered in 1957 for the areas of Chanchamayo and San Ramón (Ortiz 1969: vol. 2, 640, 920). One of the innovations that was introduced was the management of the different estates in the conglomerate as specialized production units, with processing services for major products such as coffee, concentrated on one of the estates. Roads into the interior of each of the estates were built to eliminate the use of mule teams for coffee transport and to facilitate timber extraction from the forested areas of the conglomerate. These roads joined at the Cañaveral *hacienda,* where the coffee-processing plant was located. Technological innovations also included the intensive use of fertilizers, which were prepared locally. Finally, as part of its modernization process, Sociedad Agrícola Chalhuapuquio began the construction of housing and collective facilities for their laborers. These investments were geared toward making work on the *hacienda* more attractive in order to overcome the problem of the chronic labor shortage in the valley.

Several of the new and modern agribusinesses placed more emphasis on the production of fruit crops than on coffee production. This was the case in the conglomerate formed by the San Carlos, Quisquis, and Dos de Mayo *haciendas* owned by Juan Espinosa. All of these estates originally cultivated sugarcane for *aguardiente* production. By 1956 this conglomerate was working under a model similar to that of Sociedad Agrícola Chalhuapuquio. San Carlos produced citrus crops almost exclusively. Quisquis primarily produced coffee, whereas at Dos de Mayo, coffee production was combined with cultivation of forage crops for cattle breeding based on imported stock. Facilities such as machine shops and installations for employees, seasonal laborers, and their families, who numbered nearly 500 (Ortiz 1969: vol. 2, 636), were concentrated on the first and oldest of these *haciendas*. This conglomerate was later acquired by the Peschiera Bohl family, which was the principal partner in Sociedad Agrícola San Carlos and whose lands were subsequently affected by the agrarian reform in 1970 (Reforma Agraria n.d.).

The last case to be considered is that of Negociación Agrícola Francia-Roma, established at the end of the 1940s. The two most important partners in this business were Carlos Peschiera Pastorelli and Miguel Baldini. Pastorelli had worked for Casa Tealdo for many years, later entering independently into the coffee-export business (Ortiz 1969: vol. 2, 646). This agribusiness was fundamentally devoted to fruit production, oranges being the principal staple produced by the firm. In 1956, the company owned 200 hectares of orange trees. The Francia *hacienda* was one of the most technologically advanced in the valley in terms of citrus production, the testing of new varieties, and facilities for culling and washing the oranges (Ortiz 1969: vol. 2, 636).

This technological improvement also reached the medium-sized holdings. Mid-sized coffee and fruit farms, such as those of Orlando Salvatierra and Oscar Mayor in Chanchamayo and of the Brack and Mick families in Villa Rica, became models of modern management and high profitability. The economic success generated by agribusiness in the valley may be appreciated through an evaluation of the deposits and loans in commercial banks in Chanchamayo between 1949 and 1957 (Table 2.5). During this period, loans by commercial banks grew by 386 percent, and in an even more spectacular manner, deposits grew by 1,061 percent, such that, in 1957, deposits in commercial banks in Chanchamayo exceeded loans by 83 percent. It should be noted, however, that a significant part of the earnings generated in the region remained in Lima as a result of coffee export. Thus it can be asserted that the bank deposits at the time reflected, more than anything else, the fact that small and mid-sized producers could save money.

In the 1960s, when agrarian reform became an issue in Peru, mid-sized and large property holdings in the Chanchamayo Valley had reached their maximal degree of economic development. When the agrarian reform was implemented during the government of General Velasco Alvarado, it established a maximal size for individual holdings of 80 hectares, which would potentially affect all of the *haciendas* and a large number of the modern farms of the valley. The justification for land reform on these *haciendas* differed from that used to cancel the Peruvian Corporation's concession in 1965. Whereas in the case of the Perene Colony, as in those of many southern Andean *haciendas*, the government intervened, alleging that it held great extensions of unproductive land, *haciendas* in

Table 2.5. Loans and Deposits in Commercial Banks of La Merced and San Ramón

Bank activity and locale	1949	1950	1951	1952	1953	1954	1955	1956	1957
Loans									
La Merced	1,298	2,228	3,314	3,598	2,726	3,230	3,047	4,075	6,783
San Ramón	263	647	769	1,452	1,387	1,049	1,082	654	310
Total	1,561	2,875	4,083	5,050	4,113	4,279	4,129	4,729	7,093
Deposits									
La Merced	560	1,338	2,729	2,932	3,286	5,535	6,829	7,592	7,731
San Ramón	636	691	1,150	1,365	1,379	3,398	4,011	2,621	6,157
Total	1,196	2,029	3,879	4,297	4,665	8,933	10,840	10,213	13,888

Source: Ortiz 1969: vol. 2, 952.

Note: Values are in thousands of *soles.*

Chanchamayo were reformed for the same reasons wielded to justify reform of the *haciendas* in the coastal region.

Like the coastal sugarcane-producing *haciendas,* the large coffee- and fruit-pro-ducing holdings of Chanchamayo consisted of highly capital-intensive produc-tion units with facilities for the primary processing of the product and were often closely linked to the export houses. But, in contrast to the large coastal landhold-ings, the Chanchamayan *haciendas* had not seen a labor movement develop. Thus labor conflicts were not considered a reason for the reforms.

Nevertheless, there was intense demographic pressure on the land in this area. The population of Chanchamayo grew by 144 percent between the censuses in 1940 and 1961 and by 78 percent in the intercensus interval 1961–1972 (Aramburú n.d.: 12). Furthermore, the kinds of products and intensive agricultural practices developed required abundant labor, and many *haciendas* in Chanchamayo had more than 100 working families who were hungry for land. One can state, there-fore, that the decision to reform these properties did not have as much to do with labor strife resulting from a strong labor movement as with generic social conflicts: the great disparity in the distribution of land. Moreover, the military government wanted to break up the power of the coffee-producing groups to monopolize the coffee-export business for the benefit of the public treasury.

In 1968, Chanchamayo contributed 42 percent of the national coffee output, a large percentage of which was produced on large and mid-sized holdings, which were tightly linked to commercial coffee capital. The firms Lanfranco Monier and N. B. Tealdo and Company (the two largest agribusinesses in the valley) alone controlled 13 percent and 11 percent, respectively, of the volume of coffee exported from the country in 1963 (Watson 1964: 68). To this, one would have to add the 24 percent controlled by Productos Peruanos, whose owner, Jorge Harten, was stockholder and administrator of the old Perene Colony, which was converted into the Compañía Agrícola Pampa Whaley. The fact that these three export houses, which also ran the largest *haciendas* in the Chanchamayo area, controlled 47 percent of the coffee exported, becomes even more significant if one considers that, in 1968, coffee exports represented 21 percent of the value of the total agropastoral exports of the country (Banco Central de Reserva 1970). Given this situation, control of the coffee business, which could yield high revenues, represented a strategic objective to the government.

Although in the 1960s some of the *haciendas* began to sell part of their unused land, agrarian reform affected many of these estates in the Chanchamayo and Satipo valleys. Some of the lands that were affected by the agrarian reform were allocated to individual owners, whereas 13,550 hectares were granted as joint property to nine Cooperativas Agrarias de Producción, or Agrarian Production Cooperatives. Eight of these were located in the districts of San Ramón, Vitoc, and Chanchamayo (Juan Santos Atahuallpa, José Carlos Mariátegui, José María Arguedas, Túpac Amaru, Manco Cápac, Pampa del Carmen, Santa Clara, and Juan Velasco Alvarado) and one in the Satipo Valley (La Victoria) (Table 2.6).

The agrarian cooperatives in the Chanchamayo Valley were primarily composed of the land under production on the *haciendas* and of their industrial facilities. In many cases, a cooperative consisted of several *haciendas* that had previously belonged to different owners. The eight cooperatives in Chanchamayo were granted 9,003 hectares, which represented 10 percent of the agricultural area of the San Ramón, Chanchamayo, and Vitoc districts (Recharte n.d: 116). The total number of participants in the cooperatives included more than 884 heads of households, all of them former permanent employees, contractors, *mejoreros,* or laborers on the *haciendas* (INP/PNUD 1977). The importance of the agrarian-reform process in this area was expressed by the fact that these cooperative members constituted 30 percent of the total number of beneficiaries of all of the agrarian cooperatives in the *selva alta* (Caballero y Alvarez 1980: 63).

The expropriation of the large coffee-producing *haciendas* under the 1969 agrarian reform was followed by a series of measures intended to democratize the conditions for coffee commercialization, so as to guarantee State control of its export. To achieve this, the formation of Cooperativas Agrícolas de Servicios, or Agricultural-Services Cooperatives, was encouraged, giving them priority of access to promotional credit through the Banco Agrario (Agrarian Bank).

As a result of these measures, the agricultural-services cooperatives in Peru controlled 60 percent of the coffee destined for export in 1969 (Barrenechea 1986: 16). The second objective was achieved by giving the State-run trading companies

Table 2.6. Selva Central *Haciendas* and Farms Allocated to
Agrarian Production Cooperatives, 1969–1972

Agrarian production cooperative	Farms and *haciendas* allocated
Juan Santos Atahuallpa	Chincana
	San Jacinto
	El Diamante
	El Milagro
	La Libertad
	Virginia
	Tulumayo
José Carlos Mariátegui	San Carlos
José María Arguedas	Nijandaris
	La Galarza
	La Romilda
	La Tabernuy
	La Albanesa
Túpac Amaru	Auvernia
	Naranjal
Manco Cápac[a]	Antaloma
	Puntayacu
Pampa del Carmen	San Bernardo
	Pampa del Carmen
	Sorpresa
Santa Clara	Santa Clara
Juan Velasco Alvarado	Seven *haciendas* of the Perene Colony
La Victoria	La Victoria

Source: Ministerio de Agricultura 1988.

[a]Manco Cápac apparently also included the four *haciendas* of the Sociedad Agrícola Chalhuapuquio. The list from the Agrarian Reform Archive of the Ministry of Agriculture also seems to omit several other *haciendas* that were included in the region's new production cooperatives.

(the Empresa Pública de Servicios Agropecuarios, or EPSA [1972–1974], and later the Empresa Peruana de Comercialización de la Harina y Aceite de Pescado, or EPCHAP [1974–1978], and the Empresa Nacional de Comercialización de Insumos, or ENCI [1978–1980]), a monopoly over the export of select coffee. However, the initial success of the cooperative scheme for coffee commercialization was not accompanied by similar success in the cooperative management of former *haciendas* and agribusinesses, which, as we will see, led to their dissolution and a partitioning process.

Table 2.7. Government Land Concessions in
Satipo Province

Year	Lands sold	Lands granted	Small land concessions
1899–1943	1,973	6,380	1,285
1944–1954	65,462	—	—
1955–1958	141,374	—	—

Source: Ortiz 1961: 364, 390.

Notes: Values are in hectares. Dashes denote no data.

The Case of Speculative Holdings in Satipo

During the first half of the 20th century, the rate of occupation of the Satipo Valley experienced severe fluctuations. With the construction, in 1941, of the Satipo-Concepción road, the valley became one of the most attractive areas for colonization. The destruction of the road in 1947 seemed to bring this growth process to a standstill. Nevertheless, the spectacular rise in coffee prices in subsequent years made it possible for Satipo to attract a significant number of major investors from Lima as well as numerous poor peasants from the neighboring highlands, even if most produce had to be taken out by air. During these years the government made numerous land sales to colonists. Thus, between 1944 and 1954 alone, the land area that was sold exceeded the total area that had previously been sold or granted between 1899 and 1943 (Table 2.7). Likewise, the government authorized major concessions of up to 20,000 hectares to individuals and companies in Lima (Hein and Neale 1954). Most petitions for land were speculative in nature.

Nevertheless, taking advantage of State promotional credits for the cultivation of coffee, many of these *hacienda* owners started producing coffee. This trend was accentuated with the opening, in 1953, of an office of the Banco de Fomento Agropecuario in the town of Satipo. Since the end of the 1940s, the State prioritized support for large-scale agriculture at both the national and local levels. Thus, in the period from 1953 to 1960, the Satipo office of the bank authorized 309 loans to small farmers, averaging 27,221 *soles* each, whereas the 173 loans for large-scale agriculture averaged 161,888 *soles* each (Shoemaker 1981: 88–89). The opportunistic nature of the development of *haciendas* in Satipo and the speculative nature of landownership was such that the government's contribution of credit support did not actually lead to real capital improvement. Satipo *haciendas* never reached the level of technological advancement and intensive production that was attained by those in Chanchamayo.

This paradox became evident beginning in 1959 with the relative decline in coffee prices on the international market. In spite of the fact that the road to Concepción was also reopened in 1959—thus reducing shipping costs—the high cost of coffee production, in addition to low coffee prices and low productivity, were such that *hacienda* owners in this valley only made small profits. This situation was aggravated by the lack of diversification of their holdings. All of these factors resulted in the incapacity of large *hacienda* owners to pay their debts to the Banco de Fomento Agropecuario and eventually led to the abandonment of numerous properties.

In the 1960s, Andean peasants who continued to flow *en masse* into the area as a result of the population explosion in the Andes encountered a land-tenure system that impeded their access to land (Shoemaker 1981: 97). On the one hand, there were huge concessions that had never been developed by their owners and had only speculative value. On the other, the large *haciendas* abandoned because of bankruptcy were forfeited to the Banco de Fomento and could be recovered only by payment of the outstanding debts against them. The only available land was mainly located far from roads and therefore was not very attractive. In 1960, of the 150,000 hectares legally registered in the valley, less than 4 percent was under cultivation (Shoemaker 1981: 97).

In response to this situation, a spontaneous process of agrarian reform took place. Lands on unexploited *haciendas* and farms were invaded. This kind of action was based on the experiences of the struggle for land that colonists brought with them from the Andes. In contrast to the lack of labor organization in the Chanchamayo Valley, in 1961 a union was formed by colonists with small holdings in Satipo: the Federación de Campesinos de Satipo (Peasant Federation of Satipo). This organization led the struggle for land in the area. With the appearance of the insurgent Movimiento de Izquierda Revolucionaria (Leftist Revolutionary Movement) in 1965, and in light of the growing pressure of peasants' organizations, which made the situation unmanageable, the government of President Fernando Belaúnde consented to legally sanction this spontaneous agrarian-reform movement. However, it was only later, under President Velasco Alvarado, that these colonists were granted legal property rights. Through this process, 110 large and mid-sized holdings were returned to the State and were then partitioned and legally assigned to their invaders and to new colonists (Castro de León 1982: 7).

As a result of demographic pressure and the breakdown of the *hacienda* system, the pattern of small-scale production became widespread in Chanchamayo and Satipo provinces. The growing flood of immigrants to the region resulted in the rapid occupation of the Satipo, Perené, and Villa Rica valleys, whereas the Chanchamayo and Oxapampa valleys began to be saturated. As we will see, the processes that were unleashed at the beginning of this stage led to severe land fragmentation and the generalization of *minifundios*.

A second consequence of these processes was the consolidation of the economic profile of the region. As we will see, the economic model developed by large-scale producers, which combined coffee and fruit cultivation with timber extraction, continued to predominate at the regional level, even though small-scale producers could not combine all of these activities.

The breakup of the *hacienda* system did not signify, however, a substantial loss of economic power on the part of locally dominant groups. Although agricultural production remained almost entirely in the hands of small and mid-sized producers, the power groups remained dedicated to the same two activities that they had always controlled: the buying and selling of coffee, and timber extraction and processing. It is worth noting that in spite of government control of coffee exports, private buyers continued to control 40 percent of the total volume of coffee exported in 1969. After the breakup of the state monopoly in 1980, this percentage increased, rising to 68 percent in 1986 (Barrenechea 1986: 16, 40).

This process also led to the final breakdown of the geographic unity of indigenous territories. Until the 1940s, the colonists managed to erode the frontiers of ethnic territories, but large areas remained intact. Beginning at this time, colonization fronts began to multiply, and the flow of immigrants acquired such a volume that almost none of the areas known since colonial times remained uncolonized. Given this situation, the indigenous peoples no longer had the opportunity to retreat, the stategy that they had favored since the end of the 19th century. Surrounded by colonists on all sides, they could retain only the land they actually cultivated, and not always even that. The present-day "native communities" took shape on the basis of this fragmentation of traditional indigenous territories.

Demographic Growth and the Increasing Presence of the State

The demographic growth that the region experienced beginning in the 1940s, and the pressure that the migrant population exerted on the land, resulted in the transformation of the land-ownership system that had been prevalent until then. At the political level, successive waves of Andean immigrants led to increased attention given to the area by the State. At the same time, it significantly expanded its presence in the area. Certainly, population growth was not the only element that forced the government to assert its authority. As has been described, the economic growth of the Selva Central and its increasingly significant contribution to the national economy also played an important role in this process. Finally, guerrilla activity in 1965, although brief and confined to a limited area, seems to have been the factor that convinced the State to incorporate the region more effectively into its sphere of influence.

Table 2.8. Population Growth in the Selva Central

Province	1876	1940	1961	1972	1981
Chanchamayo	2,468	14,145	34,576	61,482	98,508
Oxapampa	1,265	5,881	25,783	39,794	49,857
Satipo	—	1,642	14,360	37,660	64,595
Selva Central	3,733	21,668	74,714	138,936	212,960

Source: Maletta and Bardales n.d.: vol. 1.

Notes: Values given are total numbers of people. Dash denotes no data.

Two characteristics of the population dynamics of the Selva Central between 1876 and 1981 can be inferred from Tables 2.8 and 2.9. First, during the pioneer colonization stage (1847–1947) the cumulative annual growth rates were relatively low, whereas more recently (since the 1940s) they have accelerated. Second, there were marked variations in the rate of demographic growth within the areas that form the Selva Central—the provinces of Chanchamayo, Satipo, and Oxapampa. We will attempt to explain these patterns in detail.

Table 2.9. Annual Population Growth Rates in the Selva Central and Peru

Years and area	Chanchamayo	Oxapampa	Satipo	Peru
1876–1940				
Urban	3.68	0.85	—	1.10
Rural	2.73	3.05	—	1.49
Total population	2.77	2.43	—	1.34
1940–1961				
Urban	5.23	7.72	12.72	3.59
Rural	4.18	7.21	10.50	1.30
Total population	4.35	7.29	10.88	2.25
1961–1972				
Urban	7.79	3.80	9.51	5.03
Rural	4.77	4.07	9.07	0.46
Total population	5.37	4.02	9.16	2.88
1972–1981				
Urban	5.41	3.17	7.47	3.61
Rural	5.38	2.41	5.81	0.91
Total population	5.38	2.54	6.18	2.58

Source: Maletta and Bardales n.d.: vol. 1.

Notes: Values denote average percent increase in population per year. Dashes denote no data.

Between the censuses in 1876 and 1940, the Selva Central remained a region poorly linked with the rest of the country, in search of economic activities that would be sufficiently profitable to ensure its long-term stability. During this period there was a gradual transition from a sugarcane to a coffee-producing economy. Nevertheless, during the same period, coffee prices fluctuated enormously. These elements explain the relatively low cumulative growth rate of the population during the period between these two censuses. In spite of this, these rates were two and sometimes three times the national rate, which indicates that during this period immigration greatly contributed to population growth.

Since 1940, two phenomena have taken place that accelerated regional growth rates. First, in the period between 1940 and 1961, the entire country experienced unprecedented demographic growth due to a significant decline in the gross mortality rate. This fell from 27 per thousand to 15 per thousand, while the gross birthrate remained stable at 45 per thousand (Centro de Estudios de Población y Desarrollo 1972: 152). The demographic explosion was most strongly felt in the Andean highlands, where the predominant *hacienda* system denied extensive sectors of the population access to land, thus generating a mass of landless peasants. Second, coffee prices rose in a sustained fashion between 1940 and 1954, remaining at a relatively high level until 1965 and making migration to the tropics attractive (see Figure 2.2). As a result, a large percentage of the landless peasants of the central Andes chose to immigrate to the Selva Central.

A comparison of Figures 2.2 and 2.3 illustrates the tight correlation between the evolution of coffee prices and demographic growth in all three provinces of the Selva Central. As has been stated, the increase in coffee prices stimulated colonization. At the same time, coffee production itself generates an intense demand for hired labor during certain periods in its annual cycle. Thus, the expansion of the area planted in coffee as a result of its improved prices had, over a certain period and while certain conditions prevailed, a multiplier effect on the volume of the immigrant population.

Within this general pattern, population growth in the Selva Central occurred at different rates in the three provinces that form it. The Chanchamayo area attracted the greatest number of immigrants after the reopening of the region in 1847. Between 1940 and 1961, Chanchamayo continued to present a high rate of growth (almost double the national rate). This was, nevertheless, far below the growth rates of Oxapampa and Satipo. In spite of the destruction of the road that connected it with the highlands, Satipo was the province with the highest growth rate, appearing to be the most promising area for the settlement of Andean colonists. Its annual growth rate of 10.9 percent was almost four times the national rate. One should bear in mind, however, that, at the beginning of this period, the province had less than 2,000 colonists. Satipo was still an incipient

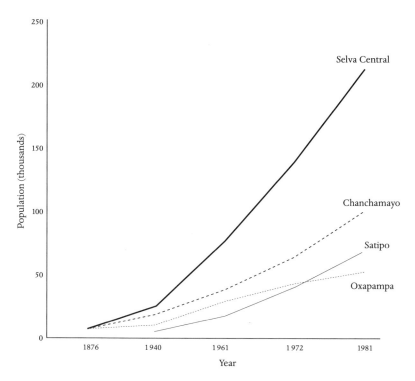

Figure 2.3. Population of Chanchamayo, Oxapampa, and Satipo, 1876–1981. *Source:* Table 2.8.

colonization front throughout this period. In contrast, the rapid growth of Oxapampa Province was due, primarily, to the opening of Villa Rica as a new expansion area and to the interest of the timber industry in the Oxapampa Valley beginning with the 1943 inauguration of the road that connected it with La Merced. Population growth in Chanchamayo resulted not so much from the opening of new areas for colonization but from the greater concentration of colonists in previously occupied areas. Table 2.10 shows that while, in 1961, Satipo and Oxapampa together had a population density of nearly 1.1 inhabitants per square kilometer, that of Chanchamayo had grown from 2.7 to 6.6 inhabitants per square kilometer.

In the subsequent period (1961–1972), Satipo maintained a growth rate almost identical to that of the previous intercensus interval. The reopening of the Concepción-Satipo road and the benefits accorded to the colonists by the first Belaúnde government (1963–1968) are some of the factors that explain the maintenance of its high growth rate. Oxapampa, on the other hand, experienced a clear decline in its growth rate, which derived from the saturation of the Villa

Table 2.10. Population Density

Province	1940	1961	1972	1981
Chanchamayo	2.7	6.6	11.8	18.8
Oxapampa	0.4	1.5	2.6	3.2
Satipo	0.1	0.7	1.9	3.3
Selva Central	1.1	2.9	5.4	8.4

Source: Maletta and Bardales n.d.: vol. 1.

Note: Values are numbers of inhabitants per square kilometer.

Rica district and the lack of a road that would have facilitated the opening of areas of expansion toward the Palcazu and Pichis valleys. Although in 1961 Oxapampa had a population 80 percent larger than that of Satipo, at the end of this period its population was only 6 percent larger. In contrast to the annual growth rate of these two provinces, that of Chanchamayo increased, primarily because of the massive invasion of colonists into the Peruvian Corporation's concession in the upper Perené Valley. The opening of this new area of expansion temporarily relieved the demographic pressure on areas that were first incorporated into this province. Nevertheless, at the end of this period, the population density of Chanchamayo had grown from 6.6 to 11.8 inhabitants per square kilometer, which demonstrates that the opening of the upper Perené Valley did not reduce the demographic pressure on the areas of early occupation over the long term; rather, it was basically colonized by people from outside of the province.

Between 1972 and 1981, Chanchamayo maintained its high growth rate, while the growth rates in Oxapampa and Satipo drastically declined. This was largely because of the inauguration of the Carretera Marginal, a penetration road that linked La Merced to Satipo and fueled the colonization process toward the upper and central Perené Valley. Oxapampa, its logical areas of expansion still lacking the necessary access roads, its valley lands saturated, and its forest resources depleted, experienced an annual growth rate during this period that was below the national rate. As a consequence, at the end of this period the population of Oxapampa moved from second to third position within the region in absolute terms. In spite of the fact that Satipo continued to have the highest growth rate in the Selva Central, it began to experience a certain degree of saturation in areas served by roads. As in the case of Oxapampa, this was because of the impossibility of connecting already occupied areas with areas of expansion in the lower Perené, Tambo, and Ene valleys. In 1981, Satipo and Oxapampa had a population density of around 3.3 inhabitants per square kilometer, far below the density in the rest of the country, which was then 13.3 inhabitants per square kilometer. Chanchamayo, in contrast, with 18.8 inhabitants per square kilometer, greatly exceeded the national average.

The three provinces began to experience a high degree of saturation and minifundization in areas that were already colonized. This situation was to change in the 1980s when the construction of the Carretera Marginal, begun during President Belaúnde's first term, was accelerated, opening the Palcazu, Pichis, and lower Perené valleys to colonization. Nevertheless, as we will see, a series of external factors interfered with the rhythm of the colonization process in these areas in the following stage.

The extensive Andean migration toward the Selva Central since 1940 was not the result of State planning. It was only at the end of the 1950s that the government began to focus on colonization, conceiving of it as a possible solution to the problems of scarcity of land that the nation faced because of the highland *hacienda* system. Since then, the Selva Central has been the subject of many studies and projects, which, from various perspectives and within a more or less limited geographical coverage, were proposed to ensure the geopolitical integration of the region and to generate new development options.

It is interesting to note that the first institution to call attention to colonization in this region was the Centro de Altos Estudios Militares (Center for Advanced Military Studies). In 1958, the center circulated a mimeographed document in which the creation of an institute for colonization and development in the Selva Central was proposed. The activities of this institute would be aimed at attaining two basic objectives: "incorporation, at low cost, of new and highly productive agricultural areas for the cultivation of diverse crops for the national and export markets," and "absorption and resettlement of human groups resulting from the process of demographic pressure" (CAEM 1958: 4). The document established, in addition, that the occupation and development of the Selva Central would avert four crises that the country was facing: (1) the nutritional crisis, (2) the occupational crisis, (3) the crisis in the balance of payments, and (4) the psychological crisis (CAEM 1958: 1). Although one may readily differ with the proposal of colonization as a solution to these four critical problems, what is certain is that the military was not misguided in its concern about the potentially explosive national situation: a few years later, the Selva Central became the setting for one of the earliest guerrilla movements in the country.

The plan of the Center for Advanced Military Studies was never put into practice, but it seems to have inspired the Peruvía project presented to the Congress by President Manuel Prado in 1960. In contrast to the project of the military, which proposed to stimulate the Satipo-Pangoa-Ene region, the Peruvía project sought to develop the Perené-Satipo-Pangoa area in order to create an axis of latitudinal integration that would connect the capital with the highlands and with the Selva Central. To this end, the government commissioned several consulting firms from the United States to do a series of studies (Rizo Patrón 1983: 92-93). These studies produced the first extensive aerial photography of the region.

One year later this project awoke the interest of the Organization of American States, which published a document titled *Integración Económica y Social del Perú Central (Economic and Social Integration of Central Peru)*. One of the conclusions that was underscored in this study was that "it is difficult to clearly evaluate timber resources because knowledge of the region is so flawed" (OEA 1961: vol. 1, 9). This vacuum was partially filled by a study undertaken in 1962 by the Oficina Nacional de Evaluación de Recursos Naturales (National Agency for the Assessment of Natural Resources), or ONERN, of the economic and social potential of the Perené-Satipo-Ene area (ONERN 1963). President Belaúnde's work *La Conquista del Perú por los Peruanos* (1959) (published in English as *Peru's Own Conquest*) formed the ideological basis for all of these projects.

With Belaúnde's rise to power in 1963, the ideology of colonization became the standard response to the problems of the country, and the image of the Selva Central as "Peru's larder" crystallized. The eruption of the guerrillas of the Leftist Revolutionary Movement in Satipo, Pangoa, and the Gran Pajonal two years later strengthened the decision of the government to reinforce its presence in the region through planned activities. The proposal to build the Carretera Marginal provided the backbone for this action. It was in this context that the government began to assume the dual role of development agent and guarantor of the internal security of the Selva Central.

The establishment of the 48th district headquarters of the Sinchis (a branch of the police force created especially for antiguerrilla action) in Mazamari and the resulting defeat of the guerrillas inaugurated a new modus operandi for the State in the region. The construction of the Satipo-Chanchamayo section of the Carretera Marginal by the Second Engineering Battalion of the Army is the best example of this new style. It persisted into the subsequent decade with the participation of the Ollantaytambo Battalion in La Merced in the construction of the tract of the Carretera Marginal from the Palcazu to the Pichis Valley.

Guerrilla activity in 1965 also forced the government to intervene directly in the regulation and distribution of land, which was a permanent source of social and political unrest. Under Belaúnde's agrarian reform, land distribution in the Perené Valley, where the Peruvian Corporation's concession was nullified, and in Satipo, where abandoned farms were reclaimed by the State and partitioned, was intended to avert the upsurgence of peasant labor unions in the Selva Central as had occurred in La Convención and Lares to the south of the country.

Priorities of the State in the region changed under the government of General Velasco Alvarado. Colonization was no longer the political bandwagon and the panacea for the problems of the country as it had been during the first Belaúnde government. Instead of encouraging massive colonization, the military government proposed, in the case of the Selva Central, to solve the land problems of its poor. Thus the large *haciendas* of the region were expropriated for the benefit of their workers, and in 1974, Decree Law 20653 was passed—the Ley de Comunidades Nativas y de Promoción Agropecuaria de las Regiones de Selva y Ceja de Selva (Law for Native Communities and Agropastoral Promotion in the Areas of the Selva and Selva Alta). We have already discussed the motivations for the 1969 agrarian reform and its effects in the Selva Central. The discussion of the context and impact of Decree Law 20653 on the indigenous population of the region will be presented in greater detail in the third part of this book. Nevertheless, it is appropriate to make a few remarks on the subject here.

To a large extent, the law of native communities was formulated in response to the specific plight of the indigenous peoples of the Selva Central (Alberto Chirif, personal communication), for it was in densely colonized areas where the indigenous population had less land. In older colonization areas, such as the Chanchamayo Valley, the indigenous peoples had been completely displaced. In the Oxapampa, Villa Rica, and upper Perené valleys, the majority of indigenous land had been colonized, and what remained was reduced to small, encroached-upon areas.

A previous 1957 law, Supreme Decree 03—Normas para la Reserva de Tierras para los Selvícolas (Norms for the Reservation of Land for Forest Peoples)—which had been issued together with the first proposals for State-sponsored colonization and was enforced only after 1960, had not solved the problem of indigenous land rights. The major deficiencies of this decree were that land was not granted as property but only in usufruct. Although the size of the allocated plots (10 hectares per person more than five years old) was barely sufficient for agricultural purposes, neither the indigenous peoples nor the officials who had to enforce the law saw the initiative as a guarantee that its provisions would be effectively put into practice. During the 17 years that Supreme Decree 03 was in effect, only 46 communal Yanesha, Ashaninka, and Nomatsiguenga reserves were created of the total of 280 settlements extant in the Selva Central by 1975 (Chirif 1974).

Before Decree Law 20653 was passed, the existence of the region's indigenous peoples had been systematically denied in ideological terms by both colonists and local authorities. As a result, they were consistently ignored in the State's development plans for the Selva Central, despite the fact that the indigenous labor force was crucial to the region's economy. The passing and subsequent enforcement of Decree Law 20653 had the effect of reinstating the indigenous peoples into the region's social and political agendas.

Finally, the passage of this law coincided with the appearance of the first indigenous organizations in the region and in many cases served as a motivating factor for the formation of others. Since then, as a result of the presence, actions, and pressures of these organizations, the existence of the indigenous sector could no longer be ignored.

In accordance with its objective of modernizing the country's social and economic structures, and following in the steps of previous governments, the military government expressed an interest in the occupation of the Selva Central. This time, however, the focus was shifted from stimulating colonization to formulating integrated development strategies (Chirif 1985: 194–195). As a complement to the proposed construction of the stretch of the Carretera Marginal from Villa Rica to Puerto Pachitea, which the U.S. consulting firm TAMS was commissioned to study, the military government commissioned ONERN to evaluate the natural resources of the Pichis and Palcazu valleys, which it perceived as the new areas of expansion in the Selva Central (ONERN 1970). On the basis of this inventory and assessment of resources, a development plan for the Selva Central was devised in 1974 under the direction of a multidisciplinary commission (Comisión Multisectorial Ad-hoc 1974), and two years later an Integrated Program for the Development of Palcazu-Pichis was implemented with the support of the Dutch government (Ministerio de Agricultura 1976). The authors of the latter document explicitly elaborated on the aspects that distinguished this project from other similar projects proposed earlier:

First, the area is not considered a zone to be colonized. Rather, we intend to encourage the development of the population that is currently living there. Second, instead of establishing an economy that is primarily based on extensive cattle ranching, we hope to achieve a balance between a subsistence agriculture and commercial agriculture entailing the highest degree possible of local industrialization, based on the intensive use of land and on the rational management of available forest resources. Finally, this economic strategy should not consist of simply applying current technologies with a major injection of capital, but be based on the creation of appropiate technology for the humid tropics and aim at improving the institutional and organizational bases of the local population and the State agencies involved. (Ministerio de Agricultura 1976: 1)

Furthermore, this proposal placed considerable emphasis on granting property rights to native communities in the area through an innovative program that would combine grants of land suitable for agriculture as community property with the establishment of communal reserves in usufruct in forested areas, and the creation of the Yanachaga National Park (Ministerio de Agricultura 1976:

96-97). This project was to be put into practice several years later in a slightly modified form.

The integrated program was never entirely applied. In 1980, only 12 days after assuming office for the second time and having visited the Pichis Valley, President Belaúnde announced the initiation of the Proyecto Especial Pichis-Palcazu (Pichis-Palcazu Special Project). Initially, this project was intended to convert the Pichis and Palcazu valleys into modern and active fronts for mass colonization.

However, the first detailed studies of land and natural resources of these valleys found that the area presented serious limitations to mass occupation (Smith 1983: 118). Apprehension regarding the probable environmental impact that such a colonization program would have had a major effect on the international organizations and foreign governments interested in funding the project. Among them were the U.S. Agency for International Development, which was to finance the Palcazu program; the Interamerican Development Bank, which backed a program in the Pichis Valley; the World Bank, which was to finance the Satipo-Chanchamayo component; the German government, which supported the Oxapampa program; and the Swiss and Belgian governments, which were to finance the activities of the Pachitea-von Humboldt program (Salazar 1984: 257-264). This forced the government to modify the original objectives of the Pichis-Palcazu Special Project. Despite the fact that at the level of political rhetoric the project continued to be touted as the great solution to the country's land and food problems, in practice it readopted, to a certain extent, the philosophy that had animated the rural-development program proposed in 1976.

The importance of the four programs of the Pichis-Palcazu Special Project in our study area (Palcazu, Pichis, Oxapampa, and Satipo-Chanchamayo) is illustrated by the fact that their budget represented 47 percent of the foreign aid that the Belaúnde government received for all of its projects in the Amazonian region (Table 2.11). However, this project received substantial funding only between 1980 and 1985 and was primarily dedicated to three activities: road construction, research and promotion of technological packages for certain productive activities, and land-ownership registration. Given the new focus of the project, and despite great expectations created by the government, there were no major migrations into the areas of expansion in the Selva Central, except in the Pichis Valley.

Increased State intervention in the region, primarily through the colonization and development projects that it initiated in the 1950s, also included the expansion of rural health and educational services. No less important at this stage was the expansion of State credit services, primarily through the Banco de Fomento Agropecuario (subsequently Banco Agrario). The number of offices that offered credit services in the Selva Central tripled between 1951 and 1984 (Table 2.12).

Table 2.11. International Loans for Special Projects, 1983

Special project	Amount (millions of US$)	% of all loans	Duration
Palcazu[a]	22.0	8.4	1983-1987
Pichis[a]	46.0	17.5	1983-1987
Oxapampa[a]	15.0	5.7	1984-1987
Satipo-Chanchamayo[a]	40.0	15.2	1984-1988
Jaén-San Ignacio-Bagua	42.8	16.3	1984-1988
Alto Mayo	49.0	18.6	1983-1987
Central Huallaga-Bajo Mayo	19.0	7.2	1979-1984
Alto Huallaga	18.0	6.8	1982-1986
Chontayacu-Purús-Ucayali	11.2	4.3	1983-1985
Pachitea-Von Humboldt	–	–	1980-?
All 10 projects	262.8	100.0	1979-1988?

Source: Salazar 1984; data elaborated by the authors.

Note: Dashes denote no data.

[a]Projects in the Selva Central.

They not only increased in absolute numbers, but some of the previously established offices were upgraded. For example, in 1969, the small La Merced office was upgraded to the second regional headquarters of the Banco Agrario in the Amazonian region, after that of Iquitos.

The way in which credit facilities developed in the Selva Central reflects not only different degrees of economic activity within the various areas of the region but also the State policies intended to stimulate business in some of these areas in particular. In 1951 there were two small offices in Satipo and Puerto Bermúdez and a larger office in La Merced. Five years later these three offices were upgraded, and a new office was opened in Villa Rica, when the area became an important coffee-production center. Although Puerto Bermúdez in the Pichis Valley was not as active a colonization front as those in Satipo and Chanchamayo, rubber extraction there justified the existence of an agency of the Banco de Fomento Agropecuario of equal rank to those in the other two areas.

The situation remained the same until 1961, when a small office was established in Oxapampa, an area that had, until then, been served by the office in La Merced. The opening of this office was closely tied to the growth of the timber industry in Oxapampa. In 1967, as a result of the decline in rubber extraction in the Pichis area, the Puerto Bermúdez agency was downgraded to inspection office. At the same time, the Villa Rica inspection office was upgraded to agency. An agency was established in Pampa Silva (in upper Perené), which after 10 years of massive invasions had become a dynamic colonization area. Throughout the rest of the decade, this situation remained unchanged, except for the establish-

Table 2.12. Evolution of Banco Agrario Credit-Service
Facilities in the Selva Central

Year	Branches	Type A agencies	Type B agencies	Offices	All facilities
1951	0	0	1	2	3
1956	0	3	0	1	4
1961	0	3	0	2	5
1967	0	2	2	2	6
1971	1	1	1	4	7
1976	1	1	1	4	7
1984	1	2	3	3	9

Sources: Banco de Fomento Agropecuario 1951-1969; Banco Agrario 1971-1984.

Note: Between 1951 and 1984, the Banco de Fomento Agropecuario, which in 1970 became Banco Agrario, changed its organizational structure several times. We have standardized the data according to the structure of credit-service facilities extant in 1984.

ment of a restricted service *(puntos de atención)* in the less consolidated areas of expansion. Table 2.13 shows the organizational structure of the credit offices of the Selva Central at the end of this stage. There are two innovations that are worth commenting on: the creation of a credit service in Pichanaki, a settlement in the central Perené Valley that experienced the most accelerated urban growth in the region in the 1980s, in response to increased logging and coffee and fruit production; and the upgrade of the Puerto Bermúdez office to a type B agency as a result of the actions of the Pichis-Palcazu Special Project.

As a result of massive colonization, greater State intervention, and the generalization of the coffee-fruit-timber economic trinomial, the Selva Central became effectively incorporated into the national and international markets. This external articulation went hand in hand with a process of internal articulation, whose characteristics will be discussed in the following section.

Toward the end of this period, the Selva Central was no longer a "frontier area," although there were still frontier areas within the region to be conquered for the market. It is not surprising, then, that in terms of relative development, and considering indicators of mortality, development and economic diversification, consumer services, and levels of consumption, by 1972 the areas that formed the Selva Central were among the five most developed basins of the *selva alta* region (Table 2.14). As we will see, however, the ecological characteristics of the region, as well as the strong demographic pressure on its natural resources, make it difficult to maintain the present-day degree of development—and even more difficult to increase it—without resorting to the continuous opening up of new colonization fronts.

Table 2.13. Banco Agrario Facilities
in the Selva Central, 1984

Type of facility	Location
Branch	La Merced
Type A agency	Satipo Villa Rica
Type B agency	Oxapampa Pampa Silva Puerto Bermúdez
Office	Pozuzo Pichanaki San Martín de Pangoa

Source: Banco Agrario 1984.

The Culmination of the Process of Internal Articulation and the Contemporary Configuration of the Region

To speak of the "culmination" of the process of internal articulation of the Selva Central is somehow misleading, for there are still uncolonized areas, and thus what we have defined as the Selva Central regional space may still be subject to numerous transformations in the future. However, for methodological purposes (but also because, in the case of sociohistorical phenomena, periods of expansion often alternate with periods of stabilization) we can state that, toward the end of this period, the colonization areas of the Selva Central had effectively become articulated with each other. It is important to bear in mind that the four original colonization fronts (Chanchamayo, Oxapampa, Pozuzo, and Satipo), which were each independently connected with the highlands, would not necessarily have formed a single region. On the contrary, the articulation of these diverse fronts was achieved thanks to the conjunction of structural factors with factors derived from historical accident.

Among the structural factors we include the successive waves of colonization centered in the towns of La Merced–San Ramón, Oxapampa, Pozuzo, and Satipo, which arose from the needs of the frontier economy. These waves of expansion were triggered by internal factors (such as necessity for new lands) or by external factors (high prices for certain tropical products, or State incentives for colonization). As a result of these various factors, the pace of occupation in each of these areas was unique. With time, however, these waves became intermingled and superimposed, thus leading to the articulation of these areas among them and the homogenization of the social and economic phenomena that were taking

Table 2.14. *Selva Alta* Basins Ranked in Order of Degree of Development, 1972

Basin	A	B	C	Total A–C	Overall rank[a]
Upper Mayo	1	2	2	5	1
Chanchamayo	5	3	1	9	2
Pichis-Palcazu-Oxapampa	3	4	4	11	3
Upper Huallaga	4	1	6	11	3
Central Huallaga-Lower Mayo	2	7	7	16	4
Perené-Ene-Tambo (Satipo)	7	5	5	17	5
Upper Urubamba	9	6	3	18	6
Upper Marañón	5	8	9	22	7
Pachitea	8	11	8	27	8
Apurímac	10	12	10	32	9
Tambopata	11	10	11	32	9
Inambari	12	9	12	33	10
Upper Madre de Dios-Manú	13	13	13	39	12

Source: Lésevic 1984: 47.

Note: The components of the overall ranking are the following:
A = ranking by mortality rate; 1 denotes lowest mortality.
B = ranking by level of socioeconomic development and diversification; 1 denotes most developed and diverse.
C = ranking by availability of basic domestic utilities and levels of consumption; 1 denotes greatest availability and consumption.

[a]A rank of 1 denotes the most developed.

place within them. If we were to plot this process, we would obtain a map like Map 2.2.

The earthquake that shook the Selva Central in the Satipo area—razing 60 kilometers of the Satipo-Concepción road and destroying all of the housing in Satipo, 80 percent of the housing in La Merced, and most of San Ramón (Ortiz 1969: vol. 2, 583-586)—was certainly among the most important random historical factors. This event was to change the course of the history of road integration in the Selva Central. The road, which represented 21 years of the colonists' efforts, could not be reconstructed without State support. Satipo colonists appealed to President José Luis Bustamante y Rivero, who promised to "remedy their distressing situation and proceed as soon as possible to reopen the road" (Ortiz 1969: vol. 2, 591).

The rise to power of General Manuel A. Odría, a year later, frustrated this possibility. Odría—a Tarma native—was opposed to the investment of public funds in rehabilitating the destroyed road, preferring instead to invest in the extension of the Tarma-Chanchamayo road and favoring the idea of constructing a road out of Satipo along the Perené River toward La Merced. Once again the old rivalries among highland cities, intensified at this point by the nascent

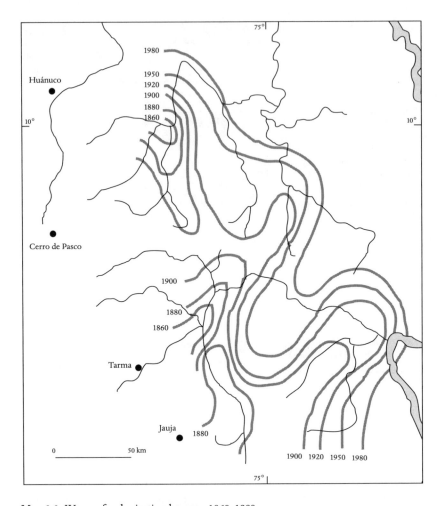

Map 2.2. Waves of colonization by year, 1860–1980.

rivalry between the various colonization areas, played a role in the configuration of the Selva Central. Another reason for not supporting the road reconstruction was the limited importance of Satipo with respect to the other colonization fronts. The price of barbasco, the principal export product of Satipo, began to fall in 1948 and bottomed out in 1953 (Shoemaker 1981: 85).

The area of Satipo would have been abandoned if world coffee prices had not increased suddenly during the same period. As we have indicated, given the natural possibilities that the area offered for coffee production, the Banco de Fomento Agropecuario established an office in Satipo in 1953. Thus this area, which until then had existed at the margin of the coffee economy, became

Table 2.15. Evolution of the Selva Central Road Network

[handwritten marginalia: How + why various sections + added —) funds, elite) co... ... ...) earthquake) war markets]

Year opened	Road section
	Lima-Tarma (231 km)
1918	Tarma-La Merced (71 km)
1928	La Merced-Puente Paucartambo (32 km)
1943	Puente Paucartambo-Oxapampa (66 km)
1965	Oxapampa-Huancabamba (27 km)
1975	Huancabamba-Pozuzo (54 km)
1956	Puente Paucartambo-Villa Rica (22 km)
1975	Villa Rica-Cacazú (58 km)
1984	Cacazú-Iscozacín (40 km)
1985	Cacazú-Puerto Bermúdez (58 km)
1941	Satipo-Concepción (209 km)
1961	Satipo-Concepción (reopening)
1973	La Merced-Satipo (124 km)
1982	Satipo-Puerto Ocopa (66 km)

Source: INADE 1985; data elaborated by the authors.

embroiled in "coffee fever." This gave rise to new *haciendas* in the area and allowed for the reopening of the road to Concepción, which was finally inaugurated in 1961. The fact that Satipo was the hinterland of Huancayo, and that Huancayo benefited from its commercial activity, also helped to make the road a reality.

By then, however, the rehabilitation of this route had become anachronistic; other processes were developing, turning the construction the Satipo-La Merced road into the most rational and far-sighted option. To begin with, Chanchamayo was clearly the most prosperous and active economic front within the region. With the construction of the Puente Paucartambo-Oxapampa road in 1943 and the Paucartambo-Villa Rica road in 1956 (Table 2.15 and Map 2.3), Chanchamayo assumed leadership over these two colonization areas. Furthermore, the shipment of products out of Satipo by air through San Ramón between 1948 and 1955 forged the first direct economic links between Satipo and Chanchamayo.

Another factor that favored the articulation of Satipo with Chanchamayo was the opening of the Perené Valley as a colonization front as a result of the massive invasion of the Peruvian Corporation's lands beginning in 1956. The Perene Colony had acted as a geographic obstacle that impeded the integration of these two areas. From a contemporary standpoint, Satipo and Chanchamayo were perceived as two locally independent fronts unlikely to be connected; the 124 kilometers that separated them were perceived by the colonists as a vast, impenetrable no man's land. The gradual breakup of the Peruvian Corporation's

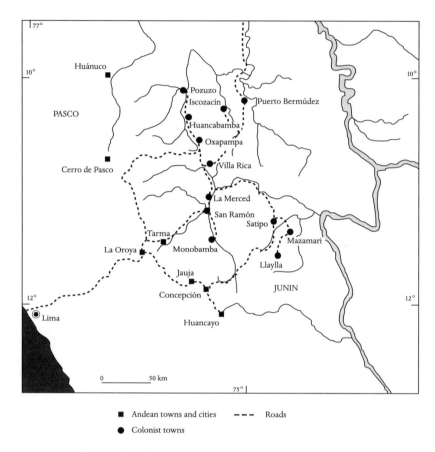

Map 2.3. Road network in the Selva Central, 1990.

monopoly of the land in the Perené Valley soon made the connection of these two areas plausible.

Thus it was only by the end of the 1950s that State development plans began to adopt the notion of the Selva Central as a distinct regional space. In fact, it was only then that the term Selva Central began to be used in place of phrases such as *"montaña de Chanchamayo"* and *"montaña de Satipo"* and that the objective and subjective conditions that were to result in the construction of the Satipo-La Merced road began to materialize. The guerrilla uprising in 1965 and the new internal security doctrine hastened the construction of this route, which became a reality in 1973, concluding the process of integration by means of road building and the socioeconomic integration of the Selva Central.

The new road had profound effects on the configuration of this regional space. Anticipating the importance that La Merced was to acquire, its Banco Agrario

office became the regional headquarters, with control over all of the offices of
the Selva Central except Satipo. The Satipo office, still under the control of
Huancayo, ultimately came under the administration of the La Merced office in
1974. Paradoxically, although the gross value of production in Chanchamayo
exceeded that of Tarma, and despite the fact that the Tarma office of the Banco
Agrario was dependent on the branch office in La Merced until 1974, Chanchamayo continued to be part of the Andean province of Tarma until 1978. A
crucial element in the creation of the province of Chanchamayo was the termi-
nation of the construction of the Satipo–La Merced road.

The construction of the Oxapampa–Pozuzo and Villa Rica–Cacazú segments
of the road in 1975 consolidated the geographic and economic integration of the
areas that were already occupied, accentuating the leadership of Chanchamayo.
The construction of new sections of the penetration road in the 1980s opened
the doors to new colonization fronts. The opening of these internal frontiers
followed the same road scheme that made La Merced the point of confluence
for trade and the gateway to the interior. Nevertheless, the connection of the
road network of the Selva Central with the Pucallpa–Lima axis by way of the
Puerto Bermúdez–San Alejandro road—inaugurated in 1985—provided new alternatives for articulation, especially for the colonization fronts of the Palcazu
and Pichis valleys. At present, it is difficult to evaluate the effects of the Puerto
Bermúdez–San Alejandro road, since it has been affected by the presence of the
Shining Path and the Túpac Amaru Revolutionary Movement.

Internal articulation was accompanied by the consolidation of the economic
profile of the region around coffee, fruit, and timber production. The integration
of the transportation network not only contributed to the expansion of this
model but also allowed the commercial capital related to each of these activities
to acquire regional scope.

Since the mid-1960s, and as a reflection of the growing stability of the region
and the economic impetus of the most recently colonized areas, the State began
to modify the existing political and administrative boundaries. As Table 2.16
shows, the number of districts doubled in the period between 1954 and 1978. At
present one can distinguish three types of areas within the Selva Central regional
space: (1) long-occupied and now consolidated central areas (Chanchamayo,
Perené, Oxapampa, Villa Rica, and Satipo valleys); (2) partially integrated peripheral areas (the Palcazu, Pichis, and lower Perené valleys), and (3) poorly articulated
areas of expansion (the lower Pozuzo, Tambo, Ene, and upper Pachitea valleys).

One of the most interesting phenomena of this final stage is the gradual
"Andinization" that the Selva Central has experienced, even in some areas with
well-defined non-Andean identities, such as the villages of German origin in
Oxapampa and Villa Rica. In 1972, nearly half of the population of the Selva

Table 2.16. Districts in the Selva Central

Province	1954	1978	1987
Chanchamayo[a]	Chanchamayo	Chanchamayo	Chanchamayo
	San Ramón	San Ramón	San Ramón
	Vitoc	Vitoc	Vitoc
		San Luis de Shuaro	San Luis de Shuaro
		Pichanaki	Pichanaki
			Perené
Oxapampa	Oxapampa	Oxapampa	Oxapampa
	Huancabamba	Huancabamba	Huancabamba
	Chontabamba	Chontabamba	Chontabamba
	Villa Rica	Villa Rica	Villa Rica
		Pozuzo	Pozuzo
		Puerto Bermúdez	Puerto Bermúdez
			Palcazu
Satipo[b]	Satipo	Satipo	Satipo
	Río Tambo	Río Tambo	Río Tambo
		Llaylla	Llaylla
		Mazamari	Mazamari
		Pampa Hermosa	Pampa Hermosa
		Pangoa	Pangoa
		Río Negro	Río Negro
		Coviriali	Coviriali

Sources: INE 1989a, 1989b.

[a]In 1954 Chanchamayo was an area composed of three districts belonging to the province of Tarma. Chanchamayo became a province in 1978.

[b]In 1954 Satipo was an area composed of two districts belonging to the province of Jauja. Satipo became a province in 1965.

Central were immigrants (Table 2.17). Of these, the great majority were of Andean origin. Far from losing their roots, Andean immigrants frequently tended to settle and to form cultural and religious associations according to their geographic origin.

However, it would be a mistake to say that these Andean immigrants were not influenced by their new geographical and cultural environments. Apart from having adopted new agricultural technologies, forms of construction, food, and so on, the confluence of tropical and Andean elements has given rise to new cultural phenomena. The tropical–Andean music of "Los Juanecos," which became popular throughout the area in the 1970s, constitutes an expression of the new identity of the colonized areas. Another element that points to a unique regional identity is the significant influence of non-Catholic religious organizations. Although there are no quantitative data regarding their influence, their presence and importance are clearly perceptible in the region.

Table 2.17. Immigrant Population in the Selva Central, 1972

Province	Total population	Immigrant population	% of total population
Chanchamayo	61,482	30,190	49.1
Oxapampa	39,794	14,169	35.6
Satipo	37,660	17,806	47.2
Selva Central	138,936	62,165	44.7

Source: Maletta and Bardales n.d.: vol. 1.

Though Amazonian indigenous peoples began to make their voices heard by forming ethnic organizations in the 1970s, the process of mass occupation had the effect of making the indigenous presence in the region practically invisible to the eyes of the colonists. The loss of political autonomy, their retreat into marginal areas, their subordination in the regional economy, and the "domestication" and appropriation of their land by the colonists as the transportation network expanded turned the indigenous sector into a merely folkloric element. After being "domesticated," the indigenous component became an acceptable heritage that could be incorporated safely into the regional identity. However, the incorporation of indigenous elements was expressed at quite banal levels, such as the folkloric presence of indigenous people in commemorative parades, the use of native names for various products or entities (the "El Campa" transport company and the "Shambari" restaurant, for example), and the use of indigenous and pseudo-indigenous pharmacopoeia.

The 1989 assassination of Alejandro Calderón, the leader of the Ashaninka organization in the Pichis Valley, at the hands of the Túpac Amaru Revolutionary Movement and the Ashaninka uprising in the area triggered by his death would once again bring indigenous strength, initiative, and organization to the forefront. Meanwhile, the indigenous peoples of the Selva Central have reinforced their identity, principally through their common struggle for land and for better living conditions. It is difficult to determine how this identity might evolve in the future, but what is clear is that after 350 years of economic, social, and cultural pressures from a broad range of Spanish and Peruvian agents, the indigenous peoples of the Selva Central have been able to maintain their cultural vitality and preserve their political utopias.

PART TWO

THE COLONIST ECONOMY

As a result of the State's growing interest in the colonization and economic incorporation of the Selva Central area, since the late 1950s a number of socioeconomic analyses, technical studies, and monographs about various aspects of this region have been written. Many of these have contributed valuable information from which the present investigation has drawn. However, the above-mentioned works present a series of important limitations. First, because they were elaborated in conjunction with colonization programs or to promote development, their objectives and achievements have been limited to a specific area or theme and cover a very limited temporal horizon. Therefore, they do not provide an integrated image of the mechanisms and dynamics of frontier expansion in the region as a whole.

Second, the economic activities that characterize this space are generally treated individually and from a predominantly technical perspective. This type of approach has impeded the identification of the many interrelationships among the diverse activities that have given the region a distinctive economic profile. Furthermore, the individual analysis of these activities has led to recommendations that are inadequate with respect to the reality of the region or that are contradictory to one another.

Third, the local nature of these studies has frequently led to the extrapolation of information corresponding to a particular area to the entire Selva Central. Thus the particular is elevated to the general, and we lose sight of the multiplicity of economic, social, and ecological situations that exist within the region. Finally, the lack of a holistic perspective and of an interest in determining the structural characteristics of the region's economy has hindered an understanding of the peculiarities of the Selva Central with respect to other areas of colonization in the *selva alta* region.

In Part Two, we propose to analyze the colonist economy from a perspective that allows us to produce an image of the agrarian economy of the Selva Central as a whole, while at the same time pointing out and explaining the differences among the several areas that compose it. In order to do this, we will consider four dimensions of the regional agrarian economy that are tightly linked with one another.

The first dimension to be considered is the economic profile of the region, a profile that, as we have seen, is the product of a series of endogenous and exogenous historical circumstances. Based on the coffee-fruit-timber trinomial, this profile not only accounts for the expansion of the agropastoral frontier in the region but also for the ways in which the region has become internally articulated. Parallel to this global vision, the particularities of the central areas, where this economic profile is more consolidated, will be contrasted with those of peripheral areas and areas of expansion. The second dimension to be considered is land tenure. As is true for the economic profile, land-tenure structure is a result of the historical processes of occupation of the region. In this sense, although the land-tenure structure of the Selva Central may be characterized in general as minifundiary, important differences are found within the area that are associated with length of occupation as well as with differential demographic pressure on "valuable land." The analysis of these two dimensions demonstrates that the economic profile and the land-tenure structure have influenced and conditioned each other, such that it becomes impossible to establish unidirectional causality between them.

These two dimensions form the structural framework within which a particular form of land use has developed. This constitutes the third dimension on which we focus to determine the degree of land-use intensity in the region. Although, in general, it might be asserted that producers in the Selva Central use land relatively intensively, there are major differences among them that are associated with the length of occupation, levels of minifundization, and the prevalent type of production pattern.

Because of their unique ecological characteristics, the environmental dimension is a fundamental aspect of tropical economies. As compared with other geographic areas that are more suitable for the intensive agriculture and monoculture favored by modern economies, in tropical areas such as the Amazonian region the environmental factor is critical to the perpetuation of local economies. Therefore, the analysis of a tropical economy such as that of the Selva Central would not be complete without an analysis of the impact of economic activities on the environment and, consequently, on its opportunities for sustainable development. As we will see, the factors related to the economic profile, land tenure, and patterns of land use are fundamental to understanding not only the mechanisms but also the level of environmental degradation that has taken place in the region in recent decades.

3

ECONOMIC PROFILE AND EXPANSION
OF THE AGROPASTORAL FRONTIER

Throughout almost 150 years of gradual occupation, the Selva Central has acquired an economic profile that is based on the crystallization and diffusion of a
certain pattern of production that has served as a model for the colonists who
continue to settle in the region. This economic profile, the result of a combination of historical, environmental, and economic factors, is based on coffee and
fruit production, as well as logging. As we will see, although all producers do
not develop all of these activities simultaneously, commercial agriculture and
logging are closely interrelated. Even as they compete for the same space, each
creates the conditions for the development of the other.

In this sense, agricultural production and timber extraction exist in a complementary, but at the same time antithetical, relationship in the Selva Central.
Their relationship is complementary insofar as timber fronts act as spearheads
for agropastoral colonization fronts. The opening of logging roads, which increase the value of the land that they traverse, make it attractive for colonization.
At the same time, the temporal and spatial stability generated by commercial
agriculture contributes to the maintenance and strengthening of the timber
industry. The antithetical nature of these two activities is manifested not only at
the level of competition for space and resources, which gives rise to conflicts
among the economic sectors involved, but also in terms of the patterns of
occupation that they generate, in which the relatively mobile nature of timber-
extraction activities contrasts with the more permanent character of coffee and
fruit cultivation. The simultaneous development of the timber industry and of
a commercial agriculture based on these two crops has contributed, with their

respective and mutual linkages, to the formation of a regional space that differs substantially from other areas within the *selva alta* region.

In the first section of this chapter, we analyze the characteristics of the predominant agricultural-production pattern to emphasize the important role that coffee and fruit cultivation has played in the economic configuration of the region. In the second section, we concentrate on an analysis of the timber industry to examine its spatial and economic effects, as well as its role in the process of regional occupation. Finally, we discuss the elements that lead us to postulate the antithetical yet complementary character of this pattern of production.

THE ROLE OF COFFEE AND FRUIT CROPS IN THE REGIONAL ECONOMY

If there is something that distinguishes the Selva Central from other colonized areas in the *selva alta,* it is its long tradition of commercial agriculture based primarily on the production of coffee and, to a lesser extent, of fruit crops. This type of agriculture has given the Selva Central a stable economic identity, making its occupation more permanent and assuring a continuous connection with national and international markets. At the same time, stable commercial agriculture and the economic and social linkages that it generates have allowed the different areas that form the region to enjoy a certain degree of prosperity for a long period of time, a phenomenon that is quite unusual in the colonization of tropical areas.

In spite of the significant expansion of the area in pasture in recent times, we have not included cattle ranching in our characterization of the economic profile of the Selva Central because it has not played a relevant role in the processes of occupation, incorporation, and economic articulation of the region. First, commercial cattle ranching is an activity that has developed only recently. Second, it has been extremely limited as an economic option by the current land-tenure structure, which is characterized by the predominance of small landholdings. As a consequence, cattle ranching is mainly concentrated in the peripheral areas of Oxapampa and Satipo provinces. Third, the contribution of cattle production to the regional and national economies is relatively small because of the extensive and low-technological character of this activity. Finally, as a result of the above-mentioned factors, cattle ranching has not had the same impact that the coffee-fruit-timber trinomial has had on the creation of a labor market, on capital accumulation, or on economic agglomeration in the region.

Developed in the late 19th century in the *haciendas* of the Chanchamayo Valley, the agricultural model based on coffee and fruit production was later widely adopted by mid-sized and small landholders, thus conditioning the modes of

Table 3.1. Cultivated Area in the
Selva Central

Year	Area (hectares)
1964	74,610
1968	101,915
1972	105,719
1976	102,695
1980	113,943
1984	134,302

Source: Ministerio de Agricultura 1963–1988.

Note: Between 1964 and 1984 the amount of area
cultivated increased 80 percent.

expansion of the agricultural frontier and determining the economic configuration of the region.

In this section we begin by analyzing the evolution of the agropastoral frontier in the Selva Central and the contribution of coffee cultivation to its expansion. We also examine the characteristics of and the trends in coffee production. Next, we analyze the linkages generated by the coffee economy and its contribution to the formation of local labor, real estate, and capital markets. We continue by analyzing the logic behind the process of diversification of commercial agriculture that took place in the region beginning in the 1950s with the development of fruit cultivation. We examine the linkage between fruit and coffee cultivation, as well as the factors that impeded the greater diffusion of this new commercial activity. Finally, we analyze the current situation of the region's agrarian economy and the prospects of the predominant pattern of coffee and fruit production.

Coffee and the Expansion of the Agropastoral Frontier

Throughout the past three decades, the area under cultivation in the Selva Central has expanded significantly, growing at an annual rate of nearly 3,000 hectares. In 1964 the agropastoral area under cultivation encompassed 74,610 hectares; by 1974 it had grown by 40 percent and by 1984 by an additional 27 percent, arriving at a total of 134,302 hectares (Ministerio de Agricultura 1963–1988; Table 3.1). This means that over the course of the two decades mentioned, a total of 59,692 hectares were incorporated into production in the Amazonian areas of the departments of Pasco and Junín, not an insignificant figure in a country that is hungry for land.

In the context of the expansion of the agropastoral frontier, coffee culture has been the principal vector for the occupation and integration of the Selva Central. Various factors have contributed to the fact that coffee became the fundamental medium for this process. First, coffee has been a commercial crop that, in spite of price variations, has had a guaranteed market for many years and has had a well-established local commercial network since at least the 1920s. Second, although it is true that road construction has favored the expansion of coffee cultivation, the fact that coffee is not a perishable product allowed its production even in some areas lacking direct road access. In this sense coffee is a "pioneer crop." Third, coffee can be developed with little capital investment and generates an income whatever its scale of production. Finally, coffee production has benefited from the management and technical knowledge that were well developed in the region decades earlier and that have facilitated its adoption by successive waves of colonists who settled in the region.

Thus, when the price of coffee increased substantially in the 1950s to two times the average 1940 price, this crop became a keystone in the colonization and production strategies of Andean immigrants, many of whom initially arrived in the Selva Central as seasonal workers attracted by the increase in demand for labor in coffee *haciendas*. Coffee cultivation provided immigrants with a fairly stable source of income and thus became a substitute for or complement to salaried work. It is not surprising, therefore, that coffee was rapidly adopted by small colonist landholders. This process was facilitated by the *hacienda* owners' own practice of employing *mejoreros* as a means of expanding their plantations, a job that provided a large number of immigrant colonists with the basic knowledge required to start small, independent farms. By taking advantage of the opening of new logging roads (often before the roads themselves were completed), by occupying uncultivated *hacienda* land, and by displacing the local indigenous population to grow coffee, immigrant colonists contributed to the process of incorporation of new areas into the regional and national economic life.

Throughout the second half of the 20th century, coffee cultivation has not only become the most important factor in attracting new colonists but has accounted for a large proportion of the region's cultivated area (Table 3.2). Furthermore, if we exclude the area devoted to pastures, coffee cultivation was responsible for 77 percent of the increase in the area under cultivation during the 1964-1984 period.

Table 3.2 presents the evolution of the percentage contribution of coffee to the total cultivated area at the provincial as well as at the regional levels. The same table shows that, between 1964 and 1984, coffee represented up to 62 percent and never less than 35 percent of the total cultivated area in the region. During this period, the area in coffee underwent a net increase of 11,267 hectares. Its evolution, however, has not been constant, presenting fluctuations that are intimately linked to coffee prices, to the progressive incorporation of new spaces for colonization, and to the appearance of plant diseases.[1]

Table 3.2. Area Cultivated in Coffee

| Year | Chanchamayo–Satipo | | Oxapampa | | Selva Central | |
	Area in coffee (hectares)	% of cultivated area	Area in coffee (hectares)	% of cultivated area	Area in coffee (hectares)	% of cultivated area
1963	30,552	—	4,522	—	35,074	—
1964	33,020	61.6	5,450	25.8	38,470	51.5
1965	34,000	69.1	5,400	27.2	39,400	57.1
1966	42,625	71.8	7,500	34.1	50,125	61.6
1967	40,819	67.8	15,300	31.9	47,919	58.1
1968	44,712	66.8	15,400	43.6	60,012	58.8
1969	47,000	61.0	13,100	42.2	62,400	55.0
1970	37,000	53.7	12,000	31.9	50,100	45.6
1971	39,000	61.0	10,600	27.8	51,000	47.6
1972	36,400	53.7	9,000	27.8	47,000	44.4
1973	37,500	55.9	9,000	24.3	46,500	44.6
1974	37,700	56.0	9,000	23.8	46,700	44.4
1975	35,500	54.9	7,240	19.5	42,740	42.0
1976	36,000	54.7	7,200	19.5	43,200	42.0
1977	36,500	54.1	6,000	20.7	42,500	44.0
1978	37,000	55.3	6,000	18.3	43,000	43.1
1979	39,000	57.5	6,000	17.6	45,000	44.2
1980	39,000	52.9	6,600	16.3	45,600	40.0
1981	39,110	53.4	6,900	14.5	46,010	38.1
1982	39,347	52.1	7,787	17.6	47,134	39.4
1983	39,237	52.6	6,710	11.6	45,947	34.8
1984	39,555	52.5	6,786	11.4	46,341	34.5

Sources: Ministerio de Agricultura 1963–1988; data elaborated by the authors.

Notes: Cultivated area includes cultivated pastures. Dashes denote no data.

A major difference among provinces is apparent in spatial terms. In the provinces of Chanchamayo and Satipo, coffee has played an important role in the incorporation of land into production, representing 52 percent to 72 percent of the cultivated area throughout this period. Furthermore, the area devoted to coffee production in these two provinces represented nearly 80 percent of the area in coffee within the region.

The area in coffee has been more stable in the provinces of Satipo and Chanchamayo than in the province of Oxapampa, both in absolute terms and in terms of its percentage incidence. Whereas in Satipo and Chanchamayo coffee production has been the predominant means of land occupation, in Oxapampa coffee cultivation has been favored only in some areas, cattle ranching being the predominant activity in peripheral areas such as the Pichis and Palcazu valleys.

As we have already stated, coffee cultivation was initially developed on the *haciendas* of the first districts to be colonized in the province of Chanchamayo

(San Ramón, Chanchamayo, and San Luis de Shuaro) long before the era of massive colonization of the region. Beginning in the 1950s, poor Andean colonists who invaded the concession of the Peruvian Corporation also adopted coffee as their principal commercial crop. In the following decades, the more recently occupied districts—Perené and Pichanaki—rapidly became the main areas of expansion for the coffee economy, a process facilitated not only by a political context that permitted the occupation of this land but also by favorable international coffee prices during this period (see Figure 2.2). It was estimated that, in 1972, 69 percent of the agricultural units in Chanchamayo dedicated a portion of their area to coffee cultivation (Maletta and Makhlouf n.d.: vol. 3, 139). During this stage, colonists expanded their coffee farms on both small (less than 20 hectares) and mid-sized (20 to less than 50 hectares) holdings, according to land and labor availability.

A similar process took place in the province of Satipo, where, before 1950, some of the large *haciendas* in the districts of Satipo and Pampa Hermosa had introduced coffee as a substitute for barbasco. In the beginning of the 1960s, the reopening of the road to Concepción, which attracted a new wave of immigrants of Andean origin, was accompanied by growth in the coffee-producing area, this time in the context of small and mid-sized holdings, in all districts in this province except Río Tambo and southern Pangoa. Thus, in 1972, it was calculated that 68 percent of the agricultural units in Satipo produced coffee (Maletta and Makhlouf n.d.: vol. 3, 139). This activity intensified in the 1970s because of a renewed rise in coffee prices and because of the opening of the Carretera Marginal, which expanded the market network and reduced the costs of transportation to Lima, where coffee was stored for export.

The expansion of coffee cultivation in the province of Oxapampa differs in some respects from that in Chanchamayo and Satipo. Before the era of massive immigration, coffee was produced on a small scale in the districts of Oxapampa, Chontabamba, and Huancabamba. This was combined with sugarcane cultivation, cattle ranching, and subsistence agriculture. The connection of these three districts with La Merced after 1943 fostered the expansion of coffee-growing areas, mainly in the mid-sized holdings of colonists of European origin. However, major growth of the coffee-producing area in Oxapampa Province took place when, at the end of the 1950s, the Villa Rica Valley, originally inhabited by the Yanesha, was almost entirely occupied by families from the town of Oxapampa and by Andean immigrants dedicated to coffee production on small and mid-sized holdings.

The appearance in the 1970s of coffee leaf rust (a disease caused by *Hemelia vastatrix*) and of the berry borer *Hypothenemus hampei* had a devastating effect on the coffee plantations of the districts of Oxapampa and Chontabamba, leading coffee growers to convert them into pastureland. In contrast, in the district of

Table 3.3. Percentage Distribution of Agricultural Units by Predominant Crop, 1988

Province and district[a]	Coffee	Citrus	Other fruits	Industrial crops	Annual crops	Pastures
Chanchamayo						
San Ramón (860)	45.8	10.6	35.8	1.6	3.8	2.4
Chanchamayo (614)	51.0	19.1	25.0	3.1	1.2	0.6
San Luis de Shuaro (318)	27.4	34.6	21.7	12.9	2.5	0.9
Perené (2,002)	72.5	13.3	12.9	0.1	0.9	0.3
Pichanaki (2,195)	80.1	9.9	5.6	2.3	1.3	0.8
All 5 districts (5,989)	66.7	13.4	15.2	2.1	1.6	1.0
Satipo						
Satipo (388)	92.8	0.8	0.5	1.0	4.9	0.0
Llaylla (19)	100.0	0.0	0.0	0.0	0.0	0.0
Río Negro (894)	91.7	0.8	0.9	2.9	1.0	2.7
Pangoa (1,241)	70.4	10.9	6.6	7.3	0.6	4.1
Pampa Hermosa (487)	87.4	0.3	7.2	0.2	0.6	4.3
Mazamari (525)	67.2	14.7	3.2	5.0	1.1	8.8
Coviriali (84)	63.1	0.0	26.2	7.1	0.0	3.6
All 7 districts (3,638)	79.9	6.1	4.6	4.2	1.2	4.0

Source: PRONAC 1990; data elaborated by the authors.

Notes: Citrus crops include orange, mandarin orange, tangerine, and grapefruit. Other fruits include avocado, papaya, pineapple, and banana. Industrial crops include annatto and cocoa. Annual crops include manioc, corn, and rice. Pastures include natural and cultivated land.

[a]Values within parentheses denote the numbers of agricultural units surveyed within the districts and provinces.

Villa Rica and in the provinces of Chanchamayo and Satipo, the areas lost to these plagues were compensated by the establishment of new plantations.

Although between 1964 and 1984 the proportion of the area cultivated in coffee tended to decrease, both overall and within each province, coffee continues to account for the largest proportion of the cultivated area. In addition to being a pioneer crop and representing a considerable percentage of the region's cultivated area, coffee presently constitutes the predominant crop in the agricultural units of all of the districts of Chanchamayo and Satipo, with only one exception. This means that even though its relative importance has tended to diminish, in most of the agricultural units in the region coffee continues to be the crop that occupies the greatest proportion of land, affecting the organization of family labor and contributing a significant part of its agricultural income.

Table 3.3, based on information collected by the Programa Nacional de Catastro (National Land Registry Program; see the appendix), indicates that in 1988 in the province of Chanchamayo, coffee was the predominant crop in 67 percent of all agricultural units, whereas in Satipo this proportion grew to 80 percent. The situation in Chanchamayo contrasts with that in Satipo. Whereas in Chanchamayo the districts with the highest proportion of agricultural units on which coffee is the predominant crop are the most recently colonized (Perené and Pichanaki), in Satipo, the highest proportion of coffee-growing agricultural units are located in the districts that have been occupied for the longest period of time (Río Negro, Satipo, and Llaylla). This phenomenon is not contradictory and can be explained by analyzing diachronically the relationships among economic options, demographic saturation, and diminishing soil productivity.

Thus, coffee is given priority by colonists when they first arrive in the region because it is the commercial product that offers the most stable price and the most secure market. In all of the recently occupied areas in the provinces of Chanchamayo and Satipo and in some districts in Oxapampa, coffee is the predominant crop on colonists' agricultural units. Its prominence tends to be maintained even when, with the passage of time, these areas begin to be fully incorporated and to develop the infrastructure necessary for carrying out other economic activities. However, eventually severe soil degradation, associated with long-term occupation, higher population pressure, and extreme land fragmentation causes such a decline in productivity that producers are forced to abandon coffee and shift to other economic activities. This is exactly what happened in the districts that had been occupied for the longest time in Chanchamayo (San Ramón, Chanchamayo, and San Luis de Shuaro). Farmers who occupy the most degraded lands have given up coffee cultivation and opted for crops that continue to yield even when grown on extremely degraded land, such as pineapple. An intermediate situation exists in the earliest occupied districts of Satipo, where coffee is grown in association with other crops.

Given that 60 percent of the agricultural units in Chanchamayo and Satipo are smaller than 10 hectares in size and that 78 percent have less than 10 hectares under cultivation, it should not be surprising that a high proportion of agricultural units on which coffee is the predominant crop are small. Unfortunately, we have been unable to correlate the size-class distribution of holdings with the predominance of coffee. However, data from the 1972 census offer some leads: at that time, the average coffee plot was 5.6 hectares (Maletta and Makhlouf n.d.: vol. 3, 139), whereas 76 percent of coffee producers owned agricultural units smaller than 20 hectares (Figueroa and Gonzales Vigil 1979). Nevertheless, because of the low productivity of small units, most of the coffee produced in the region came from medium-sized units between 20 and 50 hectares, as is still the case (Cerrón 1985). This type of mid-sized coffee farm is concentrated in the more recently occupied districts in Chanchamayo Province and in the Villa Rica district of Oxapampa Province.

Expansion of the agrarian frontier did not go hand in hand with an increase in average coffee yield. In fact, coffee yield tended to diminish with the transition from coffee cultivation on *haciendas* to its cultivation on smaller plots. Thus, in the 1920s, the *haciendas* and farms of Chanchamayo registered a yield of 13 *quintales* per hectare (1 *quintal* = 46 kilograms) (Barclay 1989). Yield increased in the 1940s and 1950s as a consequence of the modernization process initiated by *hacienda* owners. At present, the median yield in the region has fallen to slightly less than 10 *quintales* per hectare (Brack et al. n.d.: 30, 45).[2] However, these figures conceal a great variety of situations resulting from differences in land quality and availability, altitude, access to labor, management practices, and the modifications that result from the introduction of new high-yield coffee varieties.

Arabic coffee varieties predominate in the Selva Central. Robusta varieties, which are more rustic, less productive, and more adapted to lower altitudes, are found almost exclusively on small plots in the Pichis, Palcazu, and Tambo valleys. The most technologically advanced farms, and smaller holdings that make adequate use of cultivation techniques, contouring, pruning, and compost fertilization, attain yields of up to 45 *quintales* per hectare when growing the most traditional of the Arabic varieties. The fact that the average yield in the Selva Central is currently estimated to be 11.5 *quintales* per hectare, a figure higher than that for the rest of the country (Barrenechea 1986: 17), is due to the high productivity of this type of coffee-producing unit. However, it is estimated that only 16 percent of coffee-producing agricultural units in the region yield more than 10 *quintales* per hectare and that up to 13 percent of the coffee-growing area yields less than 4 *quintales* per hectare (Brack et al. n.d.: 4).

The adoption of improved Arabic varieties—caturra and bourbon—by the holders of medium-sized farms has meant a substantial increase in coffee yield per hectare, allowing them to obtain up to 108 *quintales* per hectare under optimal management conditions (Brack et al. n.d.: 142).[3] Coffee producers in Villa Rica were the first to adopt improved coffee varieties, as well as intensive management practices. This phenomenon is linked to the initially high productivity of the area, which was favored not only by its altitude and the socioeconomic characteristics of its early colonists but also by the lower degree of land fragmentation in the Villa Rica Valley. As a result, data on coffee production in this area cannot be extrapolated to the entire Selva Central. Nevertheless, because coffee cultivation in Villa Rica is the most developed, information regarding the use of improved varieties and agricultural practices there provides a reference point that allows one to infer both the current ceiling on coffee production in the region and the variability of coffee-growing situations. Mori Caro (1982) established that up to 55 percent of the agricultural units in Villa Rica have introduced improved coffee varieties and that 33 percent of the coffee-producing area in the valley is planted in these varieties. As a result of the cultivation of improved varieties and the use of fertilizers by 24 percent of the agricultural units, the average coffee yield in Villa Rica, by subarea, ranges from 20.8 to 22.6 *quintales* per hectare. Most of the producers that have adopted these practices are owners of medium-sized holdings. It is they who have been able to achieve significant levels of capital accumulation and who are well represented in the Peruvian Association of Coffee-Growers (Barrenechea 1986: 102).

In contrast, producers owning less than 5 hectares, who account for a considerable proportion of the coffee producers in the region, have serious difficulties adopting these kinds of technological improvements. Because of the limited area of available land, their commercial agricultural production does not allow them to make the capital investments necessary for the adoption of improved coffee varieties, which, because of their greater nutrient requirements, make the use of fertilizers obligatory. Furthermore, their lack of capital makes it difficult for them to hire the additional labor that is also necessary for the cultivation of these improved varieties. In effect, the productivity of coffee plantations depends to a large extent on practices of year-round maintenance: pruning, cultivation, replanting and trimming of shade trees, phytosanitary controls, and so on. This is especially true in the cultivation of improved coffee varieties. Owners of small holdings must rely on family labor, and even this may not always be available, as family members are frequently forced to accept seasonal salaried jobs to complement their agricultural income.[4]

This situation explains why, even as the temporary employment of small landholders on modern medium-sized coffee farms continues to act as a channel for the dissemination of technology by demonstrating the advantages of certain innovations, they have not been able to adopt them. Although some of the technological improvements developed on Chanchamayo *haciendas* during the 1950–1970 period could be adopted by small farmers, allowing colonists to improve their incomes, current innovations need to be adopted altogether in order to ensure a return on investments. Therefore, in the rare cases in which small farmers have adopted improved varieties, they have not been able to increase either their productivity or their level of income.

Coffee Economy and Market Formation

One of the most relevant phenomena associated with the expansion of the coffee economy is its contribution to the expansion of the sphere of capitalist relationships and therefore to market formation at a regional level. In this sense, coffee cultivation not only has been a source of monetary income for colonists but has stimulated the development of a series of nonagricultural activities; contributed to the emergence of consumer, real estate, labor, and capital markets; and led to the expansion of regional capital, thus encouraging the economic articulation and consolidation of the areas that make up the region.

In the Selva Central, the coffee economy has left its imprint on all branches of economic activity. In historical terms, its evolution has influenced the pace of development of other economic activities, stimulating or depressing the trade, service, construction, timber, agribusiness, and financial sectors, according to fluctuations in the price of coffee. Furthermore, the marked seasonal character of the coffee economy strongly influences the economic life of the region. It is enough to see the rise in economic activity during the harvest season to realize the importance and impact that the coffee economy has on the nonagricultural sectors.

Capital resulting from Chanchamayo coffee production and export since the end of the 19th century progressively enlarged its sphere of influence as the coffee-growing areas expanded. However, because the Peruvian Corporation outfitted the majority of the producers who settled on its original concession and blocked the access of other coffee buyers to the area, until the 1940s the opportunities for Chanchamayo traders to widen their playing field were limited. Later, with changes in company policies, the massive influx of Andean colonists engaged in coffee production, and the expansion of the road system, the coffee-trading firms established in La Merced extended their influence progressively over all of the recent areas of colonization where coffee became the predominant crop.

The main mechanism for the promotion and control of coffee production was the outfitting of colonists by a network of middlemen, most of whom were associated with coffee-trading firms in La Merced. Advances of money and merchandise in the months before the beginning of the coffee harvest, when there was an increased need for cash to pay laborers and to cover other related costs, obligated returns from the harvest and assured the rapid recuperation of capital invested by traders. In addition to employing agents who traveled throughout the region to outfit farmers and gather the product, these firms provided capital to mid-sized farm owners so as to allow them to hire laborers for the harvest. The fact that the most important coffee buyers also owned plants to process coffee beans and controlled coffee exports guaranteed a wide profit margin for this sector.

As a reaction to the monopolistic practices of these firms, in the early 1960s coffee producers organized themselves in marketing cooperatives. These were mainly supported by mid-range producers and were promoted by the government through the granting of low-interest credit for coffee commercialization. Coffee cooperatives were initially organized on a local basis. Such is the case of the cooperatives in both Villa Rica and Satipo. However, these cooperatives very quickly expanded their influence into other areas, competing with the traditional coffee-trading firms for control over regional production.

When the 1969 agrarian reform was implemented, two important events took place with respect to coffee marketing and its associated capital. First, the cooperative system increasingly integrated smaller producers, at the same time that the government attempted to monopolize the export business, which until then had been in the hands of private export firms. However, the growth of coffee cooperatives did not leave traditional traders altogether out of the game. Second, coffee traders in the region diversified their activities, establishing bean-processing facilities as well as other small fruit-processing plants, which allowed them to increase the value of the fruit produced in the region. This contributed to the redefinition of the role of coffee cultivation in the earliest occupied areas.

The growing economic activity around coffee trading brought about the expansion of opportunities for commerce in general, both to satisfy the demands of the coffee-production infrastructure (depulping machines, bags, cement for construction of washing tanks, and drying areas) and to satisfy a growing consumer market for food, clothing, and other manufactured goods imported from the coast and the highlands. The economic profile that crystallized in the region discouraged food production, increasing the dependence of local producers on food from sources outside the region. The coffee economy also gave a big push to the service sector and in particular to transportation.

Beyond merely stimulating regional growth and economic consolidation, coffee cultivation gave rise to the early emergence of a real estate market. In the Amazonian region, poorly integrated and with less fertile soils, what is valued is not land itself but those forest resources for which there is a demand in the national or international markets. In these areas, demand for land is largely speculative in nature, the primary interest being in the animal, mineral, or forest-related resources associated with it. When these extractive resources are exhausted or lose their value as a result of a drop in prices, land ownership becomes unimportant. In areas where agriculture based on the cultivation of crops with high commercial value—such as coffee, rice, or coca—predominates, the situation is different. In the case of the Selva Central, coffee cultivation has favored the construction of a major transportation network and the rise of a stable agricultural market. This, added to the fact that coffee is a perennial crop, has made the land more valuable, generating a real estate market that does not exist in other areas of the *selva alta* region.

We have already seen how, in the first half of this century, the expansion of the coffee market gave rise to an important process of land sales through the transfer, partitioning, or redistribution of sugarcane plantations in the San Ramón and Chanchamayo areas. The increase in international coffee prices in the 1950s produced a new reordering of property through the sale and fusion of farms and *haciendas* into more modern, large-scale production units. At the same time, even before it faced the problem of massive invasions, the Peruvian Corporation began to divide up certain sectors of its concession in order to sell them.

Finally, with the massive influx of colonists, the recuperation of coffee prices, and the development of the road network in the 1960s and 1970s, land in areas served by roads became quite valuable. Consequently a more generalized market for land developed, even though agrarian-reform regulations prohibited such transactions.

Because the sale of land was prohibited, there are no records that allow us to estimate very precisely the magnitude of this market. However, studies such as that of Recharte (n.d.) for San Ramón and of Shoemaker (1981) for Satipo enable us to conclude that the land market included not only large and medium-sized properties but also smaller holdings. These studies also show that the land market developed not only in the areas that had been occupied for the longest periods of time but also in more recently incorporated areas. Officials in charge of regional land-titling programs are aware of the difficulties involved in maintaining current records in light of the existence of this informal land market. In the case of small properties, these transfers are made under the guise of "land improvements" *(mejoras);* that is, what appears to be sold is not land but, instead, plantings, pastures, buildings, or other forms of infrastructure on a given holding. Thus despite the prohibition on land sales, the original owner is able to recover his or her investment, and land destined for commercial production can be transferred to the new owner. On official records, these transfers are registered as the abandonment of a plot and its subsequent reallocation. Despite the language and the form of the transfer, it is obvious that a dynamic land market currently exists in the region. First seen primarily within the coffee economy, today this market involves not only land where coffee is grown but also land where other commercial crops such as citrus fruits or forages are cultivated.

Another notable impact of the coffee economy has been the formation of a regional labor market. The development of the sugarcane industry in Chanchamayo during the second half of the 19th century did not give rise to a labor market, because the owners of sugarcane plantations from Tarma brought in workers from their Andean *haciendas* for the harvest season. Later, the coffee estates resorted to the extensive use of the system of coercive recruitment of labor *(enganche),* a mechanism used to meet their demand for harvest labor, which was scarce in the region. In addition to this type of seasonal labor, estate owners retained a limited number of permanent workers and *mejoreros* in their service who were responsible for maintenance tasks on the plantations throughout the year (Barclay 1989: 163–178).

With the mass migrations of the 1950s, coffee agriculture expanded significantly outside of the *hacienda* context. This growth generated greater competition for labor during the harvest season, which resulted in higher wages and in better working and sanitary conditions. Increased demand for labor on the part of small and mid-sized coffee producers resulted in the breakdown of the *enganche* system and coercive mechanisms of retention. The *haciendas* began to adjust to these new conditions through the concomitant process of technological advancement and modernization. Consequently, seasonal labor during coffee harvest became attractive not only to poor Andean peasants but also to poor colonists settled in the region and those just recently established. For the last two groups, the seasonal sale of labor allows them to complement their earnings from their petty-commodity production but also to generate a source of income until their commercial crops are mature enough to yield.

In addition to the laborers who arrive in the Selva Central independently, there are contractors operating in the region who, to meet the high demand during harvests, recruit laborers in neighboring Andean areas by giving cash advances. It should be noted, however, that although these contractors continue to use cash advances as a recruitment technique, this form of contracting has become less important and does not require the use of extraeconomic coercive mechanisms, as it did in the past. On the contrary, the scale of the coffee economy, the level of demand for labor, the opportunity to earn a respectable seasonal income, and the prospect of acquiring experience that could facilitate workers' establishment in the area as colonists has enabled the development and constant expansion of a regional labor market. Furthermore, progressive fragmentation and deterioration of the land that has been under production for the longest period of time has resulted in the permanent conversion of a significant proportion of the poorest producers into semiproletarian workers.

In this sense, we agree with Cotlear (1979: 83) in that, although *enganche* as a system for acquiring labor exhibits certain defining characteristics, it functions in various ways according to the historical and economic contexts in which it operates. Thus, in areas of expansion and in peripheral areas of the Selva Central— areas that are still not fully incorporated into the capitalist system and where there is no free labor market—this system provides the mechanism to recruit and retain labor, often through compulsory methods of an extraeconomic nature. In contrast, in central areas (such as those studied by Cotlear) that are immersed in the capitalist system, *enganche* continues to operate to facilitate the establishment of relationships between prospective Andean laborers and widely dispersed coffee producers. In such areas, the system ceases to function as a substitute for a free labor market, playing a role equivalent to that of an employment agency and having the "dual function of permitting access to a greater quantity of labor, while simultaneously depressing salaries in the valley market" (Cotlear 1979: 83).

In order to understand the importance that this labor market has in the region, it is essential to bear in mind that in Peru, coffee is the crop with the greatest labor requirements after coca plantations (Maletta 1984: 105–115). At the national level these requirements have been calculated to be between 152 and 192 days per worker per year per hectare (Gutiérrez et al. n.d.: 50; Maletta 1984: 115). However, in the Selva Central, several authors have noted the existence of important differences among the diverse coffee-growing areas. Thus, in the 1970s, the most modern agricultural areas in Chanchamayo required a labor force equivalent to 246 days per worker per year per hectare, a figure much higher than the national average (Gutiérrez et al. n.d.). The demand for labor for coffee cultivation is basically seasonal and is principally associated with harvest periods. The beginning of the harvest season is determined by the altitude of the coffee fields—the lower they are the earlier the harvest begins—whereas its duration depends on the rate at which the beans mature, which is influenced by the rainfall pattern in the preceding period. Nevertheless, the greatest demand for labor generally occurs between March and August and is characterized by its inflexibility, because the beans need to be harvested before they fall. A delay of a few days may prove to be disastrous to coffee producers.

Some authors have calculated that, in Chanchamayo and San Ramón, an average of 68 days per worker per year per hectare is required during the harvest season and that these requirements represent approximately 30 percent of the yearly labor requirement for coffee cultivation (Recharte n.d.: 146; Maletta 1984). However, the need for labor as well as the capacity to contract it depends not only on the productivity of individual coffee-growing units but also on the availability of land and capital, on coffee prices at harvest time, and on the labor requirements of other commercial crops.

On the basis of field data it can be said that a farmer who has up to 1 hectare of coffee can generally meet all of the harvest labor requirements with family labor. During peak harvest periods, coffee plots larger than 1 hectare are estimated to require approximately seven people per hectare working simultaneously to be able to gather the beans and to depulp, wash, and dry them. In this case it is necessary to contract additional labor.

The figures of the 1972 Agrarian Census show that 42 percent of the agricultural units in Satipo and Chanchamayo contracted temporary labor, whereas only 7 percent contracted permanent labor. For more recent periods, we have only the estimates of the National Survey of Rural Households (INE 1986: 418), which established that 67 percent of the agricultural units in the central *selva alta* region employed hired labor. One can safely assume that a high proportion of this labor is for coffee-related activities. These data indicate that coffee cultivation results in a high proportion of agricultural units employing extrafamilial labor, in sharp contrast to the general situation of small-plot agriculture at the national level.

Given the major influence of the cost of labor on the structure of coffee-production costs—which in the 1980s represented between 40 percent and 67 percent, depending on whether or not this included finance charges—it is not surprising that farmers of a high percentage of agricultural units depend on credit to be able to contract labor during the harvest period. Because of this need, the State Agrarian Bank has maintained a policy in the Selva Central of constantly increasing the number of loans of this type since the 1940s. On the basis of data from the National Survey of Rural Households, we can assert that in 1983–1984, 80 percent of the farmers in the Selva Central who received subsidized credit used it for coffee production and that the average area to which it was allocated was 5.4 hectares (Ccama 1987: 230–231). Thus, it can be said that the emergence of a labor market for coffee production has also contributed to the expansion of the capital market. Although traditionally this has mainly referred to State-run banks, coffee traders and the owners of some modern medium-sized farms have turned also to commercial banks for short-term loans. This, in turn, has resulted in the multiplication of internal and external economic linkages, leading to greater economic agglomeration and a more stable economy. The fact that, in a strictly economic sense, the role of the State has been relatively limited in comparison with the role that it has played in other areas of the *selva alta* region makes the development process of the Selva Central even more unique and a phenomenon that deserves to be taken into consideration in terms of the future of other areas of the Amazonian region.

Agricultural Diversification and the Development of Fruit Cultivation

In the last two decades, fruit production has become increasingly important, both from the point of view of the colonists' economic strategies and from the point of view of regional economic development. Fruit production in the Selva Central includes a wide range of perennial and semiperennial crops, which can be differentiated according to the technological requirements associated with them and the role that they play in the colonists' economic strategies as a function of the size of their agricultural units, their degree of capitalization, and their geographic location within the region. It is also important to note that because of the perishable nature of this type of product, the development of fruit production has been strongly influenced by the availability of transportation, a factor that distinguishes it from coffee production.

Regional fruit production began to be developed in the 1940s and 1950s as an attempt on the part of Chanchamayo coffee estate owners to diversify their produce and thereby to compensate for frequent variations in coffee prices, as well as to make maximal use of their permanent labor. In developing this strategy, the *haciendas* and agricultural conglomerates had the advantage of being located in areas well connected by road and of having access to permanent labor

Table 3.4. Harvest Schedule of Commercial Crops in the Selva Central

Crop	Jan	Feb	Mar	Apr	May	Jun	Jul	Aug	Sep	Oct	Nov	Dec
Tangerine	–––	–––	–––									
Mandarin orange			–––	–––								
Coffee			–––	–––	–––	–––						
Orange					–––	–––	–––					
Pineapple								–––	–––	–––		
Avocado									–––	–––	–––	–––

and to the technical resources necessary to guarantee high yields and disease control on their plantations. The same advantages were available to the Perene Colony.

The Chanchamayo *haciendas* that became involved in fruit production managed to conquer the Lima market and achieved a certain national renown (Francia oranges and Chanchamayo avocados, for example, became synonymous with good-quality fruit). As markets for these products developed, fruit production was steadily adopted by farmers on neighboring small and medium-sized holdings. In the 1950s, the majority of fruit sold by producers in the tropical areas of Junín and Pasco to coastal markets consisted of citrus fruits (55 percent), papaya (16 percent), banana (13 percent), and avocado (10 percent) (Ortiz 1969: vol. 1, 120). The bulk of regional citrus and avocado production was located on large and mid-sized holdings, whereas small farmers generally chose to develop small-scale production of banana, papaya, and pineapple, along with their coffee production. Pineapple was often cultivated in former coffee-growing areas where soils had become highly eroded but where there was good access to roads.

The opening of the road from Chanchamayo to Satipo along the right bank of the Perené River in 1973, and the improvement of the road to the coast through La Merced, allowed fruit cultivation to progressively expand into the upper and central Perené Valley, areas that were originally incorporated into the market economy through coffee cultivation. Fruit cultivation in the valley was mainly adopted by medium- and small-scale producers to obtain monetary income throughout the year, in addition to that generated by their seasonal coffee crop.

According to the harvest schedule in these areas and to the size and extent of capital input on their agricultural units, small-scale coffee producers favored the adoption of avocado, papaya, and banana, crops whose harvest seasons do not overlap with that of coffee, whereas owners of more-capital-intensive, medium-sized holdings had the additional option of cultivating citrus fruits (Table 3.4). Because of the predominance of coffee on most of the agricultural units in this area, fruit cultivation was introduced on a very limited scale. Although this enabled growers to maximize the use of family labor, it also required them to employ hired labor for fruit harvest seasons.

The development of citrus production outside of the *hacienda* context was encouraged by the establishment of private nurseries and by its profitability, which was equal to that of coffee (Swenson 1986b: 6). However, the development of citrus cultivation was uneven, in terms of both the type of citrus crop that was grown and the type of landholdings involved. Thus, whereas orange cultivation on medium-sized holdings was preferred in Perené, on the La Merced–Oxapampa axis, mandarin oranges and, later, tangerines were preferred on small holdings where coffee and banana were also grown. In Satipo, as recently as the 1980s, a significant increase in citrus production (mainly that of oranges) took place on medium-sized farms, spurred by the growing demand in the Andean areas of Huancayo and Mantaro Valley (INADE 1985).

Pineapple production constitutes a different case. Having been introduced on one of the Peruvian Corporation's *haciendas,* this crop was subsequently adopted by small-scale producers located in the areas with the most degraded land in the region: the upland areas in the districts of San Ramón and Chanchamayo (see Table 6.7). Pineapple's low nutrient requirements allowed growers to take advantage of otherwise unproductive land. This and the fact that its cultivation requires constant attention throughout the entire year led pineapple to become a monocultured crop (Recharte n.d.: 129). However, the fact that pineapple is cultivated without a cover crop in areas with steep slopes leads to further erosion and results in the irreversible degradation of much of the land where it is cultivated.

According to official figures, in 1984 there were 17,073 hectares cultivated in fruit, representing 13 percent of the total cultivated area in the Selva Central region (Table 3.5). This is quite a significant figure, considering that by then the area cultivated in coffee represented 35 percent of the total cultivated area. Although coffee and fruit production accounted for nearly 50 percent of the cultivated area in the entire Selva Central in 1984, their combined importance in the provinces of Chanchamayo and Satipo was even greater, where they occupied 72 percent of the total cultivated area.

Two other factors shown in Table 3.5 are the little weight that fruit cultivation has in the province of Oxapampa as compared with that in Chanchamayo and Satipo, and the extreme importance of citrus and banana production as compared with fruit production as a whole.

The first factor can be explained from a historico-economic and logistic point of view. When, in the 1970s, coffee plantations in the Oxapampa Valley were devastated by the coffee berry borer and by coffee leaf rust, medium-scale producers opted for cattle raising rather than fruit cultivation. In the Villa Rica Valley, coffee continued to be the predominant crop because of its comparative advan-

Table 3.5. Area Cultivated in Fruit, 1984

Fruit	Chanchamayo-Satipo	Oxapampa	Selva Central
Banana	4,807	1,895	6,702
Citrus[a]	4,745	341	5,086
Pineapple	1,800	31	1,831
Avocado	1,410	170	1,580
Papaya	1,400	51	1,451
Granadilla	—	137	137
Passion fruit	120	—	120
Mango	100	6	106
Annona	60	—	60
All	14,442	2,631	17,073

Sources: Ministerio de Agricultura 1963–1988.

Notes: Area cultivated is in hectares. Dashes denote no data.

[a]Citrus includes orange, mandarin orange, and grapefruit.

tages, and fruit production did not develop. Finally, the relative isolation of the Pichis and Palcazu valleys did not permit the development of fruit cultivation.

The second factor can be explained by the fact that citrus crops and bananas represent opposite extremes in terms of technological requirements, suitable land, capital investment, and distance from consumer markets. Thus, citrus cultivation, with investment requirements and profitability similar to those of coffee, is preferred by mid-scale producers who have land near the valley floor and are located in areas nearest to consumer markets. In contrast, banana cultivation, less demanding in terms of capital and labor investment, but also less profitable, is favored by small and mid-scale producers located in the areas furthest from centers of consumption who have less fertile land. Other fruit crops have more restricted markets or require levels of investment that are not compensated by similar levels of profitability, which make them less attractive.

In spite of the fact that, in the provinces of Chanchamayo and Satipo, fruit cultivation has developed to a greater extent than it has in Oxapampa, important differences exist within this area. Data in Table 3.3 show that agricultural production in the province of Chanchamayo is much more diversified than it is in Satipo and that, overall, fruit cultivation is much more important (29 percent versus 11 percent). This is particularly true in the case of citrus cultivation and is clearly associated with the comparative advantages of Chanchamayo as the area nearest to consumer centers. In Satipo, where the percentages of predominantly fruit-producing agricultural units are generally low for all districts, we find that only in Pangoa and Mazamari do units of this type exist at percentages equivalent to those in areas of more recent occupation in Chanchamayo. There,

Table 3.6. Fruit-Crop Yields and
Producers Exceeding Average Yields, 1983

Crop	Average yield (tons per year)	% of producers above average
Citrus	15	30
Banana	10	26
Papaya	24	22
Avocado	18	15
Pineapple	12	10

Source: Brack et al. n.d.: 44.

as in Chanchamayo, this growth has been accompanied by the establishment of citrus-processing plants, which add value and increase the profit margins of producers by offering washing, polishing, and trademarking services.

The districts of Chanchamayo that have been occupied for the longest period of time are also those that have significantly higher proportions of agricultural units predominantly dedicated to the production of "other" fruits, in this case avocado, papaya, banana, and pineapple. Among these districts, San Ramón stands out because of the predominance of agricultural units specializing in pineapple cultivation. It should be noted that, in general, several other fruit crops are frequently grown on the same holding and on agricultural units that also produce coffee. In the case of Satipo, the majority of agricultural units where production of other fruit predominates are dedicated to banana production, which is destined, in large part, for the highland market of Huancayo. Its production yields relatively high profits (Swenson 1986b: 6).

The rapid spread of papaya cultivation beginning in the 1960s was followed by the diffusion of a disease that, beginning in 1979, advanced throughout the Perené and Satipo valleys. This required growers to abandon papaya production, which explains why there is currently a very low proportion of papaya-producing agricultural units and why their yield has substantially decreased.

There are no studies that allow us to establish the average area dedicated to these crops or a producer typology according to crop and size class of agricultural unit. However, a World Bank study (1983) for the Satipo-Chanchamayo Unit of the Pichis–Palcazu Special Project suggests that small farmers who combine production of both papaya and citrus crops dedicate an average of 0.6 and 1.0 hectare, respectively, to these crops. Farms that produce avocado and bananas dedicate an average of 0.6 and 0.5 hectare, respectively, to these crops. Unfortunately, this typology excludes mid-sized fruit producers and does not indicate the area planted in coffee. Table 3.6 shows the average yields for various types of fruit in the Selva Central as well as the percentage of producers in the region whose yields exceed the average. The variability in yields reflects very different technological conditions, degrees of capitalization, scales of production, and soil conditions.

Fruit cultivation in the Selva Central has experienced significant growth in the past three decades, becoming one of the mainstays of regional agricultural activity. This additional activity has contributed to strengthening the process of internal and external articulation of the region but, at the same time, has been hindered by a series of factors that it is worthwhile to review. An initial limitation on the expansion of fruit cultivation results from its extreme dependence on the transportation system. This is not only determined by the perishability of the fruit. It is also due to the fact that the prices of produce that is sold on the farm are radically lower than prices obtained when it is sold along major roads or access routes. A second limitation is related to the scarcity of soils suitable for fruit cultivation. Fruit production can be properly developed only in areas near the valley bottoms. In contrast, coffee thrives in the most common soil types in the region, where the majority of small holdings are found.

A third limitation is that fruit production is generally more technologically demanding than coffee production. Fruit growers must regularly apply pesticides and fungicides, which require greater capital investment. In addition, the managerial and technical expertise associated with coffee cultivation is much more widespread than that necessary for fruit production, making extensive adoption of fruit crops more difficult. Fourth, small-scale coffee growers are seriously limited in their ability to supply the additional labor required for fruit production, particularly in the case of citrus crops. Even if they have access to enough suitable land to be able to diversify and expand their production of fruit, the family labor force would not often be in the position to attend to the maintenance requirements of both crops. This is made even more difficult by their lack of capital and by limitations on their access to credit. Consequently, small-scale producers prefer coffee cultivation, which involves considerably fewer risks. Finally, the marketing mechanisms for the fruit crops that are currently grown in the area, which vary depending on their volume and the location where they are produced, clearly do not favor the small-scale producer. As a result, a high proportion of producers are paid prices that are much lower than the average regional fruit prices.

In the case of fruit cultivation, capital availability and volume of production are the factors that determine how produce is marketed. Fruit buyers establish collection routes that include the access roads connecting with the Carretera Marginal. Most small-scale producers sell their fruit on the farm to this type of buyer. Cerrón (1985) estimates that approximately 75 percent of the produce sold by these small-scale producers is sold in bags at prices that do not adequately compensate for the investment in inputs and labor. Mid-scale producers, who are generally located closer to access roads, sell their produce either in the field (47 percent of producers do this, according to Cerrón) or take the fruit in crates to collection points along the road, where it is sold to fruit traders. Finally, large-scale producers consign their produce to local shipping companies, who sell it in Lima and settle accounts 5 to 15 days later. This system, which offers substantial advantages in terms of the prices that can be obtained, is not risk free. The condition of the road cannot be guaranteed, and contingencies caused by bad weather may delay the arrival of produce at the market, reducing or eliminating profits.

The combination of these factors has prevented fruit cultivation, as a diversification strategy, from becoming generalized to all of the colonization areas that make up the Selva Central and from being widely adopted by small farmers, who constitute the majority of producers in the region. However, in spite of the fact that fruit production is less important and less generalized than coffee production, it has contributed to the creation of linkages among various economic sectors and has strengthened economic relationships within the region.

Thus, for instance, fruit growing has allowed the development of a small, local agroindustry dedicated to the production of juices, concentrates, canned fruit, and jam. Of these, the oldest and most important is Industrias Alimenticias S.A. (INDALSA), established in 1968. At the same time, several industries in Lima have established collection and primary-processing centers in Chanchamayo. Processing is completed in Lima. Even though these agroindustries have had a certain degree of influence on producers' expectations, stimulating the process of agricultural diversification and production, they have not contributed to the improvement of the technological conditions for fruit production. This is principally because these industries often buy only surplus fruit of that destined for Lima. Only a few producers, such as the Juan Velasco Alvarado agrarian cooperative, have fixed contracts to supply local fruit-processing plants. In addition to the serious limitations faced by local agroindustries, the situation of violence in the region has influenced their ability to function in the last several years—for example, by affecting the availability of electrical energy.

Citrus-processing plants established in the region seem to have a greater impact on producers. Most of these are owned by mid-scale fruit producers. Of the 12 processing plants extant in 1989, 5 were located in Chanchamayo, 6 in the upper Perené Valley, and the most recent in Satipo (CDR Chanchamayo 1980–1989; CDR Satipo 1980-1989). Their main clients are medium- and large-scale fruit producers who sell their produce through shipping companies.

In addition to generating a demand for transportation and labor during periods when coffee is not being harvested, fruit cultivation has contributed to the expansion of the crating industry in the Selva Central, which has not only generated employment but also permitted the diversification of the activities of saw-mills in the areas where fine-timber reserves are virtually exhausted.

One should note that the expansion of fruit production in the Selva Central has not been the result of State promotional policies. Rather, its development has been associated with the growth experienced by the coffee economy, which contributed to the development of the transportation network and to the existence of a labor market, as well as to the circulation of capital in the region. Only in the 1980s did the government decide to promote fruit cultivation to stimulate a greater diversification of regional production and to increase producers' incomes. Its actions, however, were affected by a lack of continuity and by the limitations of their plans for the transfer of technology. In spite of the lack of State support, coffee and fruit growers have developed the expertise, production techniques, alternative sources of credit, and marketing channels, generating significant income for themselves and for the region.

Coffee and Fruit Production: The Current Situation

The expertise, technology, production patterns, and marketing connections developed by coffee growers in the Selva Central have significantly influenced the development of national coffee production. Moreover, the region contributes a large proportion of the volume of coffee produced in the country. In the 1980s, it was estimated that 39 percent of the total area in coffee was located in the Selva Central and that it produced 41 percent of Peru's total coffee production. Given that 80 percent of the coffee produced is destined for export and that coffee is the country's principal agricultural export item, one may conclude that the region contributes a considerable proportion of the foreign currency generated by the export of agricultural products.

Because of the relatively early development of fruit cultivation in the Selva Central, the region currently contributes a large proportion of the tropical fruit destined for the country's urban markets. Thanks to its advantageous location with respect to Lima, as compared with other areas of the Amazonian region, the Selva Central has maintained a primary role in the supply of this market. In 1982, it was estimated that the region contributed 85 percent of the papaya, 39 percent of the pineapple, 26 percent of the mandarin oranges, and 16 percent of the avocados produced at the national level (INADE 1985).

These achievements are threatened by the current situation of violence, which originally appeared as an exogenous factor but has become endogenous. Violence has become an outlet for a series of old internal conflicts that have little to do with the ideology or strategic objectives of the subversive groups. This climate of violence that took shape in peripheral areas and has since expanded to include parts of the central areas of the Selva Central region has resulted in a retraction of State influence, as well as the breakdown of commercial networks and the credit system. This has directly affected local farmers.

To this we must add the effects of the sharp decline in international coffee prices. At the end of the 1980s, disagreements among consumer and producer countries that signed the International Coffee Agreement led to the suspension of the quota system, which had contributed to the stabilization of international coffee prices in the last few decades. In mid-1989, the sale of accumulated stocks in the international market brought on a sharp decline in coffee prices—on the order of 30 percent. The fall in international coffee prices has aggravated the problems resulting from the spiraling violence in the Selva Central. In Chanchamayo, Satipo, and Villa Rica—important commercial-production areas that are strongly affected by violence—many of the owners of medium-sized farms dedicated to coffee and fruit production have moved away, leaving their property in the hands of administrators. In addition, the presence of the Shining Path, the Túpac Amaru Revolutionary Movement, and the armed forces has aggravated the problems of mobilizing labor for harvests. This has had a negative impact on investment levels and the upkeep of cultivated areas.

Thus, even if the situation were to return to normal as a result of peace in the region, it would be difficult to undo the effects that this situation of disorder has had on the productivity of these crops within the foreseeable future. Because of travel problems on certain routes, the devaluation of exchange rates for these products, the pressure imposed by armed groups, and the lack of credit support, the income of coffee and fruit producers in the region has shrunk.

DYNAMICS AND LIMITATIONS OF FORESTRY ACTIVITY

An analysis of timber production in the Selva Central is necessary, not so much because of its influence on the regional economy (which, even at its peak, has been much less significant than that of the agricultural sector) but for its intimate relationship with the pace and mode of expansion of the agricultural frontier and because it illustrates the limitations and degrading effects of traditional extractive systems. We begin this section with an analysis of the evolution of timber production in the Selva Central in the last three decades, attempting to explain its cyclic ups and downs, while reconstructing the spatial and economic dynamic that it has brought about. We then analyze the factors that have led some researchers to characterize timber production as a "nomadic economy" (Brack et al. n.d.: 34) and present evidence that disputes this characterization. Finally, we argue that logging activity constitutes the vanguard of the colonization process, being complementary to, but also sometimes contradictory to, agriculture. Along the same lines, we evaluate the contribution of the timber industry to the regional and national economy, in terms of the gross value of production as well as its role, together with coffee production, in the economic integration of the region.

Two cautionary notes to the reader: first, this section focuses on logging and milling operations developed in areas where rivers are not navigable and where wood is transported over land. This excludes an analysis of logging activity in the Tambo River region, where timber is shipped to Pucallpa from the Atalaya forestry district. This latter has been the subject of two important studies (Filomeno 1982; Villasante 1983). Second, because of the lack of systematic information, we have concentrated the analysis on only three of the six forestry districts in the Selva Central: Oxapampa, San Ramón, and Satipo. This excludes the Villa Rica forestry district, where timber production was important during the 1970s, and the two most recently created forestry districts: Puerto Bermúdez and Iscozacín. The exclusion of these three districts is compensated for by the fact that the three districts that we have considered are the most important, being the earliest exploited and those that contribute most to regional timber production. The forestry district of Oxapampa includes the Chorobamba, Chontabamba, Huancabamba, and Pozuzo valleys. The San Ramón forestry district covers all of Chanchamayo Province, and the Satipo forestry district includes all of Satipo Province, except for certain areas of the Tambo and Ene river valleys that fall within the Atalaya forestry district.

An analysis of the timber industry must take into consideration the natural limitations that it faces in the *selva alta* in general and in the Selva Central in particular. Forests in the *selva alta* are characterized by a high diversity of tree species. This great wealth is limited, however, by the fact that trees of a given species are widely dispersed throughout the forest, making the extraction of commercially valuable species more difficult and expensive. In addition, forests with timber-harvest aptitude — that is, those that can be exploited without a serious risk of soil erosion — are not homogeneous with respect to their potential. Thus, as one sees in Table 3.7, whereas in the Pichis Valley it is estimated that there is a potential average volume of 70.6 cubic meters of roundwood per hectare, in the Oxapampa-Villa Rica area potential production amounts to 22.4 cubic meters of roundwood per hectare. Differences in timber-production potential in these various areas are explained both by their distinctive environmental conditions and by the varied intensities with which their forests have been exploited in the past. Thus, the higher average timber-production potential recorded for the Palcazu, Pichis, and Tambo river valleys is explained, in part, by the fact that their forests have been among the least exploited in the Selva Central.

Finally, it should be emphasized that, because of the lack of detailed studies

Table 3.7. Total and Average Timber Potential, 1985

Zone	Total potential[a] (m^3 of roundwood)	Average potential (m^3 of roundwood per hectare)
Oxapampa-Villa Rica	33,772,891	22.4
Chanchamayo-Satipo	22,657,680	35.9
Gran Pajonal	8,146,723	37.7
Palcazu	5,243,311	65.9
Tambo	5,420,328	66.9
Pichis	9,087,836	70.6
All 6 zones	84,328,769	49.9

Source: Rivadeneira Cotera 1986.

[a]Total potential refers to the potentially exploitable volume of roundwood, not to the total volume of timber extant in any given area.

on the potential uses of many tree species in the region, as well as of the limitations imposed by market demands, the number of species that are currently exploited is still very low. In the forestry districts of San Ramón and Satipo, 65 percent of sawnwood consists of two species, *tornillo (Cedrelinga catenaeformis)* and *moena (Nectandra* spp. and *Occotea* spp.); whereas in Oxapampa-Villa Rica, 80 percent of sawnwood consists of different varieties of *roble amarillo* (Lauraceae) (INADE 1984). These figures reflect the underutilization of the region's timber resources. Thus, although the average timber-production potential per hectare in the region ranges from 22.4 to 70.6 cubic meters of roundwood per hectare, it is estimated that the average volume that is actually extracted does not exceed 1 to 2 cubic meters per hectare according to Malleux (1981: 3), or 2 to 4 cubic meters per hectare according to Pino Zambrano (1985: 95). This, as we will see, has been the principal limiting factor for the stability and continuity of the timber industry in the region, as well as the principal cause of the extensive plundering of its forests.

The Evolution of Timber Production

In Table 3.8, we have recorded the production of sawnwood per forestry district for the 1954-1988 period. To construct this series, we have drawn from various sources, selecting those that cover the longest periods of time and that offer information about the three districts that are considered, rather than those that offer data for only a few years or for a single district. In addition, it should be noted that since the Ministry of Agriculture itself calculates that 30 percent of sawnwood production is not recorded, these figures are probably underestimates. However, what is important here are the patterns of increases and decreases in the volume of sawnwood produced, which should be unaffected by the proportion of timber that is unaccounted for if we assume that this remains fairly constant over time.

Table 3.8 shows that the combined yield of the forestry districts of Oxapampa, San Ramón, and Satipo grew continously between 1954 and 1975, after which it declined. It recovered temporarily in 1980 but declined again progressively for the rest of the decade. By 1988, yield had fallen to 1966 levels, representing barely twice the volume registered in 1964 when the yield of the San Ramón forestry district was still reduced and that of Satipo almost insignificant. The fluctuations in sawnwood production in these three districts are illustrated in Figure 3.1. However, it is only when analyzing the evolution of sawnwood production in each of these districts (Figure 3.2) that it becomes apparent that logging activity has not had the same impact, nor developed at the same time, in the different areas that compose the Selva Central.

The first sawmills in the Selva Central were those established in Chanchamayo around 1920 (Brack et al. n.d.: 32). Twenty years later, new sawmills were established in Oxapampa, surpassing the yield of those in Chanchamayo within a few years. In 1950, the first mills were established in Villa Rica. In Satipo, commercial logging also began in the 1950s, but timber production did not take off until the 1970s, as did that of the Pichanaki area in Chanchamayo (Brack et al. n.d.: 32).

Thus, logging and timber processing in the Selva Central have been neither spatially nor temporally homogenous. On the contrary, they have developed one stage at a time, gradually involving a greater number of areas as new logging fronts opened up. The different times at which these areas entered into production have not resulted from chance; rather, they have resulted from a combination of factors, including (1) the different environments of these areas, which determine greater or lesser availability of timber resources, (2) the availability of the necessary infrastructure (essentially, roads) for large-scale logging, (3) the structural limitations of the prevailing extractive model, and (4) the economic strategies of the logging companies. In the following pages, we will see how these four variables interact to explain the differences in the dates when timber exploitation was begun and in the rates of timber production that are given in Figure 3.2.

The Oxapampa Forestry District

Although the Chanchamayo Valley (San Ramón forestry district) was the first area to enter into production, Oxapampa quickly surpassed it because of its large reserves of *ulcumano (Podocarpus utilios)*. In contrast to the majority of tree species in the Amazonian region, *ulcumano* is one of the few species that occurs in dense stands, forming relatively homogeneous forests. This makes it easier and cheaper to harvest. The presence of these timber reserves accelerated the

Table 3.8. Production of Sawnwood According to Forestry District

Year	Oxapampa	San Ramón	Satipo	All 3 forestry districts
1954	19,458	2,486	254	22,198
1955	23,079	3,295	399	26,773
1956	22,096	2,765	455	25,316
1957	20,493	3,249	425	24,167
1958	14,774	2,075	520	17,369
1959	14,024	5,544	412	19,980
1960	23,284	2,570	361	26,215
1961	15,479	7,190	480	23,149
1962	21,159	13,910	282	35,351
1963	22,078	15,941	372	38,391
1964	20,941	17,479	642	39,062
1965	23,135	15,498	959	39,592
1966	29,796	26,164	1,369	57,329
1967	35,510	25,987	2,560	64,057
1968	33,086	32,133	2,407	67,626
1969	34,058	31,159	3,356	68,573
1970	33,693	43,455	9,628	86,776
1971	37,973	35,231	14,506	87,710
1972	33,268	33,939	15,962	83,169
1973	34,106	43,078	19,473	96,657
1974	32,009	47,524	27,827	107,360
1975	32,009[a]	54,181	31,463	117,653
1976	21,292[b]	47,330	45,603	114,225
1977	21,292	35,520	30,172	86,984
1978	20,296	24,980	33,508	78,784
1979	20,296[a]	33,556	42,065	95,917
1980	23,174	46,341	63,464	132,979
1981	15,785	43,759	47,956	107,500
1982	12,484	43,115	44,330	99,929
1983	10,579	31,312	32,312	74,203
1984	7,988[c]	41,645	36,762	86,395
1985	7,988[c]	33,149	44,000	85,137
1986	7,988[c]	35,368	29,799	73,115
1987	7,988[c]	36,216	36,625	80,829
1988	5,398	20,343	28,265	54,006
1954–1988, overall	758,056	937,487	648,973	2,344,516

Sources: Banco de Crédito 1972 (for the three forestry districts, 1954–1969); David 1983 (for the three forestry districts, 1970–1974 and 1977–1981); Rivadeneira Cotera 1986 (for the three forestry districts, 1982–1983); INP/PNUD 1977 (for San Ramón, 1975–1976); CDR Chanchamayo 1988 (for San Ramón, 1985–1988); CDR Satipo 1988 (for Satipo, 1984–1988); Rodríguez del Aguila 1985 (for Satipo, 1975–1976, and San Ramón, 1984); CDR Oxapampa 1989 (for Oxapampa, 1988).

Note: Production data are given as volume of sawnwood, in cubic meters.

[a] Because of lack of data, we have used the figure for the previous year.

[b] Because of lack of data, we have used the figure for the following year.

[c] Because of lack of data, we have used the average of the 1983 and 1988 figures.

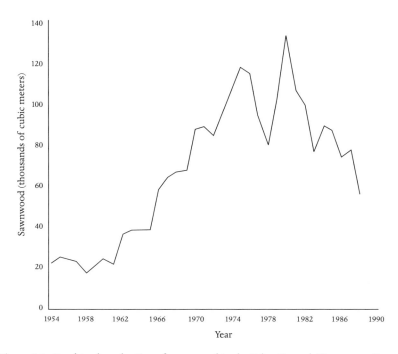

Figure 3.1. Combined production of sawnwood in the Selva Central (Oxapampa, San Ramón, and Satipo forestry districts), 1954-1988. *Source:* Table 3.8.

construction of the La Merced-Oxapampa road, which was finally inaugurated in 1943. This made it possible for Oxapampa to enter into timber production.

Between 1954 and 1970, a total of 115,714 cubic meters of sawnwood of *ulcumano* was produced in the country, approximately 60 percent of which came from Oxapampa (Banco de Crédito 1972). During the same period, Oxapampa occupied second place in importance after Pucallpa, among the large timber-producing centers in the country, reaching a maximal level of expansion in 1971 with a yield of 37,973 cubic meters. By that time, the timber reserves in the area, and reserves of *ulcumano* in particular, gave clear signs of running out. In 1975, sawnwood production plummeted by 30 percent, in comparison with the previous year, and continued to fall without any sign of recovering until 1988, when yield was only a quarter of the volume recorded 30 years earlier.

The first signs of the decline were reported in a study done by the Organization of American States in 1961. This study pointed out that timber production in Oxapampa had leveled off at around 14,000 cubic meters of sawnwood, estimating that "an economically accessible reserve of timber would be available for a period of 3-5 years, after which the cost of timber exploitation would be too high for continued large scale logging" (OEA 1961: 65). These predictions were

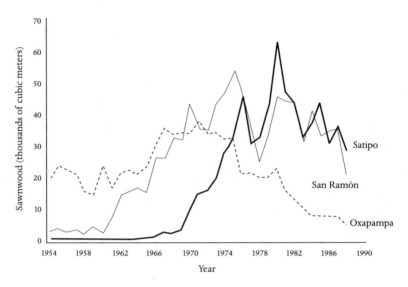

Figure 3.2. Production of sawnwood in the Oxapampa, San Ramón, and Satipo forestry districts, 1954–1988. *Source:* Table 3.8.

not completely borne out. Timber yields continued to increase as a result of the advance of the Oxapampa-Huancabamba-Pozuzo road, the investment of local sawmill owners in the construction of new logging roads, and the extraction of new species with less commercial value than those previously exploited. These factors permitted the opening of new areas and access to new timber reserves, while resulting in more intensive use of forest resources. However, the predictions were not totally inaccurate. In the 1970s, reserves began effectively to run out, which led to the bankruptcy of several sawmills and to the migration of others to other areas of the Selva Central (Villa Rica, Pichanaki, and Satipo) and even to other *selva alta* areas (Huallaga Valley).

The San Ramón Forestry District

The decline of Oxapampa as a timber-production center coincided with the takeoff of the San Ramón forestry district. Thus, in only four years (1967–1970), the production of sawnwood in this district grew from 25,987 to 43,455 cubic meters. The factor that governed this increase was the construction of new penetration roads. It was during this period that the road that was to connect the towns of La Merced and Satipo was under construction. The sections of the Carretera Marginal that were built then opened the doors of the present-day districts of Perené and Pichanaki (in Chanchamayo Province) to timber production, allowing the transfer of capital and technology into these new areas by sawmill owners from Oxapampa and La Merced.

In 1975, shortly after the inauguration of the La Merced–Satipo road, lumber production in the forestry district of San Ramón reached its highest level (54,181 cubic meters), greatly exceeding the production figures of Oxapampa, which never surpassed a threshold of 40,000 cubic meters. The production curve in this forestry district also shows that timber extraction achieved a much more accelerated pace than that registered at the height of the timber industry in Oxapampa. Thus, in a period of only 10 years, from 1970 to 1980, the volume of timber extracted and milled in Chanchamayo was equal to that produced in Oxapampa over the 18-year period from 1954 through 1971, its apogee as a timber-production center. Even though the greater intensity of timber extraction was due, in part, to improved technologies both in the logging and milling phases, certainly the motto of the timber barons of the San Ramón forestry district during the 1970s appears to have been "Extract the most timber in the shortest time possible." Several years later, this phenomenon was to be replicated in an even more accentuated way in the forestry district of Satipo.

In the 1980s, the San Ramón forestry district continued to maintain a high average annual yield, but at the expense of exhausting the resource in nearby areas and with huge investments in logging roads into the most interior areas of the right bank of the Perené River. Recently, production has declined notably because of the high cost of extracting timber in more distant areas. This, as we will see, forced the closure of many of the sawmills located in La Merced and San Ramón. In addition, the scarcity of timber has forced many small extractors to begin to engage in clandestine logging operations in protected areas, such as the Pui-Pui Forestry Reserve on the right bank of the Perené River. It is difficult to predict the future of the timber industry in the San Ramón forestry district. The trend is toward a continuously declining yield, in part because of the exhaustion of timber reserves but also because of the climate of violence in the area. However, if the authorities do nothing to preserve the Pui-Pui area, the local timber industry will be able to operate for several more years thanks to the timber reserves contained in this 60,000-hectare forestry reserve.

The Satipo Forestry District

The province of Satipo took off as a timber-production center in 1975, the last year in which Oxapampa recorded a yield of sawnwood of over 30,000 cubic meters and the year in which Chanchamayo reached a peak production of 54,181 cubic meters of lumber. The development of the timber industry in Satipo was tightly linked to the completion of the La Merced–Satipo section of the Carretera Marginal in 1973, which opened the doors to coastal markets. In only four years (1972–1975), production of sawnwood doubled, and in 1980 Satipo reached its peak with a yield of 63,464 cubic meters of lumber, the greatest volume ever extracted in a single year in a single forestry district of the Selva Central during the entire period from 1954 to 1988.

Between 1976 and 1986, a volume of timber similar to that produced in Chanchamayo between 1970 and 1980 was extracted and milled: 449,971 and 445,135 cubic meters of sawnwood, respectively. In contrast to the production curve for Oxapampa, which reflects a nearly continuous yield and no major fluctuations, those for the San Ramón and Satipo forestry districts fell as quickly as they rose. The rates of extraction in these two districts were much higher because of the greater competition that resulted from the multiplication of the number of sawmills. Whereas the timber industry in Oxapampa was in the hands of a few families that concentrated local economic and political power and had vested interests in the area, the timber industry in the new logging areas of Chanchamayo (especially in Pichanaki) and in Satipo were, for the most part, in the hands of new agents from outside the region who competed intensely among themselves. This gave rise to a strategy of extracting the greatest volume of timber in the shortest time possible.

A consequence of this strategy was a rapid plundering of the forests accessible from Satipo and a sharp drop in the volume of production, which was reduced by half between 1980 and 1988. Nevertheless, Satipo still has forest reserves. Thus, local logging companies have strongly supported the construction of the Satipo-Puerto Ocopa road and the project to extend it to Atalaya, seeing this as an opportunity to expand their timber reserves. The presence of insurgent groups in the area has put a temporary stop to these projects, which leads us to expect that the volume of production in this forestry district will continue to decline in forthcoming years.

Finally, it should be noted that the production curves in these three forestry districts register certain fluctuations that are not a result of factors intrinsic to the extractive cycle but rather result from exogenous factors. Thus, a sharp decline in the volume of production registered in 1978 is associated with the economic crisis that swept the country in the latter part of the military rule of General Francisco Morales Bermúdez. The notable upswing in yield that was registered two years later is explained, in contrast, by the expectations that were generated by the second Belaúnde government, whose "special jungle projects" promised to create new momentum in the regional economy. These expectations were not totally satisfied, insofar as the prosperity achieved was based on the injection of loans from the international banking community, which did not manage to transform or activate the bases of the region's economy.

Thus, even while the yield continued to be relatively high in the San Ramón and Satipo forestry districts, the tendency was clearly toward a reduction in yield. The opening of the Pichis and Palcazu valleys, thanks to the construction of new stretches of the Carretera Marginal, did not represent an expansion of existing forest reserves as was expected. This was largely because of the pressures of the international agencies who financed the Pichis-Palcazu Special Project and demanded a more effective control over the logging activity, thus averting inappropriate logging in protected areas and areas that were not suitable for logging. Such was the case in the Yanachaga Range, later converted into Yanachaga-Chemellem National Park, where logging companies from Oxapampa had begun to extract timber in the mid-1940s.

In summary, in the Selva Central, commercial logging activity began in the 1920s in the Chanchamayo Valley, because it was closest to consumer centers and was the only area that had the transportation infrastructure necessary to ship lumber. Toward 1940, the rich reserves in the Oxapampa Valley represented an additional incentive to finish the La Merced-Oxapampa road by 1943. This road opened the area to the exploitation of forest resources. For slightly more than 20 years, Oxapampa was one of the major centers of production of tropical hardwood in the country. In about 1974, the exhaustion of its reserves was reflected in a sharp fall in lumber production. Slightly earlier, in 1970, the advance of the La Merced–Satipo road allowed the exploitation of the timber reserves of Pichinaki on the upper Perené Valley, which contributed to a rebound in the production of lumber in the old San Ramón forestry district. This boom lasted until 1982, when yield gradually began to decline. The inauguration of the La Merced–Satipo road in 1973 was accompanied by the takeoff of Satipo and nearby valleys as the most recent timber-production areas. Since 1985, the yield on this new front has begun to decline, partly because of the exhaustion of its reserves but mostly because of the violence that swept through the area.

In Table 3.9, one may observe the changing relative contribution of the forestry districts of Oxapampa, San Ramón, and Satipo to the region's lumber production. The data presented illustrate even more clearly the two phenomena that we are interested in underscoring: (1) the expansion of timber industry activities since the 1950s, progressively incorporating nearly all of the Selva Central environment within the industry's sphere of influence; and (2) the opening and exploitation of new areas to compensate for the relative exhaustion of the reserves of previously exploited ones.

The Timber Industry: A Nomadic Economy?

By 1983, logging activity in the Selva Central entered into a period of crisis as a result of the relative exhaustion of forest reserves, the situation of violence, and the economic crisis that the country began to experience. This was aggravated by the paralyzation, shortly thereafter, of the special projects initiated by the second Belaúnde government. As a result of this crisis, the number of sawmills,

Table 3.9. Percentage Contribution of the Forestry
Districts to the Region's Production of Sawnwood

Five-year period	Oxapampa	San Ramón	Satipo
1955–1959	83.2	14.9	1.9
1960–1964	63.5	35.2	1.3
1965–1969	55.8	40.9	3.3
1970–1974	37.0	44.1	18.9
1975–1979	23.3	39.6	37.1
1980–1984	13.9	41.2	44.9
1985–1989	10.0	41.9	48.1

Sources: See Table 3.8.

the number of timber extraction contracts solicited and granted, and the volume of lumber production plummeted (Table 3.10). In Figures 3.3, 3.4, and 3.5, one can see how these three indicators of the vitality of the timber industry are interrelated in each of the provinces under consideration. Currently, only four areas of expansion for the logging activity remain in the Selva Central: the Anapati, Ene, Pichis, and Palcazu valleys. The first of these valleys is already connected by road with Satipo at one end. In contrast, the Ene Valley is isolated from this center because of a lack of roads. And although the other two have roads that connect them with La Merced and the road to Lima, the current situation of violence makes their development impossible.

The rising and falling cycles of timber production in the various areas that compose the Selva Central, as well as the constant opening of new areas of forest and the expansion of the logging activity further into the interior, has led some researchers to characterize the activity as a "nomadic economy" (Brack et al. n.d.: 34). This characterization is based on the idea that the gradual exhaustion of timber reserves in a given area forces the movement of logging companies into new, still-unexploited areas. In this view, loggers and sawmill owners are constantly moving, always looking for new reserves in the areas of expansion of colonized territories. Although there is evidence indicating that the exhaustion of forest reserves in a given area constitutes a limiting factor for the sustained development of the local timber industry, one cannot infer from this that the industry is itinerant. On the contrary, the evidence shows that the relative exhaustion of the forest reserves in one area does not result in the immediate collapse of local sawmills and their transfer into other areas. Although this does not contradict the idea that the logging activity always requires new reserves to exploit, it does have important consequences for the understanding of the processes of regional configuration in areas of the *selva alta*.

Table 3.10. Timber-Production Activity

Province[a]	1977	1980	1983	1986	1988
Oxapampa					
No. of sawmills	27	31	30	24	22
No. of contracts	64	115	48	31	34
Vol. of sawnwood (m³)[b]	38,270	36,823	25,757	7,988	5,398
Chanchamayo					
No. of sawmills	16	28	29	21	20
No. of contracts	97	111	19	45	29
Vol. of sawnwood (m³)	35,520	46,341	31,312	35,368	20,343
Satipo					
No. of sawmills	31	32	26	23	23
No. of contracts	39	94	44	34	26
Vol. of sawnwood (m³)	30,172	63,464	32,312	29,799	28,264

Sources: See Tables 3.8, 3.12, and 3.13.

Note: Values for contracts exclude permits to extract timber from one's own agricultural unit or native community.

[a]Data for the province of Oxapampa come from two of its four forestry districts (Oxapampa and Villa Rica), because information on the forestry districts of Puerto Bermúdez and Iscozacín is unreliable; data for the provinces of Chanchamayo and Satipo come from the forestry districts of San Ramón and Satipo, respectively.

[b]The volumes of sawnwood registered for the years 1986 and 1988 in Oxapampa refer only to that produced in the forestry district of Oxapampa, because we lack data for the forestry district of Villa Rica.

In the Selva Central, the various phases between timber extraction and the arrival of lumber in centers of consumption may be handled entirely by a single entrepreneur or distributed among various agents. Thus, in 1982, 46 percent of sawmill owners in Oxapampa and 39 percent of those in Villa Rica had their own extraction contracts, while the rest bought roundwood from independent loggers (Cotera 1982a, 1982b). In general, it is the owners of the largest mills who control not only the milling stage but also the extraction and transportation of wood, both from logging areas and to centers of consumption. Such control reduces costs of production, thus increasing profit margins. In contrast, the smallest mills, which depend on contracts with third parties for the supply and transport of the wood, have smaller profit margins and thus, during periods of crisis—whether due to the exhaustion of forest resources or to the reduction of market prices— are the most vulnerable.

In Table 3.11, the structure of the costs of production and marketing of a cubic meter of sawnwood from the Selva Central in 1982 is presented. Unfortunately, we do not have access to more recent data; but given that neither the technology nor the conditions of production have changed substantially in the last 10 years, we

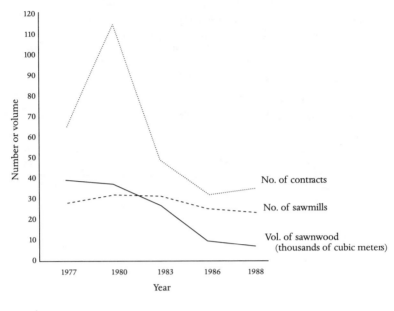

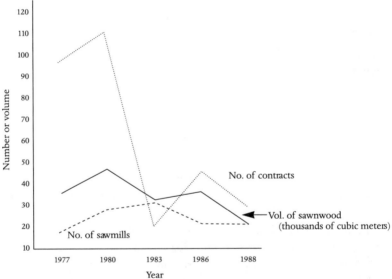

Figure 3.3 (top). Sawmills, timber-extraction contracts, and sawnwood in Oxapampa, 1977–1988. *Source:* Table 3.10.

Figure 3.4 (bottom). Sawmills, timber-extraction contracts, and sawnwood in Chanchamayo, 1977–1988. *Source:* Table 3.10.

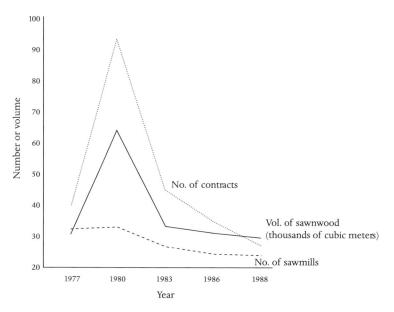

Figure 3.5. Sawmills, timber-extraction contracts, and sawnwood in Satipo, 1977–1988. *Source:* Table 3.10.

assume that this structure has remained constant and that trends that were already evident in 1982 are even more pronounced. From Table 3.11 it becomes apparent that the items that have the most effect on the cost of production of sawnwood are, in order of importance, sawing, transport of roundwood from the logging area to the sawmill, and transport of lumber to Lima. These three items represent 65 percent of the total cost of production. These are regional average figures, however, and do not necessarily reflect major variations resulting both from the type of timber extracted and from the distances that separate logging areas from the mills. Thus, for example, the cost of shipping a board foot of roundwood of *cedro* or *tornillo* to the mills in Satipo from Marankiari or Cubantía in 1984 ranged from 55 to 85 *soles*, respectively (DGFF 1985). That means that in the forestry district of Satipo, differences in the distances from the logging areas to the mills could cost a mill owner up to 55 percent more per board foot of roundwood. When the mills do not cut their own timber, buying it from small or medium-sized logging outfits instead, the place of origin is also reflected in the price paid for the wood. Thus, for class A timber, prices in Satipo ranged from 250 *soles* per board foot of round-wood extracted from Sonomoro to 350 *soles* for timber extracted from Pangoa (DGFF 1985). In the case of the Satipo forestry district, one of the most recent to enter into production, the situation was not yet as serious. In 1983, the maximal distance between logging areas and the mills ranged from 40 to 50 kilometers

Table 3.11. Cost of Production of Sawnwood in the Selva
Central, 1982

Activity	Cost per m^3 of sawnwood (US$)[a]	% of total cost
Clearing and felling	8.40	9
Construction of ramps	10.10	10
Transport of roundwood to sawmill	16.80	17
Construction and maintenance of timber-extraction roads	8.40	9
Sawing	25.00	26
Forestry tax	2.40	2
Reforestation tax	4.50	5
Transport of sawnwood to Lima	21.20	22
All activities	96.80	100

Source: David 1983: Table 16; data are for September 1982.

[a]Dollar values have been converted from *soles*. The average exchange rate in 1982 was US$1 = 760 *soles*.

(INADE 1984). For older forestry districts, the situation, in contrast, was more serious. Thus, in 1983, the maximal distance between mills in Oxapampa (where nearby forest reserves were exhausted around 1975) and logging areas was up to 90 kilometers (INADE 1984). In the case of the mills in San Ramón, the maximal distance from logging areas was 100 kilometers (David 1983). Whether or not sawmill owners cut their own timber or buy it from independent extractors, the differences in shipping costs due to the greater transport distances undoubtedly have strong repercussions in terms of their profit margins.

It is on the basis of this phenomenon that it has been asserted that logging constitutes a nomadic activity. The idea is that as the forest reserves near the mills become exhausted and the distance between the mills and the logging areas increases, transportation costs increase and profit margins are gradually reduced, until they arrive at a point at which the activity is no longer profitable. Arriving at this critical point, the only option for survival that remains for sawmill owners is to move to sites that are closer to logging areas or into other areas where forest resources are still abundant.

Although these options are feasible, the data presented in Table 3.12 show that although the number of sawmills in the Selva Central has been shrinking constantly since 1980, only in the oldest logging areas, and therefore the most degraded, has the size of the timber industry been significantly reduced. In other words, the exhaustion of forest resources in a given area does not always lead to its abandonment by logging companies.

Table 3.12. Operating Sawmills in Oxapampa, Chanchamayo, and Satipo

Province and town	1977	1980	1983	1986	1989
Oxapampa					
Oxapampa	11	12	14	10	9
Villa Rica	16	19	16	14	13
Both locales	27	31	30	24	22
Chanchamayo					
San Ramón	9	10	10	5	3
La Merced	5	5	2	2	2
Pichanaki	2	13	17	14	15
All 3 locales	16	28	29	21	20
Satipo					
Satipo	19	16	—	—	—
Río Negro	1	6	—	—	—
Mazamari	6	4	—	—	—
San Martín de Pangoa	5	6	—	—	—
All 4 locales	31	32	26	23	23[a]
Selva Central	74	91	85	68	65

Sources: DGFF 1978 (for the three provinces, 1977); CDR Chanchamayo 1989 (for the province of Chanchamayo, 1980, 1983, and 1989); CDR Satipo 1988 (for the province of Satipo, 1980 and 1986); Ministerio de Industria 1989 (for the province of Oxapampa, 1983, 1986, and 1989); Capcha Rodríguez 1986 (for the province of Chanchamayo, 1986); Cotera 1982b (for the town of Villa Rica, 1980); Ministerio de Industria 1980 (for the town of Oxapampa, 1980); Rodríguez del Aguila 1985 (for the province of Satipo, 1983).

Note: Dashes denote no data.

[a]The 1986 figure was used because of a lack of information.

In the Oxapampa forestry district, for example, where the yield of sawnwood has shrunk drastically since 1975, the number of sawmills continued to grow until 1983, when there was a renewed decline in the volume of sawnwood. Even so, in 1989 the number of mills was only slightly lower than in 1977, when the first effects of the crisis began to be felt. In the case of the Satipo forestry district, the number of sawmills rose from 1974, when logging activity experienced a sudden increase, until 1980, when production reached its peak. The swift decline in production after 1981 had an almost immediate effect on the number of sawmills in operation, which steadily declined from 32 in 1980 to 23 in 1989. Nevertheless, even in this case the number of sawmills that continue to operate is significant.

The case of the San Ramón forestry district (Chanchamayo) presents an intermediate situation. In spite of the fall in the production of sawnwood since 1975, the number of sawmills located in the towns of San Ramón and La Merced remained stable. With the entrance of the Pichinaki area into production at the end of the 1970s and a small rebound in the level of production, the number of sawmills located in this new area grew, whereas the number of mills in San Ramón and La Merced drastically declined. What is certain is that, with the exception of the areas nearest to the towns of San Ramón and La Merced, which are among the oldest and most densely populated in the region, the timber industry continues to subsist, even in those areas where yield has dropped significantly, as is the case in the Oxapampa Valley.

In a detailed study of timber transport in the Selva Central, David (1983: 15) asserts that although as a result of the exhaustion of forest reserves some sawmills in the early 1980s moved closer to the logging areas or into new areas within the region, "most of them have remained in place" in spite of higher transportation costs and reduced profit margins. Data in Table 3.12 confirm David's statement. The question that arises, therefore, is, Why don't these sawmills move? The answer is complex. Because we do not have sufficient information to offer a definitive answer, we suggest three possible explanations.

First, relocation into other areas, or into areas that are closer to the logging areas, necessarily implies an increase in the distance from consumer centers, insofar as the only outlet for products from the Selva Central is the road through La Merced. Thus, although relocation would entail a reduction in the cost of transporting logs to the mill, at the same time it would imply an increase in the cost of transportation of lumber to Lima, which is the main consumer center. Thus, sawmills that remain in areas where forest reserves are relatively exhausted — those of the San Ramón and Oxapampa forestry districts, for example — compensate for the necessity of covering greater distances from logging areas with their proximity to Lima.

Second, one of the options of mill owners who decide to stay in an area where nearby reserves are exhausted is to exploit more tree species than those logged during the early stages, making more intensive use of logging contracts granted by the State. This is possible because of the growing acceptance and demand on the part of the domestic market for timber with lower commercial value than that which has been exploited traditionally.

This seems to be the case in the San Ramón forestry district. As can be observed in Table 3.13, there is a major discrepancy between the volume of timber approved in State-granted logging contracts and the volume of sawnwood that is actually produced. The results of this comparison show that the volume of lumber produced during the peak years in this forestry district (1976–1982), when the greatest number of contracts and authorizations for logging were

Table 3.13. Timber-Production Activity in the San Ramón Forestry District

			Timber extracted	
		Vol. of timber		
	No. of	approved for	Vol.	
	contracts	extraction (m³ of	(m³ of	% of
Year	and permits	sawnwood)	sawnwood)	approved vol.
1976	222	345,284	47,330	13.7
1977	107	298,342	35,520	11.9
1978	228	206,010	24,980	12.1
1979	392	164,249	33,556	20.4
1980	138	283,212	46,341	16.4
1981	112	367,720	43,759	11.9
1982	99	380,933	43,115	11.3
1983	36	115,389	31,312	27.1
1984	49	738,700	41,645	5.6
1985	77	167,136	33,149	19.8
1986	—	161,628	35,368	41.3
1987	98	85,690	36,216	42.3
1988	56	73,229	20,343	27.8

Sources: Rodríguez del Aguila 1985 (for the period 1974-1984); CDR Chanchamayo 1988 (for the period 1985-1988).

Note: Dash denotes no data.

granted, rarely exceeded 15 percent of the volume of timber approved by the Ministry of Agriculture. Beginning in 1985, this situation changed. As a consequence of the economic crisis experienced by the region, the number of logging contracts granted and the volume of timber that could be extracted diminished between 1986 and 1988. In response to this situation, the logging companies intensified their use of forest resources, increasing the proportion of timber extracted with respect to the volume approved for extraction to up to 40 percent.

A third explanation stems from the fact that sawmill owners who decide to remain in areas where nearby reserves are exhausted have the options of (1) modernizing, employing more efficient machinery to cut down the level of waste, or (2) diversifying, venturing into the production of crates, parquetry, and furniture, thereby increasing the value of the final product and permitting them to realize larger profit margins. This was the case of 3 of the 10 sawmills in the town of San Ramón in 1983, which in 1989 stopped producing raw sawnwood in order to produce furniture (CDR Chanchamayo 1989).

All of these elements make it necessary to rethink the characterization of Brack et al. (n.d.) of the timber industry as a nomadic activity. Although the exhaustion of forest resources in an area results in the disappearance of a certain number of sawmills and the relocation of others in new logging areas, this in itself does not lead to the complete disappearance of the local timber industry.

While new logging fronts are constantly opened up, older fronts are not completely abandoned. The smaller distance to consumer centers; better access to infrastructure, such as electrical supply; and the possibility of a more intensive use of timber resources through the diversification of forest products offer older logging fronts certain comparative advantages with respect to those more recently opened. Thus, although timber resources are less abundant, logging activity may continue to be profitable for quite a long time for those sawmills that remain in the area.

However, the timber industry may turn extremely unstable in moments of crisis, triggered by either endogenous or exogenous factors or a combination of both. An analysis of the lists of sawmills registered in the Oxapampa, Villa Rica, and San Ramón forestry districts for the critical 1977-1989 period reveals that (1) only a relatively small percentage of the mills existing in 1977 still survived in 1989; (2) throughout the 1980s, a major decline in the total number of sawmills took place; and (3) rather than relocating, the biggest sawmills in areas where nearby timber resources were exhausted often opened branches in areas where resources were more abundant.

In Tables 3.14, 3.15, and 3.16, information provided in these registers has been organized so as to identify the closing of sawmills and the opening of new ones during the 1977-1989 period and thus assess the stability of the region's timber industry. We have considered a sawmill's presence to be continuous in time as long as it keeps the same name and remains in the hands of the same owner or family group. Thus, in some cases, the "disappearance" of a given sawmill only means that it has been transferred to another owner. In other cases, it means that it has closed shop. Data in these tables show that in the Oxapampa, Villa Rica, and San Ramón forestry districts, only 45 percent, 31 percent, and 38 percent, respectively, of the sawmills extant in 1977 were still in operation in 1989. The rest of the sawmills had changed ownership or closed shop. This, along with the establishment of some new mills, constitutes a clear indicator of the relative instability of the logging industry. Although the number of mills decreased throughout the 1980s, the number of those operating in 1989 shows that neither the relative exhaustion of timber reserves nor the economic crisis has led to the collapse of the timber industry in any of the areas of the Selva Central.

The observed pattern of evolution of the region's sawmills suggests that the mills that stayed in areas of relatively scarce timber resources and that remained in the hands of the same owner between 1977 and 1989 are generally the largest and oldest. In the case of the Oxapampa forestry district, these were the ones owned by Ernesto, Alberto, and Werner Müller (founded in 1952), Walter Loechle Müller (1965), A. and N. Balarín (1967), A. Kovak (1970), and Batrič Bozovich (1974). These mills belong to the two biggest economic and political

Table 3.14. Continuity of the Timber Industry in the Oxapampa Forestry District

Year sawmills opened	No. of sawmills operating in:				
	1977	1980	1983	1986	1989
1977	11	10	6	5	5
1980		2	1	1	1
1983			7	4	3
1986				0	0
1989					0
Total	11	12	14	10	9

Sources: See Table 3.12.

Table 3.15. Continuity of the Timber Industry in the Villa Rica Forestry District

Year sawmills opened	No. of sawmills operating in:				
	1977	1980	1983	1986	1989
1977	16	16	6	5	5
1980		3	0	0	0
1983			10	9	8
1986				0	0
1989					0
Total	16	19	16	14	13

Sources: See Table 3.12.

Table 3.16. Continuity of the Timber Industry in the San Ramón Forestry District

Year sawmills opened	No. of sawmills operating in:			
	1977	1980	1983	1989
1977	16	10	8	6
1980		18	16	9
1983			5	3
1989				2[a]
Total	16	28	29	20

Sources: See Table 3.12.

Note: No data were available for 1986.

[a] These two sawmills may have opened earlier.

power groups of the Oxapampa Valley: the "German group," which revolves around the Müller brothers, and the "Yugoslavian group," which revolves around the Balarín brothers (Rumrrill and Zutter 1976: 113). In 1975, the Müller group owned the largest mill in Oxapampa, whose capacity represented 20 percent of that of the entire area. The Balarín group controlled six mills that produced nearly 50 percent of Oxapampa's lumber.

These family groups did not relocate their mills as Oxapampa's forest reserves became exhausted. Rather, they expanded their activities, establishing mills on newly opened logging fronts. Thus, the Balarín Gustavson brothers, relatives of the Balarín family in Oxapampa, established two mills in San Luis de Shuaro and Pichanaki. Ernesto Hassinger Verde, related to the Hassinger family in Oxapampa, founded a mill in Pichanaki when this zone was opened for logging; and Alberto Müller and Batrič Bozovich, owners of important mills in Oxapampa, each established mills in Satipo, the most recently opened logging area in the Selva Central. As we will see, the tendency of sawmill owners in the older logging areas to expand their activities and to invest in new timber fronts, without abandoning mills in the areas where they began their operations, seems to be generally true throughout the region.

These data demonstrate that logging activity in the Selva Central does not constitute a nomadic economy in the strict sense of the term. What such a concept assumes is that a fixed number of mills would exist and that, as soon as the resources of one zone became exhausted, they would move to another area to gain access to new reserves and to be able to continue to operate. What actually happens is that the exhaustion of older logging fronts, as well as the growing demand of the market, requires a constant opening of new fronts. Some logging companies stay in the oldest colonization areas, whereas others move to more recently opened timber fronts. In addition, of those that stay, the largest and most powerful tend to open branches on new timber fronts.

In the Selva Central, where there are no major rivers to transport timber, logging activity develops in intimate relation with the construction of new roads. On the new logging fronts that arose as a result of roadway expansion, one finds various contractors—some local and others arriving from older timber-extraction areas. As the yield of older areas declines, that of new fronts increases, but sawmills in both areas continue to function. Furthermore, the fact that the major logging companies have mills in more than one zone or on more than one timber front has led to the regionalization of capital investments. This has contributed to an increased regional articulation. But, in addition, because the timber industry continues to persist in the older logging areas, it continues to contribute to their consolidation and to generate greater levels of economic agglomeration.

Greater articulation and higher levels of economic agglomeration have been achieved, however, at the cost of concentrating the timber industry in a few hands. Of the 91 sawmills extant in 1980 in the forestry districts of Oxapampa, Villa Rica, San Ramón, and Satipo, 35 percent were in the hands of 11 family groups: the Müller group, with three mills in Oxapampa and Satipo; the Scavino Reátegui group, with three mills in Pichanaki and La Merced (and others in Pucallpa); the Hassinger group, with two mills in Oxapampa and Pichanaki; the Vidalón group, with two mills in Villa Rica and Satipo; the Lizárraga group, with two mills in Villa Rica and Satipo; the Raschio Jordán group, with two mills in San Ramón; and the Solórzano Aste group, with two mills in Pichanaki. Each group owned an average of almost three mills, the majority usually located in different areas or on different logging fronts.

In conclusion, the timber industry in the Selva Central cannot be characterized as nomadic. Rather, being controlled by a few and powerful family groups, it tends to constantly expand, including an ever greater number of logging areas. Oligarchic control becomes more accentuated as a result of the depletion of timber resources in the most accesible areas. This increases production costs by requiring larger investment in the construction of logging roads and in the transport of timber from the logging areas. Only groups that have a large supply of capital and that control various phases of timber extraction, manufacture, and marketing are able to pay for these costs, resulting in a tendency toward even greater concentration of the logging activity in a few hands. Thus, it is not by chance that in the San Ramón forestry district it is precisely the mills belonging to the most important economic groups (Solórzano, Balarín, and Hassinger) that hold the largest timber-extraction contracts and that, of these, the two largest own warehouses in Lima in order to market directly the lumber that they produce. The same may be said of the Müller and Balarín groups in Oxapampa.

THE DIALECTICAL RELATIONSHIP BETWEEN AGROPASTORAL ACTIVITY AND TIMBER EXTRACTION

Timber extraction and agriculture are dialectically related, insofar as they are complementary while at the same time antithetical economic activities. This characteristic is manifested both in terms of their economic and political importance in the regional economy and in their use of the area and its resources. Moreover, this dialectical relationship has determined the forms and the rhythms of the occupation of the region, rendering its analysis indispensable.

In the 1950s and 1960s, timber produced in the Selva Central contributed significantly to national timber production, representing 36 percent of the national total in 1968. In later years, production continued to increase, reaching an initial peak of 117,653 cubic meters of sawnwood in 1975 and a second peak of 132,979 cubic meters in 1980. However, the importance of regional yield with respect to the national total has steadily declined, representing less than 20 percent of the national product in 1980 (Table 3.17).

In terms of its contribution to the gross value of production in the region, the "forestry sector" has not been very important either. In 1975 its contribution to the gross value of production represented 10 percent of the total (Table 3.18). It is worth noting, however, that the data provided by the National Planning Institute does not specify whether the contribution of all of the mills is included in the forestry sector, or only that of mills whose small number of employees exclude them from being classified as industrial enterprises. Thus it is possible that part of the contribution of the logging activity to the gross value of production is being counted as "industrial activity." In spite of this possibility, and even if we assume that the entire contribution of the industrial sector is associated with the timber industry, which is certainly not the case, the aggregate contribution of the forestry and industrial sectors (35 percent) to the regional gross value of production is still far less than the contribution of the agricultural sector (62 percent). In spite of their age, these data are relevant in that they correspond to a time when timber production in the region reached its first peak, exceeded only by the yield registered in 1980. If, in one of the major booms of logging activity, the contribution of this sector to the gross value of production ranged between 10 percent and 35 percent, one would expect that currently, in a time of crisis in the timber industry, these figures would be much lower.

Breaking these figures down, one finds that, in all of the provinces but particularly in Chanchamayo and Satipo, the agricultural sector contributes much more to the gross value of production than does the forestry sector. In spite of this, and in spite of the fact that in the Selva Central the forestry sector only employs 2 percent of family units, as compared with 75 percent employed in the agricultural sector (Brack et al. n.d.), logging activity has received equal or greater attention than this latter sector in regional development plans, on local political platforms, and in the perception of important social actors.

This is explained by the oligarchic nature of the region's timber industry. Whereas profits from the logging activity are distributed among a very small group, earnings generated by agricultural activity are distributed among thousands of peasant families. Thus, powerful economic interests revolve around the timber industry, seeking, and finding, support from the government and from local political forces. As a consequence, logging activity has been given a priority that does not correspond to its real importance in the regional economy. This

Table 3.17. Sawnwood Production in Peru and the Selva Central

		Selva Central	
Year	Peru's total production (m^3)	Total production (m^3)	% of Peru's total production
1954	85,576	22,198	25.9
1955	96,213	26,773	27.8
1956	99,615	25,316	25.4
1957	104,924	24,167	23.0
1958	82,120	17,369	21.2
1959	82,178	19,980	24.3
1960	95,666	26,215	27.4
1961	99,123	23,149	23.4
1962	124,471	35,351	28.4
1963	124,891	38,391	30.7
1964	141,795	39,062	27.5
1965	154,006	39,592	25.7
1966	214,503	57,329	26.7
1967	201,158	64,057	31.8
1968	187,927	67,626	35.9
1969	209,328	68,573	32.8
1970	312,000	86,776	27.8
1971	380,000	87,710	23.1
1972	380,000	83,169	21.9
1973	388,000	96,657	24.9
1974	465,000	107,360	23.1
1975	514,000	117,653	22.9
1976	497,000	114,225	22.9
1977	474,000	86,984	18.4
1978	476,000	78,784	16.6
1979	526,077	95,917	18.2
1980	606,594	132,979	21.9
1981	643,343	107,500	16.7
1982	523,977	99,929	19.0
1983	380,083	74,203	19.5
1984	474,348	86,395	18.2
1985	524,736	85,137	16.2
1986	606,656	73,155	12.1

Sources: Data for Peru: Banco de Crédito 1972 (for the period 1954-1969); Schrewe 1981 (for the period 1970-1979); DGFF 1987 (for the period 1980-1986). Data for the Selva Central: see Table 3.8.

Table 3.18. Gross Production Values, 1975

Production sector[a]	Oxapampa		Chanchamayo		Satipo		Selva Central	
Agriculture	104.0	(23.3%)	1,120.0	(71.5%)	274.4	(68.9%)	1,498.4	(62.2%)
Cattle raising	37.2	(8.3%)	26.4	(1.7%)	7.7	(1.9%)	71.3	(2.9%)
Forestry	77.0	(17.3%)	61.2	(3.9%)	93.4	(23.4%)	231.6	(9.6%)
Industry	228.1	(51.1%)	357.9	(22.9%)	23.0	(5.8%)	609.0	(25.3%)
All 4 sectors	446.3	(100.0%)	1,565.5	(100.0%)	398.5	(100.0%)	2,410.3	(100.0%)

Source: INP 1981: 16.

Note: Values are given in millions of *soles*. The percentage of the region's total that the value represents is in parentheses.

[a]We have excluded the mining sector, which is relevant only in Chanchamayo Province, because it distorts the relative weight of the other sectors at the regional level.

incongruity further aggravates conflicts between loggers and farmers in situations where there is competition for resources.

It is an often-reported fact that, following in the footsteps of timber extractors, an ever-growing number of colonists arrive on new logging fronts. In order to maximize yield, logging activity must be developed in areas of virgin forest where the most commercially valuable timber species are still found in abundance. To achieve this, sawmill owners build logging roads extending away from the network of roads built by the State. As we will see in the following chapter, in the Amazonian areas, land only acquires value for the colonists when it is served by roads that allow them to gain access to the market. Although unintentionally, roads opened by loggers bestow value on land. For the same reason, the opening of a road immediately attracts colonists who have recently arrived in the area or local colonists in search of less degraded land than they currently own.

This competition for the use of space is manifested in the high number of logging concessions that are invaded by colonists each year. In 1983, of 79 concessions in the province of Chanchamayo, 58 percent were invaded by colonists; in Satipo, this figure reached 93 percent (Table 3.19). Altogether, 77 percent of the concessions in the Selva Central were invaded by colonists in 1983. This has created continual conflicts between loggers and colonists. Loggers complain that colonists invade their land and ask for certificates of ownership from the Ministry of Agriculture, thus reducing the area in which they can exercise their timber-harvesting rights and thus the volume of timber they extract. Loggers also argue that the cutting and burning of forested land necessary for the clearing of agricultural plots results in the loss of valuable timber resources. This situation is aggravated by the fact that the construction costs for logging roads rest almost completely on the backs of the loggers; thus, the invasion of concessions by

Table 3.19. Invasions of Timber-Extraction
Concessions by Colonists, 1983

Province	No. of concessions	% invaded
Oxapampa	79	58
Chanchamayo	92	71
Satipo	131	93
Selva Central	302	77

Source: Brack et al. n.d.: Table 8.

colonists does not allow them to recover their investment. In response to the loggers' complaints, colonists simply argue that logging companies try to reserve enormous areas of land for themselves that could be better used for the development of agricultural activities.

What is certain is that, although these two activities constitute antithetical options for the use of space, there is an important level of complementarity between them, in the sense that timber extraction functions as a spearhead that facilitates the opening of spaces for the development of agropastoral activity. Thus, the predominant form of occupation of the Selva Central has become a progression from timber extraction to agropastoral activity . Loggers open new timber-extraction fronts, which are almost immediately occupied by colonists and are transformed, in time, into agricultural or pastoral fronts.

It should be mentioned, however, that in certain areas one encounters the opposite dynamic, which also demonstrates the antithetical and at the same time complementary character of these activities. Thus, in some cases, loggers take advantage of and even encourage colonist invasions into reserved or protected areas so as to pressure local authorities to lift legal restrictions and permit them to harvest timber. In this case, it is the loggers who benefit from the opening of areas by the colonists. In situations like this, the argument used by the loggers is that, given that the invading colonists will inevitably cut and burn the forest in order to establish their farm plots, it is better to authorize the previous extraction of all of the timber that has commercial value.

Although the general dynamic indicates that timber extraction serves the purposes of colonization and agropastoral expansion—in the sense that it constantly opens up new areas—in the Selva Central colonization also serves the purposes of timber extraction. This is so because the permanent transformation of logging fronts into agropastoral fronts creates certain infrastructural conditions that are indispensable for the development and greater stability of the timber industry: road improvement, availability of fuel and electricity, repair services, and availability of food, parts, and other goods. This only occurs when older logging fronts are consolidated as agropastoral fronts and these become articulated with formerly colonized areas. In this dialectical relationship — where loggers appear as the vanguard that opens new economic fronts and colonists are the retroguard who disputes these areas, bringing them permanently into the market sphere — the synthesis that results is the making of a new regional space.

4
LAND TENURE, *MINIFUNDIOS,* AND LANDS WITH ECONOMIC VALUE

In the previous chapter we referred to the economic profile that characterizes the Selva Central and pointed out its implications with respect to the spatial and economic configuration of the region. In this chapter we analyze the characteristics of the land-tenure structure that resulted from the decomposition of the *hacienda* system and the increasing internal articulation of the region. The new land-tenure structure is not only an expression of the driving logic behind the previously analyzed mass-occupation process but also reflects and influences the predominant pattern of production. Thus, the characteristics of this land-tenure structure, along with the economic profile prevalent in the region, provide an indispensable framework for the study of land-use patterns and their environmental impact, topics that will be considered in the following chapters.

In contrast to that of other geographic regions of the country, the land-tenure structure in the Amazonian region has received little attention from agrarian researchers. This can be explained, to a large extent, by the fact that the land in this region has often been considered an "unlimited" good—like air or solar energy. This perception has given rise to the notion that land-tenure in tropical areas is open and unstable, being characterized by the constant formation of new agricultural fronts and the abandonment of the oldest areas. According to this view, because of its extreme fluidity land tenure in the Amazonian region has not given rise to the formation of a real land-tenure "structure." As we will try to demonstrate, this is only half true. Although land is not yet a scarce resource in the Amazonian region, access to markets constitutes a serious limiting factor. As a result, only a small proportion of Amazonian land has real "value." This in turn has led to a situation of intense demographic pressure on this type of land, giving rise, at least in the case of the Selva Central, to the development of a minifundiary land-tenure structure.

A second reason why the structure of land tenure in the Selva Central has been poorly studied is the scarcity of reliable data, as well as the methodological difficulties inherent in its analysis. Of the two agrarian censuses that have been conducted, the first, in 1961, is of little use because definitive results were never published, and preliminary results, in the opinion of experts, contain substantial errors (Maletta and Makhlouf n.d.: vol. 3, 9). The 1972 census, organized on a provincial rather than a district basis, presents difficulties for researchers focusing on the Selva Central because the present-day province of Chanchamayo was then a district of the province of Tarma, and data from the two can not always be differentiated. Since 1972 there has not been another attempt to determine land-tenure structure in the Selva Central, with the exception of a few microregional studies such as those conducted in the Pichis (Dirección General de Empleo 1982) and Palcazu (INADE 1988) valleys, and several very limited approaches to the subject based on small samples of coffee producers (Gutiérrez et al. n.d.), on the fragmentary records of the Rural Land Registry Office (Recharte n.d.), and on local land censuses (Pineda 1982).[5] In contrast, the information that we use in this chapter, corresponding to 1988, is based on a highly representative sample of agricultural units from the most active provinces in the region: Chanchamayo and Satipo (see the appendix).

Data from the Programa Nacional de Catastro (National Land Registry Program), or PRONAC, are based on a sample of 10,361 agricultural units under individual management, with a total area of 124,348 hectares. The sample does not include units under collective management, such as the agrarian production cooperatives created after the 1969 agrarian reform. The PRONAC sample would represent approximately 57 percent of the total number of agricultural units estimated by the Ministry of Agriculture for these two provinces in 1984 (Cerrón 1985: 23). More conservative estimates allow us to assert that the PRONAC sample represents at least a third of the agricultural units in these two provinces.

An analysis of the agrarian economy and of land tenure in the Selva Central should not focus exclusively on the colonist sector, to which the PRONAC data refer. Obviously, it is necessary to include the land-tenure situation of the indigenous peoples. Nevertheless, for expository purposes and to achieve maximal clarity in the presentation and analysis of this information, we have decided to treat this topic in the third part of the book, which specifically addresses the process of integration of the indigenous sector.

We begin the present chapter with a presentation of the statistical information that allows us to characterize the current land-tenure structure in the Selva Central, as well as the transformations that have occurred in the last 30 years. In a second section, this information will be critically interpreted, beginning with an attempt to define the category *"minifundio"* in the *selva alta* region. After determining that the land-tenure structure in the Selva Central is minifundiary, we analyze the factors that explain this phenomenon, beginning with the notion of "valuable land" and the role that the State has played in the reproduction of this structure.

EVOLUTION AND CHARACTERISTICS OF LAND TENURE

To help the reader understand the transformation of the land-tenure structure in the Selva Central in general, and in Chanchamayo and Satipo in particular, we first present the information that portrays its current configuration, and then analyze the changes that have taken place in the last several decades. To provide a more complete picture of the situation, we will then present the available information about land-tenure structure in the province of Oxapampa.

The Case of Chanchamayo and Satipo

In Table 4.1, we present the percentage distributions of the number and area of agricultural units according to size class of holding in Chanchamayo and Satipo. The first aspect that comes to our attention is the high incidence of small landholdings. In Chanchamayo, 34 percent of the agricultural units are smaller than 5 hectares, whereas as many as 60 percent are smaller than 10 hectares in size. The situation is very similar in Satipo, where 31 percent of the agricultural units are smaller than 5 hectares and 57 percent are smaller than 10 hectares. Intense human population pressure on the land is even more evident when one considers the average area per agricultural unit in the size classes of 0 to less than 5 hectares and 5 to less than 10 hectares for each province. Thus, the data indicate that in the Selva Central, a third of the colonists conduct their agricultural activities on units of less than 2.7 hectares, and more than half work plots smaller than 7.3 hectares.

The second salient aspect is that the greatest percentage of the registered area is concentrated in agricultural units in the size class of 10 to less than 20 hectares (30 percent), whereas, in general terms, it can be shown that the majority of the land area registered is concentrated on agricultural units whose sizes range from 10 to 50 hectares (63 percent). Agricultural units that are larger than 50 hectares (slightly less than 2 percent of those in Chanchamayo and slightly more than 2 percent in Satipo) represent at least 13 percent and 15 percent, respectively, of the registered area. All of this seems to indicate the absence of *latifundios* and a relatively homogeneous distribution of land resources.

Table 4.1. Agricultural Units in Chanchamayo and Satipo, 1988

Region and size class of holding	No. of AUs	% of total no. of AUs	Area of AUs	% of total area of AUs	Average area per AU
Chanchamayo					
0 to <5	2,199	33.5	5,912.82	7.7	2.7
5 to <10	1,727	26.3	12,500.95	16.3	7.2
10 to <20	1,596	24.3	22,399.44	29.1	14.0
20 to <30	620	9.4	14,996.26	19.5	24.2
30 to <50	296	4.5	10,899.47	14.2	36.8
50 to <100	109	1.7	7,233.10	9.4	66.4
100 to <200	17	0.3	2,362.11	3.1	138.9
≥200	2	0.0	571.92	0.7	285.9
All size classes	6,566	100.0	76,876.07	100.0	11.7
Satipo					
0 to <5	1,162	30.6	3,152.72	6.6	2.7
5 to <10	981	25.9	7,140.36	15.0	7.3
10 to <20	1,007	26.5	14,212.22	29.9	14.1
20 to <30	373	9.8	9,046.23	19.1	24.3
30 to <50	187	4.9	7,051.76	14.9	37.7
50 to <100	70	1.9	4,745.36	10.0	67.8
100 to <200	13	0.3	1,623.10	3.4	124.9
≥200	2	0.1	500.33	1.1	150.2
All size classes	3,795	100.0	47,472.08	100.0	12.5
Chanchamayo–Satipo					
0 to <5	3,361	32.4	9,065.54	7.3	2.7
5 to <10	2,708	26.2	19,641.31	15.8	7.3
10 to <20	2,603	25.1	36,611.66	29.5	14.1
20 to <30	993	9.6	24,042.49	19.3	24.2
30 to <50	483	4.7	17,951.23	14.4	37.2
50 to <100	179	1.7	11,978.46	9.6	66.9
100 to <200	30	0.3	3,985.21	3.2	132.8
≥200	4	0.0	1,072.25	0.9	268.0
All size classes	10,361	100.0	124,348.15	100.0	12.5

Source: PRONAC 1990; data elaborated by the authors.

Notes: Size classes and area measurements are in hectares. AU denotes agricultural unit.

The absence of *latifundios* is due to the effects of the agrarian reform in the region, a factor that has been discussed in Chapter 2. As to land distribution, although Table 4.1 allows us to verify a certain homogeneity or at least the absence of a significant process of land concentration, it does not eliminate concern that the agricultural units in the size class of 0 to less than 5 hectares, which represent 32 percent of the agricultural units in both provinces, only account for 7 percent of the registered area. A similar disparity is observed if one considers the size class of 0 to less than 10 hectares: in the case of Chanchamayo,

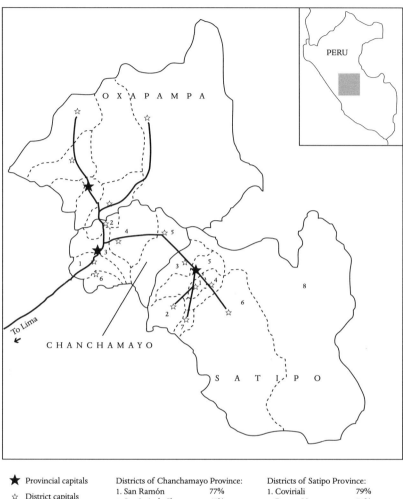

PERU

★ Provincial capitals
☆ District capitals
—— Province boundaries
---- District boundaries
—— Carretera Central

Districts of Chanchamayo Province:
1. San Ramón   77%
2. San Luis de Shuaro   65%
3. Chanchamayo   63%
4. Perené   55%
5. Pichanaki   54%
6. Vitoc   no data

Districts of Satipo Province:
1. Coviriali   79%
2. Pampa Hermosa   71%
3. Río Negro   62%
4. Mazamari   59%
5. Satipo   56%
6. Pangoa   45%
7. Llaylla   5%
8. Río Tambo   no data

Map 4.1. Percentage of minifundiary agricultural units by district in Chanchamayo and Satipo provinces, 1988. *Source:* PRONAC 1990.

Table 4.2. Distribution of the Agricultural Units According to Size Class of Holding, 1988

Province and district	0 to <5 hectares	5 to <10 hectares	10 to <20 hectares	20 to <30 hectares	30 to <50 hectares	50 to <100 hectares	100 to <200 hectares	≥200 hectares	All size classes
Chanchamayo									
San Ramón	616 (55.5%)	243 (21.9%)	164 (14.7%)	44 (3.9%)	23 (2.0%)	12 (1.0%)	7 (0.6%)	0 (0.00%)	1,109 (10.7%)
Chanchamayo	227 (33.9%)	195 (29.1%)	153 (22.9%)	57 (8.5%)	21 (3.1%)	10 (1.4%)	5 (0.7%)	0 (0.00%)	668 (6.4%)
San Luis de Shuaro	134 (39.0%)	88 (25.6%)	72 (20.9%)	25 (7.2%)	17 (4.9%)	7 (1.8%)	0 (0.0%)	0 (0.00%)	343 (3.3%)
Perené	612 (28.2%)	571 (26.3%)	568 (26.1%)	235 (10.8%)	130 (5.9%)	50 (2.3%)	3 (0.1%)	1 (0.04%)	2,170 (20.9%)
Pichanaki	610 (26.8%)	630 (27.6%)	639 (28.0%)	259 (11.3%)	105 (4.6%)	30 (1.3%)	2 (0.08%)	1 (0.04%)	2,276 (21.9%)
All 5 districts	2,199 (33.5%)	1,727 (26.3%)	1,596 (24.3%)	620 (9.4%)	296 (4.5%)	109 (1.7%)	17 (0.2%)	2 (0.03%)	6,566 (100%)
Satipo									
Satipo	106 (25.6%)	127 (30.7%)	102 (24.6%)	54 (13.0%)	17 (4.1%)	7 (1.6%)	0 (0.0%)	0 (0.00%)	413 (3.9%)
Llaylla	0 (0.0%)	1 (5.2%)	8 (42.1%)	9 (47.3%)	1 (5.2%)	0 (0.0%)	0 (0.0%)	0 (0.00%)	19 (0.2%)
Río Negro	316 (33.9%)	259 (27.7%)	219 (23.4%)	71 (7.6%)	48 (5.1%)	16 (1.7%)	1 (0.1%)	2 (0.20%)	932 (8.9%)
Pangoa	315 (24.5%)	263 (20.4%)	413 (32.1%)	155 (12.0%)	83 (6.4%)	42 (3.2%)	12 (0.9%)	0 (0.00%)	1,283 (12.4%)
Pampa Hermosa	224 (42.9%)	144 (27.6%)	104 (19.9%)	32 (6.1%)	15 (2.8%)	2 (0.3%)	0 (0.0%)	0 (0.00%)	521 (5.0%)
Mazamari	160 (29.7%)	158 (29.3%)	146 (27.1%)	48 (8.9%)	23 (4.2%)	3 (0.5%)	0 (0.0%)	0 (0.00%)	538 (5.2%)
Coviriali	41 (46.0%)	29 (32.5%)	15 (16.8%)	4 (4.4%)	0 (0.0%)	0 (0.0%)	0 (0.0%)	0 (0.00%)	89 (0.9%)
All 7 districts	1,162 (30.6%)	981 (25.9%)	1,007 (26.5%)	373 (9.8%)	187 (4.9%)	70 (1.9%)	13 (0.3%)	2 (0.05%)	3,795 (100%)
Chanchamayo and Satipo	3,361 (32.4%)	2,708 (26.1%)	2,603 (25.1%)	993 (9.6%)	483 (4.6%)	179 (1.7%)	30 (0.3%)	4 (0.04%)	10,361 (100%)[a]

Sources: PRONAC 1990; data elaborated by the authors.

Notes: Data are given as number of agricultural units, followed by the percentage of the province's total agricultural units in parentheses.

[a] Chanchamayo represents 63.4% of this total, and Satipo represents the other 36.6%.

this size class, which represents 60 percent of the total number of agricultural units, only accounts for 24 percent of the registered area, whereas in Satipo the same size class, which includes 56 percent of all agricultural units, encompasses 22 percent of the area.

This information suggests that a significant percentage of landholders are seriously limited in their access to land, even though there is no corresponding process of extreme concentration of this resource. This situation, which we could characterize as minifundization in the absence of *latifundios,* merits a more detailed discussion, which we present in the following section.

The third aspect that comes to our attention in Table 4.1 is a great similarity in the percentage distribution of the number and area of agricultural units in both provinces. The absence of major differences in this respect, in spite of the fact that both provinces experienced different historical processes of colonization, seems to indicate that the generalization of this land-tenure structure has resulted from the dissemination of a single pattern of production, based on coffee and fruit cultivation. The key elements necessary for understanding this homogenization process are the effects of the 1969 agrarian reform, the functioning logic of the dominant pattern of production, and the local perception of "valuable land." Some of these elements will be treated in depth in the following section. Others have been discussed in previous chapters and will be taken up again in the following chapter.

In Table 4.2, the number and percentage of agricultural units according to size class of holding for these two provinces are broken down at the district level. This table is extremely useful in that it allows us to visualize differences and similarities in land tenure on a spatial level, as well as some deficiencies of the PRONAC sample. Thus, there are districts for which the information is based on extremely small sample sizes (for example, Coviriali with 89 agricultural units, or Llaylla with only 19), whereas sample sizes in other districts are more representative. When analyzing the data as a whole, this unequal district representation could lead to a biased interpretation insofar as, in general, the districts that have been colonized for the longest periods of time are those that present the greatest degree of fragmentation, whereas in those more recently colonized, land resources are more abundant (Map 4.1).

In effect, as becomes apparent in Table 4.2, the districts that have been colonized for the longest periods of time in Chanchamayo (San Ramón, San Luis de Shuaro, and Chanchamayo) and in Satipo (Coviriali, Pampa Hermosa, Río Negro, and Mazamari) have the greatest percentage of agricultural units in the size class of 0 to less than 5 hectares. Nevertheless, given that in the PRONAC sample the more recently colonized districts (Perené and Pichanaki in Chanchamayo, and Pangoa in Satipo) have a greater number of registered agricultural units, the resulting bias would tend to underestimate rather than overestimate the percentage of agricultural units in the size class of 0 to less than 5 hectares. This is important for our argument since, in spite of this bias, the overall results indicate that a high percentage (32 percent) of agricultural units in both provinces are less than 5 hectares in size.

Some of the data in Table 4.2 merit more detailed explanation. The very high percentage of agricultural units in the size class of 0 to less than 5 hectares in San Ramón (56 percent) is explained by the fact that this district was the first to be colonized in all of the Selva Central, beginning in 1847. To this one must add the fact that, since the inauguration of the La Merced–Satipo road in 1973, San Ramón became a gateway into the Selva Central and the point of entry for the majority of immigrants. Its strategic location and the demographic pressure in this area have combined to accelerate the land-fragmentation process. The same may be said of the Chanchamayo and San Luis de Shuaro districts, with 34 percent and 39 percent, respectively, of agricultural units in the size class of 0 to less than 5 hectares.

In the case of Satipo Province, something similar occurs in the districts of Pampa Hermosa and Coviriali (with 43 percent and 46 percent, respectively, of agricultural units with less than 5 hectares), which were the gateways to this area on the old Concepción–Satipo route. It is surprising, in contrast, that the greatest percentage of agricultural units in the district of Satipo (31 percent) are within the size class of 5 to less than 10 hectares, because this district was colonized during the same period as the two previously mentioned districts. The explanation seems to stem from the fact that cattle ranching, with its greater land requirements, has existed in this area since early times. Pastoral activity is not as significant in districts that have been colonized for a longer period of time in Chanchamayo Province.

Land-tenure data confirm something that was clear from direct observation: that the gateway areas served by roads, where public services and facilities are concentrated, are the most attractive for colonization. This, in itself, is not new. What is new is that the process of land overfragmentation in the Selva Central, which had already been noted by Recharte (n.d.), has affected most of the region and that the percentage of minifundios is much higher than that estimated by Recharte in the early 1980s. Thus, whereas, on the basis of a sample of 1,865 agricultural units in the Vitoc, San Ramón, and Chanchamayo districts, Recharte concluded that 23 percent of these were in the size class of 0 to less than 5 hectares, the PRONAC data give a figure of 47 percent for the districts of San Ramón and Chanchamayo alone.

A different situation is observed in more recently occupied districts. In Pichanaki, for example, the largest percentage of agricultural units (28 percent) are

Table 4.3. Agricultural Units in the Perené-Satipo Zone

Year and size class of holding	No. of AUs	% of total no. of AUs	Area of AUs	% of total area of AUs	Average area per AU
1963					
0 to <10	162	5.1	903	0.3	5.6
10 to <20	229	7.2	3,510	1.2	15.3
20 to <50	673	21.3	16,112	5.6	23.9
50 to <100	362	11.4	22,169	7.6	61.2
100 to <200	1,502	47.5	156,098	53.6	103.9
≥200	236	7.5	92,413	31.7	391.6
All size classes	3,164	100.0	291,655	100.0	92.2
1988					
0 to <10	4,127	54.5	20,614	21.0	4.9
10 to <20	2,087	27.7	29,504	30.0	14.3
20 to <50	1,228	16.2	35,069	35.7	28.6
50 to <100	106	1.4	9,805	9.9	92.5
100 to <200	18	0.2	2,286	2.3	127.0
≥200	4	0.0	1,072	1.1	268.0
All size classes	7,570	100.0	98,350	100.0	12.9

Sources: ONERN 1963 (for the 1963 data; the sample includes 1,146 titled agricultural units and 1,718 untitled agricultural units located in the Perené-Satipo-Ene colonization axis); PRONAC 1990 (for the 1988 data; the sample includes 7,570 agricultural units belonging to the present-day districts of Perené and Pichanaki in the Chanchamayo Province and of Satipo, Río Negro, Mazamari, and Pangoa in the Satipo Province, all of which are located along the Perené-Satipo-Ene axis).

Notes: Size classes and area measurements are in hectares. AU denotes agricultural unit.

in the size class of 10 to less than 20 hectares. The same is true for the district of Pangoa, with 32 percent of agricultural units in this range. In the Perené district, recently created but colonized before the other two, one encounters an intermediate situation, with nearly the same proportion of agricultural units in the size classes of 0 to less than 5, 5 to less than 10, and 10 to less than 20 hectares. Unfortunately, the PRONAC information does not include the Río Tambo district, the more recently colonized area of expansion in the Selva Central, which prevents us from contrasting the land-tenure situation in districts that have been colonized for a long time with the most recently occupied districts. Information on the Pichis and Palcazu valleys will partially make up for this limitation.

As Table 4.3 demonstrates, the land-tenure structure presently observed in Chanchamayo and Satipo provinces is of recent origin. To organize this table we used as a baseline a sample of 3,164 agricultural units from the Perené-Satipo-Ene axis studied by ONERN in 1963 with the intention of promoting its colonization. In modifying the PRONAC information to make it comparable with the ONERN data, information from only the districts of Perené and Pichanaki

(Chanchamayo) and from Satipo, Río Negro, Mazamari, and Pangoa (Satipo), encompassing most of the area studied by ONERN, was used. The results obtained are revealing. Whereas in 1963 only 5 percent of agricultural units consisted of less than 10 hectares, in 1988 this figure rose to 55 percent. This situation becomes worse when one considers the average area per agricultural unit within this size class, which fell from 5.6 to 4.9 hectares.

The 1963 figures, with 55 percent of agricultural units in the 100-hectare and greater size class and only 12 percent of agricultural units with less than 20 hectares, depict a situation of initial colonization, in which land resources are abundant and available in spite of indigenous presence and resistance. In 1963, the population centers of Satipo and La Merced were still not interconnected by the Carretera Marginal, and the Perené Valley had been opened for colonization only recently. The fact that agricultural units in the size class of greater than 200 hectares, representing 7 percent of the total, accounted for 32 percent of the area seems to indicate a trend toward the emergence of *latifundios* and to a land-tenure structure similar to that found in the Satipo and Chanchamayo valleys at the time. This structure changed radically in the 1960s, with the invasion of large landholdings occurring in Satipo and the enforcement of agrarian reform in Chanchamayo.

In general, demographic pressure on the land and its subsequent fragmentation is expressed as a decline in the average area per agricultural unit, which fell from 92.2 to 12.9 hectares per agricultural unit in this area. As we will see in the analysis of the case of the Kivinaki zone (in the central Perené Valley), changes in opportunities for access to land resulted from the construction of the Carretera Marginal, which increased the value of land and resulted in the arrival of a greater number of colonists. On the other hand, the increase in the average area per agricultural unit observed in the size classes of 20 to less than 50 and 50 to less than 100 hectares is surprising. This seems to indicate that currently the largest holdings (in relative terms) are concentrated in these size classes. There is a smaller percentage of agricultural units in the size class of 20 to less than 100 hectares (declining from 33 percent to 18 percent), but these represent a higher percentage of the total area, which increased from 13 percent to 46 percent.

To conclude this global description, it is worth noting that, in spite of the fact that half of the districts that make up the 1963 sample have been colonized during the last three decades, today their land-tenure structure has the same characteristics as that of the Chanchamayo and Satipo provinces taken together. This, as we will see, is an indicator that the logic of the occupation process in the region inevitably leads to a land-tenure structure that is minifundiary in character.

Table 4.4. Agricultural Units in the Chorobamba Valley, 1983

Size class of holding	No. of AUs	% of total no. of AUs	Area of AUs	% of total area of AUs	Average area per AU
0 to <5	14	14.0	42	1.6	3.0
5 to <10	23	23.0	170	6.3	7.4
10 to <20	22	22.0	316	11.7	14.4
20 to <30	12	12.0	268	10.0	22.3
30 to <50	17	17.0	633	23.6	37.2
50 to <100	7	7.0	474	17.7	67.7
100 to <200	4	4.0	469	17.5	117.2
≥200	1	1.0	311	11.6	311.0
All size classes	100	100.0	2,683	100.0	26.8

Source: PEPP 1983.

Notes: Size classes and area measurements are in hectares. AU denotes agricultural unit.

The Case of Oxapampa

Information regarding land tenure in Oxapampa Province is poor in relation to that from the other two provinces of the Selva Central. This is especially true in reference to the districts colonized for the longest periods of time. In contrast, there is more information available for those districts that have recently been the object of road-building and State colonization programs. In Tables 4.4 and 4.5, we present land-tenure data for two areas in the district of Huancabamba: the Chorobamba Valley, the longest occupied, and the Palcazu Valley, colonized for a long time but not accessible by road until 1985. In 1987, this latter area was separated from the district of Huancabamba to form the district of Palcazu. Data in the first table come from a list of colonists settled on both banks of the Chorobamba River. Those in the second table come from a sample of 481 agricultural units from a total of 511 reported in the valley.

By comparing these two tables it is possible to confirm that differences in period of occupation and in the rate and type of occupation result in notable differences in land-tenure structure. In the Chorobamba area, as in Chanchamayo and Satipo provinces, the highest percentage of agricultural units is found in the size class of 5 to less than 20 hectares. However, the percentage of agricultural units smaller than 5 hectares (14 percent), still relatively high, is less than that recorded in the 1972 National Agrarian Census for the entire province of Oxapampa (19 percent) and that recorded in the PRONAC sample for Chanchamayo and Satipo combined (32 percent). This may be a result of the nature of the sample, which was designed for a land-grant program and not for an evaluation of land tenure, but also because Huancabamba, in spite of having been colonized

Table 4.5. Agricultural Units in the Palcazu Valley, 1988

Size class of holding	No. of AUs	% of total no. of AUs	Area of AUs	% of total area of AUs	Average area per AU
0 to <50	61	12.7	2,525	4.7	41.1
50 to <100	255	53.0	20,145	37.4	79.0
100 to <150	94	19.6	11,665	21.7	124.1
150 to <200	39	8.1	6,626	12.3	169.9
200 to <300	14	2.9	3,538	6.6	252.7
300 to <600	14	2.9	6,264	11.7	447.4
600 to <900	4	0.8	2,994	5.6	748.5
All size classes	481	100.0	53,757	100.0	111.8

Source: INADE 1988.

Notes: Size classes and area measurements are in hectares. AU denotes agricultural unit.

since early times, is not among the most dynamic districts or those with high population density and less available land, as is the case in other districts within Oxapampa Province (i.e., Oxapampa, Chontabamba, and Villa Rica).

The case of the Palcazu Valley is entirely different. Unfortunately, the classification system used does not break down the size class of 0 to less than 50 hectares. Nevertheless, the fact that 87 percent of the agricultural units fall into the size class of more than 50 hectares seems to indicate that in the Palcazu Valley, in contrast to Chanchamayo and Satipo, access to land does not yet constitute a problem, providing greater economic opportunities for producers within the area. However, these data may be misleading. Although in Palcazu mid-sized and large holdings prevail, the income study conducted by Camones (1986: 6), based on the same sample, indicates that 47 percent of landholders received no income for sales of agricultural products in 1985. Moreover, of the landholders who had monetary income in the same year, 83 percent received less than US$928.00, which placed them in the small-producer category. Based on these results, Camones concludes that the rural economy of the valley can be characterized as one of subsistence (Camones 1986: 6). This contrasts with the situation of the *minifundio* holders in Chanchamayo and Satipo, who, in spite of severe limitations on access to land, sell the bulk of their agricultural production and depend almost entirely on the market for their subsistence.

The Palcazu situation suggests, therefore, that land-tenure analysis in the Selva Central may not be based simply on an appreciation of the gross area of agricultural units. Rather, the notion of valuable land should be incorporated. Before 1985, land in the Palcazu Valley, with the exception of large ranches that could export their produce by air, was considered valueless land because it lacked a connection to the market. Thus, the fact that most colonists in the valley owned agricultural units of more than 50 hectares is not significant in terms of their level of income.

In summary, although we do not have recent, representative, and reliable information on land-tenure structure for Oxapampa Province, we do find trends identical to those observed in Chanchamayo and Satipo: a preponderance of agricultural units of less than 10 hectares in areas that have been colonized for a long period of time, in contrast to the prevalence of mid-sized and large holdings in more recently occupied areas.

DETERMINING THE LIMITS OF THE AMAZONIAN *MINIFUNDIO*

The Amazonian *minifundio* has received little attention from agrarian researchers and State planners. As we have seen, this is because of the assumption that, in the Amazonian region, land as a resource is an unlimited good. This assumption is not completely false if all of the land in the region were to be considered. However, given current technology and production systems, scarcely 11 percent of the land can be considered suitable for agriculture. Furthermore, not all land suitable for agriculture has value from the perspective of the colonist, who migrates to the Amazonian region to become involved in commercial agriculture. Only land that is at least minimally connected with consumer markets has value and is therefore attractive for colonization. As a result of these constraints, there has been a process of demographic pressure on land, particularly in the most economically active areas of the *selva alta*.

In general, rather than focusing directly on the question of the Amazonian *minifundio,* researchers have preferred to determine the optimal sizes that agricultural and pastoral units in this region should have, based on ecological, technological, or socioeconomic factors, or a combination of the three. The underlying assumption is that below these limits one would face a *minifundio* situation. In the current section, we analyze these proposals to determine what may be considered a *minifundio* in the *selva alta* and then critically analyze the statistical data on the Selva Central presented in the preceding section.

The first aspect that comes to our attention is that the issue of the Amazonian *minifundio,* as such, is principally limited to a few studies carried out in the late 1960s and up to the 1972 National Agrarian Census. In later works, the term *minifundio* almost disappears. Paradoxically, interest in the *minifundio* question declined precisely at the time when the land-fragmentation process in the Selva Central intensified. The second interesting aspect is that the studies completed immediately before the 1969 agrarian reform, such as that carried out by the

Table 4.6. Land-Tenure Categories for the *Selva Alta* and *Selva Baja* Regions as Determined by CIDA, 1966

Category	Selva alta	Selva baja
Large multifamilial	≥100	≥200
Medium multifamilial	20 to <100	100 to <200
Familial	10 to <20	20 to <100
Subfamilial or *minifundio*	0 to <10	0 to <20

Source: CIDA 1966: 200-203.

Note: Values denote areas of land plots in hectares.

Comisión Interamericana de Desarrollo Agrícola, or CIDA (1966), treat the topic of the *minifundio* from an analytical perspective, attempting to define the type of unit according to ecological characteristics of the region. In contrast, more recent studies treat the Amazonian *minifundio* from a descriptive point of view, presenting, as we will see, a distorted view of the reality of land tenure in the region (e.g., Eguren 1987).

To consider the land-tenure issue in Peru, the CIDA study defined four land-tenure categories: large multifamilial, medium-sized multifamilial, familial, and subfamilial or *minifundio*. The size classes within which they are placed were defined by the CIDA team according to ecological differences observed among the coastal, highland, and Amazonian regions, as well as according to geographic distinctions within this latter region. Thus, in the case of the Amazon, the CIDA study defined different size classes according to the location of these categories in the *selva alta* or the *selva baja* (Table 4.6). According to this study, a *minifundio* is considered to be any unit of less than 10 hectares when it is located in the *selva alta*, and any unit of less than 20 hectares in the *selva baja*.

A few years later, in its evaluation of the economic potential of the Perené-Satipo-Ene region, ONERN determined the minimum recommended farm sizes to be granted to families in these areas according to "soil economic categories" (1963: 3-4). Soils were classified not according to their agronomic quality but rather according to the crop types appropriate for each category (see Table 4.7). In determining the minimum sizes for land grants by soil category, ONERN set three criteria (1963: 4):

(a) provide colonist families with an acceptable standard of living, defined as a minimum family income of US$1,268 per year;
(b) solve the problem of the availability of labor for farm production by taking into account that farmers would need to contract addi-

Table 4.7. Minimum Holding Size per Family for the Perené-Satipo-Ene Zone as Recommended by ONERN, 1963

Soil category	Area	% of total area (all soils)	Recommended minimum area per family	Appropriate crops
First	15,210	8.3	5.50	Citrus, avocado, banana, papaya, and tobacco
Second	18,550	10.2	9.25	Banana, papaya, coffee, manioc, corn, and pineapple
Third	146,340	80.3	15.00	Pastures, banana, pineapple, coffee, manioc, annatto, and papaya
Fourth	2,130	1.2	19.00	Jute, beans, corn, and rice

Source: ONERN 1963: 3–5.

Note: Area measurements are in hectares.

tional labor equivalent to up to 67 percent of family labor during periods of high demand; and

(c) enable each family to pay for the land without much effort by guaranteeing a total income of US$1,720 per year per family.

The minimum sizes for agricultural units within each soil category that ONERN determined on the basis of these considerations are shown in Table 4.7. Unfortunately, it is difficult to establish equivalencies between the soil categories defined by ONERN in 1963 and those used by the same institution in subsequent studies. Nevertheless, what is relevant is that, according to ONERN, in no case should a family farm have an area of less than 5.5 hectares. Moreover, given that the third category of soils makes up almost 80 percent of the study area, one could conclude that the minimum size recommended by ONERN for the majority of agricultural units established in this area was 15 hectares.

In contrast to the previous studies, the work of Varese (1974), conducted after the 1969 agrarian reform, presents much higher figures for minimum land-size requirements. On the basis of "the model established by the Agrarian Reform Law," but without stating it explicitly, Varese related the soil-quality factor to minimum land area per family to obtain the values that are presented in Table 4.8. The average minimum size of landholding on soils suitable for agriculture would be, according to Varese, 30 hectares per family, a limit three times larger than the CIDA estimate and double that of ONERN.

Caballero and Alvarez (1980), like Varese, base some of their estimates on the minimum land size recommended by the agrarian reform for "family units."

Table 4.8. Minimum Holding Size per Family for the
Peruvian Amazonian Region as Recommended by
Varese, 1974

Use capacity of soils	Minimum area per family
Intensive agriculture (type A)	20 hectares
Perennial agriculture (type C)	40 hectares
Cattle raising (type P)	200 hectares

Source: Varese 1974: 25.

Table 4.9. Minimum Holding Size per Family for the
Selva Alta Region as Recommended by Smith, 1983

Use capacity of soils	Minimum area per family
Intensive agriculture (type A)	10 hectares
Perennial agriculture (type C)	30 hectares
Cattle raising (type P)	50 hectares

Source: Smith 1983: 73.

These requirements should allow "(a) the use of all of a family's labor force without requiring extra labor, except in specific periods of the agricultural cycle, and never greater than a fourth of the annual family labor capacity; and (b) the farmer to earn a net income that is sufficient to support a family and to fulfill the corresponding obligations for paying off the land and accumulating a certain margin of savings" (Caballero and Alvarez 1980: 43).

These considerations are similar to those described in the 1963 ONERN study. According to the agrarian reform, the minimum size of the family agricultural unit should range between 3.5 and 4 hectares on irrigated coastal land. Caballero and Alvarez use the conversion factor of 1 hectare of irrigated land in the coastal region as equal to 1.6 hectares of irrigated land or 3.4 hectares of nonirrigated land in the Amazonian region (1980: 17). On the basis of these conversion factors, the minimum size for a family unit in the Selva Central, where there is no irrigated land, would range from 11.9 to 13.6 hectares, figures that are intermediate in comparison with estimates given in the CIDA and ONERN studies.

The equivalencies used by Caballero and Alvarez are reasonable. However, in the Amazonian region the current fundamental difference in soil capacity is not due to the presence or absence of irrigation but rather to the agricultural quality and gradient of the land. On the basis of these considerations and on agronomic research conducted in the Pichis and Palcazu valleys, Smith (1983: 72-73) con-

Table 4.10. Comparison of Minimum
Recommended Holding Sizes per Family
for the Peruvian Amazonian Region

Source	Minimum area per family
CIDA 1961	10 hectares*
Caballero and Alvarez 1980	≈13 hectares
ONERN 1963	15 hectares*
Smith 1983	30 hectares*
Varese 1974	40 hectares

Note: Asterisks mark the values that apply only to the
selva alta. The unmarked values apply to the Peruvian
Amazonian region.

cludes that 1 hectare of type A soil (suitable for annual crops) is equivalent to 3
hectares of type C soil (suitable for perennial crops), or to 5 hectares of type P
soils (suitable for pasture). These conversion factors, along with the results of a
study conducted by Pool (1981), in which he concludes that the minimum size for
intensive production of annual crops in type A soils is 8 to 10 hectares, allow Smith
to determine the size of minimum landholdings that we present in Table 4.9.

In Table 4.10 we present a summary of the results of these studies. In the case
of the results obtained by Caballero and Alvarez, we present an average. In the
case of the studies of ONERN, Varese, and Smith, the minimum size recommended for type C soils was chosen because they represent the majority of soils
suitable for agriculture in the *selva alta* in general and in the Selva Central in
particular. We have not considered estimates for soils that are suitable as pastureland, since cattle ranching is relatively insignificant in the provinces of Chanchamayo and Satipo, to which the PRONAC data refer.

From our point of view, Smith's estimates for minimum land-holding size in
the *selva alta* are the best substantiated and those which probably best approxi-
mate the current ecological, technological, and socioeconomic reality of the
region. Nevertheless, because of the methodological necessity of defining the
minifundio in the *selva alta* in keeping with identical definitions for minimum
land-holding size in the rest of the country, we have chosen to combine the
results of the Caballero and Alvarez study with those of Smith. To do so we have
assumed that the equivalence of 1 hectare of irrigated coast land to 3.4 hectares
of nonirrigated Amazonian land pertains to type C soils, which represent 79
percent of the soils suitable for agriculture in the Selva Central. We have applied
this conversion factor to the minimum size for family agricultural units established by the Agrarian Reform Law, obtaining a minimum of 11.9 to 13.6 hectares

Table 4.11. Estimates of Minimum Recommended
Holding Size per Family for the *Selva Alta* Region

Use capacity of soils	Minimum area per family
Intensive agriculture (type A)	3.9 to 4.5 hectares
Perennial agriculture (type C)	11.9 to 13.6 hectares
Cattle raising (type P)	19.5 to 22.5 hectares

Sources: Caballero and Alvarez 1980; Smith 1983; data elaborated by the
authors.

for type C soils. Next, we have applied equivalencies suggested by Smith to these
data (1 hectare of type A soils = 3 hectares of type C soils = 5 hectares of type
P soils), obtaining the results shown in Table 4.11.

The results obtained this way are low in comparison with estimates by Varese
and Smith and are similar to those proposed by ONERN. Given that type C soils
account for almost 80 percent of all the soils suitable for agriculture in the Selva
Central, for the purposes of this study we have assumed that any agricultural
unit under the minimum recommended size for this type of soil constitutes a
minifundio. To avoid an overestimate of the percentage of *minifundios* in the
region, and given that land-tenure information jumps from the size class of 5 to
less than 10 hectares to that of 10 to less than 20 hectares, we have chosen to use
a value of 10 hectares as the limit below which we consider an agricultural unit
to be a *minifundio.* This decision, far from posing a problem, lends even greater
force to our argument. Since this value is significantly lower than those determined by the studies that we reviewed, we can assert without a doubt that all of
the agricultural units that are less than 10 hectares in size can be classified as
minifundios, whereas those with areas of less than 5 hectares are what we will
designate "extreme *minifundios.*"

Taking these criteria into account and based on PRONAC data for Chanchamayo and Satipo, we may conclude that 59 percent of the agricultural units
registered fall within the *minifundio* category, whereas 32 percent are in a critical
extreme-*minifundio* situation. The average area per agricultural unit in these two
provinces (12.5 hectares) is exactly at the limit of our definition of *minifundio.*
This allows us to characterize the land-tenure structure of the region as one
undergoing a process of complete minifundization. These data contradict the
conclusions that Eguren (1987) reached in his analysis of land-tenure data from
the 1984 National Survey of Rural Households. On the basis of a descriptive
definition of the *minifundio* (all agricultural plots with an area of less than 2
hectares), applied to the entire country regardless of geographic and ecological
differences, Eguren concludes that in the *selva alta minifundios* are of little relative

Table 4.12. Minifundiary Agricultural Units in Peru's
Amazonian Region

Year and size class of holding	No. of AUs	% of total	% increase in no. of AUs from previous decade[a]
1961			
0 to <10 hectares	82,216	91.8	—
≥10 hectares	7,363	8.2	—
All sizes	89,630	100.0	—
1972			
0 to <10 hectares	90,339	60.4	9.8
≥10 hectares	59,307	39.6	705.4
All sizes	149,646	100.0	66.9
1984			
0 to <10 hectares	195,142	61.2	116.0
≥10 hectares	123,542	38.8	108.3
All sizes	318,684	100.0	112.9

Sources: CIDA 1966: 200–203 (for 1961 data, based on the First National Agropastoral Census in 1961); Eguren 1987: 181–183; Maletta et al. n.d.: vol. 2 (for 1972 data, based on the Second National Agropastoral Census, in 1972); Eguren 1987: 181–183 (for 1984 data, based on the National Survey of Rural Households).

Note: AU denotes agricultural unit.

[a]That is, the increases from 1961 to 1972 and from 1972 to 1984.

importance (1987: 179). Had Eguren applied the homogenization coefficients used by Caballero and Alvarez in their work, he probably would have arrived at conclusions similar to ours in respect to the Amazonian *minifundio*.

In order to compare the land-tenure data from Chanchamayo and Satipo with that for the entire Amazonian region, and in light of the definition of *minifundio* used here, we have composed Table 4.12, in which we compare information provided by the National Agrarian Censuses of 1961 and 1972 with that provided by the National Survey of Rural Households for 1984. Three phenomena come to our attention in an examination of this table. The first is the sharp decline in percentages of agricultural units of 0 to less than 10 hectares in the period between 1961 and 1972, a phenomenon that should be attributed to the impact of the 1963 and 1969 agrarian reforms in the region, which did not benefit the *minifundio* farmers settled there but instead primarily benefited salaried laborers from the *haciendas* and a new wave of Andean immigrants. This explains the fact that the percentage variation in the number of agricultural units in the size class of less than 10 hectares in this period was less than 10 percent, whereas that of the agricultural units in size classes of 10 hectares and above is on the order of 700 percent.

The second phenomenon that becomes apparent is that, although the total number of Amazonian agricultural units doubled between 1972 and 1984, the percentage of minifundiary agricultural units remained practically constant with respect to the previous period. This indicates that a major proportion of the newly established colonists in the Amazonian region during the 1972–1984 period settled directly into *minifundio* conditions and suggests that, in the last two decades, rather than a process of progressive land fragmentation there has been a continuous process of replication of the minifundiary land-tenure structure. The reason for this replication will be the object of a more detailed discussion in the following section.

Finally, we should note that the percentage of agricultural units of less than 10 hectares as established by the National Survey of Rural Households for the entire Amazonian region (61 percent) is nearly identical to that which results from the PRONAC information for Chanchamayo and Satipo (59 percent). This indicates that the situation of minifundization observed in the Selva Central is not an exceptional case and that, moreover, one encounters the same general trends in this region that are observed throughout the Peruvian Amazonian region.

CAUSAL FACTORS IN THE MINIFUNDIZATION PROCESS

A reading of the statistical information regarding land tenure in the Selva Central in light of our definition of the Amazonian *minifundio* clearly demonstrates that the process of minifundization in the region does not follow the same causal process as that in other geographic areas of the country. To begin with, the Selva Central *minifundio* does not have a *latifundio* counterpart. With the exception of the Pichis and the Palcazu valleys, where there are still large cattle ranches, in the Selva Central *latifundios* disappeared with the agrarian reform of the 1960s. If we apply the definition given in the CIDA report, which identifies all holdings larger than 100 hectares as *latifundios* or as "large multifamily systems," we find that, according to PRONAC, only 0.34 percent of agricultural units in Chanchamayo and Satipo fall into this category, making up slightly more than 4 percent of the total registered area.

PRONAC information does not include jointly owned property, which, from a certain point of view, could be considered to be within the category of large holdings under State control. This, nevertheless, does not change the global picture. The agrarian cooperatives of the Selva Central have embarked upon a process of land fragmentation that began to take shape in 1983 with that of the Juan Velasco Alvarado cooperative (formerly the Perene Colony) and that has deepened in the last several years.

The case of the partitioning of the José Carlos Mariátegui cooperative in the Chanchamayo Valley is a clear example of the replication of the *minifundio* pattern. Thus 58 percent of the owners of new plots from the former agrarian cooperative hold plots of less than 10 hectares, whereas 47 percent are in an extreme *minifundio* situation, with plots smaller than 5 hectares (CDR Chanchamayo 1989).

Demographic Pressure on Land with Economic Value

How do we explain the minifundization process without the simultaneous existence of a clear-cut process of land concentration? The explanation lies in the process of intense demographic pressure on the land. To evaluate this process we constructed Table 4.13, in which the rural population density—that is, the number of rural inhabitants per square kilometer—per district was calculated for the period 1961-1981. The results show that the rural population density of Oxapampa and Chanchamayo doubled in the 1961-1981 period, whereas that of Satipo increased more than four times. The Chanchamayo case is special in that its rural population density in 1981 was much higher than that of the other two provinces and three times higher than the rural population density estimated for the entire country.

Another element to emphasize is that values for rural population density vary significantly at the district level, with the highest figures corresponding to the districts that have been colonized for the longest period of time. If the hypothesis that *minifundios* arise where there is higher demographic pressure is true, one would expect districts with greater population density to have a higher percentage of minifundiary agricultural units. However, when one correlates the two variables, this is not always the case.

Thus, in the San Ramón district, which has a rural population density of 11.5 inhabitants per square kilometer, 77 percent of agricultural units are smaller than 10 hectares, whereas in San Luis de Shuaro, with a rural population density three times greater, the percentage of *minifundios* is smaller, reaching 65 percent. A similar situation is found on analysis of the data corresponding to the districts of Pampa Hermosa and Satipo.

These discrepancies make it obvious that the explanation for the existence of *minifundios* in the Selva Central is not merely excessive population pressure on "available" land. Except in Chanchamayo Province, where the general population density is high, in the Selva Central, land resources, in terms of total area, are still relatively abundant. Therefore, if demographic pressure is an important

Table 4.13. Rural Population Density and Percentage of Minifundiary Agricultural Units

Province and district	Area (km²)	1961 Rural pop.	1961 Rural density	1972 Rural pop.	1972 Rural density	1981 Rural pop.	1981 Rural density	% of AUs of <10 hectares in 1988
Oxapampa								
Oxapampa	982	6,626	6.7	6,018	6.1	7,368	7.5	—
Chontabamba	365	939	2.6	1,610	4.4	2,177	6.0	—
Huancabamba	4,048	2,029	0.5	2,819	0.7	6,733	1.7	—
Puerto Bermúdez	10,988	5,074	0.5	7,390	0.7	9,863	0.9	24.8
Villa Rica	896	4,579	5.1	8,900	9.9	8,380	9.4	—
Pozuzo	1,394	2,114	1.5	2,027	1.5	5,938	4.3	—
All 6 districts	18,673	21,361	1.1	32,878	1.8	40,459	2.2	—
Chanchamayo								
Chanchamayo	2,021	20,713	7.4	39,423	14.0	39,131	19.4	63.0
San Luis de Shuaro	177	—	—	—	—	6,862	38.8	64.6
Pichanaki	1,619	—	—	—	—	8,933	5.5	54.4
San Ramón	592	5,964	10.1	6,050	10.2	6,822	11.5	77.4
Vitoc	314	1,747	5.6	1,965	6.3	4,208	13.4	—
All 5 districts	4,723	28,424	6.0	47,438	10.0	65,956	14.0	59.8
Satipo								
Satipo	732	11,168	1.3	6,017	8.2	10,087	13.8	56.3
Coviriali	145	—	—	2,878	19.8	2,979	20.5	78.5
Llaylla	180	—	—	1,530	8.5	2,264	12.6	5.2
Mazamari	333	—	—	2,280	6.8	3,631	10.9	59.0
Pampa Hermosa	567	—	—	1,958	3.5	2,049	3.6	70.5
Pangoa	6,197	—	—	6,914	1.1	15,808	2.6	44.9
Río Negro	715	—	—	4,554	6.4	6,974	9.8	61.6
Río Tambo	10,562	274	0.03	3,603	0.3	7,679	0.7	—
All 8 districts	19,431	11,442	0.6	29,734	1.5	51,471	2.6	56.5
Selva Central	42,827	61,227	1.4	110,050	2.6	157,886	3.7	—
Peru	1,285,215	5,208,568	4.1	5,479,713	4.3	5,945,329	4.6	—

Sources: INE 1989b (for data on area in square kilometers); Maletta and Bardales n.d.: vol. 1; PRONAC 1990 (for data on percentage of agricultural units of less than 10 hectares in 1988).

Notes: Rural density is calculated as the rural population ("pop.") per square kilometer. Because in 1961 and 1972 the districts of San Luis de Shuaro and Pichanaki had not been separated from that of Chanchamayo, data for these two years correspond to this last district. Because in 1961 the districts of Coviriali, Llaylla, Mazamari, Pampa Hermosa, Pangoa, and Río Negro had not been separated from that of Satipo, data for this year correspond to this last district. AU denotes agricultural unit. Dashes denote no data.

Table 4.14. Rural and Agricultural Population Density and Minifundiary Agricultural Units in Satipo, 1981

District	Area (km^2) Total	Suitable for agriculture	Rural population Total no.	Density	Agricultural population density	% of AUs of <10 hectares
Río Tambo	10,562	940	7,679	0.7	8.2	—
Llaylla	180	150	2,264	12.6	15.1	5.2
Pangoa	6,197	680	15,808	2.6	23.2	44.9
Coviriali	145	100	2,979	20.5	29.8	78.5
Mazamari	333	120	3,631	10.9	30.3	59.0
Pampa Hermosa	567	60	2,049	3.6	34.2	70.5
Río Negro	715	200	6,974	9.8	34.9	61.6
Satipo	732	250	10,087	13.8	40.3	56.3
All 8 districts	19,431	2,500	51,471	2.6	20.6	56.5

Sources: INE 1989b (for data on area in square kilometers); CDR Satipo 1981 (for data on area suitable for agriculture); República del Perú 1985 (for rural population data); PRONAC 1990 (for data on percentage of agricultural units of less than 10 hectares).

Notes: Agricultural population density is calculated as the rural population per square kilometer of land suitable for agriculture. AU denotes agricultural unit. Dash denotes no data.

determining factor, it is not in terms of available land in general but in terms of a specific type of land. Originally, we thought that this specific type of land would be the "best" land—that is, land suitable for agriculture. With this new hypothesis in mind, we developed Table 4.14. Unfortunately, data on the area suitable for agriculture per district are not available for all of the provinces in the Selva Central. Nevertheless, an analysis of the case of Satipo Province, for which these data do exist, is sufficient to test this hypothesis.

The results in this table diminish the previously observed discrepancies. Thus, districts in which the total rural population density was low (Pampa Hermosa, Pangoa, and Río Negro) appear to have higher values for population density when we consider only the areas suitable for agriculture. In general, one can verify a correlation between rural agricultural density (rural inhabitants per square kilometer of land suitable for agriculture) and the presence of *minifundios*. However, as one observes in this table, there is no strict correlation between higher rural agricultural densities and a greater percentage of minifundiary agricultural units.

Given that the variable of demographic pressure seems to be closely linked to the *minifundio* phenomenon, and given that indicators of rural population density and rural agricultural density do not appear to be enough to explain differences in the relative importance of *minifundios* at the district level, we decided to correlate this variable with a variable that we term "valuable land." This latter

Table 4.15. Ranking of Districts Within Their Provinces According to Degree of Demographic Pressure on Lands with Economic Value

Province and district[a]	A	B	C	D	E	F	G	Total, A–G	Overall ranking[b]
Chanchamayo									
Chanchamayo (63.0%)	2	1	2	1	1	1	1	9	1
San Ramón (77.4%)	3	1	1	2	1	1	1	10	2
San Luis de Shuaro (64.6%)	1	2	3	3	1	2	1	13	3
Perené (54.5%)	2	3	4	4	2	1	1	17	4
Pichanaki (54.4%)	4	4	5	5	2	1	1	22	5
Satipo									
Satipo (56.3%)	2	2	2	1	1	1	1	10	1
Coviriali (78.5%)	1	2	3	2	2	2	2	14	2
Pampa Hermosa (70.5%)	6	1	1	5	1	2	1	17	3
Río Negro (61.6%)	5	2	4	3	2	1	1	18	4
Mazamari (59.0%)	4	3	5	4	2	1	1	20	5
Pangoa (44.9%)	7	4	6	6	2	1	1	27	6
Llaylla (5.2%)	3	5	7	7	2	2	2	28	7

Sources: PRONAC 1990; INE 1989a; data elaborated by the authors.

Note: The components of the overall ranking are the following:

A = ranking by rural density (1981 data); 1 denotes greatest density. We assigned the same rank to Perené and Chanchamayo, because in 1981 they had not yet been separated into two districts.

B = ranking by length of occupation; 1 denotes the longest occupation.

C = ranking by proximity to extraregional markets, in terms of road distance; 1 denotes closest proximity.

D = ranking by proximity to main local urban center, in terms of road distance; 1 denotes the closest proximity.

E = direct access to main colonization roads; 1 denotes direct access, and 2 denotes no direct access.

F = access to secondary colonization roads; 1 denotes access, and 2 denotes no access.

G = location of district capital; 1 denotes a capital that is a passage point, and 2 denotes a capital that is a road-terminal point.

[a]The value in parentheses following each district name is the percentage of the district's agricultural units that are less than 10 hectares.

[b]A rank of 1 denotes the highest demographic pressure on lands with economic value.

variable has been defined not according to agronomic criteria but rather according to the economic perception of the colonist-producer. In Table 4.15 we have ranked the districts of Chanchamayo and Satipo provinces according to their relative level of minifundization. This ranking has been correlated with the variables "demographic pressure" and "valuable land." For the first, we have used total rural population density as an indicator; for the second, we have combined a series of indicators. Some of these are taken into account by the producer when he or she decides to settle in a given area. Others result from criteria that are not necessarily considered by the producer. It is important to note, however, that none of these indicators taken alone explains differences in the relative weight of *minifundios* at the district level.

For each indicator considered, we have ranked the districts within each province, assigning them values according to their relative positions. The combination of these indicators with that of rural population density, expressed as the sum of the assigned values, shows that there is a strong correlation between the level of minifundization and the level of demographic pressure on valuable land.

Before commenting in greater detail on Table 4.15, we briefly present the indicators that were selected to define the variable "valuable land." The first— length of occupation—although not consciously considered by the producer, is often essential to understand the reasons for his or her decisions. Areas that have been colonized for the longest periods of time are generally better connected, are closer to consumer markets, and have better services. However, long-term occupation does not guarantee the existence of these other conditions, as the case of Pozuzo (which was colonized beginning in 1854 but remained relatively isolated until 1974) demonstrates.

Distance from extraregional consumer markets is a factor that is definitely taken into consideration by producers. Given the commercial and export character of agriculture in the Selva Central, a large part of its produce is consumed outside the region. In general, the districts that are closest to these markets have been colonized for the longest period of time and are the obligatory gateways for immigrants who arrive to colonize the region. Many of them, as we will see, tend to establish themselves there, rather than heading toward more distant areas where production and living conditions are more difficult, in spite of greater land availability.

Distance from primary urban centers is another factor considered by producers. La Merced, San Ramón, and Satipo offer the majority of banking, educational, health, and other State services in the region, in addition to providing the primary markets for the buying and selling of products. Proximity to these urban centers, therefore, offers major advantages to producers.

The last three indicators are related to the availability of roads and to the frequency of transport means. It would be ideal to have access to quantitative information regarding principal and secondary roadways according to their condition (paved, improved, unimproved) at the district level. Unfortunately, the available information is organized on departmental and provincial levels. Lacking these figures, we have considered the presence or absence both of main colonization roads that connect the region with the coast and of secondary roads that connect the region internally. In addition, we distinguish district capitals that constitute a passage point from those that are road terminal points, assuming that land in districts with towns that are passage points are more attractive because they have better transportation facilities and more intense commercial flows. For all these indicators, the lowest values asigned correspond to the most attractive conditions that increase the value of land: long-term occupation, proximity to extraregional markets and local urban centers, better road access, and better transportation flow.

The data in Table 4.15 demonstrate that the combination of these indicators is closely correlated with existing levels of minifundization, suggesting that the minifundization process throughout the Selva Central is a result of intense demographic pressure on valuable land. What the data do not indicate is the total area of currently existing valuable land. This would allow us, on the one hand, to estimate levels of demographic pressure more accurately, and on the other, to understand the phenomena that are unleashed as a result of the combination of opening new roadways with the other key indicators that we have identified. This information would be indispensable, in turn, in designing more rational settlement plans and avoiding the process of extreme minifundization that is currently observed.

Both objectives can be achieved. To do this, it would be necessary to have better information about soils according to their use capacity at the district level. Second, it would be necessary to have more detailed information about the transportation system in the region at the district level, including not only the length of main roads but also the extent of the network of secondary roads. This would allow us to progress from general statements to more exact and reliable results regarding the areas that are given value by a certain type of road. Finally, it would be necessary to have more detailed information about the colonists' production and marketing strategies to determine the maximal distances with respect to transportation that would guarantee colonists a level of production that—from the perspective of the producer and in accord with the type of product he or she wants to sell—provides a significant profit margin. The interrelation of these indicators would provide a more precise characterization of valuable land than that offered in Table 4.15. Meanwhile, we must be content with this initial approximation.

The results in Table 4.15 are very consistent. The sum of the values assigned demonstrates that the greater the demographic pressure on valuable land, the higher the level of minifundization. There are two notable exceptions, however—the districts of Chanchamayo and Satipo. They both have very high rural population densities and the highest valued land. However, they do not present the highest levels of minifundization. The explanation for this lies in the fact that the capital towns of these two districts are also the capitals of their respective provinces: La Merced and Satipo. Local elites reside in these towns, and the oldest *haciendas* in the region were established in these districts. Even though these *haciendas* disappeared as a result of the agrarian reform, some became mid-sized farms. Thus, a significant percentage of valuable land (about 40 percent) has remained in holdings in intermediate size classes (20 to less than 100 hectares), which coexist with a large number of *minifundios* and extreme *minifundios*. In these districts, it is the presence of these mid-sized holdings, which are generally quite modern and highly productive, that has prevented the process of mini-fundization from acquiring the proportions that it assumes in other districts with similar characteristics in terms of demographic pressure on valuable land. Thus, we may conclude that the correlation that we have established generally works for valuable land but not for lands with the highest absolute value in the region, which tend to be concentrated in holdings in intermediate size classes.

In conclusion, in the Amazonian region, land itself has no value per se from the colonists' perspective. It acquires real (exchange) value when conditions are such that the products resulting from its use yield monetary profit. Lacking these conditions (access to roadways and transportation, to local and extraregional markets, and to banking, educational, and medical services), the land has only use value. In certain cases, areas that have not previously been considered valu-able suddenly acquire exchange value when it becomes known that these condi-tions will soon materialize (for instance, when it is known that the construction of a road is imminent). However, as we will see, the process of valorization of Amazonian lands is a catch-22 in the sense that it is accompanied by innumerable ecological problems, endangering not only the possibilities for regeneration of the tropical ecosystem but also for the reproduction of the economic system that it sustains.

The State and the Multiplication of *Minifundios*

In the preceding pages, we have shown how the process of minifundization responds to demographic pressure, not on the land in general but on valuable land, which constitutes a limited good. In districts where land is more valuable and therefore more attractive to immigrant colonists, it has been subjected to a process of excessive fragmentation, with the subsequent appearance of extreme forms of *minifundio*. The question that arises is whether these elements are sufficient to explain the phenomenon of minifundization. Like all social phenom-ena, the process of minifundization that characterizes the region cannot be reduced to a single causal factor. Bearing this in mind, we have analyzed State land-distribution activities in the region over the last 20 years.

According to official data, in the period from 1967 to 1982 the government distributed a total of 38,551 hectares to 2,111 families in the province of Chan-chamayo and Satipo (Aguila 1983: 58), an average of 18.2 hectares per agricultural unit. In the period from 1983 to 1988, the government intensified its land-alloca-tion activities in these provinces, granting a total of 85,393 hectares to 4,796 families, with an area of 17.8 hectares per agricultural unit (Table 4.16). We

Table 4.16. Area of Granted Lands in Chanchamayo and Satipo

	Chanchamayo			Satipo		
Year	Area	No. of beneficiary AUs	Average area per AU	Area	No. of beneficiary AUs	Average area per AU
1983	2,248	90	24.9	2,639	145	18.2
1984	3,947	199	19.8	2,921	125	23.4
1985	1,910	93	20.5	8,641	421	20.5
1986	12,134	690	17.6	6,258	314	19.9
1987	18,038	1,114	16.2	7,711	525	14.7
1988	10,136	547	18.5	8,810	533	16.5
1983–1988, overall	48,413	2,733	17.7	36,980	2,063	17.9

Source: PDR Chanchamayo-Satipo 1988.

Notes: Area measurements are in hectares. AU denotes agricultural unit.

Table 4.17. Area of Granted Lands Suitable for Agriculture in Chanchamayo and Satipo

	Chanchamayo			Satipo		
Year	Area	No. of beneficiary AUs	Average area per AU	Area	No. of beneficiary AUs	Average area per AU
1984	2,868	199	14.4	1,713	125	13.7
1985	912	93	9.8	3,984	421	9.4
1986	5,900	690	8.5	3,307	314	10.5
1987	9,490	1,114	8.5	4,212	525	8.0
1988	6,443	547	11.7	6,115	533	11.4
1984–1988, overall	25,613	2,643	9.6	19,331	1,918	10.1

Source: Chávez 1989.

Notes: Area measurements are in hectares. AU denotes agricultural unit.

should note, however, that during both periods, holdings of less than 2 hectares were also granted.

If the land that was granted had consisted entirely of land suitable for agriculture, the average size of land grants would be significantly larger than the size limit for *minifundios* that we have established here. Until 1983, land records in the region did not specify what proportion of the land awarded had agricultural value; thus it is difficult to draw specific conclusions regarding this point for earlier dates. Beginning in 1984, however, the government began to differentiate between "land granted in property" (that suitable for agriculture) and "land ceded in use" (that unsuitable for agriculture). In Table 4.17, we concentrate solely on the area of land granted in property between 1984 and 1988.

The data in this table show that the average area suitable for agriculture that was granted during this period was generally under, or barely above, the limit that we established for *minifundios*. One can assume that average awards of land suitable for agriculture for the period before 1984 were similar. In conclusion, we can assert that the State, far from preventing excessive land fragmentation, aggravated the minifundization process. This, as we will see, has forced (or will force in the near future) colonists to use for agricultural purposes lands that are unsuitable for agriculture, thus accelerating the processes of deforestation and soil degradation in the region.

5
PATTERNS AND INTENSITY OF LAND USE

In the preceding chapters we examined the pattern of production and land-tenure structure that characterize the colonist economy in the Selva Central. In this chapter we analyze current land-use patterns with three goals in mind: (1) to determine the degree of land-use intensity and to analyze the factors that influence it; (2) to determine the nature of the process of land-use intensification and to discuss its causes and the appropriateness of extant explanatory models; and (3) to substantiate the need for a qualitative analysis of the process of land-use intensification in the *selva alta* region.

The analysis of current land-use patterns and of the nature of land-use intensification has important implications in terms of the present and future sustainability of the region's agrarian economy. As we will demonstrate, the pattern of production that has crystallized in the region and the constraints imposed by the land-tenure structure have resulted in relatively intensive land use in the Selva Central. This land-use intensity, which is manifested as a more continued use of soils and a relatively low proportion of land left fallow, is not in this case a result of a process of qualitative land-use intensification. On the contrary, these land-use patterns have led to soil overexploitation and, as we will see in the next chapter, to the degradation of the region's resource base. Basing our analysis on historical and socioeconomic variables—as opposed to environmental and cultural variables, which some authors have emphasized (Aramburú n.d.; Dourojeanni 1981a)—allows us to introduce additional considerations into the explanatory models for the process of land-use intensification formulated for the *selva alta* region.

CURRENT LAND-USE PATTERNS

There are two factors that are important to consider with regard to land-use patterns in contextualizing the analysis of land-use intensity in the region: on the one hand, the relationship between land availability and the way that land is used; and on the other, the type of crop that is cultivated. Both factors are closely associated with the structural constraints that we have previously analyzed. Nevertheless, their analysis allows us to illustrate other dimensions of these constraints from a land-use perspective. We will again draw on PRONAC data (1990) that correspond to Chanchamayo and Satipo provinces.

Land Availability and Use

In Table 5.1, we present averages of cultivated areas and granted areas according to district, province, and size of holding. The data demonstrate that agricultural activity in the Selva Central takes place in a context of limited land availability. Nevertheless, one should note that districts in Satipo Province generally tend to have larger averages than do those in Chanchamayo. As stated previously, colonization processes in Chanchamayo are much older, and therefore landholdings have undergone more fragmentation.

   In spite of these overall differences, within each of these provinces we find that the longer a district has been occupied, the more the average area of landholdings and of land under cultivation tends to shrink. The situation is particularly extreme with respect to the size classes of 0 to less than 5 hectares and 5 to less than 10 hectares. The average cultivated areas are 1.98 and 4.80 hectares, respectively, for the two provinces. This indicates that 32 percent of producers in Satipo and Chanchamayo provinces — those working land in the "extreme *minifundio*" size class — obtain farm income on the basis of a very limited cultivated area: barely 2 hectares. Furthermore, it is evident from this table that at a more general level the average cultivated area according to district is always less than 10 hectares. In the Selva Central, 77 percent of the producers have less than 10 hectares under cultivation, whereas up to 49 percent have less than 5 hectares under cultivation (PRONAC 1990). This situation needs to be considered in any planning activity related to technical assistance or credit policy.

   Table 5.2 shows the percentages of cultivated areas and areas in use with respect to the average area of holding, according to district and size of holding. The area in use is composed of both cultivated areas and fallow areas *(purmas)*, which form an integral part of the production system for farmers who practice land-use rotation. A comparison of the two indicators is important, insofar as it permits us to better understand the proportion of land used by holders of land

Table 5.1. Average Cultivated Area per Average Granted Area by Size Class of Holding, 1988

Province and district[a]	0 to <5 hectares	5 to <10 hectares	10 to <20 hectares	20 to <30 hectares	30 to <50 hectares	50 to <100 hectares	100 to <200 hectares	All size classes[b]
Chanchamayo								
San Ramón	1.6/2.3	4.3/7.0	6.7/13.5	11.0/23.3	15.0/36.0	20.6/72.7	62.7/139.3	4.2/8.2
Chanchamayo	1.8/2.8	4.3/7.3	6.8/13.8	11.1/24.2	15.9/36.8	24.8/65.8	66.7/144.8	5.8/11.5
San Luis de Shuaro	1.7/2.6	3.3/7.0	7.0/14.3	11.2/24.3	12.2/37.6	23.5/72.4	0.0/0.0	4.9/10.9
Perené	2.2/2.8	5.4/7.3	10.0/14.0	16.8/24.3	23.3/37.6	36.0/64.4	105.0/142.1	8.9/13.0
Pichanaki	2.2/3.0	4.6/7.3	7.3/14.2	11.5/24.2	15.9/35.9	31.5/65.8	33.6/118.4	6.5/12.3
All 5 districts	1.9/2.7	4.4/7.2	7.6/14.0	12.3/24.0	16.5/36.8	27.3/68.2	67.0/136.1	6.0/11.7
Satipo								
Pampa Hermosa	2.0/2.6	5.0/7.3	7.9/13.7	11.4/24.4	16.6/36.5	48.5/68.0	0.0/0.0	5.2/8.7
Satipo	2.5/2.9	5.8/7.2	9.8/14.0	18.5/24.6	27.4/37.4	47.1/60.3	0.0/0.0	9.2/12.3
Río Negro	2.2/2.7	5.8/7.3	10.6/13.8	17.7/24.1	26.6/37.9	50.4/67.1	77.3/107.5	8.7/11.8
Coviriali	1.8/2.6	5.6/7.5	11.2/13.6	19.5/23.5	0.0/0.0	0.0/0.0	0.0/0.0	5.4/6.8
Mazamari	2.0/2.6	4.7/7.1	9.3/14.6	15.4/24.5	18.4/37.7	49.1/68.7	0.0/0.0	6.9/11.0
Pangoa	2.1/2.9	4.7/7.3	8.3/14.2	12.6/24.1	20.2/37.9	30.0/68.2	65.9/126.3	8.6/15.6
Llaylla	0.0/0.0	5.1/9.9	7.4/15.1	11.8/24.6	8.5/32.0	0.0/0.0	0.0/0.0	9.4/20.2
All 7 districts	2.1/2.7	5.2/7.7	9.2/14.1	15.3/24.3	19.6/36.6	45.0/66.5	65.9/116.9	7.6/12.5
Chanchamayo and Satipo	2.0/2.7	4.8/7.3	8.4/14.1	13.8/24.2	18.0/37.2	36.1/66.9	66.5/132.8	6.8/12.0

Source: PRONAC 1990; data elaborated by the authors.

Note: All data are in hectares.

[a] Districts within each province have been ordered according to relative length of occupation, from the longest to the shortest.

[b] The calculations of the overall average areas also include the size class of 200 or more hectares.

Table 5.2. Percentage of Granted Land Area Put to Use, Particularly in Cultivation, by Size Class of Holding, 1988

Province and district[a]	0 to <5 hectares		5 to <10 hectares		10 to <20 hectares		20 to <30 hectares		30 to <50 hectares		50 to <100 hectares		100 to <200 hectares		All size classes[b]	
	A	B	A	B	A	B	A	B	A	B	A	B	A	B	A	B
Chanchamayo																
San Ramón	67	93	61	87	49	80	47	78	41	74	28	75	44	76	50	82
Chanchamayo	64	89	58	86	49	77	45	73	43	71	37	61	46	84	50	79
San Luis de Shuaro	63	87	47	65	48	66	46	60	32	40	32	39	0	0	44	59
Perené	80	96	74	93	71	87	68	85	61	74	55	71	73	87	68	85
Pichanaki	73	89	63	80	51	70	47	64	44	60	47	59	28	42	52	70
All 5 districts	69	90	60	81	53	75	50	71	44	63	39	60	47	76	57	77
Satipo																
Pampa Hermosa	78	88	68	83	57	72	46	58	45	56	71	79	0	0	59	73
Satipo	85	99	80	98	70	94	75	96	73	88	71	95	0	0	74	95
Rio Negro	82	97	79	97	76	97	73	95	70	92	75	93	72	72	74	94
Coviriali	68	80	75	87	82	92	82	99	0	0	0	0	0	0	79	91
Mazamari	75	91	65	88	63	87	62	77	48	73	71	83	0	0	62	83
Pangoa	72	92	64	87	58	85	52	76	53	77	43	65	52	65	55	79
Llaylla	0	0	52	99	48	73	47	62	26	63	0	0	0	0	46	67
All 7 districts	78	94	69	92	64	85	62	80	58	81	67	83	61	65	63	84
Chanchamayo and Satipo	74	93	68	88	61	82	58	76	54	73	51	71	51	73	60	80

Source: PRONAC 1990; data elaborated by the authors.

Notes: A = percentage of granted land that is cultivated. B = percentage of granted land that is in use.

[a] Districts within each province have been listed in order of relative length of occupation, from the longest to the shortest.

[b] The calculations of the overall average percentages also include the size class of 200 or more hectares.

Table 5.3. Average Forested Area per
Agricultural Unit, 1988

Size class (hectares) of holding	Chanchamayo	Satipo
0 to <5	0.19	0.16
5 to <10	1.00	0.61
10 to <20	2.95	1.68
20 to <30	5.94	4.39
30 to <50	11.74	7.31
50 to <100	22.53	14.64
100 to <200	30.35	43.42

Source: PRONAC 1990; data elaborated by the authors.

Note: Data are in hectares per agricultural unit.

in different size classes, as well as the availability of land for the expansion of cultivated areas.

Table 5.2 shows that the smaller the amount of land available to producers, the greater the proportion of land that is cultivated or in use. This is not surprising given the extremely low average size of land grants in the size classes of 0 to less than 5 hectares and 5 to less than 10 hectares. In these size classes, 93 percent and 88 percent of the available area is in use. This implies that *minifundio* holders have almost no land onto which they can expand their activities. In effect, holders of extremely small *minifundios* in Chanchamayo and Satipo provinces have access to an average of 0.19 and 0.16 hectare, respectively, of primary forest for the expansion of their activities (Table 5.3). In these cases, and as a result of the lack of capital to acquire such agricultural means as fertilizers or pesticides, the only opportunity for these producers to increase their production and their income is to overexploit the land that is available to them.

We can estimate the percentage of fallow land according to district and size class of holding from the difference between the percentage of area cultivated and the total percentage of area in use. This allows us to verify that in the *minifundio* size classes, the percentage of fallow land is always smaller than it is in other size classes, generally varying between 10 percent and 20 percent. This implies that in these size classes producers cannot leave their land fallow long enough for it to partially recover its fertility. What takes place in these cases is an acceleration of the rate of land rotation, resulting in declining productivity. The only apparent exceptions to this rule are the earliest colonized districts in the region: San Ramón, Chanchamayo, and San Luis de Shuaro. In these cases one finds a higher proportion of fallow land (20 percent to 30 percent). As we will see, part of this fallow land is no longer integrated into the production system and exists as overexploited and extremely degraded land that cannot be used productively.

To summarize, agricultural activity in the Selva Central develops in a context of limited land availability and on the basis of average cultivated land areas that, in most cases, are less than 10 hectares. The small size of landholdings forces the majority of producers to make use of almost all of their land. Prolonged occupation and logging activities have resulted in a high proportion of primary forest on valuable land being cut, and therefore in landholders having only very small areas of forested land available for the expansion of their activities. This, and the need to use a large proportion of the land for the development of agricultural activities, has resulted in an accelerated pace of fallow-land rotation by *minifundio* holders. In the case of the earliest colonized districts, fallow land has been degraded to such an extent that it has ceased to be productive.

Incidence of Crop Types

Land information from PRONAC allows cultivated areas to be broken down according to type of crop and district. This information is relevant to our analysis of current land-use patterns, insofar as each one of these crop types imposes distinct demands in terms of the area employed, capital, and labor. We have previously indicated that (1) coffee is the predominant crop in almost all of the districts of Chanchamayo and Satipo; (2) coffee and fruit represent a high percentage of the cultivated land per agricultural unit; (3) in general, on the agricultural units belonging to colonists in the Selva Central, only a small proportion of the land is used for food crops; and (4) cattle ranching, of growing importance in certain areas, is extensive.

The data in Table 5.4 confirm the predominance of perennial crops at the provincial level for both Chanchamayo and Satipo, where they represent 94 percent and 92 percent of the cultivated area, respectively. Among perennial crops, however, there is a clear predominance of agricultural crops over cultivated pastures. This preference, which has historical roots, is currently reinforced by the limited availability of land per agricultural unit. Perennial agricultural crops, such as coffee and fruit, have the double advantage of providing a fairly stable source of income and of being cultivable in relatively small areas. The productive life of the most common variety of coffee is roughly 25 years, and farmers in general partially replant to prolong the useful life of their coffee plantations. The same advantages are shared by many fruit crops. In this sense, an agricultural system based on perennial agricultural crops is currently in concordance with the strong presence of *minifundios* in the region.

However, a striking difference emerges when we contrast the provinces of Chanchamayo and Satipo with regard to perennial crops. Whereas, in

Table 5.4. Distribution of Cultivated Area According to District, 1988

Province and district	Annual agricultural crops			Perennial agricultural crops			Cultivated pastures			Total cultivated area
	Area	%	Average area per AU	Area	%	Average area per AU	Area	%	Average area per AU	
Chanchamayo										
San Ramón	247.32	5.4	0.24	4,063.02	88.1	4.05	302.76	6.5	0.27	4,613.10
Chanchamayo	183.63	4.8	0.29	3,492.39	90.3	6.56	190.06	4.9	0.28	3,866.08
San Luis de Shuaro	246.87	14.8	0.92	1,311.00	78.5	4.89	111.75	6.7	0.33	1,669.62
Perené	997.46	5.2	0.47	17,975.59	92.6	8.57	430.85	2.2	0.20	19,403.90
Pichanaki	903.80	6.1	0.41	13,110.10	88.9	5.98	783.39	5.0	0.32	14,752.29
All 5 districts	2,579.08	5.8	0.41	39,952.10	90.2	6.46	1,773.81	4.0	0.28	44,304.99
Satipo										
Pampa Hermosa	126.55	4.7	0.25	2,073.86	76.9	4.11	497.51	18.4	0.95	2,697.92
Satipo	462.81	12.2	1.13	2,734.25	71.9	6.68	604.80	15.9	1.46	3,801.86
Río Negro	1,172.44	14.4	1.28	6,142.58	75.5	6.73	825.54	10.1	0.89	8,140.56
Coviriali	24.22	5.0	0.27	388.78	80.4	4.41	70.48	14.6	0.79	483.48
Mazamari	148.72	4.0	0.28	2,887.36	77.7	5.46	681.15	18.3	1.27	3,717.23
Pangoa	468.61	4.2	0.37	8,932.07	80.6	7.07	1,684.27	15.2	1.52	11,084.95
Llaylla	16.41	9.2	0.86	129.50	72.4	6.81	33.02	18.4	1.73	178.93
All 7 districts	2,419.76	8.0	0.65	23,288.40	77.4	6.25	4,396.77	14.6	1.24	30,104.93
Chanchamayo and Satipo	4,998.84	6.7	0.50	63,240.50	85.0	6.38	6,170.58	8.3	0.78	74,409.92

Source: PRONAC 1990; data elaborated by the authors.

Notes: This table is based on data for those agricultural units (AUs) that had part of their lands cultivated at the time of the survey. Area measurements are in hectares.

Chanchamayo, 90 percent of the cultivated area is devoted to perennial agricultural crops, in Satipo, these account for 77 percent. This difference in land use is a consequence of (1) Satipo's more recent linkage to the coastal markets, which means that coffee cultivation has been massively adopted only since the 1960s; (2) greater land availability, which has allowed Satipo's colonists to combine perennial agricultural crops with pastures and annual crops; and (3) government promotion of annual food crops in Satipo, which in the mid-1980s involved the granting of zero-interest loans. Whereas the first two factors are structural, the last has been mainly junctural, making it hard to predict whether Satipo's farmers will maintain this land-use pattern in the future.

The districts of Chanchamayo Province generally have land-use patterns that are much more homogeneous than those in Satipo. With the exception of San Luis de Shuaro, we find that in the districts of Chanchamayo the area devoted to perennial agricultural crops fluctuates between 88 percent and 93 percent of the total cultivated area. Similar homogeneity is found in the proportion of land dedicated to annual crops and to cultivated pastures. This indicates that the region's predominant pattern of production is more consolidated and stable in those districts that are located nearer to consumer centers and that have land with higher value. San Luis de Shuaro is an exceptional case, insofar as it has a relatively high percentage of cultivated area dedicated to annual crops (15 percent). This can be explained by the presence of farmers who have accumulated a small amount of capital and are dedicated to the production of annual or semiperennial crops (such as corn or pineapple) with the concomitant intensive application of chemicals.

The districts of Satipo present a greater heterogeneity with respect to the combination of perennial and annual agricultural crops and cultivated pastures. Here, there seems to be no strict correlation between the length of occupation and certain production options. Thus, the incidence of cultivated pastures is high by Selva Central standards, both in districts occupied for the longest periods of time, such as Pampa Hermosa, as well as in some that were occupied more recently, such as Pangoa and Mazamari. Given the larger average size of granted land in Satipo, the option of sowing grass is associated with the possibility of immediately incorporating into production those fallow lands generated by the cultivation of annual crops. In Chanchamayo's small landholdings this option is out of the question. It should be noted, nevertheless, that in Satipo cattle raising is generally carried out in relatively small areas, the average area in pastures oscillating between 0.79 and 1.73 hectares. Unfortunately we do not have information correlating average area per type of crop and size class of holding, which would have allowed us to identify the kind of agricultural unit most commonly devoted to cattle raising in Satipo.

In summary, agriculture in the Selva Central is based on the cultivation of perennial crops. This pattern of production has been stable over time and is still predominant in both Chanchamayo and Satipo. Although there are differences in the extent to which this pattern has been adopted, these variations do not constitute a substantially distinct production pattern: cattle raising in the region's central areas remains a marginal and fairly unproductive activity.

The evolution of this pattern of production—which originally was associated with the crisis of the sugarcane economy and with the allure of higher prices of coffee in the international market—is now tightly linked to the severe land fragmentation experienced by the region. As we will see, these two elements— land fragmentation and cultivation of perennial crops—have resulted in a relatively intensive use of land.

INTENSITY AND INTENSIFICATION OF LAND USE

Authors who have analyzed agricultural development in the *selva alta* (e.g., Aramburú and Bedoya 1987; Bedoya 1991, n.d.; Dourojeanni 1981b, 1990; Grobman 1983) generally consider that, given the ecological and demographic conditions of this subregion, the only way to make more rational use of tropical resources and thus lessen the environmental impact of agricultural activities is to intensify land use. For these authors, intensification is achieved when an area in production has only a small proportion of fallow land. This can only take place when the traditionally migratory agriculture is stabilized. According to this view, stabilization and land-use intensification may take three forms: (1) the development of an agriculture based primarily on perennial agricultural crops and forages; (2) the development of annual and biannual crops in a stable manner, based on regular fertilization and irrigation; and (3) the development of agroforestry, based on an agricultural system that contributes to the regeneration and simultaneous management of harvestable forests.

Perennial Agriculture and Land-Use Intensity

The Selva Central seems to have spontaneously taken the first of these paths early in its development. As a function of the definitions proposed by these authors, agriculture based on perennial crops and pastures makes more intensive use of the land than does shifting agriculture, insofar as it significantly reduces the rate at which fallow land is generated. Therefore, the proportion of an area planted in perennial crops in relation to the total cultivated area is a basic indicator of the degree of land-use intensity in a given region. According to this criterion, the higher the proportion of perennial crops, the higher the land-use intensity. However, one must caution that this is a very rough indicator, since it does not differentiate among the economic and ecological implications of the various perennial and annual crops.

Applying this criterion, we find that the estimated proportion of total cultivated area planted in perennial crops is significantly larger in the Selva Central than it is in the *selva alta* as a whole: 79 percent versus 60 percent, respectively (Table 5.5). The notable differences between the Selva Central and the rest of the *selva alta* are due to the presence of coffee, fruit crops, and pasture in the Selva Central. In contrast, in most colonization areas of the *selva alta*, where development took a very different direction as a result of state credit and pricing policies, the area planted in annual crops (particularly rice and corn[6]) during the past 15 years has increased significantly. The data in Table 5.5 permit us to conclude that, at least in these terms, relatively intensive use is made of the land in the Selva Central. Nevertheless, it should be emphasized that this is not

Table 5.5. Distribution of Cultivated Area in the *Selva Alta* and the Selva Central

Type of crop	Selva alta (%)	Selva Central (%)
Annual crops	40.3	21.0
Perennial crops		
Agricultural crops	36.6	47.1
Cultivated pastures	23.1	31.9
All perennial crops	59.7	79.0

Sources: Grobman 1983: 57 (for the *selva alta* in 1983); Ministerio de Agricultura 1963-1988 (for the Selva Central in 1980).

necessarily the result of improved technical management. Within the framework of intense pressure on valuable land, the "sedentarization" of agriculture in the Selva Central appears to be more a result of the size constraints of the agricultural units and the predominant pattern of production than of the adoption of technological innovations. In fact, rather than an increase in productivity as a result of land-use intensification, the region has witnessed a progressive reduction in the average yields of its principal crops (see Chapter 3).

In the Selva Central, the high proportion of perennial crops is not a recent phenomenon. However, since the appearance of the classic works of Conklin (1963), Crist (1969), and Watters (1971) describing the migratory character of tropical agriculture, and in spite of the publication of studies that question the relevance of their findings to areas that have been colonized for a long period of time (e.g., Recharte n.d.), authors and planners tend to assume that shifting agriculture is not only characteristic of all tropical areas but is practiced by all colonists in the initial stages of settlement. Some authors (e.g., Aramburú n.d.) have tended to emphasize the "peasant" nature of colonist agriculture and to characterize the appearance and development of an agricultural system based on perennial crops as a function of the transition from subsistence to commercial agriculture. Contrary to this assumption, in the Selva Central one finds that even colonists settled in recently incorporated areas plant, from the very beginning, commercial crops that make permanent use of the land: coffee, fruit, and forages.

As we have seen, on the colonists' holdings in the Selva Central, the importance of food-crop agriculture (for consumption by the producer or for sale) is limited and tends to decline when perennial commercial crops, introduced early on, mature and produce monetary income. Table 5.6 highlights the stability of the economic profile of the Selva Central and, with it, the fact that the intensity of land use, measured in gross terms, has remained practically constant over the past 30 years.

Table 5.6. Distribution of Cultivated Area in the Selva Central

Year	Annual crops (%)	Perennial crops (%)		
		Agricultural crops	Cultivated pastures	All perennial crops
1964	20.5	59.4	20.1	79.5
1966	15.5	69.2	15.3	84.5
1968	16.1	68.4	15.5	83.9
1970	18.8	55.1	26.1	81.2
1972	15.4	56.7	27.9	84.6
1974	17.9	54.5	27.6	82.1
1976	19.1	50.9	30.0	80.9
1978	19.5	51.2	29.3	80.5
1980	21.0	47.1	31.9	79.0
1982	18.5	43.0	38.5	81.5
1984	17.3	41.6	41.1	82.7

Source: Ministerio de Agricultura 1963–1988.

As a result of variations in the pattern of production at the provincial level, the proportion of annual crops to perennial crops in Chanchamayo and Satipo provinces differs substantially from that in Oxapampa Province. In the provinces of Chanchamayo and Satipo taken together, the proportion is 1 hectare of annual crops per 3.3 hectares of perennial crops, this ratio remaining basically stable between 1964 and 1984 (Ministerio de Agricultura 1963–1988).[7] In Oxapampa Province, annual crops are relatively less important and clearly show a decreasing trend in favor of the establishment of pastureland. Thus, in 1964, for every hectare of land planted in annual crops in Oxapampa, there were 6.1 hectares of land planted in perennial crops, and in 1984 this relationship was 1 to 8.5 (Ministerio de Agricultura 1963–1988).

The distinction between perennial agricultural crops and cultivated pastures is useful to introduce qualitative criteria into the analysis of land-use intensification. Although both perennial agricultural crops and pastures are stable and generate a small proportion of fallow land, their profitability and ecological impact are quite distinct. Cattle ranching in the Selva Central is extensive, rather than intensive. This means that, although the use of land for pastures is relatively stable over time, yield per hectare is quite low. Thus, some authors estimate an average requirement of 4 hectares of pasture per head of cattle (e.g., Grobman 1983). More-moderate estimates indicate that the average is approximately 1.6 hectares per head of cattle and that, under current conditions, a hectare of pastureland yields nearly 31 kilograms of beef per year (Staver 1981). Further-

more, the development of pastureland, which involves complete, long-term deforestation, quickly exhausts soils, whereas perennial agricultural crops offer
some protection, thus slowing soil degradation. These economic and ecological
considerations demonstrate that cattle ranching, as it is practiced in the region,
does not really make intensive use of the land. As a result, including cultivated
pastureland in calculations to determine the degree of land-use intensity distorts
the agrarian reality of the region, making indispensable the development of
models that reflect it more adequately.

Land-Use Intensification and Deintensification

Among the studies that analyze the colonists' production pattern and the dynamic nature of agropastoral frontiers in tropical areas, the detailed works of
Bedoya (n.d.) and Aramburú and Bedoya (1987) are particularly valuable, for they
offer a hypothesis for land-use intensification in the *selva alta* region. Aramburú
and Bedoya construct their model based on a comparison of land-use patterns
in three zones of colonization in the upper Huallaga Valley, occupied at different
points in time: (1) Tingo María, the oldest zone, where, in the 1980s, nearly 50
percent of the colonists had been established for 20 years; (2) Aucayacu, where
a similar proportion of colonists had been established for between 11 and 20
years; and (3) Tocache–Uchiza, the most recently occupied zone, where more
than 60 percent of the colonists had been established for less than 10 years (1987:
129). Analyzing the information regarding land-use patterns in these three zones,
and inspired by Esther Bosrup's ideas about the relationship between demographic pressure and agrarian change, Aramburú and Bedoya found "evidence
of a land use intensification process" (1987: 116) in this region. According to
Bedoya (n.d.: 60), in this process "the length of occupation explains the level of
intensification."

The hypothesis of these authors is that, in areas that have been occupied for
the longest time, (1) there is higher population pressure, which is correlated with
greater land fragmentation, and (2) producers are better linked with the market,
resulting in the transition from a subsistence shifting agriculture to a commercial
agriculture based on perennial crops. These two factors result in land-use intensification, which takes the form of (1) a reduction in cultivated area per agricultural unit and (2) a reduction in the proportion of fallow land.

To determine the degree of land-use intensity, Aramburú and Bedoya developed a formula that relates total cultivated area with total area in use (cultivated
area plus fallow area) (1987: 159):

$$\frac{\text{area in perennial crops} + \text{area in annual crops}}{\text{area in perennial crops} + \text{area in annual crops} + \text{fallow area}}.$$

According to this formula, the greater the proportion of cultivated area with respect to the total area in use, the higher the coefficient of land-use intensity. Coefficients of land-use intensity range from 0.0 to 1.0. The lowest values correspond to more extensive land use, whereas the highest values, near 1.0, correspond to more intensive land use. Aramburú and Bedoya established five categories of land-use intensity (1987: 158):

Degree of Intensity	Coefficient of Intensity
Very low	0.1–0.2
Low	0.3–0.4
Moderate	0.5–0.6
High	0.7–0.9
Very high	1.0

Applying this formula to the data from the upper Huallaga Valley, Bedoya (n.d.: 74-76) confirmed a close correlation between length of occupation and land-use intensity. Thus, Tingo María, the zone occupied for the longest period of time, which has the lowest average granted areas, has an overall coefficient of land-use intensity of 0.55. Aucayacu, an intermediate zone both in terms of length of occupation and land fragmentation, has an average coefficient of 0.43; whereas Uchiza–Tocache, most recently occupied and with higher average granted areas, has a coefficient of 0.40 (Table 5.7). In addition, Bedoya found that, within each of these zones, the coefficient of land-use intensity increased as size class of holding decreased. In general, according to the classification proposed by Aramburú and Bedoya, the resulting coefficients of land-use intensity correspond to the medium and lower range of land-use intensity.

Table 5.7. Coefficients of Land-Use Intensity in the Upper Huallaga Valley According to Zone

Size class of holding	Tingo María	Aucayacu	Uchiza–Tocache
0 to <5 hectares	0.77	0.62	0.47
5 to <10 hectares	0.70	0.51	0.57
10 to <20 hectares	0.58	0.47	0.48
20 to <30 hectares	0.43	0.39	0.37
All size classes	0.55	0.43	0.40
	(19.50)	(26.75)	(30.07)

Source: Bedoya n.d.: 85–87; data elaborated by the authors.

Note: Values in parentheses are average areas (hectares) per agricultural unit within the given zones.

Data from the upper Huallaga Valley confirm the hypothesis formulated by Aramburú and Bedoya (1987: 157-162). However, when we apply this formula to the districts of Chanchamayo and Satipo provinces, we find that here their hypothesis is only partially confirmed. Data in Table 5.8 show that the correlation between length of occupation and coefficient of land-use intensity is partially substantiated for the districts of Satipo but not for those of Chanchamayo, where the earliest colonized districts have lower coefficients of land-use intensity. On the other hand, whereas there seems to be a general correlation between land fragmentation and coefficient of land-use intensity (as is true for the province of Chanchamayo), this is not the case in Satipo, where because of the presence of larger areas of pastureland, the agricultural units in the highest size class have coefficients of land-use intensity as high as those calculated for the minifundiary size classes.

If we accept Aramburú and Bedoya's hypothesis to the extent that (1) length of occupation is correlated with greater land fragmentation, (2) lower land availability results in reduced opportunities for rotation, and (3) the higher the proportion of perennial crops the lower the proportion of fallow land, what explains the fact that, in the case of the Selva Central, the hypothesis of these authors cannot be confirmed? Why is there no clear correlation between greater length of occupation and greater land-use intensity?

We believe that this lack of correlation can be explained by the fact that the temporal scale of occupation and exploitation is considerably shorter in the cases studied by Aramburú and Bedoya than it is in the districts of the Selva Central. In effect, whereas the earliest zone to be occupied in the upper Huallaga Valley was settled in the 1940s, the first areas to be occupied in the Selva Central were already settled by the end of the 19th century. Furthermore, at that time these areas were already linked to the market through a system of permanent, commercial agricultural production. Therefore, commercial production in the Selva Central has been much more constant and is much older than that of the upper Huallaga Valley. These differences are reflected in the fact that all of the average coefficients of land-use intensity for the districts of Chanchamayo and Satipo correspond to the range of high land-use intensity proposed by these authors. In all cases, the coefficients are higher than the highest coefficients reported for the upper Huallaga Valley. Therefore, the consideration of other, more-qualitative variables that reflect the peculiarities of its process of land-use intensification seems to be indispensable in the case of the Selva Central.

In order to enrich Aramburú and Bedoya's hypothesis, we will correlate length of occupation not only with property fragmentation and coefficient of land-use intensity but also with three other variables that we believe more adequately reflect the economic and ecological reality of the Selva Central: (1) the presence

Table 5.8. Coefficients of Land-Use Intensity by Size Class of Holding, 1988

Province and district[a]	0 to <5 hectares	5 to <10 hectares	10 to <20 hectares	20 to <30 hectares	30 to <50 hectares	50 to <100 hectares	100 to <200 hectares	All size classes[b]
Chanchamayo								
San Ramón	0.71	0.69	0.52	0.60	0.55	0.37	0.58	0.61
Chanchamayo	0.71	0.67	0.63	0.61	0.60	0.60	0.54	0.63
San Luis de Shuaro	0.72	0.71	0.72	0.75	0.78	0.81	0.00	0.74
Perené	0.82	0.78	0.81	0.79	0.82	0.77	0.83	0.89
Pichanaki	0.82	0.78	0.72	0.72	0.72	0.79	0.66	0.75
All 5 districts	0.75	0.72	0.69	0.69	0.69	0.66	0.65	0.77
Satipo								
Pampa Hermosa	0.88	0.81	0.79	0.79	0.79	0.89	0.00	0.81
Satipo	0.85	0.81	0.74	0.78	0.82	0.74	0.00	0.78
Río Negro	0.84	0.81	0.78	0.76	0.75	0.80	0.00	0.79
Coviriali	0.86	0.85	0.89	0.82	0.00	0.00	0.00	0.88
Mazamari	0.82	0.73	0.72	0.80	0.65	0.85	0.00	0.75
Pangoa	0.78	0.72	0.68	0.67	0.68	0.66	0.80	0.70
Llaylla	0.00	0.52	0.66	0.77	0.41	0.00	0.00	0.69
All 7 districts	0.83	0.78	0.76	0.77	0.73	0.78	0.80	0.74
Chanchamayo and Satipo	0.79	0.75	0.72	0.73	0.71	0.72	0.72	0.76

Source: PRONAC 1990; data elaborated by the authors.

[a]Districts within each province have been ordered according to relative length of occupation, from the longest to the shortest.

[b]The calculation of the overall average coefficient also includes the size class of 200 or more hectares.

of agricultural units with a coefficient of land-use intensity of 1.0, (2) the presence of agricultural units with a coefficient of land-use intensity of 0, and (3) the relative weight of perennial crops. We have selected five districts that belong to the provinces of Chanchamayo and Satipo for this exercise, ordering them according to the length of time that they have been occupied: (1) San Ramón, which was first occupied in the middle of the 19th century and began to receive a massive influx of immigrants in 1890; (2) Pampa Hermosa, which was first occupied in 1920; (3) Coviriali, whose occupation dates from 1940; (4) Perené, which has been massively occupied since 1960; and (5) Pichanaki, whose occupation began in 1970 with the inauguration of the Carretera Marginal.[8]

Property fragmentation was analyzed in the previous chapter, and its strong correlation with length of occupation has been established. For the present exercise, we have chosen the percentage of minifundiary agricultural units — that is, those that have been allotted less than 10 hectares — as the first variable. As we have seen, because of limited land availability, agricultural units in this range tend to have a higher proportion of land under cultivation and a smaller proportion of fallow land. The second variable is degree of land-use intensity according to the coefficients obtained with the formula proposed by Aramburú and Bedoya, which were presented in Table 5.8. As we have seen, these coefficients tend to be higher when property fragmentation is greater.

The third variable, presence of agricultural units with a coefficient of land-use intensity of 1.0, is particularly important in the context of intense demographic pressure on valuable land. In effect, in areas of long-term occupation, levels of minifundization are so high that in a considerable proportion of agricultural units all of the land area is in use. In these agricultural units there is no fallow land. Therefore, they would represent the highest degree of land-use intensity. In Table 5.9, we present the percentages of agricultural units that have coefficients of land-use intensity of 1.0 according to size class of holding and district. The data in this table confirm that with greater property fragmentation there is a greater percentage of agricultural units with coefficients of land-use intensity of 1.0. In the minifundiary size classes, this percentage is extremely high, rising to almost 60 percent for the size class of 0 to less than 5 hectares and to almost 40 percent for the size class of 5 to less than 10 hectares.

The fourth variable to be considered is the presence of agricultural units with coefficients of land-use intensity of 0, which, in this case, refers to those agricultural units in the sample that do not have cultivated plots but have areas of fallow land. Given that in many cases these agricultural units are well situated with respect to roads and markets, we assume that if they are not cultivated, it is because the land is extremely degraded and their productivity does not justify the investment of labor and capital required. If the formula developed by

Table 5.9. Percentage Distribution of Agricultural Units with Coefficients of Land-Use Intensity of 1.0, by Size Class of Holding, 1988

Province and district[a]	0 to <5 hectares	5 to <10 hectares	10 to <20 hectares	20 to <30 hectares	30 to <50 hectares	50 to <100 hectares	All size classes
Chanchamayo							
San Ramón	48.1	37.2	18.1	21.4	21.7	0.0	38.5
Chanchamayo	49.2	31.5	23.8	10.7	0.0	20.0	32.1
San Luis de Shuaro	50.0	31.2	25.0	13.0	7.6	16.6	34.0
Perené	63.8	45.2	34.5	27.3	23.8	14.0	43.2
Pichanaki	65.2	43.1	26.6	21.2	24.0	20.0	40.4
All 5 districts	57.8	40.7	28.3	22.3	21.4	14.8	39.9
Satipo							
Pampa Hermosa	71.9	35.9	26.2	16.1	26.6	50.0	47.8
Satipo	66.9	43.3	21.7	18.5	35.2	0.0	39.6
Río Negro	62.0	39.6	29.3	23.9	14.5	12.5	41.4
Coviriali	65.0	41.3	46.6	25.0	0.0	0.0	52.3
Mazamari	63.2	37.2	28.0	35.4	17.3	33.0	41.3
Pangoa	57.5	50.5	11.8	12.3	59.6	14.2	26.0
All 6 districts	63.4	35.9	21.1	19.1	15.6	14.3	37.1
Chanchamayo and Satipo	59.8	38.9	25.5	21.1	19.1	14.6	38.9

Source: PRONAC 1990; data elaborated by the authors.

Note: Holdings of size classes of 100 hectares or more have not been included, because none have a coefficient of land-use intensity of 1.0.

[a]Districts within each province have been ordered according to relative length of occupation, from the longest to the shortest.

Aramburú and Bedoya is applied without considering the implications of including this type of agricultural unit, both fallow land that is effectively integrated into the system of production and land rotation as well as older fallow land that is in a state of extreme degradation (and that can no longer be worked) would be integrated into the denominator with the same value. As a consequence, the current coefficient of land-use intensity would be reduced, even if it adequately reflects the long-term pattern. This should be considered when analyzing the information presented in Table 5.8.

The percentages of agricultural units with coefficients of land-use intensity of 0 are presented in Table 5.10. This table shows that the greater the degree of property fragmentation, the greater the percentage of agricultural units whose soils have become completely degraded and are no longer cultivated. This is particularly obvious in the case of the extreme-*minifundio* size class in the earliest colonized districts in the region, where the percentage ranges from 13 to 24 percent of the total number of agricultural units. This would indicate that in the

Table 5.10. Percentage Distribution of Agricultural Units with Coefficients of Land-Use Intensity of 0.0, by Size Class of Holding, 1988

Province and district[a]	0 to <5 hectares	5 to <10 hectares	10 to <20 hectares	20 to <30 hectares	30 to <50 hectares	50 to <100 hectares	All size classes
Chanchamayo							
San Ramón	13.1	6.2	6.1	4.5	0.0	0.0	9.7
Chanchamayo	14.0	4.1	3.9	1.8	4.8	0.0	7.2
San Luis de Shuaro	23.8	27.2	16.7	8.0	23.5	14.3	21.9
Perené	8.6	2.1	1.2	0.4	0.0	0.0	3.4
Pichanaki	5.2	3.1	3.6	3.5	1.0	0.0	3.8
All 5 districts	12.9	8.5	3.6	2.4	2.0	0.9	5.9
Satipo							
Pampa Hermosa	4.4	3.4	1.0	3.1	0.0	0.0	3.3
Satipo	2.8	0.0	1.0	0.0	0.0	0.0	1.0
Río Negro	5.0	0.7	0.5	0.0	0.0	0.0	2.1
Coviriali	2.5	0.0	0.0	0.0	0.0	0.0	1.1
Mazamari	3.1	3.1	0.0	0.0	0.0	0.0	1.9
Pangoa	3.5	0.8	1.7	0.6	0.0	0.0	1.6
All 6 districts	3.5	1.2	1.0	0.5	0.0	0.0	1.9
Chanchamayo and Satipo	8.2	3.2	2.6	1.7	2.0	0.9	4.5

Source: PRONAC 1990; data elaborated by the authors.

Note: Holdings of size classes of 100 hectares or more have not been included, because none are uncultivated.

[a]Districts within each province have been ordered according to relative length of occupation, from the longest to the shortest.

minifundiary size classes (in areas that have been occupied for a long period of time), two concomitant and contrasting processes occur: on the one hand, a process of land-use intensification, with high percentages of agricultural units with the maximal coefficient of land-use intensity; and, on the other hand, a process of decline over time in land-use intensity that reflects a greater presence of agricultural units with coefficients of land-use intensity of 0.

The last variable that we will consider is the relative weight of perennial crops, including both perennial agricultural crops and cultivated pastures. One of the mechanisms for achieving greater land-use intensity is the development of an agriculture based primarily on the production of perennial crops. Thus, a greater percentage of perennial crops would indicate a higher degree of land-use intensity. We have used data from Table 5.4 to evaluate the contribution of this variable.

In Table 5.11, we have correlated these five variables with length of occupation for the five previously mentioned districts. In the same table, the districts have been arranged according to relative length of occupation. For each of the vari-

Table 5.11. Ranking of a Sample of Chanchamayo and Satipo Districts According to Length of Occupation and Degree of Land-Use Intensity, 1988

District, by length of occupation	A	B	C	D	E	Total, A-E	Overall rank[a]
San Ramón	4	1	2	1	1	9	1
Pampa Hermosa	3	3	4	3	4	17	4
Coviriali	5	4	5	5	3	22	5
Perené	2	5	3	2	2	14	3
Pangoa	1	2	1	4	5	13	2

Notes: The districts are listed in order from the longest occupation to the shortest. The components of the overall ranking are the following:

A = ranking by percentage of agricultural units (AUs) that are minifundiary (area of 0 to <10 hectares; see Table 4.2); 1 denotes the lowest percentage of minifundiary AUs.

B = ranking by coefficient of land-use intensity (see Table 5.8); 1 denotes the lowest coefficient of land-use intensity.

C = ranking by percentage of AUs with the maximum coefficient of land-use intensity (i.e., 1.0; see Table 5.8); 1 denotes the lowest percentage of AUs with coefficients of 1.0.

D = ranking by percentage of AUs with the minimum coefficient of land-use intensity (i.e., 0.0; see Table 5.8); 1 denotes the highest percentage of AUs with coefficients of 0.0.

E = ranking by percentage of cultivated area in perennial crops (including cultivated pastures; see Table 5.4); 1 denotes the lowest percentage of areas in perennial crops.

[a]A ranking of 1 denotes the lowest intensity of land use.

ables considered, the districts in the sample have been assigned a relative value of between 1 and 5, according to the degree of land-use intensity associated with this variable. In column A, which registers the incidence of minifundiary agricultural units, larger values have been assigned to the districts that have the highest percentages of *minifundios*. In column B, in which coefficients of land-use intensity are registered, higher values correspond to the districts that have the highest coefficients. In column C—presence of agricultural units with coefficients of land-use intensity of 1.0—higher values have been assigned to districts that have the highest percentages of agricultural units in this category. In column D, higher values have been assigned to districts that have lower percentages of agricultural units with coefficients of land-use intensity of 0. Finally, in column E, higher values have been assigned to districts that have higher percentages of perennial agricultural crops and cultivated pastures. The values assigned according to variable and according to district have been summed to obtain the figures shown in the last column. In this column, the largest numbers correspond to the highest degrees of land-use intensity.

Results obtained in this fashion partially confirm the hypothesis of Aramburú and Bedoya. In the districts of Coviriali, Perené, and Pangoa, occupied between 1940 and 1970 and representing the same temporal horizon as the cases studied by these authors in the upper Huallaga Valley, one finds that the longer the land

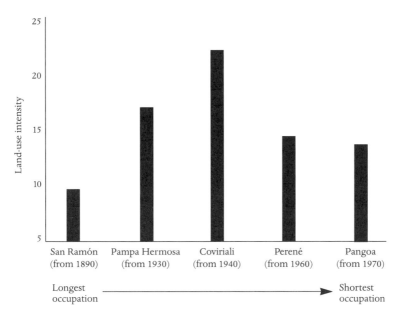

Figure 5.1. Land-use intensity in relation to date of settlement in Chanchamayo and Satipo, 1988. *Source:* Table 5.11.

has been in use, the higher the coefficient of land-use intensity. However, when the temporal horizon is broadened to include areas of more prolonged occupation, we find that the degree of land-use intensity tends to diminish to even lower levels than those recorded in the areas most recently occupied.

This process may be better appreciated with an examination of Figure 5.1: the degree of land-use intensity increases according to the increase in length of occupation, until it arrives at a point of decay. This curve illustrates both the processes of land-use intensification in areas of fairly recent occupation and the processes of deintensification that result from the progressive degradation and total deterioration of soils in those areas of most prolonged occupation. This last process takes place in spite of the fact that some producers invest in chemicals and the like in order to maintain or increase their productivity.

It should be noted, however, that this deintensification process does not imply that the economy in these areas reverts to an earlier state or loses its commercial character. On the contrary, because of the comparative advantages conferred upon them by their location, it is precisely in these areas where there is greater economic agglomeration. Therefore, in areas where agriculture is based on perennial crops that offer sustained marketing opportunities, such as coffee or fruit, even those areas that undergo a process of land-use deintensification continue to be strongly linked with the market economy. However, it is important to note that if no solution is found to the current process of soil degradation and the concurrent process of deintensification of land use, in the following decades environmental deterioration in these areas will reach a critical and irreversible point that will lead to their abandonment, at least in terms of agricultural production.

In summary, data on the process of land-use intensification in the Selva Central do not completely invalidate Aramburú and Bedoya's hypothesis. Rather, it shows that the hypothesis should be expanded to take into account areas in which there has been long-term land use. The fact that even the areas of the Selva Central that were occupied first present high coefficients of land-use intensity with respect to those reported for the upper Huallaga Valley should not be taken as evidence that there is a more rational use of resources in the region. On the contrary, far from indicating a truly intensive land use — which would require actions aimed at protecting and regenerating the resource base — the high coefficients of land-use intensity found in the region indicate that its soils are being overexploited. The consequences of this trend will be analyzed in the next chapter.

6

ECONOMIC ARTICULATION AND ENVIRONMENTAL DETERIORATION

Constant expansion of economic frontiers over nearly a century and a half has had a negative impact on the natural resources of the Selva Central. In the present chapter we analyze the progressive deterioration of the resource base from the perspective of the effects caused by agropastoral activities and timber extraction. Like the rest of the Amazonian region, the Selva Central is a fragile ecosystem. Nevertheless, it is not homogeneous ecologically. Thus, although certain patterns of production and resource use have become generalized, the extent of their impact on the environment varies, as a function both of preexisting natural conditions and of the specific forms and rates of disturbance and occupation taking place in different areas. We begin by briefly presenting the general ecological conditions of these areas. We then evaluate and discuss the impact that the predominant forms of resource exploitation have had in the region. Finally, to complement this general view with a more detailed close-up of these processes, we present a case study of the Kivinaki zone in the central Perené Valley. We use information from aerial photographs and land records to demonstrate the interrelationships among the several variables that determine the nature, pace, and degree of environmental deterioration from a diachronic perspective.

The analysis of this theme assumes that (1) although coffee and fruit cultivation has a lesser immediate impact on soils than other patterns of production, in the long term it has a negative impact on the resource base; (2) the functional linkage between logging and agriculture leads to the continual incorporation of land unsuitable for agriculture into production, with serious consequences in terms of erosion and soil degradation; and (3) the intense demographic pressure on valuable land leads to overexploitation of available resources, not only as a

Table 6.1. Population Density, 1990

Province	Area (km^2)	Population[a]	Population density[b]
Chanchamayo	4,723	158,274	33.5
Satipo	19,431	123,533	6.4
Oxapampa	18,673	66,025	3.5
Selva Central	42,827	347,832	8.1

Sources: Maletta and Bardales n.d.: vol. 1; Ministerio de la Presidencia 1989.

[a]We estimated 1990 population figures by applying the 1972–1981 cumulative rates of population growth to the 1981 census figures.

[b]Population density is calculated as number of inhabitants per square kilometer.

result of the scarcity of land but also as a result of a scarcity of capital that makes it virtually impossible for minifundiary producers to modernize their operations.

It can thus be asserted that the patterns of occupation and production that characterize the colonization of the Selva Central have imposed serious constraints on the region's possibilities of attaining a sustained development. The impact of these patterns can currently be perceived in areas that have been occupied for the longest periods of time, offering a dramatic portrait of the future of the region's economy. Exploiting those areas within the region that have yet to be made "valuable" is no solution in the face of the present degradation process, which in the long term will have an even greater impact because of the exponential increase in environmental damage.

ECOLOGICAL CHARACTERISTICS OF THE SELVA CENTRAL

The Selva Central, as defined in this study, has a total area of 42,827 square kilometers (Table 6.1). This area is largely a part of what has been called the *selva alta,* the region of tropical forest that is located on the eastern slopes of the Andean range, between 400 and 2,500 meters above sea level. As a result of its location on the Andean piedmont, the Selva Central presents an irregular landscape, where valleys alternate with mountain ranges, including the San Carlos massif and the Yanachaga, San Matías, and Sira ranges.

Within the region, Joseph Tosi (1960) has identified four types of ecological formations: dry tropical forest, humid subtropical forest, very humid subtropical

Table 6.2. Ecological Formations in the Selva Central

Zone	Tropical dry forest	Subtropical wet forest	Subtropical very humid forest	Tropical humid forest
Oxapampa-Villa Rica	-	+	+	+
Pichis-Palcazu	-	-	+	+
Chanchamayo	-	-	+	+
Perené	+	+	-	-
Satipo	-	-	-	+
Ene	+	-	-	-
Tambo	+	+	-	+

Source: SINAMOS 1975: 21.

Note: + = presence; - = absence.

forest, and humid tropical forest. Thus, the Selva Central is formed by a mosaic of ecological areas that present different advantages and limitations to the development of economic activities (Table 6.2).

The dry tropical forest formation includes the Ene, Tambo, and lower Perené river basins. Because of its moderate levels of precipitation (around 2,000 millimeters per year), distributed more or less uniformly throughout the year, and moderately cool temperatures, these valleys are considered to have an average potential for agropastoral activities.

The humid subtropical forest formation is found in the upper reaches of the Perené Valley, in some areas of the left bank of the Tambo River, and on the northern flanks of the San Carlos massif in the Oxapampa-Villa Rica area. Part of this area consists of a combination of forest and grassland. Because of its location at more than 700-1,000 meters above sea level, this formation includes a rugged area with slopes as steep as 70 degrees. This, and the relatively high level of rainfall (2,000-4,500 millimeters per year), makes its soils highly susceptible to erosion. In addition, these soils tend to be moderately acid to acid.

The very humid subtropical forest is found in some parts of the Oxapampa-Villa Rica, Pichis, and Palcazu valleys, at altitudes from 600 to 1,700 meters above sea level. This formation is composed of very dissected land. High precipitation (up to 6,000 millimeters per year) and relatively low average annual temperatures (19°C) result in reduced evapotranspiration. Therefore, 60 percent of the precipitation ends up as surface runoff and leads to a high erosion rate in deforested areas.

Finally, the humid tropical forest is found in the areas of lower altitude (less than 600-700 meters above sea level) in the Chanchamayo, Satipo, Oxapampa, Villa Rica, Pichis, Palcazu, and Tambo valleys. High levels of rainfall here are compensated for by high temperatures (around 25°C), which favor evapotrans-

Table 6.3. Distribution of Land According to Physiographic
Units in the Perené-Satipo-Ene Zone

Physiographic unit	Vernacular categories	% of total area
Alluvial terraces	*Pampas*	10
Low hills	*Faldas*	20
Medium to high hills	*Laderas cultivables*	35
Mountainous areas	*Laderas no cultivables*	35

Sources: Shoemaker 1981: 48; adapted by the authors according to the classification
given in Aguila 1983.

piration and reduce the washing action on soils in deforested areas. The zone
presents areas of alluvial deposits, high terraces, and gentle rolling hills suitable
for the development of agropastoral activities.

The landscape in the region consists of three physiographic units: alluvial
terraces, hills (low, moderate, and high), and mountain ranges (Aguila 1984: 17).
The alluvial terraces, known locally as *pampas,* are located in valley bottoms in
areas of flat or gently undulating topography with a 1 degree slope. Their deep,
medium-grained, well-drained soils, with a pH between 4.6 and 7.0, are considered among the most fertile in the region; they are also the rarest soil type in
the Selva Central. Because of the high agronomic value of these soils, they are
the first to be occupied. The low foothills, known locally as *faldas,* have gentle
slopes of no more than 20–30 degrees. Their fairly deep, good-textured, well-
drained soils vary in fertility. The hills of medium and high altitude with slopes
of more than 30 degrees are known as *laderas.* The soils in these areas are also
not uniformly fertile: they tend to be acid and to support a limited selection of
crops where tree cover has not been completely eliminated. Finally, because of
their steep slopes, the highest and roughest mountainous areas are unsuitable for
agriculture or even timber extraction because deforestation exposes readily erod-
able soils and tends to produce landslides, leaving the bedrock exposed.

In Table 6.3, we present the percentage distribution of these physiographic
units in the Perené-Satipo-Ene area according to a study conducted by ONERN
in 1962. The best land in this region represents only 30 percent of the total,
whereas most of the area consists of land with limited or no agronomic value
because of its low fertility, acidity, or steep slopes. As a result of the physiographic
configuration of the region, most of the valleys are long and narrow. In the
Chanchamayo Valley, for example, 90 percent of the land used for agriculture is
located on *laderas* with slopes ranging from 25 degrees to more than 70 degrees
(Recharte n.d.: 106).

Information about the distribution of soils according to their use capacity

Table 6.4. Distribution of Area According to Soil Type and Zone

Soil type[a]	Satipo–Chanchamayo		Oxapampa		Palcazu		Pichis		Selva Central	
	Area	%	Area	%	Area	%	Area	%	Area	%
A soil	17,769	2.6	3,864	0.8	5,802	1.4	14,900	2.4	42,335	1.9
C soil	45,178	6.6	9,227	1.8	42,882	10.9	59,900	9.8	157,187	7.2
P soil	11,594	1.7	34,850	6.7	22,502	5.7	80,400	13.2	149,346	6.7
A, C, and P soils	74,541	10.9	47,941	9.3	71,186	18.0	155,200	25.4	348,868	15.8
F soil	212,091	31.2	363,218	70.8	68,334	17.3	221,900	36.4	865,543	39.4
X soil	393,466	57.8	101,880	19.8	254,523	64.6	232,700	38.1	982,569	44.7
F and X soils	605,557	89.0	465,098	90.6	322,857	81.9	454,600	74.5	1,848,112	84.1
All soils	680,098	100.0	513,039	100.0	394,043	100.0	609,800	100.0	2,196,980	100.0

Source: Rivadeneira Cotera 1986.

Note: Area measurements are given in hectares.

[a]Soil types are as follows:
  A = suitable for annual crops.
  C = suitable for perennial agricultural crops.
  P = suitable for pastures.
  F = suitable for timber extraction.
  X = protected land.

provides us with a more comprehensive view of their agricultural and timber potential. Unfortunately, as both Tello (1981) and Dourojeanni (1990) point out, evaluation of Amazonian soils and, in particular, of soils in the Selva Central has yielded very disparate results, not only because of technical and methodological difficulties but also because of the interference of political interests that affect their interpretation. In this context, the information presented in Table 6.4 seems to be the most reliable, insofar as it results from intensive research on the use capacity of soils in four areas, which comprise a total of 2,196,980 hectares, or 51 percent of the total area of the Selva Central.

As shown in this table, land that is suitable for agropastoral activities represents only 16 percent of the total land in the sample, with values ranging from 9 percent for the Oxapampa-Villa Rica area to over 25 percent for the Pichis Valley. These figures are similar, although a bit more optimistic, to those given in the Soil Classification Map produced by ONERN (1982) for the Selva Central. On the basis of an estimated total area of 4,270,000 hectares, ONERN concludes that only 11 percent of the land is suitable for agropastoral activities, whereas 89 percent is suitable for timber extraction or is not suitable for any exploitation, being classified as areas that should be protected (Map 6.1).

It is important to note that the system applied by ONERN to classify soils according to use capacity is based not only on characteristics of the soils themselves but also on currently existing technologies and production systems. Thus, both the application of new technologies and progressive soil deterioration could redefine this view of regional resources in the near future.

THE ENVIRONMENTAL IMPACT OF AGROPASTORAL AND LOGGING ACTIVITIES

On the basis of the description of the physiographic conditions of forest types in the Selva Central and on soil classification according to its use capacity, there are two factors that we will consider here in order to evaluate environmental deterioration: first, the degree of disturbance of ground cover, and second, the ways in which previously analyzed land-use patterns affect the ground cover.

No general evaluation of the current level of ground-cover disturbance in the Selva Central and its surroundings is available. The most recent study, conducted in 1982 by the Universidad Nacional Agraria-La Molina (UNA 1982), refers specifically to the Chanchamayo-Satipo area but does not include the Pangoa, Ene, or Tambo areas to the east. The province of Oxapampa as a whole has not been the object of such an assessment. The environmental impact of economic activity has only been evaluated in its Palcazu and Pichis valleys.

The evaluation of Chanchamayo-Satipo by the Universidad Nacional Agraria, which covers an area of 630,098 hectares, reveals the presence of very extensive areas (41 percent of the total area) that have been subject to conditions of severe disturbance, as a result of both agropastoral activity and logging. Of this extremely disturbed area, 49.6 percent is used for agricultural purposes and includes land planted in annual and perennial crops, pastureland, fallow land, and areas abandoned as a result of soil degradation, whereas 50.4 percent was disturbed exclusively by logging activities. This study concludes that, in these extremely disturbed areas, forests in their original state are practically nonexistent, although certain forested areas retain some logging potential. The areas that are partially affected by agropastoral activity and where there is reduced logging disturbance represent 35 percent of the total area that was evaluated, whereas areas of limited disturbance represent only 24 percent (Table 6.5).

In terms of specific effects on existing forests, in the study area 69 percent of the forested area was extremely disturbed, whereas 31 percent was little disturbed. These distinctions were based on an estimate of the potential volume of timber per hectare (UNA 1982). In summary, the evaluation of the Chanchamayo-Satipo area shows that, although the degree of intervention in the forests

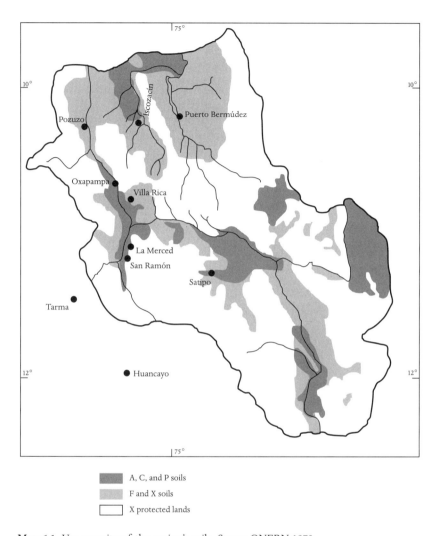

Map 6.1. Use capacity of the region's soils. *Source:* ONERN 1970.

of the Selva Central is not the same everywhere, at least in this area a high proportion of the land has been disturbed and directly affected by agricultural and logging activities. Though timber extraction does not imply massive deforestation, if we consider the close ties between logging and agriculture, we can conclude that, in the long term, the majority of the areas affected by logging will eventually be completely deforested and will be occupied by colonists involved in agricultural production.

To estimate the impact of colonist occupation, various authors have developed

Table 6.5. Distribution of Area According
to Degree of Human Disturbance in
Chanchamayo and Satipo, 1982

Degree of disturbance	Area (hectares)	% of total area
Severe	260,860	41.4
Moderate	219,274	34.8
Light	149,964	23.8

Source: UNA 1982: Table 10.

Note: Human disturbance includes agropastoral and forestry-related activities.

models that simulate the degree of forest disturbance (Dancé 1979; Dourojeanni
1990; Agreda n.d.). These simulations and calculations tend to be based on
generic models of land use, models that consider "shifting agriculture" the predominant production system in the Amazonian region. Based on this premise
and on a detailed study by Dourojeanni (1981a) in the Huallaga area,
Dourojeanni (1990) and Agreda (n.d.) have extrapolated the information obtained to construct a simulation model applicable to the entire Amazon and thus
to estimate the area affected and the degree of deforestation in the region. This
model employed the following assumptions: of the total agricultural area, (1) 10
percent is composed of areas of permanent agriculture without fallowing (includes both annual and perennial crops); (2) 40 percent is under rotation, with
fallow periods of 2-7 years for every 1 to 3 years of use; and (3) 50 percent
corresponds to areas worked under a pattern of shifting agriculture, that is, are
used for 3 to 4 years and then abandoned, becoming fallow land that eventually
regenerates as secondary forest.[9]

Based on the assumption that shifting agriculture is the prevailing pattern of
land use in the Amazon basin, most authors agree with the calculations provided
by Dourojeanni (1990: 81), who estimates that for every 4 hectares that are deforested, 1 is under actual cultivation and 3 are abandoned, either as fallow land or
as land in a state of complete deterioration. Without questioning the validity of
Dourojeanni's data for the Huallaga Valley, it is necessary to remember that the
Selva Central differs because of the predominance of an agriculture based on
perennial crops and pastures, which, as we have seen, has given rise to very specific
land-use patterns. In this sense, the model developed by Dourojeanni to evaluate
the expansion of the agricultural frontier and its impact in terms of deforestation
does not apply to the Selva Central, as we anticipated in the preceding chapter. In
fact, on the agricultural units in Chanchamayo and Satipo, as well as in Oxapampa,

the average ratio of fallow to cultivated land is the inverse of that proposed by Dourojeanni. That is, for every 4 hectares that are cut, 3 are in production and only 1 is lying fallow or is abandoned (see Table 5.2).

In the Selva Central, extreme property fragmentation has led to an intensification of land use but is also responsible for the overexploitation of soils. Land-use intensification is not often accompanied by management practices that could contribute to recovering soil nutrients or to alleviating erosion on steep slopes.

At the same time, given the complementary nature of agropastoral and logging activities, areas that are deforested by logging and "made valuable" by the construction of logging roads tend to be almost immediately incorporated into agricultural activity, no matter the actual capacity of its soils. This deterioration process is further accelerated by logging activities, which, after exhausting the most accessible forests, begin to exploit areas farther from the valley floor in the higher, more steeply sloping areas of the region.

Thus, the low proportion of land suitable for agropastoral activities, the excessive demographic pressure on valuable land, the often inadequate agricultural practices, and the spatial overlapping of agropastoral and logging activities have given rise to two closely related phenomena, which together have serious consequences for the environment in the Selva Central: (1) the generalized use of areas unsuitable for agriculture, and (2) the progressive exhaustion and erosion of soils under agropastoral use. The second phenomenon has already been substantiated in the previous chapter and is quantified in Table 5.11 and Figure 5.1.

The very frequent use of land unsuitable for agriculture may be appreciated in Table 6.6. On the basis of a survey conducted among farmers in the Selva Central, the German Forestry and Agroforestry Project of the Selva Central established that, in 1983, an extremely high proportion of the cultivated area in the region—in use as agricultural land or pastureland—was in lands classified by ONERN as suitable only for forestry-related activities (type F soils) or as land to be protected (type X soils) (Brack et al. n.d.: 24-28). Breaking this information down to the provincial level, one finds that more than 60 percent of the cultivated area in Chanchamayo occupies land unsuitable for agriculture, whereas in Oxapampa, it is almost 40 percent, and in Satipo, almost 20 percent.[10]

Data for the province of Chanchamayo show that the districts of San Ramón, Chanchamayo, and Vitoc present the highest percentages of cultivated area on soils classified as F and X. This information is consistent with the fact that these areas have been occupied for the longest periods of time and are those with higher relative land "value," in an economic, not agronomic, sense. In turn, in the province of Oxapampa, in all of the districts that have been occupied for an extended period of time or that, since the 1950s, have been the object of major migratory influxes, 40 percent of the area under cultivation occupies soils of type

Table 6.6. Distribution of Cultivated Area
According to Soil Type and District, 1983

Province and district	% cultivated in F and X soils	% cultivated in A, C, and P soils
Chanchamayo		
San Ramón	63	37
Chanchamayo	69	31
Vitoc	71	29
San Luis de Shuaro	56	44
Pichanaki-Perené	51	49
All 5 districts	62	38
Oxapampa		
Oxapampa	40	60
Chontabamba	45	55
Huancabamba	50	50
Pozuzo	60	40
Villa Rica	46	54
Puerto Bermúdez	10	90
Palcazu	10	90
All 7 districts	37	63
Satipo	19	81

Source: Brack et al. n.d.: Tables 1, 3, and 6.

Note: Soil types are as defined in footnote to Table 6.4.

F or X. In the Palcazu and Pichis valleys, which have been subject to less massive demographic pressure and which have a greater proportion of land suitable for agriculture, Brack et al. (n.d.) found that 10 percent of land under cultivation occupies soils classified as F or X. Unfortunately, information at the district level for Satipo Province is unavailable.

Brack et al. (n.d.: 44) estimate that in the Selva Central most of the cultivated area in types F and X soils is planted in perennial or semiperennial crops, though pastures and annual crops can also be found (Table 6.7). Their study also indicates that 65 percent of the coffee plantations in the region are located on these types of soils, which means that as many as 30,000 hectares of coffee could be located on land that is inappropriate for its cultivation. This may be one of the principal factors that explains the reduction in the average yield of coffee plantations in the region. Because the livelihood of colonist families, as well as of the regional economy, is based on coffee production, these data are of great economic significance. In addition, this source indicates that the same is true for 55 percent of the land planted in citrus fruits, the most important commercial crops after

Table 6.7. Distribution of Cultivated Area
According to Soil Type and Crop in the Selva
Central, 1983

Crop	% in F soils	% in X soils	% in A, C, and P soils
Banana	20	10	70
Citrus crops	35	20	45
Coffee	50	15	35
Corn	30	30	40
Manioc	32	23	45
Papaya	40	20	40
Pasture	18	13	69
Pineapple	60	40	0
Potato	20	0	80
Rocoto chili	32	41	27

Source: Brack et al. n.d.: Table 14.

Note: Soil types are as defined in footnote to Table 6.4.

coffee, and 31 percent of the pastureland. The finding that a large proportion of the area planted in pineapple, corn, and manioc (crops that are planted without tree cover) consists of F and X soils is also of great concern.

Since we do not know the methodology employed by Brack et al. to project their survey results, we must interpret these data cautiously. However, they allow us to consider one of the fundamental problems that settlement in the Selva Central has brought with it. The high percentage of cultivated area with soils classified by ONERN as F and X is undoubtedly associated with major demographic pressure on the land and with the process of minifundization, which encourage colonists to make use of available "valuable lands," including some that were granted to them temporarily for timber extraction under forest contracts.

Although we cannot disregard the influence of cultural or cognitive factors, or the effects of the use of technologies adapted to other environments, the explanation of the destructive nature of the Andean colonists' economic practices cannot be reduced to such variables. In fact, in some native communities of the Selva Central, where various studies have shown that the population possesses detailed knowledge of the land and of the requirements of various crops (Salick n.d.), similar situations occur, which demonstrates that the primary factor that explains this situation is demographic pressure on allocated land. Thus, Smith (1983: 75) found that in the Palcazu, where communal indigenous lands have become insufficient as a result of population growth and the development of extensive cattle ranching, some communities have also been forced to cultivate crops on F and X soils.

Prolonged occupation and land use, in combination with steep slopes, average and high rainfall, and inappropriate use of soils, has given rise to a severe process of soil erosion in the Selva Central, as various studies have shown (Felipe-Morales et al. 1978; Alegre 1978). In the San Ramón area, Alegre (1978: 73) found that as a result of topsoil erosion, 119 metric tons of soil per hectare per year were lost on bare soils and 148 metric tons per hectare per year were lost from fallow land repeatedly used for the cultivation of annual crops, such as corn, potatoes, and beans. Erosion results in the loss of significant quantities of nutrients, particularly nitrogen, calcium, potassium, and magnesium, elements that are generally deficient in the soils of the region.

It is worth noting that, although the adoption of certain techniques may help to reduce erosion on slopes, the cost of replacing lost nutrients with the use of fertilizers is extremely high for owners of small agricultural units. The cost of replacing soil nutrients at a rate corresponding to the erosion rates mentioned has been calculated to be US$6.50 per metric ton of soil lost, that is, between US$773 and $962 per hectare per year (Rivadeneira 1986:11). Poor colonist farmers, who tend to be settled in the steepest areas, lack the capital to make this sort of investment. The burning of stubble, brief intervals between periods of cultivation, and pineapple production are, in these cases, the prelude to the abandonment of lots that are completely degraded. In the case of coffee plots in soils unsuitable for agriculture, declining production is barely attenuated by the addition of nitrogen by shade trees (*Inga* spp.) and by the practices of hilling and replacing old plants with young ones. Thus, at a certain point, yields become so low that it is no longer worthwhile to invest labor for harvest. In the Selva Central it is this process, rather than the practice of shifting agriculture (which is often considered the main cause of deforestation), that leads to the exhaustion and abandonment of agricultural plots.

It is not surprising to find, therefore, as we have seen in the previous chapter, that in some agricultural units there are areas that appear to be fallow land but that actually have completely lost their fertility and productive capacity. Soil deterioration in these cases is so severe that not even adequate access to roads justifies their use for agriculture. As we have seen, the percentage of these holdings is significantly high in the size class of 5 to less than 10 hectares in the three earliest and continuously occupied districts in the province of Chanchamayo, ranging from 14 percent to 24 percent (see Table 5.10).

The soil deterioration resulting from the interaction of occupation, deforestation, and soil erosion on land unsuitable for agriculture has a serious impact on the entire environment of the region to the extent that they affect evapotranspiration and run-off, which in turn affect rainfall and the frequency of landslides. Such disturbances ought to be evaluated in cost-benefit terms and in terms of opportunity cost, in order to internalize the environmental costs that are incurred in the exploitation of the region's resources, as has been proposed by Christensen (1989), Daly (1990), and Page (1990), among others. Environmental deterioration not only affects the income of producers by reducing the yield and profitability of their crops but also results in enormous losses in terms of the irreversible destruction of certain natural resources and the failure to make good use of the public and private investment required to incorporate land and expand the agricultural frontier. Thus, environmental damage ought to be incorporated in calculations of the feasibility and economic evaluation of colonization projects, not only as a lateral and "qualitative" variable but also in terms of its real economic costs.

ENVIRONMENTAL DETERIORATION IN KIVINAKI: A CASE STUDY

To illustrate more clearly the factors that coalesce to accelerate environmental deterioration, in this final section we will analyze in greater detail the impact that agropastoral and logging activities have had on an area located halfway down the Perené Valley: the Kivinaki zone. This case study will also enable us to determine the pace of the deforestation process along a temporal axis of more than 30 years.

The selection of the Kivinaki zone was based on the following criteria:(1) there are aerial photographic records for this area, taken both before (1957) and after (1977 and 1983) the opening of the Carretera Marginal; (2) the zone was included in the land-registration program conducted between 1984 and 1987 by the Satipo-Chanchamayo Rural Development Program of the Pichis-Palcazu Special Project, from which detailed information regarding soil classification, land-tenure structure, and current land use is available; and (3) thanks to the activities of the Land Registration Program of the Pichis-Palcazu Special Project, it was possible to establish a spatial relationship between the soil-classification information and maps based on 1983 photographs. Because of the opportunity to combine all of this information, the Kivinaki zone appeared to be an ideal case for determining the pace and type of environmental deterioration that had occurred in the Selva Central as a result of the colonization process.

Note that the Kivinaki zone is neither one of the oldest occupied zones, such as the districts of San Ramón or Chanchamayo, nor one of the most recently opened zones, such as the districts of Palcazu or Puerto Bermúdez. Therefore, our findings regarding environmental impact will reflect an intermediate situation and thus may be taken as a reference point for the entire region.

The area that we selected corresponds to that delimited by aerial photograph 343/83-A/19 taken by the National Aerial Photography Service in October 1983 (see Figure 6.3). This aerial photograph has been used as a spatial reference point to reconstruct not only the 1957 and 1977 aerial images but also the historical, demographic, and land-tenure and land-use information from the other sources mentioned.

The Kivinaki zone is located in the central Perené Valley in the district of Perené. Until the 1950s this area was almost exclusively inhabited by Ashaninka families, many of whom worked as coffee harvesters in the Perene Colony and resided temporarily in Adventist missions during the 1920s to 1940s. With the increased influx of colonists during the 1950s, this local indigenous population gathered in the present-day native communities of Kivinaki and Pumpuriani, located on the right bank of the Perené River, and in Bajo Chirani and Santa Rosa de Ubiriki, located on its left bank (see Map 6.2). Until the 1950s, Kivinaki had no road connection with Chanchamayo. At the end of that decade, construction began on a road that connected Quimirí, in the Chanchamayo Valley, with the Marankiari zone, along the right bank of the upper Perené River. The rise in coffee prices and a dispute over the Peruvian Corporation's property rights attracted many colonists to the upper Perené Valley, who then took advantage of the existence of this section of the road to settle in the area and advance toward the east. Kivinaki was among the areas occupied by these colonists.

When the construction of the La Merced–Satipo road was initiated in the 1960s, the Perené Valley became the new forest reserve in the Selva Central, resulting in a sudden increase in the volume of timber extracted and processed by the sawmills in the forestry district of San Ramón beginning in this period (see Table 3.8). This advance of the logging front meant the opening of new logging roads into the Kivinaki zone, which were constructed along three streams that flow into the Perené: the Pumpuriani, the Potochiari, and the Kivinaki. The roads attracted more colonist families, who settled on Ashaninka land. As a consequence, even before the road that was to unite Satipo and La Merced was finished, there were already numerous colonists in the Kivinaki zone who were involved in coffee production. At the same time, some Ashaninka families began to produce coffee, drawing on their experience as laborers in the Perene Colony and taking advantage of the new opportunity to sell their produce to intermediaries who soon arrived in the area. Currently, there are 93 agricultural units belonging to colonists distributed among three sectors: Pumpuriani, Potochari, and Kivinaki. In addition, there are 175 Ashaninka fam-

Table 6.8. Distribution of Area Granted to Colonists According to Soil Type and Sector in the Kivinaki Zone, 1987

Sector	% in A soils	% in C soils	% in P soils	% in F soils	% in X soils	% in all soil types
Pumpuriani	0.0	40.3	0.0	17.9	41.8	100.0
Potochari	0.0	44.5	1.2	31.5	22.8	100.0
Kivinaki	10.9	53.5	4.9	16.1	14.6	100.0
All 3 sectors	4.1	47.2	2.3	23.5	22.9	100.0

Source: PDR Chanchamayo-Satipo 1984-1987.

Note: Soil types are as defined in footnote to Table 6.4.

ilies living in the native communities of Pumpuriani, Kivinaki, Bajo Chirani, and Santa Rosa de Ubiriki.

Ecological Characteristics, Production, and Land-Tenure Structure

In the context of the Selva Central, the Kivinaki zone is a relatively privileged area: 54 percent of the land that has been appropriated to colonists is classified as being suitable for agropastoral activities (type A, C, and P soils), type C soils, those suitable for perennial crops, being the most common (Table 6.8).

Kivinaki's economic profile is consistent with that of the region. Perennial crops represent 98 percent of the total cultivated area, and coffee and fruit are the predominant crops for 98 percent of the agricultural units in the zone. Pastureland accounts for only an infinitesimal proportion of the cultivated area, corresponding, in fact, to a single agricultural unit. As is evident from the high proportion of perennial crops, the area in annual crops is extremely limited, revealing the enormous dependence that the majority of colonist families have on the market to supply their needs for food (Table 6.9).

Given that very few agricultural units registered annual crops, it is not surprising that 52 percent of them had no fallow land (Table 6.10). It is surprising, however, that in spite of the above, fallow land represents 31 percent of colonist landholdings in Kivinaki. Unfortunately, on the basis of available information, it is impossible to determine the current condition of this fallow land and how it is used. However, from aerial photographs it seems evident that the majority of fallow lands are not in the process of regeneration; rather, they are located in areas with deteriorated soils that, because of their loss of fertility, have been completely abandoned by farmers (see Figure 6.3 and Map 6.2). In Kivinaki, this situation seems to be associated with the high proportion of area under cultivation in types F and X soils. Given that only 2 of the 93 agricultural units owned by colonists in this zone include

Table 6.9. Distribution of Cultivated Area According to Crop in the Kivinaki Zone, 1988

Crop type	Area cultivated	% of total area cultivated	Average area cultivated per AU	% of AUs[a]
Annual crops	15.39	1.8	1.1	0.9
Perennial agricultural crops	827.24	97.8	9.0	98.0
Pastures (natural and cultivated)	3.06	0.4	3.1	1.1
All types	845.69	100.0	9.1	100.0

Source: PDR Chanchamayo-Satipo 1987; data elaborated by the authors.

Notes: AU denotes agricultural unit. Area measurements are given in hectares.

[a]The percentage of agricultural units in which a type of crop predominates.

patches of primary forest, current fallow lands, no matter how degraded they may be, constitute the only areas available for crop rotation. In time, this will undoubtedly lead to the overexploitation and irreversible depletion of local soils.

Kivinaki is a relatively recently colonized zone within Chanchamayo Province, where, accordingly, land fragmentation has been less accentuated (Table 6.11). Nevertheless, 57 percent of colonists' agricultural units have areas of less than 10 hectares, whereas 25 percent have less than 5 hectares. Although these figures are smaller than those from districts in the province that were occupied earlier — such as the district of Chanchamayo, which shows percentages of 63 percent and 34 percent for these two size classes — they show that Kivinaki is also undergoing a process of progressive minifundization.

However, colonists' agricultural units in Kivinaki still exhibit some of the characteristics of more recently occupied but already well-established areas. Thus, in this zone, the average area in perennial crops per agricultural unit is higher than that recorded for the provinces of Satipo and Chanchamayo taken together: 9.0 hectares versus 7.2 hectares (see Tables 5.4 and 6.9). This situation could change in the near future because of the extreme scarcity of primary and secondary forests and reuseable fallow land.

As we will see in the following chapters, in the Selva Central, the fragmentation characteristic of the land-tenure structure of the colonist sector has been replicated within the native communities. Thus, in the communities of Kivinaki and Bajo Chirani, the average area per family is only slightly above the extreme-*minifundio* limit, whereas in the community of Pumpuriani the average per family is barely above that of the *minifundio* (Table 6.12).

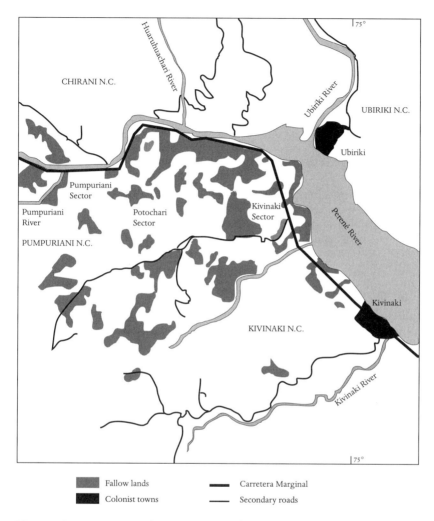

Map 6.2. Access routes, population centers, and fallow lands in the Kivinaki zone, 1987. *Source:* Programa de Catastro PEPP: Sheet 18-495-8795 152/3.

Even so, given that the average area cultivated per Ashaninka family is smaller than that of the colonists (see Chapter 8), there are still forested areas located on communal land. This can be appreciated in Figures 6.3 and 6.6. According to Swenson (1986b: 9), Pumpuriani, Bajo Chirani, and Santa Rosa de Ubiriki are communities where coffee accounts for most of the cultivated area. In the community of Kivinaki, which is not included in Swenson's sample, coffee is also the predominant crop.

Table 6.10. Percentage of Forested and Fallow Area in Colonists' Agricultural Units in the Kivinaki Zone, 1987

Type of land	Area (hectares)	% of area of AUs	% of AUs[a]
Fallow	363.0	29.9	48.4
Forested	7.1	0.6	2.1
All types	370.1	30.5	—[b]

Source: PDR Chanchamayo–Satipo 1987; data elaborated by the authors.

Note: AU denotes agricultural unit.

[a]Percentage of colonists' agricultural units with fallow or forested area.

[b]Not applicable.

Signs of Environmental Disorder in Kivinaki

Evidence of resource deterioration in Kivinaki is less visible than in areas occupied for longer periods of time, where extensive sloping areas and hill tops not only are denuded but have produced major landslides. However, after nearly 30 years of continuous occupation, the replication of certain patterns of soil and forest exploitation typical of areas of long-term occupation can already be observed. As in the rest of the Selva Central, in Kivinaki we find that a high percentage of the cultivated and fallow areas are located on land unsuitable for agriculture. There seem to be two factors that contribute to this phenomenon. The first is that, because land titling took place years after the area was completely occupied but before the government decided to grant in property only land suitable for agropastoral activities, colonist lots currently include areas classified as appropriate only for logging or as land that should be protected. The second factor is the high proportion of minifundiary agricultural units, which forces colonists to exploit even those portions of their lots that have poor soils.

Thus, the long-overdue land-titling program has sanctioned the structure of land-tenure and land-use patterns that developed in the absence of State intervention. This is true both for small as well as for medium-sized agricultural units. Thus we find that, in 1987, 46 percent of the cultivated area in the colonists' agricultural units in the Kivinaki zone occupied soils classified as F or X (Table 6.8). This percentage is similar to the 51 percent reported by Brack et al. (n.d.: 26) for the Pichanaki–Perené area in 1983.

The high proportion of cultivated area on F or X soils and the high incidence of fallow land in the Kivinaki zone (with an average of 4 hectares per agricultural

Table 6.11. Distribution of
Colonists' Agricultural Units in the
Kivinaki Zone, 1987

Size class (hectares) of holding	No. of AUs	% of all AUs
0 to <5	23	24.7
5 to <10	30	32.2
10 to <20	22	23.6
20 to <30	10	10.7
30 to <50	4	4.4
50 to <100	4	4.4
≥100	0	0.0
All size classes	93	100.0

Source: PDR Chanchamayo-Satipo 1987; data elaborated by the authors.

unit, which is surprising given the predominance of perennial crops) seem to confirm the close relationship existing between the use of soils unsuitable for agropastoral activities and the total exhaustion of certain areas, which eventually are completely abandoned. The use of land unsuitable for agriculture as a correlate of the logging activity and as a result of the lack of a timely program of legalization of land tenure has accelerated the deterioration of the resource base in Kivinaki. This is reflected in the decreasing productivity of its cultivated areas. In addition, land fragmentation resulting from the cycle of reproduction of the peasant domestic units, and the sale of plots whose productivity has decreased, tend to aggravate the overexploitation of the area's resources.

To determine the rate of deforestation that has resulted from the agronomic practices of the colonists and, to a lesser extent, of indigenous peoples, we have turned to a comparative analysis of aerial photographs taken between 1957 and 1983. With the 1983 photo as a reference (Figure 6.3), we have identified the images corresponding to the same quadrant taken on flights by the National Aerial Photography Service in 1977 and in 1957. To adjust these images to the reference photo, it was necessary to work with more than one photograph from each of the flights, since the route and altitude of each flight were different. These photographs were carefully mounted to make them coincide with the area of the reference photo and to avoid the distortions resulting from these differences. On the basis of this work, we obtained Figures 6.1 and 6.2, which, when compared with the reference photo, offer a striking view of the evolution of the local landscape.[11] In Figure 6.1, we see the area, crossed by the Perené River,

Table 6.12. Average Titled Area per Family in Native
Communities in the Kivinaki Zone, 1989

Native community	Titled area	Area ceded in use	No. of families	Average titled area per family
Pumpuriani	478.5	0.0	45	10.6
Kivinaki	441.0	0.0	81	5.4
Bajo Chirani	214.2	141.6	37	5.8
Ubiriki	237.3	0.0	12	19.8
All 4 communities	1,371.0	141.6	175	7.8

Sources: PEPP 1986, 1987; data elaborated by the authors.

Note: Area measurements are in hectares.

flowing from left to right, as it looked in 1957. The Carretera Marginal had not yet been extended through the area, nor had logging roads been opened. In this photo the forest is only broken by small clearings—where Ashaninka settlements, their gardens, and fallow land were located—and, in some places, by fairly large areas of natural grasslands.

The second photograph, taken 20 years later (1977), corresponds to a time when the Carretera Marginal, built along the right bank of the Perené River, had linked the Satipo and Chanchamayo valleys. The advance of the colonist occupation along the axis of the Carretera Marginal and particularly in the Kivinaki sector is visible in the lower right-hand corner, where the small town of Kivinaki was established (see Map 6.2). In the lower part of the photograph one can clearly see logging roads and, along them, the colonist advance into the now-valuable land. Note that the left margin of the river, composed of extremely unstable, broken terrain, was still scarcely occupied. The colonists' agricultural units on this margin were located primarily along the shores of the Perené and Ubiriki rivers, in the upper right-hand quarter, but a logging road is already visible near the Huaruhuachari stream, in the center of the top half of the photo.

The third and most recent photograph (1983) exceeds all predictions based on the previous images. It becomes difficult to locate the areas of virgin forest and of partially recovered secondary forest. A large part of the image is covered by small cultivated plots and of cleared but uncultivated areas, especially along the right margin of the Perené River. Also, the town of Kivinaki has expanded and become more densely populated. Along the left bank, where several logging roads are visible, we observe a situation similar to that which was encountered along the right bank in 1977.

To determine the rate of deforestation in the Kivinaki zone during the period

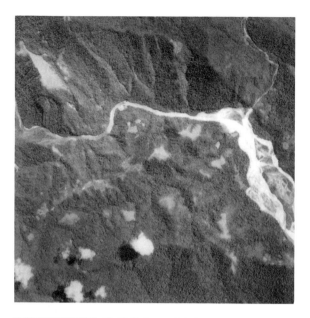

Figure 6.1 (top). Aerial photograph of Kivinaki zone, 1957. *Source:* Servicio Aerofotográfico Nacional, August 1957 (Photos 8700-167 and 8700-168).
Figure 6.2 (bottom). Aerial photograph of Kivinaki zone, 1977. *Source:* Servicio Aerofotográfico Nacional, May 1977 (Photos 4333, 4334, 4347, and 4348).

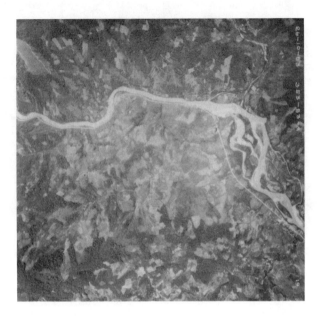

Figure 6.3. Aerial photograph of Kivinaki zone, 1983. *Source:* Servicio Aerofotográfico Nacional, October 1983 (Photo 353-83-A).

1957–1983, in our analysis of the aerial photographs we distinguished between forested areas and areas without forest cover (Figures 6.4, 6.5, and 6.6). Areas without forest cover include not only cultivated areas and fallow land but also natural grasslands and bodies of water. The results of this procedure are shown in Table 6.13.

These data are impressive. Whereas, in 1957, 86 percent of the area analyzed was forested, in 1983 this was reduced to merely 24 percent of the total area. We stress that the 1957 figure does not necessarily imply that 14 percent of the selected area had already been "deforested," because within this percentage bodies of water are included (8 percent of the selected area) along with natural grasslands. In other words, the actual deforested area, resulting from the agricultural activities of the Ashaninka in the area, was extremely limited, representing not more than 6 percent of the total area.

If we compare the information provided in these three photographs, we find a clear acceleration in the deforestation rate during the short period that separates the last two photographs. Thus, whereas between 1957 and 1977 the forested area shrank by 27 percent, between 1977 and 1983 it was reduced by 62 percent. The overall reduction between 1957 and 1983 was 72 percent. On the basis of these data, we can calculate the annual rate of deforestation for the two intervals (Table 6.14).

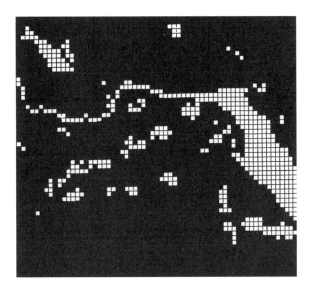

Figure 6.4 (top). Forested area (black squares) in the Kivinaki zone, 1957. *Source:* Figure 6.1.

Figure 6.5 (bottom). Forested area (black squares) in the Kivinaki zone, 1977. *Source:* Figure 6.2.

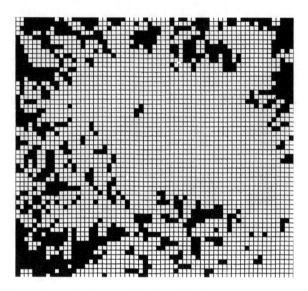

Figure 6.6. Forested area (black squares) in the Kivinaki zone, 1983. *Source:* Figure 6.3.

The annual deforestation rate for Kivinaki in the 1957-1983 period grossly exceeds the rate recorded for the entire Peruvian Amazonia in a study released by FAO/UNEP in 1981: 2.8 percent versus 0.5 percent per year (Dourojeanni 1990: 82). More serious still is the contrast between the rates of deforestation registered in the area for the periods 1957-1977 and 1977-1988: 1.3 percent and 12.4 percent per year, respectively. Both figures demonstrate that in the Selva Central, the deforestation process not only is massive but accelerates as demographic pressure on valuable land increases. Clearly, the solution to this problem does not consist of making more land valuable by building new roads. This would simply act as a short-term solution to the *minifundio* and land-shortage problems; in the medium and long term it would certainly mean the destruction of all of the tropical forest in the region.

Environmental deterioration has been an intrinsic element in the occupation of the Selva Central, in spite of the fact that it is not as acute as it could have been because of its particular pattern of production. At the local level, the destruction of natural resources is manifested in the process of erosion and irreversible loss of soil fertility, which leads to the abandonment of agricultural land in detriment to the country. It is also manifested in an increase in the occurrence of landslides, with the resulting loss of farmland, public and private investments, and even lives.

At a more global level, the effects of massive deforestation in general and the use of type F and X soils in particular have cumulative effects that accelerate the

Table 6.13. Forested and Deforested
Areas in the Kivinaki Zone

Year	% deforested area	% forested area
1957	13.8	86.2
1977	36.9	63.1
1983	76.2	23.8

Sources: Data are derived from Figures 6.1, 6.2, and 6.3.

process of environmental deterioration. Colonist producers are conscious of some of these effects, but others go unnoticed. Massive deforestation and the excessive pressure on animal resources affect not only terrestrial and arboreal wildlife populations, influencing the way trophic chains function, but also fish populations. At the same time, soils tend to lose their natural fertility and to change their texture and water-retention capability, resulting in leaching and thus the total loss of their productive potential. This, in turn, produces changes in the levels of evapotranspiration and runoff, which have repercussions that influence the environmental equilibrium (Gentry and López Parodi 1983).

Each of these occurrences has been reported in the Selva Central. And although in some cases they are irreversible phenomena, it is possible and necessary to take steps to reduce the rate of resource deterioration. These necessary steps include reducing the migratory fluxes toward the *selva alta,* which in turn requires modification of the social and economic conditions of the Andean peasants. At the same time, it is necessary to pay attention to studies that propose integrated resource management that focuses not exclusively on commercial monocultures but, rather, on the association of crops with natural vegetation or a type of vegetation that contributes to soil-nutrient recycling. Contrary to what is commonly thought, this type of integrated management would not deny opportunities for economic income to producers, forcing them to limit their activities to subsistence or very small-scale commercial production but, instead, could contribute to an increase in their income (see Brack et al. n.d.). At the same time, a qualitative rather than quantitative intensification of land use, in combination with an increase in productivity, would lead to a reduction of deforestation rates and the use of soils unsuitable for agriculture, lessening the rate of destruction of natural resources in the region.

To achieve this, it is indispensable not only to raise consciousness among colonists regarding the destructive nature of some of their economic practices but to design and disseminate commercially profitable alternatives to these prac-

Table 6.14. Annual Deforestation
Rate in the Kivinaki Zone

Period	Annual deforestation rate (%)
1957–1977	1.3
1977–1983	12.4
1957–1983, overall	2.8

Sources: Data are derived from Figures 6.4, 6.5, and
6.6.

tices through training programs. Nevertheless, for these measures to have the desired effect, it is necessary for the State to retain its role not only as regulator of land tenure but also of resource use in the region. Although excessive State intervention in the economy may result in significant distortions, when the natural resources of the country and the survival of future generations of citizens are at stake, the State cannot neglect its obligations. In the current context of State modernization, the safeguarding of natural resources of the country should take first priority among its obligations.

PART THREE

INDIGENOUS INTEGRATION

An analysis of the agrarian economy of the Selva Central would be incomplete without taking into account the forms of participation of the indigenous population in the economic and political life of the region. Both the Yanesha and the Ashaninka have played an important role in the development of the regional economy: indirectly, as laborers, and directly, as agricultural producers. In addition, one must consider the demographic significance of this sector, which represents 21 percent of the rural population in Chanchamayo and Satipo provinces, and 22 percent of the rural population of Oxapampa (Barclay et al. 1991: Appendix II.9). In spite of these two factors, the attention of regional planners and analysts has focused on the colonist sector, which explains why the economic contribution of the indigenous sector has not been adequately assessed. In Part Three, we propose to fill this gap by offering a general overview of the process of integration of the region's indigenous population.

In Chapter 7, we analyze the historical process by which "native communities" were founded. From there, we proceed to a more specific comparison of land tenure in the indigenous and colonist sectors. In Chapter 8, we analyze the various forms of participation of the indigenous peoples in the region's economy, both as peons and through commercial agricultural production. Finally, in the last chapter, we deal with the relationship between their economic and political strategies, placing special emphasis on the situation of violence that currently affects indigenous peoples in the Selva Central.

These subjects are closely related to the problem of integration or the lack thereof of the indigenous sector, which seems to be of great concern to the State and which has been used as an argument to deny their demands for land and, particularly, their requests for the expansion of their communal lands. Even now, the State continues to insist on the necessity of integrating the indigenous peoples into national life, while it continues to cite their lack of integration to justify colonization programs. In this context, "integration" is viewed by the State and the region's elite as equivalent to "producing for the market"—that is, to be integrated it is necessary to be productive. As we will see, the indigenous peoples of the Selva Central have been on the road to integration for quite some time. This, however, has not been a passive process. Rather, it has been a response to a combination of factors, among which the indigenous peoples' own desire to "become integrated" has played an important role. This has lent a particular character to their process of integration. As will become clear through an analysis of the political strategies of indigenous organizations, the objectives that this sector pursues with their strategy of economic integration do not always coincide with those advocated by the State. The response of the indigenous community to the violent situation that they currently face constitutes even clearer evidence of these differences in perspective, especially with respect to the terms in which their integration has been defined and what they are willing to accept.

7
TERRITORIAL DESPOLIATION, NATIVE COMMUNITIES, AND LAND TENURE

The Selva Central is the ancestral home of two Arawak-speaking indigenous peoples who have played an important role in the economic history of the region: the Yanesha, also known as Amuesha, with an estimated population of 5,791 in 1981; and the Ashaninka, or Campa, with an estimated population in 1981 of 32,112. The Ashaninka are further divided into several subgroups that speak different but mutually intelligible dialects and that have distinct identities. Although the languages of the Yanesha and Ashaninka are not mutually intelligible, the fact that they belong to the same linguistic family and that they occupy contiguous territories has resulted in both groups sharing numerous cultural features.

Table 7.1 and Map 7.1 show the geographic location of the Yanesha and of the Ashaninka and their subgroups. Data in the table are arranged by province and by valley. As evidenced in our description of the history of this region, these peoples are distributed across areas with extremely different colonization processes. Colonization and the expansion of the market economy have affected different groups in different ways, resulting in various means by which each has become involved in the region's economy.

The Yanesha are divided into three sectors: two in the earliest colonized areas of the provinces of Oxapampa (Oxapampa and Villa Rica valleys) and Chanchamayo (Yurinaki and Metraro zones), and a third along the Palcazu River and at its headwaters. This latter zone is one of the most recent colonization fronts and the traditional refuge for Yanesha who have been displaced from other areas by colonists. The dialect groups of the Ashaninka have suffered the same terri-

231

Table 7.1. Geographic Location of Indigenous Peoples in the Selva Central

Province and indigenous peoples	Dialect groups	Zones and valleys inhabited
Oxapampa		
Yanesha	(not applicable)	Oxapampa, Villa Rica, Cacazú, and Palcazu
Ashaninka	Ashaninka	Pichis
	Asheninka	Gran Pajonal
Chanchamayo		
Yanesha	(not applicable)	Metraro and Yurinaki
Ashaninka	Asheninka	Upper Perené
Satipo		
Ashaninka	Ashaninka	Lower Perené, Satipo, Ene, and Tambo
	Asheninka	Gran Pajonal
	Nomatsiguenga	Pangoa, Sanibeni, Anapati, and Kiatari

Source: Ribeiro and Wise 1978; data elaborated by the authors.

torial despoliation and resulting land fragmentation. Part of the Ashaninka proper are found in areas of severe colonist population pressure, such as the Satipo Valley and the central Perené Valley, whereas two other subgroups occupy areas that are relatively isolated: the Pichis, Ene, and Tambo river valleys. The case of the Asheninka dialect group is even more extreme: a segment is located in the upper Perené Valley, an area that has been colonized extensively since the 1950s, whereas another inhabits the Gran Pajonal, still one of the most inaccessible and marginal areas of the Selva Central. Finally, the Nomatsiguenga are divided into two groups, one of which inhabits the area closest to Satipo (Pangoa, Sanibeni, and Kiatari) and the other of which inhabits the Anapati area, in a territory that has only recently become an object of interest to colonists and loggers.

Their location in central and peripheral areas, or in areas of expansion, has not only resulted in different relationships with the forces and agents of the market economy but has also influenced their opportunities for access to land and natural resources. Therefore, we cannot speak of a generic "indigenous economy" or "native community." The reality of the indigenous peoples in the Selva Central is not homogeneous and, therefore, requires a case-by-case analysis of specific geographic areas. However, one can generally assert that all of the indigenous peoples of the Selva Central have experienced or are currently experiencing a transition from a primarily subsistence economy to an economy that combines subsistence production with seasonal sale of labor, and from there to a peasant economy that combines subsistence with commercial production.

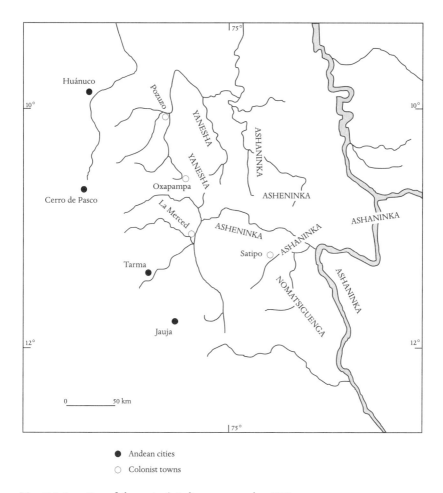

Map 7.1. Location of the region's indigenous peoples, 1988.

THE FORMATION OF NATIVE COMMUNITIES

The formation of present-day native communities in the region has taken two directions. In areas of early colonization, native-community formation was preceded by other legal means of access to land, some of which go as far back as the end of the 19th century. In contrast, in the peripheral areas and in areas of expansion, the process of native-community formation is much more recent. It has taken shape since the 1970s under completely different socioeconomic and sociopolitical conditions. In the following sections, we will present the most relevant landmarks on these two paths.

Native Communities in the Earliest Colonized Areas

Between 1847 and 1890, the colonist advance occupied the axis formed by the Chanchamayo, Paucartambo, Chorobamba, Huancabamba, and Pozuzo rivers in the Andean piedmont, displacing most of the Ashaninka and Yanesha who inhabited these valleys. Indigenous people who did not die in confrontations with the colonists or retreat to areas that had not yet been colonized were confined to increasingly more limited areas. In this context of extreme social disintegration, the indigenous peoples, especially the Yanesha, accepted the protection offered by Franciscan missionaries. The Quillazú Mission had already been founded in the Chorobamba Valley in 1881. The arrival of Father Gabriel Sala in the region in 1885 gave new impetus to Franciscan missionary activity. A year later, the mission of San Luis de Shuaro was established on the lower Paucartambo River (Barclay and Santos-Granero 1980: 47–48). Since their foundation, both missions had dual objectives: to concentrate the Yanesha population and to act as catalysts for colonization. In both cases, the second objective was achieved. Near Quillazú, the colonist town of Oxapampa was founded in 1891, and San Luis de Shuaro became the point of departure for the Via Central del Pichis road that same year.

However, this strategy had negative effects on the achievement of the religious goals of the missionaries. Facing growing pressure from the colonists, converts began to abandon the missions, especially in San Luis de Shuaro. In response, Father Sala opted for a new strategy: to secure land for the indigenous population in relatively isolated areas to ensure their sedentarization and to facilitate their conversion, while at the same time providing them with the "benefits of civilization." San Luis de Shuaro was a lost cause; consequently this strategy was put into practice in Quillazú and in Sogormo, a mission established on the banks of the Paucartambo River in 1891. Since the establishment of Sogormo, Father Sala "took the necessary steps so that the Indians would have access to an area adequate for use as their exclusive homeland, granting them free ownership and land use rights in Sogormo" (Ortiz 1969: vol. 1, 348). At the end of 1895, the government granted this land to the Apostolic Prefecture of San Francisco Solano (Ortiz 1969: vol. 1, 348).

The legal formula used to allocate this land was termed *condominio*. Under this procedure, the land was granted in the names of both the Yanesha and the mission, the former being under the tutelage of the latter. A similar legal step was taken at the Quillazú Mission, which received title to 1,226 hectares from the prefect of Junín in 1905 (Smith 1974: 55). These were the first two precedents for legal land grants to small indigenous collectives in the Selva Central. However, these two were to have a very different outcome. Whereas Sogormo, gradually invaded by colonists and abandoned by the Yanesha, gave up its status as a mission in 1920 (Barclay and Santos-Granero 1980: 50), Quillazú became the subject of a long litigation process for ownership of the land between the missionaries and the indigenous residents of the mission, which began in 1929 and was concluded only recently, in 1988, when the case was decided in favor of the Yanesha community of Tsachopen. Because of the aforementioned difficulties, the *condominio* model did not become established in other areas of the Selva Central.

A second set of events in the formation of present-day native communities took place in the upper Perené Valley at the end of the 1940s. During this period, the Perene Colony, property of the Peruvian Corporation, was invaded along its northern border in the El Palomar area. To arrive at an agreement with the invading colonists and to set a precedent that would allow the company to protect its interests, the Peruvian Corporation asked the Ministry of Agriculture to mediate. In October 1949, an agreement was signed by the litigants through which the Ministry authorized the Peruvian Corporation to offer contracts for the sale of the land to the colonists (Manrique n.d.: 53). Thus, the Peruvian Corporation maintained its right to the ownership of the concession that it had obtained from the State at the end of the 19th century and established the purchase of land as the only means of access to its property.

After the land in El Palomar-Puñizas was divided into lots, three other land partitionings were made for several other groups of colonists. Simultaneously, several partitionings were made on behalf of the Yanesha and Ashaninka living in proximity to the headquarters of the Perene Colony. In this case, partitionings were not intended to resolve the invasion problem but, as Manrique suggested, were intended "a) to concentrate the natives from the vast territory of the Colony into a single nucleus; [and] b) to provide a specific location for a population that could be relied upon during coffee harvest periods" (n.d.: 55).

The partitioning of Chicama Alto and Medio Yurinaki-Sancachari, a 1,877-hectare zone, was conducted on behalf of 125 Yanesha families, and the partitioning of Río Vayós, with 1,500 hectares, benefited 100 Ashaninka families (Manrique n.d.: 55). In neither of these cases was payment for the land required, although a fee per hectare was charged for its delimitation (Barclay 1989: 230). In order to partition these areas, the Peruvian Corporation formally referred to Law 1220 (Ley de Tierras de Montaña, passed in 1909), which was conceived primarily to stimulate the colonization of the Amazonian region and did not deal explicitly with land grants to indigenous peoples.

Allotment of land to the Yanesha and Ashaninka was organized through their local leaders *(capitanes),* each of whom had a certain degree of influence over a fairly numerous group of extended families. The beneficiaries were generally heads of extended families who had maintained long traditions as laborers for the British colony. The requirement of payment for the right to have the land delimited meant that those who were more involved as seasonal laborers could afford larger extensions of land. The most privileged, therefore, were the *capitanes*, a fact that was reflected, as we will see in the following chapter, in the expansion of coffee production within these early communities. The second effect was that the settlements that were established as a result of land partitioning were organized from the start on the basis of the individual ownership of lots. Partitioning of land among the Yanesha eventually gave rise to the communities of Alto Yurinaki, Sancachari, and Palomar, as well as to other indigenous settlements, such as Sanchirio, Yapaz, and Purús (Barclay and Santos-Granero 1980: 56). The present-day community of Alto Yurinaki, with plots that range from 0.5 to 40 hectares, is a good example of the type of community that was formed as a result of land partitioning (Barclay and Santos-Granero 1980: 57).

The communities that emerged as a result of such partitionings were at a great disadvantage as compared with the colonists who purchased land from the Perene Colony. Whereas the colonists involved in the first four land partitionings conducted by the Peruvian Corporation received an average of 37.8 hectares per lot, the Yanesha and Ashaninka received an average of 15 hectares. Forty years later, the indigenous population began to experience the effects of this initial disadvantage. Currently, the average holding per family in Alto Yurinaki is 7.9 hectares. In Palomar, the average holding is 4.5 hectares, and in Sancachari, only 3.3 hectares, despite major emigration from these three communities. A similar situation is found in the Ashaninka community of Mariscal Cáceres, which was formed as a result of the partitioning of Río Vayós: currently, the average land area per family is 8.8 hectares (PEPP 1987). These two land partitionings were not the only ones conducted on behalf of the local indigenous population. As Barclay (1989: 220–233) demonstrates, through a series of mechanisms (leases, *mejorero* contracts, free land grants, and land sales), the Peruvian Corporation attempted to sedentarize the indigenous families living within its concession to ensure that they would be a permanently available labor force for its coffee *haciendas* or that they would become small-scale coffee producers forced to sell their produce to the company. These strategies gave rise to a series of small Yanesha and Ashaninka communities along the Perené River.

At almost the same time, when the Peruvian Corporation began to formalize its first land sales, the State issued Supreme Decree 03 on March 1, 1957, establishing the procedures to reserve land for indigenous populations. Reserves only guaranteed land-use rights; property was not recognized, nor were the rights of ownership associated with it. In the Selva Central, this decree benefited 8 Yanesha settlements and 35 Ashaninka settlements (Table 7.2). Some of the groups that benefited from the sell-offs conducted earlier by the Peruvian Corporation sub-

Table 7.2. Indigenous Reserves, 1957–1974

| | No. of reserves | | | Area (hectares) | | |
Province	Yanesha	Ashaninka	No. of beneficiaries[a]	Total	Average per reserve	Average per beneficiary
Chanchamayo	1	9	688	3,522.62	322.26	5.12
Satipo	0	22	1,229	3,896.40	177.10	3.17
Oxapampa	7	4	1,747	35,966.73	3,269.70	20.58
Selva Central	8	35	3,664	43,385.75	1,008.97	11.84

Source: SINAMOS 1975; data elaborated by the authors.

[a]This category includes only those age 5 or older.

sequently applied for reserves, as was the case of the Yanesha settlement of Palomar.

This law was primarily enforced in older colonization areas in the present-day provinces of Satipo and Chanchamayo but was also applied in some of the peripheral areas that were beginning to be colonized. This was the case in the Pichis and Palcazu valleys. The average size of the reserves that were created varied from one zone to another, depending on colonist population pressure. These differences can be observed in Table 7.2. Whereas the 32 reserves created in areas of severe colonization pressure received an average of 231.8 hectares, the 11 reserves created in the peripheral areas of Oxapampa Province received an average of 3,270 hectares. This marked difference is also reflected in the average areas granted per beneficiary. If we were to transform these averages based on five-member family units, we would find that whereas in the Pichis and Palcazu valleys an average of 102.9 hectares per family unit were awarded, in Satipo and Chanchamayo, average areas of 25.6 and 15.8 hectares per family, respectively, were appropriated. These differences in opportunities for access to land stimulated the gradual indigenous migration into peripheral areas, giving rise to new settlements.

In spite of its shortcomings, Supreme Decree 03 was the first step toward more effective legislation of indigenous lands and was the first legal instrument made available to the Amazonian indigenous peoples to guarantee, although only partially, legal access to their land. We should indicate that, in the case of the Selva Central, this law was not applied on a large scale until President Velasco Alvarado came to power in 1968. This seems to indicate that previous governments did not have the political will to enforce it. Of the 38 reserves for which we have information, only 2 (5 percent) were granted before 1968, whereas the rest were granted between 1968 and the passing of the Law of Native Communities (Decree Law 20653) in 1974. In a survey of the indigenous population of the region conducted in 1974, 146 indigenous settlements were identified in the area that has been defined by this study as the Selva Central (SINAMOS 1975). Of these, only 26 percent had obtained protection as reserves.

In some areas of extreme colonist pressure where Supreme Decree 03 was not applied, indigenous families opted to solicit land under individual title. This was the case for many Ashaninka families who inhabited the right bank of the upper Perené Valley within the Peruvian Corporation's concession. In 1950, the corporation sold lots in Marankiari, Pichanaki, Pumpuriani, Ubiriki, Sutziki, and Pucharini (Barclay 1989: 232). These settlements were later subject to the 1974 Law of Native Communities. In Satipo, where colonist pressure on indigenous land was very intense, the Ashaninka were displaced from their lands over and over again because they did not have legal entitlement to them. Alberto Quinchoquer, one of the first Ashaninka leaders to address the problem of land before the State, explained:

First they displaced me to Coviriali. In Coviriali another colonist came and told me: "This isn't your farm. It's mine!" I moved to Pauriali. Then another colonist came. He said: "This is my land!" So I came to Teoría. I had been in Teoría before, in 1936.

Well then, so that they don't throw me out again and again, I will buy land here. What would I build my house for, plant my crops for, if some colonist is going to come to throw me out? . . . No way! That's what I told the engineer. (Fernández 1986: 38)

However, this option presented difficulties, since local officials, as is evident from this and other testimonies, often refused to grant land to indigenous families. It was thus that the struggle for the right to their own lands became, as we will see, their principal demand, forming the backbone of the indigenous movement since the 1960s.

By the 1950s and 1960s, as a result of the large-scale occupation of the earliest colonized areas, the indigenous population began to abandon their traditional pattern of dispersed settlement and to gather in small areas surrounded by colonist lands. Although the experience of nucleated settlement predates this period, this is when it began to be widespread in the region. The first moves of this type took place in the 1920s and 1930s as a result of the evangelical work of the Adventists within the Perene Colony. In 1922, the missionary Fernando Stahl established a mission post in Metraro, receiving 300 hectares from the colony, where, as he said, "the *chunchos* could enter and settle, forming a permanent labor force" (Barclay 1989: 122). In 1929, this missionary post was moved to Cascadas, on the lower Perené River, and a year later to the mouth of the Sutziki River, where it attracted 300 Ashaninka. Along with the mission in Sutziki, other missionary centers were created at the mouth of the Ipoki River in Kivinaki and in Soteni, the latter with an area of 150 hectares (Barclay 1989: 125). When, in 1948, the Perene Colony expelled the Adventist missionaries who were no longer complying with the agreement to supply labor, some Ashaninka converts stayed in the missionary centers or formed new settlements in Metraro, Kimariaki, Kivinaki, and Marankiari. Some of these settlements were later registered as native communities.

Although both Catholic and Adventist mission posts played an important role in concentrating the indigenous labor force and in disseminating the idea of the convenience of nucleated settlement, the role of schools was no less important. In fact, part of the attraction of the Adventist mission in Sutziki was the school. The same could be said of the Catholic mission in Puerto Ocopa, founded at the mouth of the Pangoa River in 1920 (Ortiz 1978: 171). However, it was not until the 1950s, with the arrival of the Summer Institute of Linguistics in the area, that the phenomenon of a community with a school as a gathering point for the indigenous population became widespread. As a consequence of the impetus provided by the missionaries of this institution and the growing interest on the part of the indigenous peoples in access to formal education, in 1974 there were a total of 100 schools distributed among 97 Yanesha and Ashaninka settlements (SINAMOS 1975: 211, 214). By then, 69 percent of the region's indigenous settlements had managed to establish local schools, thereby adopting a pattern of nucleated settlement.

The progressive concentration of the region's indigenous population is clearly evident in a comparison of the size of settlements between 1974 and 1988. Whereas in 1974 only 35 percent of the indigenous settlements had populations of over 100 people, in 1988, 56 percent had populations between 100 and 350 people, and a striking 21 percent had over 350 inhabitants (Table 7.3). As we will see, this phenomenon has had important consequences in terms of the social and political organization of the region's indigenous peoples.

Native Communities in Peripheral Areas and in Areas of Expansion

In peripheral areas and in areas of expansion, the process of native-community formation assumed a different character. In these areas, pressure from colonists was weaker and therefore did not contribute to the concentration of the indigenous population. The factor that drove the formation of small villages was primarily the migration of indigenous families from areas where extreme colonist population pressure existed. The phenomenon of indigenous migration from central areas into peripheral areas began at the end of the 19th century, but it was only from the 1940s onward that it began to have an effect on traditional indigenous settlement patterns. In effect, until the 1940s, peripheral areas consti-

Table 7.3. Distribution of Legally Registered Native
Communities According to Population Size Class

Population size class	1974[a]		1988	
	No. of communities	% of total	No. of communities	% of total
1–49	36	24.8	7	3.4
50–99	59	40.7	42	20.3
100–149	23	15.9	43	20.8
150–199	16	11.0	31	14.9
200–249	6	4.1	20	9.7
250–299	3	2.1	12	5.8
300–349	1	0.7	9	4.4
≥350	1	0.7	43	20.7
All size classes	145	100.0	207	100.0

Sources: SINAMOS 1975: 34; PEPP 1986, 1987.

[a]We have included all of the native communities considered in the
SINAMOS study except for those in Zone I, which is located outside the
area we have defined as the Selva Central.

tuted refuge areas for those indigenous families from the earliest occupied areas who resisted the adoption of the mores and values of the national society. Thus, this migration strategy constituted an attempt to maintain a traditional way of life. Since the 1940s, indigenous families who have migrated into peripheral areas have done so for other reasons: primarily because they no longer have access to sufficient land in their areas of origin. Furthermore, indigenous migrants in this more recent wave are individuals who have interacted significantly with the market economy, primarily as laborers for the colonists but also as independent producers.

This is the case for many Yanesha families in Oxapampa, who, since the 1940s, began to migrate into the Palcazu basin, across the Yanachaga range that separates the two valleys. Thus, the leading families of the Villa America sector in the present-day community of Siete de Julio came from Oxapampa. The same may be said of other Yanesha communities in this area, such as Santa Rosa de Chuchurras, Alto Iscozacín, and Alto Lagarto.

The Palcazu Valley also became the home of one of the groups of Ashaninka Adventists that left the Perene Colony in 1948, after the Adventist missionaries were expelled by the British company (Barclay 1989: 128). Later, several Yanesha families joined this group, giving rise to the present-day communities of Loma Linda and Laguna (Santos-Granero 19991b: 177–180). The migrants from both the

Oxapampa and Perené valleys brought with them their experience of working with colonists and continued to be linked to the market through their consumption of manufactured goods. Today, these communities stand out from others in the same valley for their "modern" and "entrepreneurial" spirit. The way of life of these migrants and their struggles to own land and to establish schools served as an example for the original inhabitants of the Palcazu Valley, spreading the concept of nucleated settlement as a way of ensuring their survival. Thus it is not surprising that the earliest Yanesha reserves were located in this area.

A similar process gave rise to the first nucleated settlements on the Pichis, Ene, and Tambo rivers. One of the Ashaninka groups that left the Perene Colony when the Adventists were expelled went to the Pichis River, founding the community of Nevati (Ortiz 1978: 199). The stimulus to migrate came from one of the missionaries expelled from the British colony, who had gone to the Pichis River to explore the possibility of establishing a new mission. According to the testimony of an Ashaninka, the missionary wrote to the converted who had stayed in Perené, telling them: "'Come here. There's no danger here. Animals are abundant. There's no shortage of food as there is in the Perené!' In his letter he told us that we should walk to the promised land, and that to arrive in the promised land, we would have to suffer quite a bit. But that milk and honey were to be found there. And that we should listen to the sweet voice of the prophet: in choosing any other way, we would lose our lives forever" (Narby 1989: 65).

Inspired by this messianic belief, many Ashaninka families from the Perené migrated into the Pichis Valley, settling in Nevati and later founding other settlements. In time, the Nevati Mission acquired major importance. In the 1970s Nevati became a native community under Law 20653. This community played a significant role in the dissemination of Adventism and of the concept of "civilized life." Thus, according to Villasante, the Ashaninka community of Betania, founded on the Tambo River at the end of the 1950s, used Nevati as a model. Betania was founded by Ashaninka families from the Ene River area who were organized by Ubiare, a local leader. Having converted to Adventism, Ubiare had lived for some time in Nevati (Villasante 1983: 96). After several successive moves, Ubiare and his followers settled in an area near the colonist town of Atalaya. According to Villasante, the reasons given by the founders of Betania for their migration were "to have more contact with civilization, to work for the logging *patrones* and to obtain the goods necessary to improve their social advancement [such as salt, kerosene, tools, and clothing]" (Villasante 1983: 100).

Messianic beliefs also played an important role in the migration of a group of Ashaninka who, during this same period, moved from Mazaranquiari, in the Satipo Valley, into the Ene Valley, after news arrived that a white missionary lived there who claimed to be Intomi Pavá, an envoy of the Ashaninka solar divinity

(Fernández 1986: 111). According to an oral testimony, this missionary "was an evangelist. I don't remember his name but I saw him. They believed he was Itomi Pavá. Yes! They said: 'Our god comes from Lima by plane'" (Fernández 1986: 111). In this particular case, migration was prompted not only by the messianic hope that underlies Ashaninka religious thought but also by the expectation of obtaining, through Intomi Pavá, Western material goods and technology, which had become indispensable for the Ashaninka. Unfortunately, the attempt to found a new settlement in the Ene Valley failed. Some of the migrants died on the trip when their raft overturned, and others died of malaria shortly after settling in the area. This and other examples show how messianism, character-istic of traditional Yanesha and Ashaninka religious beliefs, found an echo in Adventism and Evangelism, making the Christian discourse attractive to the indigenous population. But in these cases, messianism did not represent an at-tempt to take refuge in the past. Rather, it represented a search for the benefits of "civilization" with an eye toward the future. In other words, migrating into uncolonized areas and gathering in villages organized around a mission was not only inspired by the hope for salvation but by the expectation of having the same access as colonists to the technological advancements offered by Western culture. Although the messianic sentiment has declined in the last two decades as other expectations have replaced it, the "civilizatory drive" has been preserved in many of the communities that originated as Adventist or Evangelical settlements.

The origin of the Ashaninka communities of Quempiri and Camantabishi on the Ene River bears more similarities to that of the Yanesha communities of the central and lower Palcazu Valley. Founded in 1961 and 1970, respectively, these two settlements were mostly composed of immigrants coming from the Apurímac River valley, especially from the San Francisco area and the Mantaro River area (Mayer 1971: 19). As one resident stated, "We have come from the Apurímac because we are used to having land and there was none left there, because the colonists are moving in" (Mayer 1971: 19). These two settlements and the Catholic mission of Cutivireni were the first nucleated villages in the valley. According to the data from Mayer based on 52 heads of households in Quempiri in 1971, 33 percent came from massively colonized areas.

It is noteworthy that, in 1971 in both Quempiri and Camantabishi, leadership was in the hands of indigenous immigrants from Apurímac, and, as in other cases, they were driven by a religious zeal, this time inspired by the Evangelical Church. Mayer's observation coincides with similar ones in other cases:

An initial conclusion regarding these villages is that, generally, they form as a result of an initiative and under the leadership of people who have been displaced from colo-nized areas. They have been in contact with modern society and have realized the need to unite and to establish schools to be able to better defend themselves from the harmful effects that accompany social change in the *selva alta*. Both leaders are Protestants, and both towns are influenced by Protestant missionaries. The conversion to Protestantism opened the doors to contacts with the Summer Institute of Linguistics, which helped to found schools and offered their support. (Mayer 1971: 21)

In all of these areas (central, peripheral, and remote areas of expansion), the process of native-community formation was accelerated by the actions of the Sistema Nacional de Movilización Social (National System of Social Mobilization), or SINAMOS, which was created under the government of Velasco Alvarado. This agency played an important role in the diffusion of the Law of Native Communities, informing indigenous peoples about the advantages that it offered. SINAMOS also played an important role in promoting nucleated settlement and indigenous organization, thus reinforcing the new "native community" model. As an Ashaninka resident in Betania said:

In our grandparents' day, there was no community. Recently, since SINAMOS has arrived, it is called community. . . . When everyone gets together to work, it's called community. . . . I think that the school is bringing everyone together. . . . Before, in our grandparents' day, there was no school. . . . Almost everyone wandered here and there. [They] only [gathered] when they drank manioc beer. . . . When they were finished everyone went home, and later, they invited everyone to get together again. . . . In the past we never heard about community, only about hamlets . . . where several families lived, but alone. . . . Now we live in a community. . . . In the past, we didn't; . . . in the past everyone wandered about freely to hunt, built houses wherever they wanted to. . . . Now we all work together; . . . therefore, it's a community. With SINAMOS came birth certificates, personal documents, . . . [and] authorities. . . . Before it wasn't like that. . . . We did not know how old we were. . . . Now we are civilized. (Villasante 1983: 108)

Colonist population pressure on indigenous territories, the need to ensure their rights to the land, the influence of schools, missionary activity based on a messianic and civilizing world view, the example of the indigenous migrants from colonized areas arriving in peripheral areas, and the activities of SINAMOS constituted the basic factors that, combined in various ways, gave rise to present-day Yanesha and Ashaninka communities. In all cases, however, native communities result both from despoliation and fragmentation of indigenous territories at the hands of the colonists and as a form of defense in the face of this process.

   Because they result from a historical process imposed from outside, the native communities of the Selva Central are social units that do not reflect traditional

Table 7.4. Legally Registered Native Communities

	1975–1980		1981–1985		1986–1988		All 3 periods	
Province	No.	%	No.	%	No.	%	No.	%
Chanchamayo	31	21	11	26	6	40	48	23
Oxapampa	39	26	20	48	0	0	59	29
Satipo	80	53	11	26	9	60	100	48
Selva Central	150	100	42	100	15	100	207	100

Sources: PEPP 1986, 1987, 1989.

Note: Each percentage value is the percentage of native communities registered in the particular province in relation to the total number registered in all three provinces.

settlement patterns. Nevertheless, this fact has been overcome by the appearance of new forms of social interaction based on kinship ties. Several anthropological studies of present-day communities in the region (Mayer 1971; Smith 1976; Barclay 1980; Santos-Granero 1991b; Narby 1989) have shown that the Yanesha and Ashaninka have arrived at creative solutions to the challenges presented by this new settlement pattern, developing new mechanisms of integration and control of possible conflicts. This process has not yet ended, and the scarcity of land now felt in the earliest colonized areas imposes new social and economic challenges.

LAND TENURE IN THE INDIGENOUS SECTOR

In 1989, 15 years after Decree Law 20653 was issued, 207 native communities were registered by the Ministry of Agriculture in the Selva Central (Table 7.4). Of these, 87 percent have been granted land titles. Although it is estimated that between 10 and 20 indigenous settlements are still not registered and that 13 percent of the registered settlements are not yet titled, one can generally say that by 1989 the State had recognized and legally protected the majority of indigenous settlements in the Selva Central. However, the land-tenure situation in Yanesha and Ashaninka communities remains problematic and is far from homogeneous. Actually, as we will demonstrate, there are clear differences in the opportunities for access to land between those communities established in the earliest colonized areas and those located in peripheral areas and in areas of expansion.

The majority of indigenous settlements in the Selva Central were legally registered between 1975 and 1980, under the government of General Morales Bermúdez. Later, the registration of native communities slowed, although by

Table 7.5. Titled Native Communities

Province	1975-1980		1981-1985		1986-1988		All 3 periods	
	No.	%	No.	%	No.	%	No.	%
Chanchamayo	15	22	19	22	8	32	42	23
Oxapampa	27	40	23	26	0	0	50	28
Satipo	26	38	45	52	17	68	88	49
Selva Central	68	100	87	100	25	100	180	100

Sources: PEPP 1986, 1987, 1989.

Note: Each percentage value is the percentage of titled native communities in the particular province in relation to the total number titled in all three provinces.

1989 the majority of indigenous settlements in the region had been registered. The distribution of communities by province clearly demonstrates that it has been in Chanchamayo, the area of highest colonist pressure, where native peoples have been subjected to the most severe process of despoliation of their traditional territories and of spatial displacement. As a result, only 23 percent of the registered native communities are found in Chanchamayo, and, of these, the majority are found in the upper and central Perené Valley in the districts of Perené and Pichanaki. The situation of the indigenous population in Oxapampa Province is similar. Having been expelled from the earliest areas of occupation (Oxapampa, Huancabamba, and Pozuzo), the majority of the indigenous population in this province is now found in the most recent areas of colonization: the Cacazú, Palcazu, and Pichis valleys. In contrast, nearly half of the region's legally registered native communities are located in the province of Satipo, where most of the poorly integrated areas of expansion are found.

The relatively high percentage of titled communities distinguishes the Selva Central from other areas in Peruvian Amazonia, where most of the communities still have not been granted land titles. This advantageous situation is mainly explained by pressures exerted by local indigenous organizations during the second term of President Belaúnde Terry, a period when the Pichis–Palcazu Special Project was initiated. These pressures were echoed by international organizations, which made titling of indigenous land a condition for their financial support of the special project. Thus, it is not surprising that of the 180 titled communities in 1989, 48 percent had received their titles precisely during the 1980-1985 period (Table 7.5).

Although the proportion of titled communities is relatively homogeneous throughout the region, ranging between 85 percent and 88 percent of the total number of legally registered communities, when we consider the proportion of

Table 7.6. Titled Native Communities and Their Families in Relation to All Legally Registered Communities, 1989

Province	Communities		Families	
	No. registered	No. (%) titled	No. in registered community	No. (%) in titled communities
Chanchamayo	48	42 (87.5%)	1,831	1,612 (88.0%)
Oxapampa	59	50 (84.7%)	2,472	1,795 (72.6%)
Satipo	100	88 (88.0%)	5,414	3,744 (69.1%)
Selva Central	207	180 (86.9%)	9,717	7,151 (73.5%)

Sources: PEPP 1986, 1987, 1989.

Note: We estimated the 1989 indigenous population by applying a cumulative annual growth rate of 2.5 percent to figures provided at the time the communities were legally registered.

the indigenous population living in titled communities as compared with that living in all registered communities we find one important difference. This can be seen in the fact that, in the provinces of Satipo and Oxapampa, where there is a larger number of peripheral areas and areas of expansion, the proportion of indigenous population living in untitled communities is higher than it is in Chanchamayo, the earliest occupied province (Table 7.6).

If we look at the same information for the Selva Central as a whole, we find that, although 87 percent of the legally registered communities have already been titled, these include only 74 percent of all indigenous families. This demonstrates that the entitlement process for indigenous land is far from complete and that it is urgent that legal access to land be guaranteed for more than a quarter of the indigenous population of the region.

Indigenous land ownership varies according to the degree of colonist pressure experienced in the various areas that form the region. On the basis of the data in Table 7.7, we can assert that in areas of greater colonist pressure, there are fewer native communities, and that in average these have smaller areas. Thus, whereas in Chanchamayo up to 45 percent of the titled communities are less than 300 hectares in size, in Satipo and Oxapampa 23 percent and 4 percent fall in this size category, respectively. When we consider the regional space as a whole, we find that a significant proportion of the titled communities are less than 300 hectares in size (23 percent), whereas almost half (47 percent) are less than 1,000 hectares. These figures are indicative of the severe land-fragmentation process in traditional indigenous territories, a situation that is aggravated by the fact that titled land is frequently located in areas of difficult terrain, far from

Table 7.7. Distribution of Titled Native Communities by Size Class of Communal Holding, 1988

Size class (hectares) of communal holding	Chanchamayo		Oxapampa		Satipo		Selva Central	
	No.	%	No.	%	No.	%	No.	%
0–299	19	45	2	4	20	23	41	23
300–999	16	38	8	16	19	22	43	24
1,000–2,999	6	14	21	42	10	11	37	21
≥3,000	1	3	19	38	39	44	59	32
All size classes	42	100	50	100	88	100	180	100

Sources: PEPP 1986, 1987, 1989.

transportation routes. This places the indigenous sector at a disadvantage in comparison with the colonist sector with respect to opportunities for commercial production. Most of the communities located in the upper Perené Valley, in the Villa Rica Valley, and near the town of Satipo are under these severe constraints.

When we consider the average land area per family, important differences within the region are also seen (Table 7.8). Once again, the factor that explains these differences is the length of time that a given area has been under colonization. Thus, in Chanchamayo, indigenous families in titled communities have an average of only 12.2 hectares at their disposal, a figure at the limit of what we have defined as *minifundio* in the Amazonian region. In contrast, in Satipo, where titled communities are found both in areas of long-term occupation and in peripheral and expansion areas, the average landholding per family rises to 40.2 hectares. Finally, in Oxapampa, where the majority of titled communities are found in more recently colonized areas, the average land area per family is 84.3 hectares. These imbalances diminish as young indigenous families migrate from the most densely populated areas to communities in peripheral or expansion areas. Such was the case for many Yanesha and Ashaninka families from Villa Rica, Yurinaki, and the upper Perené Valley, who migrated into the Pichis and Palcazu valleys, and of the Ashaninka from the most densely populated parts of Satipo, who migrated into the Ene and Tambo valleys. This migration, which replicates the constant process of displacement that the Yanesha and Ashaninka have suffered since the mid-19th century, has begun to reach a limit. In the last few years, the inhabitants of many communities located in peripheral areas, which had previously accepted indigenous migrant families from heavily colonized areas, have decided to restrict the entry of new families. This is the case in the Yanesha communities of San Pedro Pichanaz, Loma Linda–Laguna, and

Table 7.8. Average Area per Community and Family in Titled Native
Communities, 1989

Province	No. of titled communities	No. of families	Area titled (hectares)[a]		
			Total	Average per community	Average per family
Chanchamayo	42	1,612	19,684	469	12.2
Oxapampa	50	1,795	151,306	3,026	84.3
Satipo	88	3,744	150,661	1,712	40.2
Selva Central	180	7,151	321,651	1,787	44.9

Sources: PEPP 1986, 1987, 1989.
[a]Excluded are areas granted in use, which legally cannot be utilized for agropastoral purposes.

Shiringamazú, in the Palcazu Valley. As a result, there is increased pressure on
the land in communities in the most densely populated areas, such as Chanchamayo, where already 53 percent of the communities register average areas per
family of less than 10 hectares (PEPP 1986, 1987, 1989). Thus, we can predict
that, in the very near future in this province and in areas of higher colonist
population pressure in the province of Satipo, native communities will undergo
a process of overfragmentation similar to that which has been observed in the
colonist sector.

ACCESS TO LAND IN THE COLONIST AND INDIGENOUS SECTORS

When comparing land tenure in the indigenous and colonist sectors, we find that
the indigenous peoples appear to own larger average areas of land than do the
colonists. To compare the two sectors, in Table 7.9 we have considered the total
land area granted to each — that is, the sum of titled land and areas "ceded in use."

From Table 7.9 it becomes evident that the differences between the two sectors
with respect to land access vary considerably among colonization areas. The
differences within the provinces of Chanchamayo and Oxapampa are smaller
than those within Satipo. In the case of Chanchamayo, this smaller difference is
a result of the extreme population pressure on the land in this area, which affects
the indigenous and colonist populations alike. This means that people from both
sectors have access to small areas of land only. The relatively small difference
between the two sectors in Oxapampa is primarily a result of the fact that the
sample of colonist and indigenous families was taken mostly from peripheral

Table 7.9. Average Granted Area per Family in Indigenous and Colonist Sectors, 1988

Sector and variable	Chanchamayo	Oxapampa	Satipo	Selva Central
Indigenous sector				
Area	25,711	136,022	490,264	651,997
No. of families	1,612	1,677	3,744	7,033
Average area per family	15.9	81.1	130.9	92.7
Colonist sector				
Area	76,876	162,426	47,472	286,774
No. of families	6,566	2,494	3,795	12,855
Average area per family	11.7	65.1	12.5	22.3

Sources: For the indigenous sector: PEPP 1986, 1987, 1989 (based on data for 42 titled communities in Chanchamayo, 42 in Oxapampa, and 88 in Satipo). For the colonist sector: PRONAC 1990 (for the provinces of Chanchamayo and Satipo); Mori Caro 1982 (for the Villa Rica district of Oxapampa Province, based on data for 971 colonist families); PEPP 1983 (for the Pichis Valley of Oxapampa Province, based on data for 795 colonist families); Ministerio de la Presidencia 1989 (for the Palcazu Valley of Oxapampa Province, based on data for 728 colonist families).

Note: Area measurements are in hectares.

areas where landholdings tend to be larger. Both situations contrast with that in the province of Satipo, where members of native communities have significantly larger average land areas per family. This is primarily a result of the fact that most of the land granted to the indigenous population in this province is located in poorly colonized areas of expansion. As a result, in Satipo, 44 percent of the native communities hold average land areas greater than 3,000 hectares (Table 7.7). However, since most of these communities are located in areas where road access is limited or nonexistent, their inhabitants have few opportunities to produce for the market.

From the preceding information, it would appear that the indigenous sector is in a better position than the colonist sector with respect to land tenure. However, when one considers other elements, this impression changes substantially. First, it should be remembered that the Yanesha and Ashaninka have been completely displaced from two districts of Chanchamayo (San Ramón and San Luis de Shuaro) and from one in Satipo (Pampa Hermosa) and have been almost completely displaced from three districts of Oxapampa (Oxapampa, Huancabamba, and Pozuzo). Second, in the most densely colonized areas, natives have been displaced from the more fertile land in the valley bottoms to higher areas where steep slopes result in higher levels of erosion. Furthermore, in these areas many native communities are located far from roads, which makes transport and marketing of their produce more difficult and expensive.

The discrimination experienced by indigenous peoples in terms of land distri-

Table 7.10. Area Suitable for Agriculture in Relation to All Granted Area in the Indigenous and Colonist Sectors, 1988

Sector and variable	Chanchamayo	Satipo	Both provinces
Indigenous sector			
Area granted	13,279	462,156	476,156
Area suitable for agriculture	7,252	123,271	130,271
% suitable for agriculture	54.6	26.6	27.4
Colonist sector			
Area granted	43,026	31,963	74,989
Area suitable for agriculture	24,403	18,112	42,515
% suitable for agriculture	56.7	56.6	56.7

Sources: For the indigenous sector: PEPP 1986, 1987, 1989 (based on data for 27 communities in Chanchamayo and 66 communities in Satipo titled between 1978 and 1988 under Decree Law 22175). For the colonist sector: PEPP 1989 (based on data for 2,481 colonists from Chanchamayo and 1,744 from Satipo who were granted lands between 1984 and 1988).

Note: Area measurements are in hectares.

bution becomes even more apparent when one considers the proportion of the total amount of land granted to them that is suitable for agropastoral activities. Since Decree Law 22175 was issued in 1978, modifying Decree Law 20653, a distinction was made (in granting land to both indigenous peoples and colonists) between areas suitable for agriculture, which are granted in property, and those with logging capacity, with are only ceded in use and where the development of agropastoral activities is not allowed. In Table 7.10, we present the percentages of area suitable for agriculture in two samples of the indigenous and colonists sectors in the provinces of Chanchamayo and Satipo. It shows that although the difference that exists between both sectors is smaller than in Satipo, when both provinces are considered, the colonist sector has in relative terms twice as much land suitable for agriculture as the indigenous sector.

Although we do not have similar information for Oxapampa as a whole, the 1988 data for the area covered by the Palcazu Rural Development Project allow us to assess the differences in access to land suitable for agriculture by both sectors. On the basis of the information presented in Table 7.11, it becomes apparent that, even in this recently colonized area, the colonist sector has received more and better land than did its original occupants. Whereas 70 percent of the land granted to colonists is suitable for agriculture, only 44 percent of the land granted to Indians is. Furthermore, although the difference between the average areas of land held by the colonist and indigenous populations is substantial (104.6 hectares versus 74.4 hectares, respectively), the gap increases even

Table 7.11. Area Suitable for Agriculture in Relation to All Granted Area in the Indigenous and Colonist Sectors in the Palcazu Valley, 1988

Variable	Indigenous sector	Colonist sector
Total area granted	40,859	76,178
Area suitable for agriculture	17,982	53,259
% suitable for agriculture	44.0	69.9
No. of families	549	728
Average area granted per family	74.4	104.6
Average area suitable for agriculture per family	32.8	73.2

Source: Ministerio de la Presidencia 1989; data elaborated by the authors.

Note: Based on data for the indigenous and colonist sectors within the jurisdiction of the Palcazu Rural Development Project. Area measurements are in hectares.

more when considering the average amount of land suitable for agropastoral activities per family unit. Thus, as in Chanchamayo and Satipo, colonist families in the Palcazu Valley hold almost twice the area of land suitable for agropastoral activities as indigenous families.

In summary, land tenure within the indigenous sector in the Selva Central varies substantially as a function of historical differences in the occupation of each area. This has led to unequal access to land, which, when combined with differences in the degree of access to the market, results in less advantageous opportunities and different relationships with the regional and national economy for the indigenous sector. These differences require careful consideration in an evaluation of the participation of the indigenous sector and call attention to the fact that generalizations about the indigenous peoples of the Selva Central do not adequately reflect their reality. Finally, even when native communities appear to have a better land-tenure situation in terms of absolute area, a more detailed analysis shows that, in the three provinces of the Selva Central, indigenous families have in relative terms half as much area suitable for agriculture as colonist families. From a long-term perspective, these severe constraints pose a threat to the survival of the region's indigenous peoples.

8

INDIGENOUS PARTICIPATION IN
THE REGIONAL ECONOMY

In the last four decades, the forms of participation of the Yanesha and Ashaninka in the region's economy have experienced important transformations. These changes are reflected both in the development of a wider range of commercial productive activities and in the evolution of the mechanisms and terms of exchange by which value is generated and transferred from indigenous production units. This process of change varies as a function of the location of the indigenous population in different colonization areas and is manifested in a sort of geographic specialization among the extant native communities.

We can identify two turning points with respect to indigenous participation in the regional economy. The first coincides with the beginning of mass colonization in the 1950s, which radically affected the demographic and spatial organization of the central areas in the region and which resulted in the incorporation of a large segment of the indigenous population as laborers in agropastoral and logging activities. The second coincides with the consolidation of the Selva Central as a distinct regional space in the 1970s, a period when the diverse areas that form the region became economically, socially, and politically integrated. During this second stage, a model of economic participation based on commercial agropastoral production became widespread among the Yanesha and Ashaninka. However, a clear distinction still exists between central and peripheral areas, where commercial agropastoral production has become the principal productive option for the indigenous population, and areas of expansion, in which the income of indigenous families derives mostly from salaried activities such as logging. As we will see, the areas inhabited by indigenous peoples are not isolated entities. Rather, the processes of change that affect some of them have consequences for others in terms of opportunities for employment, migration, and productive and organizational experience.

Before embarking on an analysis of the current forms of involvement of the indigenous population in the market economy, it is useful, given the marked differences that are still present within the region, to sketch briefly the characteristics of several different indigenous areas at the beginning of the period of mass occupation of the Selva Central.

By 1950, in Satipo, Pangoa, and the central Perené Valley, segments of the Ashaninka and Nomatsiguenga population that had been expelled from their lands began to work for local *patrones,* or large landowners, to avoid further displacement and to have access to manufactured goods (Shoemaker 1981: 92-95; Fernández 1986). These indigenous peons were concentrated mainly on local coffee farms and performed such tasks as clearing areas for coffee cultivation and harvesting coffee beans.

To a certain extent, this replicated the process that had taken place in previously colonized areas (Chanchamayo, Villa Rica, and the upper Perené Valley) several decades earlier (Barclay 1989: 115-118). Beginning in the early 1950s, and after this initial phase, the Yanesha and Ashaninka from these latter areas became involved in small-scale independent coffee production, although they did not completely abandon seasonal work on local coffee *haciendas.*

In the Palcazu Valley, the establishment of an oil-prospecting camp by the Cerro de Pasco Corporation in the 1950s stimulated the local economy, leading local cattle ranchers to buy land to expand their pastures. Yanesha and Ashaninka families who migrated from the upper Perené Valley served as cheap labor for the ranchers (Smith 1983). In the Pichis Valley, the indigenous population of Ashaninka origin also became a reserve of manual labor for the local cattle-ranching *haciendas.* However, this group also continued to work as loggers and rubber tappers for local *patrones.*

In the areas of expansion along the Tambo and Ene rivers, indigenous men were recruited en masse beginning in the 1950s to work on logging on the lower Tambo, Urubamba, and upper Ucayali rivers. Finally, in the same period, in the Gran Pajonal, the Ashaninka who had settled around the Catholic mission of Oventeni became indentured peons on large cattle-ranching *haciendas* (Hvalkof 1986-1987).

Thus, between 1950 and 1970, a growing number of indigenous families were incorporated into the economic activities of the colonist sector as manual labor through various forms of *habilitación* and *enganche* (see below), in which debt played a central role. With the progressive formation of native communities, the expansion of the educational system, the growth of the regional network of roads, and the appearance of intercommunity organizations, significant changes began to occur both in the way the indigenous population became involved in the regional economy and in the expectations surrounding this participation. The strategy that was initially adopted by communities in the upper Perené Valley and in Villa Rica was embraced in nearly all of the indigenous areas of the region. This strategy favored commercial agriculture (coffee, fruit, and cattle raising) over seasonal work for colonists as a means of obtaining cash and thus access to market goods. In peripheral areas and in poorly articulated areas of expansion, where marketing commercial products is more difficult, the indigenous population combined commercial agriculture with the seasonal sale of labor. However, as a result of the above-mentioned changes, even in these areas working conditions began to improve.

INDIGENOUS LABOR AND THE DEBT-BONDAGE SYSTEM

As in most of the Amazonian region, the traditional form of indigenous labor employment in the Selva Central has been based on *habilitación* and *enganche,* local forms of the debt-bondage system. In its purest form, *habilitación* of indigenous populations is associated with the creation of certain needs for manufactured goods in situations in which there is only a single option for access to them: the sale of labor under nonnegotiable terms of exchange. *Habilitación* operates where free labor markets have not yet developed and where workers produce most of their means of subsistence but already have needs that cannot be satisfied by the indigenous economy or through traditional systems of exchange.

The most important factor that is necessary for this system to function is the control of socioeconomic conditions by the *patrón,* which enables him to manipulate the terms of exchange with indentured laborers arbitrarily in his own favor. It is this complete control of both production and exchange that characterizes the system of *habilitación* and *enganche.* Because of this, the system develops more successfully where the State has a weak presence or is represented by the *patrones* themselves. The outfitter or *habilitador* is part of a commercial chain, whereby capital flows in one direction and products flow in the other. He gives his workers advances, which traditionally consist of manufactured goods or, currently, a combination of goods and cash. In addition, throughout the period of work, the outfitter offers additional merchandise to be paid in work. The value of this merchandise is generally calculated in terms of the quantity of product to be turned in to the *patrón.*

The work is not measured in terms of hours or the amount of effort invested, so it acquires the characteristics of a job that is paid according to yield. But the most important characteristic of *habilitación* is the creation of a distorted system of equivalence between the goods handed in by the outfitter (the price of which, in the absence of a local free market, is fixed by the *patrones* themselves) and the produce that the worker must deliver in exchange. The monopoly of local trade allows the *patrón* to fix the value of the products he receives. Thus, labor is never quantified, remaining invisible behind the equivalence fixed by the *patrón*. The workers may be perfectly conscious of this inequality, but because they do not have other economic alternatives and because the local sociopolitical structure allows the *patrones* to exercise an almost absolute power over them, there is little they can do to escape from the state of permanent indebtedness resulting from this system.

Because indigenous families' needs for manufactured goods are limited, as a result both of cultural patterns and of the fact that they supply most of their needs through their own activities, to gain access to their labor the *patrón* offers advances by which he engages *(enganche)* indigenous workers. At the same time, to retain their laborers, *patrones* resort to a combination of physical violence (punishment) and economic violence (debt and overpricing) in a complex relationship based on paternalism, pseudoreciprocity, and dependence.

Habilitación and *enganche* are, therefore, two sides of the same coin. Payment of an advance enables the worker to do the job *(habilitación),* while he is simultaneously "hooked" *(enganche)* since a debt is generated that may only be repaid by turning over the fruit of his labor. Finally, it should be pointed out that, in these areas, the system of debt bondage is a means to generate a labor supply where conditions for the existence of a free labor market do not exist. In the earliest colonized areas, *habilitación* and *enganche,* as becomes evident in the work of Cotlear (1979), serve other functions.

Indigenous Labor in Logging Activities

In the Selva Central, debt bondage became the prevalent form of indigenous involvement in mercantile activities in peripheral and expansion areas, particularly in logging activities. However, in the last 20 years, the traditional practice of *habilitación* has undergone various modifications in these areas in response to the emergence of alternative forms of access to goods and the transformation of the prevalent sociopolitical conditions. One of the most visible changes is the fact that *patrones* no longer have control over large segments of the indigenous population, which was the case until the beginning of the 1970s. Thus, there are currently no reports of logging *patrones* such as those who, in the lower Pichis Valley, used to control between 300 and 500 young boys and men who were indentured for timber extraction (Bodley 1976; Narby 1989). In the Tambo Valley, Villasante (1983) reported that until the 1970s nearly 90 percent of the men from the Ashaninka community of Betania worked for several months a year in logging activities. A decade later it was reported that only 40 percent of the men were so involved.

The declining participation of the Ashaninka in logging activity within the *habilitación* system is clearly linked to the formation of native communities in areas of expansion and the appearance of alternatives for access to manufactured goods. The first of these alternatives consists of seasonal work in agricultural activities developed in the central areas of the region. Although, theoretically, this possibility had always existed, hostile relations among local Ashaninka groups had limited this option. The practice of organizing raids to obtain indigenous labor, which was promoted by the *patrones* between 1870 and 1940, involved the mobilization of indigenous leaders allied with certain *patrones* to capture indigenous men and women from neighboring groups. This practice deepened traditional rivalries and worsened the already poor communication among indigenous groups in contiguous areas. Once the practice of raiding had disappeared after 1948, new links were established among indigenous populations from different areas, which made possible the seasonal movement from peripheral and expansion areas to older colonized areas to do agricultural work. Thus, as the native communities of Satipo and Perené became involved in coffee production, Ashaninka families from the Tambo, Ene, and Pichis valleys chose to work as harvesters on indigenous coffee plantations, developing a new circuit of labor and manufactured goods that is still exists today.

The second alternative available to indigenous families in peripheral and expansion areas consists of becoming directly involved in agricultural production through the cultivation of such crops as cacao, annato, coffee, rice, and corn. This produce is sold to river traders, who increased their presence in these areas in the early 1980s as a result of the expansion of the colonization fronts on the Ucayali River basin.

The same forces that have led the indigenous population of the Selva Central to look for alternatives to debt bondage in logging activities have produced a series of changes in the system of *habilitación* itself. First, a growing number of indigenous workers demand to be paid in cash or in a combination of money and goods, not simply with goods as they were in the 1960s (Villasante 1983: 204). This trend was already evident in 1974. According to data from an official survey, 11 percent of the outfitted workers who were interviewed were paid exclusively with goods, 67 percent in cash and goods, and 22 percent exclusively in cash (SINAMOS 1975: 101).

Second, since the 1980s, payments to indigenous laborers began to approach the level of payments to nonindigenous loggers, even though neither group managed to achieve the legal minimum daily wage. Filomeno (1982: 56) reported that, in 1981, in the Tambo Valley, Ashaninka loggers working in the

Inuya River basin received payments equaling 89 percent of the pay received by *mestizo* workers.

Third, some men who continue to work in logging activities now tend to leave their communities to look for *patrones* who will employ them, rather than waiting to be hired through the *enganche* and *habilitación* system in the area where they live. This allows them to negotiate the terms of their contract from a better position. Finally, with the establishment of native communities and the enforcement of the Forestry Law (1975), in the last few years indigenous families have begun to exploit timber resources on their lands independently.

Indigenous Labor in Agropastoral Activities

Throughout the present century the use of indigenous labor for the development of agropastoral activities has taken different forms in the Selva Central. Among these, *enganche* and *habilitación* for coffee harvest was one of the primary forms in which the Yanesha and Ashaninka participated in the region's economy between 1920 and the late 1960s. The engagement of indigenous laborers for coffee cultivation and harvest was a practice introduced by the Peruvian Corporation in its Perene Colony. Initially the company recruited indigenous labor through Adventist missionaries operating within its boundaries. In exchange for the right to establish mission posts, the missionaries agreed to persuade indigenous converts to work as coffee harvesters for the company. Every year they convinced the leaders of local indigenous settlements to return to the colony's *haciendas*, reminding them of their debts to the company store (Barclay 1989: 122). Yanesha and Ashaninka labor was cheaper than that of Andean indentured laborers because payments were lower and did not include travel or housing expenses. Furthermore, indigenous labor was easier to organize to meet the needs of the company. Thus, during the 1940s, indigenous workers recruited for coffee harvest represented up to 39 percent of the total labor employed by the colony (Barclay 1989: 122).

Based on the example set by the Perene Colony, *enganche* and *habilitación* of indigenous labor expanded throughout the coffee-growing areas of the Selva Central. Through this system, hundreds of indigenous laborers (not only men but also women and children) were persuaded to work for two to three months a year on the coffee farms of Chanchamayo, Villa Rica, Oxapampa, and Satipo. These workers were kept in a constant state of indebtedness by being provided with advances in cash or manufactured goods. Goods were always overvalued, and other dishonest practices, such as cheating in the weighing of the coffee harvested by indigenous peons, were not uncommon. Greater political organization beginning in the 1950s, and a greater awareness of the exploitative character of the *enganche* and *habilitación* system, persuaded many indigenous families to stop working for the colonists and to venture into commercial agriculture (mainly coffee and fruit). Currently, most of the Yanesha and Ashaninka in these areas have become independent producers or work seasonally as paid laborers for other indigenous producers.

In areas of expansion where the trade networks necessary for the development of commercial agriculture are not accessible to the indigenous population, they sell their labor on a contract basis to nearby colonists. Labor contracts, or *contratas*, are a form of seasonal labor arrangement that involves either a person or a group of people. The value of their labor is agreed upon based on the type of work and the area where they will be working. Most of these labor contracts fall within the category of debt bondage, insofar as workers are recruited by means of an advance payment and maintained as a labor reserve through relationships of permanent indebtedness. This form of labor recruitment is widespread in cattle-ranching areas.

As we have already mentioned, most of the pastureland on cattle-ranching *haciendas* in the Palcazu Valley was cleared between 1950 and 1970 by Yanesha laborers working on contract. In 1977, Yanesha men and boys were still working an average of two months per year for local cattle ranchers, which permitted them to acquire tools, clothing, medicines, school supplies, and cooking utensils (Barclay, Basurto, and Santos-Granero 1977). A study conducted in 1986 based on a sample of 509 colonists' agricultural units in the Palcazu Valley indicates that 64 percent of them employed laborers under the *contrata* system (Camones 1986: 31). Nevertheless, as a consequence of the reluctance of the indigenous population to work on the colonists' holdings and of the arrival of poor colonists in the valley, in 1986 only 37 percent of the peons employed by *hacienda* owners were indigenous (Camones 1986: 31). In contrast, in 1985 in the Pichis Valley, 95 percent of the colonists employed indigenous laborers, and the Ashaninka continued to work for local *hacienda* owners for an average of 10 weeks per year (Narby and Swenson 1985: 23).

Another mechanism employed in the Palcazu Valley to guarantee access to indigenous labor consisted of payment for work with calves. In 1977, a Yanesha man had to work intermittently for the same *patrón* for a period of two years in order to be paid one head of cattle (Barclay, Basurto, and Santos-Granero 1977). The system proved to be doubly beneficial for the *patrones*. First, they inflated the price of the cattle that they exchanged for indigenous labor, and second, by controlling the local market, they could set cattle and beef prices, thus reducing the value of cattle raised by indigenous producers.

As a result of better education, the development of community projects, and the strengthening of community organizations, the contract system has undergone the same modifications as did other forms of indigenous labor: the import-

Table 8.1. Indigenous Paid Labor, 1974

Area	Indigenous group	Sample size (no. of men)	% paid for labor	Mode of employment
Tambo-Ene	Ashaninka	683	5.8	*Habilitación* for timber extraction
Satipo-Pangoa	Ashaninka-Nomatsiguenga	677	0.7	*Habilitación* for coffee harvesting Contracts for agricultural labor
Perené	Ashaninka	327	3.4	*Habilitación* for coffee harvesting Contracts for agricultural labor
Oxapampa-Villa Rica	Yanesha	342	38.6	Contracts for agricultural labor
Pichis-Palcazu	Ashaninka-Yanesha	1,339	37.8	Contracts for labor on cattle ranches

Source: SINAMOS 1975; data elaborated by the authors.

Note: The sample groups included men older than 14 who had worked as paid laborers in the previous 12 months.

ance of cash payments has grown, the rate of payment between indigenous and nonindigenous peons has become standardized, and the level of indebtedness has decreased. At the same time, since the late 1970s, the indigenous population in these valleys stopped working for local *patrones* with the same frequency, preferring as an alternative to work as coffee harvesters or on contract for other indigenous producers in the communities of the upper Perené Valley.

An analysis of the conditions of sale of indigenous labor in 1974 reveals important differences in the means of employment and in the rate of employment in the different areas that form the region. In Table 8.1, we list the percentages of indigenous men who sold their labor by various means in the 12 months preceding a survey by SINAMOS. The results reveal the varying degrees of participation in the market through the sale of labor that have resulted from the distinctive historical processes occurring in different colonization areas.

The areas where only small percentages of the indigenous men sold their labor — Satipo and Pangoa, with 0.7 percent of the sample, and Perené, with 3.4 percent — were the earliest occupied areas, where the indigenous population had worked for the colonists in the past but where they now had enough land and had chosen not to continue to work for them, developing instead their own commercial production. In contrast, the areas where a higher proportion of the indigenous men sold their labor were either old colonization areas, such as Oxapampa and Villa Rica, where native communities were too small and land scarcity did not allow the development of commercial agriculture, or recently colonized areas, such as Pichis and Palcazu, where poor access to the market and the monopoly of local trade by *patrones* forced indigenous men to work as paid laborers. Finally, areas where a moderate proportion of the indigenous men sold their labor were those most isolated from the sphere of market relations, such as the Tambo and Ene valleys, where the conditions for the development of commercial agriculture did not exist and where the volume of market-related activities and the opportunities to sell labor were limited.

At present, in the central areas the current tendency is to develop independent commercial agriculture based on coffee and fruit cultivation, along with a minimal sale of labor to colonists. In peripheral areas, the trend is toward a reduction in the time spent working for coffee-producing colonists or on cattle-ranching *haciendas* and toward an increase in the development of commercial agropastoral activities, insofar as land ownership and market conditions permit. Finally, in areas of expansion, the general tendency is toward a reduction in the time spent working for the local large landholders, toward an improvement in the conditions of the sale of labor, and toward the development of commercial agropastoral production. These new trends are a result of (1) the establishment of new sociopolitical conditions in the various areas under consideration, (2) the dissemination of patterns of production based on the experiences gained by the indigenous peoples in the earliest colonized areas, and (3) the development of new economic strategies by indigenous peoples and organizations, whose goal is to achieve greater economic autonomy with respect to local colonists and *patrones*.

In conclusion, indigenous labor has been crucial for the expansion of mercantile activities, as well as for the economic consolidation of the different colonization areas that compose the Selva Central region. It has also been, for a long time, the mechanism through which the indigenous peoples were able to acquire manufactured goods. At present, however, most Yanesha and Ashaninka have abandoned their role as cheap laborers for colonists and timber extractors to become independent producers. In the following section, we will examine the advantages and disadvantages of this new strategy.

COMMERCIAL AGROPASTORAL PRODUCTION

The expansion of commercial agropastoral production in the native communities of the Selva Central is a phenomenon that began to gain momentum in the 1970s. This process is closely linked to the despoliation of indigenous territories, the growing demographic pressure on land and traditional forest resources (game, fish, and wild fruits), and the increasing need for consumer market goods. But it is also the result of an important change in the economic strategy of the Yanesha and Ashaninka. This transformation is illustrated by the testimony of an Ashaninka leader, who in the 1950s exhorted his people with the following

Table 8.2. Average Cultivated Area per Family in Native Communities, 1974

Zone	No. of hectares per family
Upper Perené-Villa Rica	3.1
Central Perené	2.7
Satipo-Pangoa	3.3
Palcazu-Pichis	3.9
Tambo	1.5
Ene	0.7

Source: SINAMOS 1975: 71; data elaborated by the authors.

words: "We have to work for ourselves, not for the colonists. No, now we have to work for ourselves, so that we have food. Now we have to grow coffee to sell, so that we can buy merchandise and tools" (Fernández 1986: 45).

In the earliest colonized areas, this strategy was implemented beginning at the end of the 1940s, encountering stubborn opposition from local landowners and *patrones.* To demonstrate how this strategy became widespread and how it varies according to the prevailing conditions in different colonization areas, we will analyze this phenomenon in four zones for which we have comparative information: upper Perené-Villa Rica, central Perené, Satipo-Pangoa, and Palcazu-Pichis. In addition, in some cases we will present information about the Tambo-Ene zone to highlight some contrasts. The historical processes of colonization and formation of native communities in these four areas, treated in the second chapter and in the preceding chapter, respectively, provide the framework for the analysis of this phenomenon.

In general, the expansion of commercial agropastoral production has caused, as an immediate and very obvious result, an increase in the area cultivated per family. According to studies by Johnson (1974), Denevan (1979), Hvalkof (1986-1987), and Salick (1989), traditionally the Yanesha and Ashaninka maintained a variable number of agricultural plots, with various combinations of crops at various stages of maturity. On average, these small plots added up to an area that ranged from 0.5 to 2.0 hectares. Agricultural production for family consumption, for limited exchange, and for festivals and ritual ceremonies was complemented with food from fishing, hunting, and gathering trips. Table 8.2 shows that, by 1974, most of the Yanesha and Ashaninka had departed from this traditional economic model. By then, the average area under cultivation per family had increased significantly in certain zones, ranging from 2.7 to 3.9 hectares.

The growth in the average cultivated area per family was clearly associated with the adoption of commercial agropastoral activities. Thus, by 1974 commercial coffee and fruit cultivation was reported in the areas of Satipo-Pangoa, upper Perené-Villa Rica, and central Perené, whereas cattle ranching and, occasionally, rice cultivation were reported in the area of Palcazu-Pichis. In contrast, in the Tambo River basin, an area of expansion where the indigenous population had only recently become involved in commercial agricultural production, the average cultivated area per family was 1.5 hectares, and in the Ene Valley, an even more isolated area, the average resembled that of the traditional economic system.

Although there is a clear correlation between greater access to roads and greater incidence of commercial agropastoral activities, there are other factors that determine the degree of involvement of the indigenous population in these kinds of activities. Thus, although the road network in the Satipo-Pangoa zone is not as old as that of the upper Perené-Villa Rica zone, the average cultivated area per family is greater because of greater relative availability of land. In contrast, although the indigenous population in the Palcazu Valley had no access to roads, they began to raise cattle in the 1970s, taking advantage of greater land availability and the existence of alternative means of transportation—by air to the town of San Ramón and by river to the town of Pucallpa.

Before analyzing how the average cultivated area per indigenous family continued to increase throughout the region in the subsequent decade, it is appropriate to link the preceding information with data on the availability of nonagricultural food for subsistence purposes. In Table 8.3, we can see that by 1974, the availability of wildlife was already severely affected in three of the four areas under consideration. The visible reduction in the practice of hunting in at least two of these areas reflects not only an overall reduction in wildlife resources but also the consequent necessity of traveling farther and investing more time in locating prey. The same table reveals that in several of the areas that were most seriously affected in terms of the availability of game animals and fish, such as the upper Perené-Villa Rica, the gathering of other food resources to complement protein intake intensified. The range of what could be gathered, however, was notably restricted. Data from the areas of expansion in the Tambo and Ene valleys stand out in contrast to similar data from more integrated areas. In these areas, all of the communities practiced traditional hunting and fishing activities and, in most, traditional food-collecting activities. A comparison of Tables 8.2 and 8.3 shows that there is a certain correlation among the level of economic integration, the availability of forest resources, and the average cultivated area. Thus, in the most integrated areas, where forest resources were becoming increasingly scarce, there was a reduction in fishing, hunting, and gathering activities, as well as an increase in commercial agropastoral activities, reflected in higher cultivated-area averages.

Table 8.3. Participation in Hunting, Fishing, and Gathering by Native Communities, 1974

Zone	Hunting	Fishing	Gathering
Upper Perené-Villa Rica	66.6	75.0	75.0
Central Perené	64.2	85.7	21.4
Satipo–Pangoa	96.5	89.6	31.0
Palcazu	100.0	100.0	54.1
Tambo-Ene	100.0	100.0	72.2

Source: SINAMOS 1975: 109.

Note: Each value represents the percentage of native communities in a particular zone that engage in the activity.

This trend has become more acute since the 1970s, especially in the first three areas. Therefore, currently, access to fats and proteins depends, to a great extent, on the raising of poultry and on the sale of commercial crops in order to purchase canned goods and other processed foods. This factor indirectly influences the degree of intensification of commercial agriculture and accounts for the spatial differences that are involved in this process.

The expansion of commercial production among the indigenous population is more evident today. In Table 8.4, data on average cultivated area per family in 1974 are compared with data from three studies conducted between 1982 and 1986. Data from the upper Perené Valley are based on eight Yanesha and Ashaninka communities from a larger sample taken by Swenson (1986a, 1986b) that expressly excluded communities with greater commercial production. In contrast, data for the Satipo-Pangoa area were obtained from the work of Rodríguez, based on a sample of six Ashaninka communities "that are better linked with the market" (1990: 421). The information from the Palcazu Valley comes from a sample of 9 of the 11 native communities located in this area (Smith 1983).

Table 8.4 shows that the trend toward an increase in the average cultivated area per family in native communities has continued into the 1980s. This indicates, on the one hand, that a greater amount of time is dedicated to agriculture in comparison with hunting, fishing, and food collection and, on the other, that the increase in commercial agropastoral activities is necessary to guarantee constant access to manufactured goods and food. The surprisingly high averages for the Palcazu Valley are primarily due to pastureland (70 percent); average cultivated area per family excluding pastures is estimated to be 3.3 hectares, a figure similar to that encountered in other areas. We can thus conclude that the tendency to place increasing emphasis on agriculture not only has become common

Table 8.4. Average Cultivated Area per
Family in Native Communities

Zone	1974	c. 1986
Upper Perené–Villa Rica	3.1	3.8
Central Perené	2.7	3.5
Satipo–Pangoa	3.3	3.5
Palcazu	3.9	10.8

Sources: SINAMOS 1975 (for 1974 data); Swenson 1986a,
1986b (for communities located in the Upper Perené–
Villa Rica and Central Perené zones); Rodríguez 1990
(for the Satipo-Pangoa zone); Smith 1983 (for the
Palcazu zone).

Note: Values represent average number of hectares per
family.

among native communities but has also resulted in the consolidation of an agricultural pattern that is reflected in very similar average cultivated areas (between 3.3 and 3.8 hectares) for the four zones under consideration.

Coffee Production in Native Communities

The adoption of coffee cultivation by the indigenous sector has clearly been a strategy that, from its inception, went beyond purely economic considerations. Thus, the first producers who adopted this crop not only were trying to guarantee themselves a monetary income but were also concerned about reducing their dependence on the *patrones* and guaranteeing their rights in order to avert displacement from their land. The seizure of indigenous land was often justified on the premise that the indigenous population was not "productive" in mercantile terms. Thus, the adoption of coffee cultivation became a way of proving that the indigenous peoples, too, could be productive and therefore demand respect for their rights to the land.

The cultivation of coffee in native communities was facilitated by the experience that the Yanesha and Ashaninka of upper Perené and Villa Rica had acquired while working for the Perene Colony as harvesters and *mejoreros*. Under this system, implemented beginning in the 1940s, *mejoreros* were each given a plot on which they had to plant coffee seedlings from company nurseries. They were also permitted to plant an additional area in subsistence crops. In the sixth year, when the coffee plants had begun to yield, these areas reverted to the colony, and indigenous *mejoreros* were assigned new plots (Barclay 1989: 213–220).

In 1947, the inhabitants of the indigenous settlements in the areas of Villa Rica and Metraro solicited from the Peruvian Corporation lots of 5 hectares per family to plant their own coffee plots (Barclay 1989: 220-227). The idea was to use their experience as *mejoreros* to become independent coffee producers and thus have a new source of monetary income and greater economic autonomy. Instead of selling them lots, the company leased them. Five years later, however, when the first leases expired, the company attempted to expel the indigenous producers, paying them for the improvements that they had made and offering them new leases in other areas. This move was meant to hinder indigenous *mejoreros* and peons from becoming independent producers and, thus, to retain them as a cheap labor force. It was also meant to discourage the indigenous population from settling permanently on lands that were seen by the company as future areas of expansion for its *haciendas*. Although the company was able to expel some indigenous families from these areas, they were unable to displace those who had planted their own coffee plots.

As a result, demands for land leases by Yanesha and Ashaninka families soared on the left bank of the upper Perené River as well as on both banks of its central course. The experience of continuous displacement and of working as harvesters and *mejoreros* enabled the indigenous population to gain an understanding of colonist ideology. Experience had demonstrated that growing coffee provided a certain security against being displaced, for once they engaged in commercial production they became "civilized" in the eyes of the colonists and thus acquired some rights previously denied to them—for instance, the right to the land they occupied. The fact that the Peruvian Corporation was unable to displace indigenous families who had planted coffee plots confirmed that this strategy was successful.

In later years, the expansion of indigenous coffee cultivation was fostered by the Peruvian Corporation itself. Unable to expel the growing number of colonists who were invading its concession, in the late 1950s the company decided to grant collective lots to local indigenous groups in order to protect its borders and to deny legitimacy to the demands of the invading colonists. In these communal lots, granted freely or in exchange for token payments, the prohibition on establishing commercial crops no longer held. This contributed to furthering the expansion of indigenous coffee farms in the area.

In spite of the current process of diversification of commercial production in native communities, which replicates that taking place in the region as whole, coffee continues to be the most important commercial crop. Thus, in the Perené Valley, 50 percent of the native communities have between 30 percent and 59 percent of their total cultivated area planted in coffee, whereas in 17 percent of these communities, coffee fields occupy more than 60 percent of the cultivated land (CECONSEC 1981, 1988). In the native communities of Satipo, where coffee represents about 26 percent of the cultivated area, it is also the most important commercial crop (Rodríguez 1990).

Table 8.5. Average Area Cultivated
in Coffee per Family in Native
Communities, 1988

Zone	No. of hectares per family
Upper Perené-Villa Rica	3.6
Central Perené	3.3
Satipo-Pangoa	1.3

Sources: CECONSEC 1988 (for the Upper Perené-
Villa Rica and Central Perené zones; based on nine
communities); Rodríguez 1990 (for the Satipo-
Pangoa zone; based on six communities).

Although coffee is cultivated in practically all of the communities in the valleys of Perené and Satipo, the intensity with which it is cultivated varies as a function of the length of the occupation process and the average land area available per family. These factors determine the average area planted in coffee per family (Table 8.5).

Table 8.6 shows that in the upper Perené-Villa Rica area, average plot sizes vary—from 2.1 hectares of coffee per family to 6.3 hectares. However, included in these averages are some individual farms as large as 18 hectares. This variability is also evident in the central Perené Valley, where the average size of a family coffee holding in the various communities ranges from 1.1 to 6.3 hectares. In this area, one finds coffee holdings of up to 25 hectares per family. Because the sample from the Satipo-Pangoa zone is composed exclusively of communities that are closely linked to the market, it is not possible to establish a range of variation at a more general level. Even so, the averages found in this sample are extremely variable, from 0.8 to 1.7 hectares of coffee per family (Rodríguez 1990: 428).

Taken together, the average area planted in coffee per family in the native communities of the upper Perené-Villa Rica and central Perené areas is 3.4 hectares. This figure contrasts with the average area planted in coffee per colonist's agricultural unit in Chanchamayo Province, which in 1972 was 5.6 hectares (Gutiérrez et al. n.d.). Differences can also be found at the level of productivity. Whereas the average coffee yield in the native communities of the Perené Valley is about 4 *quintales* per hectare, the overall average yield in Chanchamayo in 1982 was estimated as 8 *quintales* (Cerrón 1985: 35). These differences stem from the varying availability of capital and, above all, from different economic strategies.

Indigenous coffee growers lack the resources to contract labor to increase the

Table 8.6. Percentage Distribution of Coffee Plots According to Plot Size Class in Native Communities in the Perené Zone, 1988

Zone and community[a]	0.1–1 hectare	1.1–3 hectares	3.1–5 hectares	5.1–10 hectares	>10 hectares
Upper Perené-Villa Rica					
Alto Yurinaki (2.1)	40.9	42.4	13.6	3.0	0.0
Alto Sancachari (6.3)	0.0	37.5	16.6	29.2	16.7
Palomar (2.6)	60.0	20.0	0.0	20.0	0.0
All 3 communities (3.6)	33.6	33.3	10.1	17.4	5.6
Central Perené					
Pucharini (2.5)	14.6	68.3	14.6	2.4	0.0
Pumpuriani (3.8)	0.0	48.1	37.0	14.8	0.0
Inchatingari (2.3)	16.6	75.0	8.4	0.0	0.0
Bajo Aldea (1.1)	85.2	14.8	0.0	0.0	0.0
Palmapampa (6.3)	0.0	29.6	33.4	18.5	18.5
Alto Incariado (4.0)	21.7	43.5	21.7	8.7	4.4
All 6 communities (3.3)	23.0	46.5	19.3	7.4	3.8
Upper Perené-Villa Rica and Central Perené (3.4)	28.3	39.9	14.7	12.4	4.7

Source: CECONSEC 1988; data elaborated by the authors.

[a] Values in parentheses are the average area (hectares) in coffee per family.

size of their coffee plots and to carry out all of the activities required to enhance productivity. Not only do they depend heavily on the family labor force, but, because they tend to combine commercial with subsistence agricultural activities, they have to distribute their efforts among these different crops. Thus, indigenous families have little time to prune, systematically cultivate, or practice phytosanitary controls. Moreover, the majority have neither the resources nor the expertise to invest in and apply chemical fertilizers or pesticides. Indigenous coffee producers do, however, use hilling techniques to prevent erosion on sloping land, weed their coffee plantings periodically, and make use of shade trees.

It should be emphasized that the lower productivity of coffee farms in native communities is due not only to lack of capital, scarcity of labor, and the failure to use modern technologies but also to the lower density of their plantings. Indigenous coffee fields have an average 1,000 plants per hectare, whereas the most productive coffee fields of the colonists have between 4,000 and 6,000. This lower density has its advantages, however, in the sense that it lessens the risk of the spread of disease (Swenson 1986a).

A few indigenous farmers, particularly in the upper Perené Valley, have begun to grow the caturra variety of coffee. The expansion of the cultivation of this variety, which offers a greater yield per hectare, is rather limited in native communities, as well as on colonist small landholdings, because it requires periodic fertilization and a greater labor investment throughout the year. The fact that more-productive coffee varieties such as caturra have a shorter productive life is also an important consideration for indigenous producers.

As we have already pointed out, coffee production has generated a growing demand for seasonal labor within native communities. Nevertheless, the volume of labor that is needed varies greatly, not only as a function of the size of the areas under cultivation but also as a function of the availability of working capital and the attitude of farmers. On their less densely planted coffee plots, many indigenous producers do not employ extrafamilial labor during the harvest season even if they own plots larger than 1 hectare. Families who have more than 3 hectares of coffee generally employ salaried labor for the harvest. There is no information that enables us to quantify the total demand for extrafamilial labor in coffee-producing native communities. For the Perené area, however, it is reported that at least 35 percent of the indigenous coffee producers hire laborers, a much lower percentage than that observed among colonists (see Chapter 3). In Satipo, Rodríguez (1990) estimated that 20 percent of the families in the communities of his sample contracted salaried labor, presumably for coffee harvest.

Not all coffee-producing communities nor the individual plots within them require labor at the same time, since coffee matures according to the altitude of the fields. In addition, in higher areas the harvest tends to be more gradual than in the lowlands, where maturation is more uniform. Therefore, some indigenous coffee producers often also work as harvesters for other indigenous farmers during part of this period. As on the colonists' farms, coffee harvesters are paid on the basis of the amount of coffee picked. Most seasonal laborers who are contracted by indigenous coffee producers come from native communities in non-coffee-producing areas: the Palcazu, Pichis, Tambo and Ene valleys, and, more recently, the Gran Pajonal. Harvesters often come from communities with historical ties to coffee-producing communities resulting from former migrations and, in many cases, have kinship ties with the family for whom they are working.

In summary, coffee cultivation has become the main source of income for a large number of indigenous families and is at present one of the most important mechanisms of indigenous integration into the regional and national market economy. Moreover, coffee production has permitted some indigenous producers to accumulate enough capital to allow them to buy trucks, establish small grocery stores, or educate their children in the cities of Huancayo or Lima (Gasché, Trapnell, and Rengifo 1987). However, it should be underscored that coffee cultivation has not been adopted merely for economic reasons but, above all, for political reasons. In effect, by adopting coffee cultivation, indigenous families have been able to legitimize their claims to the land they occupy, thus avoiding further displacement and creating the conditions for forming native communities.

The Diversification of Commercial Agriculture

In the past several years, the indigenous sector has begun to diversify its commercial agricultural production. Communities in the upper Perené Valley have been the first to experiment with these new commercial crops, especially fruits. As the keystone of the indigenous strategy for economic integration, coffee is cultivated along the entire Chanchamayo–Satipo axis, independently of the altitude of native communities and of their access to transportation routes (Swenson 1986b: 4). In contrast, diversification of commercial agriculture at the community level reflects a certain specialization. Whereas coffee can be cultivated even in the communities farthest from the road, where it is transported by pack animal or on the shoulders of the producers to collection points without deteriorating, in the case of fruit production, producers clearly must consider the accessibility of the market. Thus, fruit production has tended to be concentrated in the areas closest to major roads.

The diversification of commercial agriculture has also been influenced by requirements for technical knowledge and investment. Certain fruit crops, such as citrus trees, demand a greater investment than coffee, as well as knowledge related to their maintenance that is harder to come by: for example, grafting, pruning, and disease control. As a result, citrus production has been adopted mainly in areas where indigenous families have been able to achieve a certain level of capital improvement. In contrast, commercial cultivation of other, more traditional fruit crops, such as banana, papaya, and pineapple, has become more widespread.

The adoption of commercial crops other than coffee by the indigenous population also seems to have been dependent on the existence of well-established commercial channels. Thus, in the 1980s indigenous producers in the Chorobamba Valley began producing rocoto chili (a large variety of peppers in the Solanaceae family), following in the footsteps of Andean colonists who had introduced this crop in previous years. It was only after highland buyers started to visit the area regularly that indigenous producers decided to venture into this kind of production. In turn, in the Pichis Valley, native communities began to produce annato at the end of the 1970s and introduced dryland rice in the mid-1980s, in response to the establishment of government loan programs and storage centers (Holshouser 1972: 184; Narby 1986: 15). Finally, the adoption of cocoa cultivation in the communities of the central Perené, Satipo, Tambo, and Ene valleys has occurred in response to the presence of traders who traveled throughout the region to promote its production.

Table 8.7. Percentage of Native Communities Growing
Commercial Crops

Crop	1974		1986	
	Upper Perené– Villa Rica	Central Perené	Upper Perené– Villa Rica	Central Perené
Avocado	16.6	42.8	100.0	81.2
Cocoa	16.6	14.3	–	–
Coffee	83.3	57.1	100.0	100.0
Lemon	0.0	7.1	100.0	68.7
Orange	0.0	21.4	100.0	68.7
Papaya	16.6	42.8	0.0	62.5

Sources: SINAMOS 1975: 78; Swenson 1986b: 3.

Note: Dashes denote no data.

As shown in Table 8.7, between 1974 and 1986, the adoption of commercial crops other than coffee has increased in areas that have better ties to consumer markets, whereas coffee has remained the predominant crop in the region as a whole.

Whereas the process of diversification of commercial agriculture in the indigenous sector has developed more or less along the same lines as it has in the colonist sector, there is a significant difference between these sectors with respect to the relative importance of subsistence agriculture in their respective economic strategies. As we have pointed out, when colonists arrive in the region to grow commercial perennial crops, they initially plant annual food crops to ensure the survival of the family until their coffee crop matures. This strategy is complemented by the seasonal sale of their labor. When coffee plots begin to yield, food crops tend to lose their importance in the economic strategy of the colonists. In fact, in 1986 only 15 percent of the total cultivated area in colonists' agricultural units was dedicated to food crops (Ministerio de Agricultura 1963-1988).

In contrast, among indigenous producers food crops retain a much greater importance. Thus, even in areas such as Perené and Satipo, where the indigenous population is heavily involved in commercial agriculture, an average of 30 percent of the cultivated area is planted in manioc and other native tubers, corn, beans, and bananas (Swenson 1986b: 4; Rodríguez 1990: 427). The larger proportion of the area in food crops seems to be associated with the express intent of maintaining a certain autonomy with respect to the market in terms of food supply.[12] Thus, although both sectors are linked to the market through commercial agriculture, the indigenous sector appears to resist complete dependence on the sale of this type of production for its subsistence.

How much longer indigenous producers will be able to maintain this strategy of combining commercial and subsistence agriculture is difficult to say. In those native communities located in the earliest colonized areas—where families own, on average, less than 10 hectares—increasing land scarcity is preventing producers from producing enough food. In these communities, which represent 53 percent of all the communities in the province of Chanchamayo, indigenous families have planted up to 80 percent of their land in commercial crops (Swenson 1986a). This means that in these communities the strategy for expansion and diversification of commercial production has reached its limit and that land constraints have begun to affect the complementary strategy of food self-sufficiency. Lacking areas for agricultural expansion, the land in use is subjected to ever-shorter fallow periods. In these communities, the necessity to increase productivity is evident. However, they lack the technical assistance and capital improvements necessary to further intensify land use. What constitutes an immediate challenge to these communities seems to be the fate awaiting the region's other communities in the near future.

Indigenous Production of Cattle

In the Yanesha communities of the Palcazu Valley, cattle production has become the primary link to the market. As we have already indicated, this economic pattern developed in the context of a local economy characterized by the presence of large cattle *haciendas*. Although in other areas such as the Pichis, Satipo, Pangoa, and Villa Rica valleys, a few indigenous farmers own cattle, only in the native communities of the Palcazu Valley do we find a significant proportion of the total cultivated area planted in pasture for cattle ranching.

The development of cattle production among the Yanesha of the Palcazu Valley began in the 1960s, when a growing number of indigenous families began to raise their own cattle. This practice was encouraged by local *hacienda* owners through the system of *crianza al partir*. Most producers involved in this system were associated with local *patrones* as indentured peons. Under this system, a local *patrón* would give a peon a cow, which he had to raise in his own pastures. After several years, the *hacienda* owner would have the right to reclaim the cow, along with half of its offspring. The system proved to be doubly rewarding for the *patrón*: on the one hand it maintained and reinforced the dependent relationship of his laborers, while, on the other, it transferred the costs and risks of cattle raising to his indigenous "associate." To ensure that the quality of his stock would not deteriorate, from time to time the *hacienda* owner provided his associate with a bull for breeding. Since *hacienda* owners controlled the marketing and transport of beef in the valley, the expansion of cattle production in native communities (since it did not affect the overall supply of indigenous labor) proved to be beneficial for them (Barclay, Basurto, and Santos-Granero 1977).

Table 8.8. Percentage of Cultivated
Pastures in Relation to Total Cultivated
Area in Native Communities in the
Palcazu Zone, 1981

Native community	% in pasture
Siete de Junio	85.8
Santa Rosa de Chuchurras	86.8
Buenos Aires	89.8
Alto Iscozacín	72.0
Shiringamazú	80.0
Loma Linda–Laguna	46.2
Santa Rosa de Pichanaz	43.7
San Pedro Pichanaz	31.6
All 8 communities	64.7

Source: Smith 1983: 75.

For the Yanesha families involved in this system, this was the only opportunity to develop a commercial activity. Because of the prevailing debt-bondage system in the valley, to acquire a head of cattle an indigenous farmer had to invest several months over several years working for a local *hacienda* owner. In contrast, this breeding system offered the opportunity to immediately obtain a cow without having to make a large initial labor or cash investment. Moreover, like coffee cultivation for the indigenous population in the Perené Valley, for the indigenous people in the Palcazu Valley, cattle became a way to affirm the right to their land, which had been gradually invaded by *hacienda* owners. Thus, the practice of cattle ranching not only provided the only commercial production option but was also a strategy to avert the seizure of their land in the short term while reducing their long-term dependence on cattle ranchers. As a result, cattle breeding spread among all of the native communities in the valley, progressively giving rise to individual herds, which no longer depended on the continuation of the system of *crianza al partir* for their growth. By 1976, it was reported that only one third of the cattle in native communities in the valley continued to be raised under this system (Smith 1983: 51).

The importance of cattle breeding varies from one community to another according to the type of land that is available and on the history of the relationship with local *haciendas*. Thus, whereas in five of the communities pastures accounted for 70 percent to 90 percent of the land under cultivation in 1981, in three other communities they accounted for between 30 percent and 46 percent (Table 8.8).

Not all of the indigenous families in the Palcazu Valley raise cattle. Moreover,

Table 8.9. Cattle Ownership in Native
Communities in the Palcazu Zone, 1974

Native community	% of families that own cattle	Average herd size per family
Santa Rosa de Chuchurras	80.0	11
Loma Linda	42.8	8
Laguna	42.3	3
Buenos Aires	30.4	10
Shiringamazú	17.7	19

Source: CENCIRA 1974: 178.

the sizes of family herds vary substantially over a relatively short time. This is so because, for most indigenous families, cattle breeding works as a system of savings that enables them to deal with emergencies requiring health care or to spend or invest larger sums of money. Cattle diseases and difficulties in acquiring medicine and veterinary services are also responsible for major fluctuations in the sizes of family herds. Data from Table 8.9 demonstrate the variability that exists among communities in terms of the number of families engaged in cattle raising and the average number of head of cattle per family.

Cattle breeding requires a significant initial labor investment. To clear pastureland, a family generally invites several men from the community who help to fell trees in an area in exchange for equivalent assistance in the future. Forage crops, usually kudzu *(Pueraria thunbergiana)* and *toro urco (Panicum pilosum),* are broadcast-planted by the nuclear family, often where rice has been previously introduced. Once pastureland has been prepared, the area is fenced with barbed wire or with living fences, depending on its location. To maintain the nutritional value of pastures, they need to be cultivated two to five times annually, depending on the variety. In native communities, family labor is generally employed for this task.

In the *haciendas* of the Palcazu Valley, the overall average area in pasture per head of cattle is 1.6 hectares. In contrast, in native communities the average area of pasture per head of cattle is approximately 0.8 hectare (CENCIRA 1974: 173; Smith 1983: 51). This smaller average area is not indicative, however, of a more intensive system but instead reflects native producers' difficulties in clearing and maintaining larger areas of pasture, since they also have to tend their subsistence plots, as well as hunt and fish. To this can be added communal activities and the temporary wage labor of one or more family members.

To confront these labor shortages and the increased costs of individual cattle production, since the 1970s indigenous farmers in the Palcazu Valley have chosen among two alternative strategies. The first consists of the establishment of informal associations of between two and five families linked by kinship ties, who generally form a residence group within the community. According to this scheme, these "associates" take care of their pastures and tend their cattle together. If the association dissolves, the cattle and pastures are redistributed, and calves and their profits are equally divided among all of the members.

A second strategy, communal cattle breeding, has been attempted in several communities but has proved to be successful in only one case. During the second half of the 1970s, at least six communities in the Palcazu Valley began communal cattle-breeding projects, encouraged by the opportunity to increase their stocks of cattle through access to donations of cattle, fencing, and medicine. Communal cattle production was aimed not only at lowering the costs of cattle reproduction and the per-family labor requirements but also at organizing a more systematic marketing strategy for the beef, thus creating a more stable income for its members. In the community of Puerto Laguna, these goals were achieved. However, most of the attempts to organize communal cattle-production projects have failed.

Cattle ranching in Yanesha communities, consisting of cattle raised by individual families, community-owned cattle, and herds bred from *hacienda* owners' stock, accounts for 28 percent of all cattle in the Palcazu Valley, estimated at 13,139 head of cattle in 1989. Indigenous pastures represented approximately 25 percent of the total area in pasture in the valley (Smith 1983; Watson 1985; INADE 1988: Table 2). Although these data indicate that cattle production in native communities has grown significantly, this activity has not provided a level of income proportionate to the investent in time, land, and labor it demands. This is basically because local *hacienda* owners control the beef trade and pay low prices to indigenous producers. The arrival of the Carretera Marginal in 1985 has not contributed toward eliminating this monopoly.

The degree of success of the cattle-production strategy developed by Yanesha communities in the Palcazu is difficult to assess. On the one hand, the adoption of cattle breeding has been a determining factor in changing the government's approach to indigenous peoples in the valley. As a result, indigenous farmers have managed to assert their right of ownership over 35 percent of the land granted in the valley. Concomitantly, they have achieved greater autonomy with respect to *hacienda* owners. However, the income generated by this activity does not prevent young men and adults from having to abandon their own productive activities periodically in order to work temporarily in neighboring *haciendas* or on coffee farms in the Perené and Villa Rica areas. Furthermore, in a study of changes in the indigenous agricultural systems of the Palcazu Valley, Salick (n.d.: 14) pointed out that both the expansion of cattle ranching and the necessity to work for wages are, to a large extent, responsible for the loss of diversity of traditional Yanesha agriculture and for the deterioration of their subsistence base.

The expansion of cattle production has also modified traditional patterns of land use in the communities of the valley. In 1981, the area of pastureland greatly exceeded the available land considered suitable for cattle raising (type P soils), the proportion of area in pasture being 34 percent greater than the area suitable for cattle production (Smith 1983: 68–78). This means that, by that point, a large proportion of the land suitable for agriculture (type A and C soils) was being used for cattle production. As a result, several communities were experiencing a shortage of land suitable for agriculture, and in at least two of them, people found it necessary to make agricultural use of areas suitable only for logging (type F soils) (Smith 1983: 75).

*   *   *

To summarize, as a strategy for avoiding having to work for colonists under unfair labor conditions, while at the same time ensuring monetary income and access to manufactured goods, indigenous commercial production has surely been successful. It has also been successful as a strategy for confirming their rights to ancestral lands. In the eyes of colonists and State officials, the development of commercial agriculture has endowed a greater legitimacy to indigenous land claims than that derived from the argument of ancestral ownership. However, the adoption of commercial production has brought with it a series of unforeseen side effects.

One of these has been the need to expand the area under cultivation while a large proportion of the native communities of the region are experiencing land scarcity. This has resulted in a gradual decrease of the area cultivated in subsistence crops in favor of that cultivated in pastures or commercial crops. In some communities, the expansion of these perennial crops has taken over most of the land suitable for agropastoral activities, leaving little room for subsistence agriculture. This has affected the subsistence base of the indigenous population, while at the same time making indigenous families more dependent on the market for their livelihood.

Furthermore, increased commercial production in a context of land scarcity, particularly in areas closest to roads, has reduced the time that land lies fallow, leading to the overexploitation and degradation of soils. It has also led to the exploitation of lands that are only suitable for forestry activities or that should be protected. As a result, yields of both subsistence and commercial crops have decreased, forcing many indigenous families to move to communities that have greater land availability.

Table 8.10. Commercial Crops or Pastures in Native
Communities, 1986

Province	Area (hectares)	No. of families	Average no. of hectares per family
Chanchamayo	4,211	1,831	2.3
Satipo	6,497	5,414	1.2
Oxapampa	9,571	2,472	3.9
Selva Central	20,279	9,717	2.1

Sources: Swenson 1986a, 1986b; CECONSEC 1988; Rodríguez 1990;
Smith 1983; Narby 1986; Villasante 1983; Ordoñez 1985.

INDIGENOUS CONTRIBUTION TO THE REGIONAL ECONOMY

It is difficult to quantify the contribution of indigenous commercial production to the region's economy. There are, however, two indicators—percentage of total cultivated area in commercial crops and percentage of total cultivated area—which, when correlated with the demographic relative weight of the indigenous peoples, can contribute toward this goal.

To estimate the percentage of total cultivated area in commercial crops corresponding to the indigenous sector, we have used the average areas cultivated in commercial crops per family in native communities of the provinces of Chanchamayo and Satipo as estimated by Swenson (1986a, b), CECONSEC (1988), and Rodríguez (1990). As there is no similarly reliable information for the native communities of Oxapampa Province, we have extrapolated data from areas of Chanchamayo and Satipo to areas of Oxapampa where native communities have similar patterns of production.

We have thus estimated that roughly 30 percent of the indigenous population of the Oxapampa Province—approximately 740 Yanesha families living in the districts of Villa Rica and Oxapampa—has an average of 3.8 hectares of land per family planted in commercial crops, primarily coffee. Another 30 percent of the indigenous population, composed of members of Yanesha communities located in the Palcazu Valley in the district of Iscozacín, has an average of 7.5 hectares of pasture and land planted in commercial crops. Finally, 40 percent of the population—the Ashaninka living in the Pichis Valley in the district of Puerto Bermúdez—has an average of 1.2 hectares per family, planted in annato, rice,

Table 8.11. Total Cultivated Area in Native
Communities, 1986

Province	Area (hectares)	No. of families	Average no. of hectares per family
Chanchamayo	6,775	1,831	3.7
Satipo	15,160	5,414	2.8
Oxapampa	13,995	2,472	5.7
Selva Central	35,930	9,717	3.7

Sources: See Table 8.4.

and pasture. The estimates of the total area in commercial crops and pastures for all of the native communities in the Selva Central are given in Table 8.10.

On the basis of these calculations, we can estimate that the total area planted in commercial crops or pastures in the native communities in the Selva Central is around 20,300 hectares. In 1988 this represented 15 percent of the total area in commercial agropastoral production in the region (Ministerio de Agricultura 1963–1988). Taking into consideration that the indigenous population constitutes 21 percent of the region's total rural population, their contribution to commercial agriculture would be below their demographic relative weight. However, given that the indigenous peoples have adopted this kind of production only recently and that, in contrast with colonists, they have had little or no government support, the fact that they are responsible for 15 percent of the total area cultivated in commercial crops acquires a much greater relevance.

The economic importance of the indigenous sector increases when one considers its weight in terms of percentage of total cultivated area, that is, the area planted in both commercial and subsistence crops. As shown in Table 8.11, Yanesha and Ashaninka producers are responsible for 23 percent of the region's total cultivated area, a figure slightly above their demographic relative weight.

The fact that indigenous producers devote an average of almost 44 percent of their cultivated area to subsistence production distinguishes them from colonists — who devote an average of 15 percent — and suggests that although they have pursued economic integration, their model of integration does not seek to replicate that of the colonist sector. In effect, the maintenance of a significant subsistence production acts both as an economic strategy (by ensuring a steady food supply, it makes indigenous families less dependent on the market) and as a cultural strategy (it preserves a social space where traditional economic practices prevail).

Although the economic strategy of the Yanesha and Ashaninka seems to conform to the integrationist stance of both colonists and government officials, it in fact opposes it. Advocates of the "civilizing" ideology assert that the economic integration of indigenous peoples is indispensable to achieving their incorporation into national society and culture and turning them into "real" Peruvian citizens. By this, they mean generic Peruvians who share a common culture and history. In contrast, the type of economic integration advocated by the indigenous peoples and their political organizations does not require the shedding of their ethnic identities. On the contrary, it is conceived as an instrument in the struggle to survive and maintain their culture and identities in an adverse environment. Thus, in spite of some of its negative side effects, commercial agropastoral production has provided the indigenous peoples of the Selva Central an opportunity to redefine their relationship with the national society and the State. The indigenous strategy of integration has both an economic dimension, that of ensuring better living conditions, and a political dimension, that of guaranteeing respect for their identity as full, yet differentiated, citizens.

9
INDIGENOUS ORGANIZATION AND POLITICAL STRATEGIES

The emergence of indigenous organizational movements constitutes a political response to the challenges posed by integration. Current ethnic organizations are a result of the confrontation between the indigenous peoples and the colonist sector, which is frequently favored by the State. This struggle has been manifested not only as physical confrontations between these two sectors but also as a confrontation between two different concepts of society. The State and, to a lesser extent, the dominant colonist groups have based their discourse on the premise of "one state, one nation" and on the notion of "integration" as a homogenizing mechanism. Indigenous peoples, on the other hand, have insisted on claiming their right to maintain a degree of autonomous decision making and action within a pluriethnic and multicultural society.

Integration is not only an ideological concept within the State discourse regarding indigenous peoples but a historical project to which a diversity of social, economic, and political agents, not always acting in coordination with the State, have contributed. Although, since the earliest stages of colonization, the State has proposed the incorporation of indigenous peoples, this was not always been accompanied by concrete actions that would effect their integration. Until late in the 20th century, the forces of integration were mostly in the hands of nongovernmental agents, primarily Catholic and Protestant missionaries. However, even these efforts had relatively insignificant effects in comparison with those of the social forces and economic pressures that began to influence the Yanesha and Ashaninka as a result of large-scale colonization beginning in the 1950s.

The creation of new consumer needs, the increasing restrictions on access to land and natural resources, and the desire to avoid being exploited and discriminated against have led the indigenous peoples of the Selva Central to attempt to integrate themselves into the regional economy. Therefore, indigenous integration is not the exclusive result of State actions but a consequence of a combination of external pressures that are beyond indigenous peoples' control and their will to integrate on their own terms as a strategy in their struggle to survive.

EMERGENCE AND EVOLUTION OF CONTEMPORARY INDIGENOUS MOVEMENTS

The indigenous organizational movements that have arisen in the last several decades are part of the indigenous strategy for integration. The implicit ideology that inspires these movements is the need to struggle within the system—with the tools and in the political arenas that it provides—to achieve certain objectives not shared by it, including respect for indigenous autonomy in decision making as peoples with their own histories and identities. It is necessary to note, however, that, in this region, contemporary indigenous organizations are the product of a previous defeat. Thus, when these organizations emerged, the Yanesha and Ashaninka were already territorially, socially, and politically divided. With most of their territory already occupied, with their traditional political systems in shambles, with a population shrunk by epidemics and slave trafficking, and with their power for armed struggle neutralized to a great extent, the Yanesha and Ashaninka found themselves facing a historical choice: to integrate themselves as individuals into the dominant regional society, denying or disguising their ethnic identity, or to integrate as a distinct people.

The indigenous organizations that have emerged in the region do not form a homogeneous block. There are significant differences among them as a result of the specific political and economic conditions of the various areas that form the Selva Central. It should also be noted that the struggle between colonists and the indigenous peoples is not, nor has it ever been, a confrontation between two monolithic blocks. Just as the indigenous peoples have been exposed to various methods of integration, the colonists also differ as a function of the length of their presence in an area, their access to land and capital, and their ethnic origin. Because of this variety of factors, indigenous movements have arisen in response to different problems, emphasizing one claim or another and establishing distinct relationships with various nonindigenous groups. These differences have also affected the scale, capacity for action, and platform of each organization.

The forms that these organizations have assumed have also been dependent to a large extent on the legal alternatives and political opportunities offered by the State and by civil society at the time of their formation. Thus, for instance, the changes introduced in the relationship of the State with grassroots organizations during the government of General Velasco Alvarado had major repercussions in the way indigenous peoples organized in the region.

The emergence of indigenous organizations based on Western schemes (agrarian associations, civil associations, federations, and so on) represented a significant rupture with traditional models of political organization. To begin with, in the pre-Hispanic period, indigenous political systems were based on the existence of local leaders whose power base rested on their influence over extensive groups of families and on alliances established with similar groups by marriage. These leaders had no formal coercive means of imposing their authority. Furthermore, beyond local leadership there was no other stable political authority that exercised influence over the entire ethnic group. In some cases, when the entire ethnic group, or extensive segments of it, were involved, leadership was shared among various local headmen. The nature of this leadership varied among the Yanesha and Ashaninka. Yanesha leaders had an eminently politico-religious character, whereas Ashaninka leaders had a politico-military character. The informal and decentralized political systems of the indigenous peoples were extremely fluid, gaining or losing strength during periods of peace or of crisis, such as intra- or intertribal wars, epidemics, natural catastrophes, and the presence of invaders.

The new organizations, on the other hand, were based on more formal and centralized schemes and frequently assumed a supralocal or supracommunity character, which in some cases (among the Yanesha, for example) have enabled them to unite the entire ethnic group. Nevertheless, these new organizations have maintained the fluidity characteristic of traditional political systems and, in general, seek a wide consensus as the basis for their actions. In the stage of transition to a more modern style of organization, it was the traditional leaders who assumed the role of defenders of the rights of their people. Later, when the first supralocal organizations emerged, their leadership sometimes fell back on these traditional chiefs. In a third stage, and with the intention of confronting the kinds of problems posed by integration under better conditions, traditional leaders ceded to younger leaders, who had generally received a formal education, could read and write in Spanish, and had a better understanding of the ways of the dominant nonindigenous peoples. In many cases, these young leaders also had the benefit of kinship ties with authorities and families with traditional prestige. In other cases, the new leaders were also Protestant or Adventist ministers, combining their political authority with a religious component that was always present in traditional forms of leadership.

In the following sections, we offer examples of these various forms of leadership as we analyze the process of the emergence and evolution of some of the indigenous organizations of the Selva Central.

Organizational Movements of the Perené Ashaninka

The last indigenous uprising in the Perené Valley occurred at the beginning of the 1930s after a severe smallpox epidemic (Barclay 1989: 129) When this uprising was quelled, there seemed to be only two options left for the Ashaninka population to ensure their access to land and to conserve their freedom of movement. Some local groups chose to become involved in commercial agriculture and to negotiate with the Perene Colony to rent or buy lots; others, particularly after 1948, chose to leave the area to form Adventist settlements in other places, especially in the Pichis and Palcazu valleys.

The increasing number of colonist invasions of the Perené Valley, beginning in the 1950s, affected not only the Peruvian Corporation's concession but also many indigenous settlements located in the upper and central areas of the valley. The Perene Colony showed a greater propensity to favor the claims for land posed by local indigenous leaders, with the dual objective of legitimizing its position in the region and of slowing the colonist advance. The colonists, who had formed the Comité de Colonización Nacional (National Colonization Committee) and were confronting the company, sought an alliance with the local indigenous population to strengthen their claims before the State (Casanto 1985: 227). The alliance with the indigenous peoples was not based, however, on respect for their ancestral land rights or on their rights as autonomous people but was rather opportunistic and aimed at protecting and advancing their own interests.

In this context, in which local Ashaninka leaders were unsure whether to establish an alliance with the Peruvian Corporation or with the invading colonists, a third option arose based on the example of the colonists' organization itself: to form an independent indigenous organization, which, by turning to legal actions and pressure on the government, could confront the monopoly held by the British firm (Casanto 1985: 226). Coincidentally, this also attracted some young Ashaninka leaders trained in Adventism, who had moved to the Pichis Valley but who returned to their place of origin, drawn by "news of State recognition of land rights in the Perené" (Casanto 1985: 226). This group of leaders, who had experience in supralocal organizations thanks to their participation in the activities of the Adventist Church, contributed significantly to the establishment of a new understanding between local indigenous leaders, thus laying the foundation for the future organization. Some of these leaders were later to play key roles in the emergence of the indigenous organization in the Pichis Valley.

With the understanding that the political struggle of the colonists was just, and with confidence in their own ability to assure their rights, the Ashaninka leaders of the upper and central Perené Valley agreed to form the Asociación de

Nativos Campas del Perené (Perené Indigenous Campa Association) in 1959 and to offer their support to the National Colonization Committee (Casanto 1985: 226). A few months later, both organizations met to draw up an agenda of demands, which included the establishment of schools for both groups and an agreement to build landing strips that would allow both groups to ship produce and thus break up the trading monopoly of the Perene Colony. These agreements were later endorsed by various other Ashaninka leaders in the Perené Valley, whom the Peruvian Corporation attempted to intimidate by requesting their incarceration (Casanto 1985: 226).

As the colonization process continued to accelerate, the National Colonization Committee lost influence. By 1961, the Ashaninka leaders denounced the abuses that were committed by the colonists, who did not pay their indigenous workers the salaries that had been agreed upon. In addition, as Casanto points out, "the natives felt impotent to make the colonists—who continued to invade their reserves—understand that these lands were theirs" (1985: 229). This situation precipitated not only the rupture of the alliance formed in 1959 but also the dissolution of the indigenous organization. With the uncontrollable avalanche of colonists and the consequent downfall of the British concession, the indigenous peoples continued to lose land without being able to escape from debt bondage or from exploitation by coffee and fruit buyers.

The arrival of General Velasco Alvarado in office encouraged the establishment of native reserves in the Selva Central. In addition, beginning in 1970, agrarian-reform officials took the initiative to organize annual meetings of local leaders, taking advantage of previous organizational experience and drawing inspiration from the first Congreso Amuesha or meeting of Yanesha leaders in 1969 (see below). In four consecutive annual meetings organized under their auspices, attendees of the Congreso Campa del Perené, or meeting of Perené Ashaninka leaders, discussed the problems and needs of the local indigenous population. Although these congresses did not result in the establishment of an independent organization, the meetings did help to create a new dynamic of interaction between communities, to prepare leaders to assume new functions and forms of action, to accelerate the creation of reserves, and to lobby for the establishment of schools and public health centers in the area.

With the passage of Decree Law 20653, the Ashaninka settlements in the Perené Valley began to be registered and titled as "native communities." As this process advanced, the Ashaninka became interested in the creation of a new kind of organization that could function as a trading committee to assure a means of marketing for their commercial agricultural produce. Beginning in 1975, they tried several different formulas in the style of community or multicommunity committees. These experiences led to the creation in 1978 of the Central de

Comunidades Nativas de la Selva Central (Central Committee of Native Communities of the Selva Central), or CECONSEC, which took steps to become recognized, obtain loans from the Banco Agrario, and become licensed to export coffee. In the years that followed, CECONSEC extended its sphere of influence to the Pichis Valley, where the Ashaninka had stopped holding their annual congresses (see below). The economic difficulties that they encountered limited the capacity of CECONSEC to assume the task of marketing the bulk of coffee and annato from the Perené and Pichis native communities, limiting it to an annual average of 2,000 *quintales* of coffee and the irregular sale of annato. Added to these difficulties was the fact that the coffee export quota that had been obtained by CECONSEC was expropriated by an export firm whose services had been contracted because of CECONSEC's own lack of capital.

Although CECONSEC was initially created as a business initiative, it immediately assumed union functions: defending territorial and civil rights and demanding government training for indigenous teachers, health workers, and community leaders. At the same time, CECONSEC sought to address the problem of the environmental impact of agricultural production. Also, being an Ashaninka organization, CECONSEC intervened to defend Ashaninka communities in areas that were originally outside of its jurisdiction, such as the Gran Pajonal, the Ene, the Tambo, and Atalaya, where it lobbied for land titling, charged *patrones* with abuses, and promoted community organization. In the last several years, CECONSEC has extended its work into the Satipo area.

Currently, CECONSEC, with headquarters in La Merced and an office in Satipo, epitomizes the strategy of struggle and survival defined by the communities of Perené and Satipo: economic integration as a means of struggle against political, economic, and cultural subordination. The duality intrinsic to this strategy is reflected in the structure and function of the organization, in which although some communities are associated for business reasons only, together they all form its organizational base.

Because of the historical importance of the communities of the Perené Valley in the promotion of indigenous organization in the Selva Central, CECONSEC plays a pivotal role for all of the Ashaninka organizations in the region. As a result, in recent years CECONSEC has become the focus of new and serious conflicts derived from the current situation of violence experienced by the region. In this context, native communities, their leadership, and CECONSEC have had to take on new and difficult political challenges.

The Yanesha Organizational Movement

The situation of the Yanesha of Oxapampa, Villa Rica, and Palcazu was radically different from that of the Perené Ashaninka. Although several segments of the

Yanesha people had worked for the Perene Colony, most remained at its margin. Therefore, when the conflict between the colony and invading Andean migrants began, most of the Yanesha did not perceive themselves as involved in it, nor did they feel forced to take part or establish strategic alliances with any of the groups involved.

Moreover, most of the colonists established in Yanesha territory had ethnic origins and economic situations different from those of the poor Andean peasants who settled in the Perené Valley. In Oxapampa, an area that had been occupied for a long time, colonists of German origin who were engaged in coffee and cattle production and in logging operations formed the elite of the valley and concentrated some of the most important capital resources in the region. In Villa Rica, colonists descended from Germans who had originally settled in Pozuzo and Oxapampa dominated the economy of the zone and owned large coffee *haciendas,* which made extensive use of Yanesha labor force. Finally, in the Palcazu, colonists of German origin owned large cattle ranches and controlled trade in the valley.

The colonization of the rest of the Yanesha territory did not have the same massive character as it had in the Perené Valley. However, the economic and political power of the colonists who had settled there and their control of the best land had forced the Yanesha to work for them as the only form of access to monetary income or manufactured goods. Without any legal protection for their land and with a colonist sector in full economic expansion, the Yanesha (especially in Oxapampa and Villa Rica) saw their survival become more and more endangered.

Supreme Decree 03 gave the Yanesha the legal option to claim their ancestral land rights in 1957, but it was not enforced until much later. Thus, between 1957 and 1968, only two Yanesha reserves were established. When General Velasco Alvarado came to power, there was a political change with respect to indigenous land rights. The Summer Institute of Linguistics, which had been doing missionary and linguistic work in Yanesha territory since 1953, along with some volunteers from the Peace Corps, began to propose the idea of a meeting of leaders to seek legal protection for the land.

This first meeting took place in Miraflores (presently Tsachopen) in 1969, with a gathering of representatives from 20 Yanesha settlements in the Palcazu, Villa Rica, and Oxapampa valleys. As a result of the meeting, a memorandum detailing the agreements that were reached was presented to the government. Two of these dealt with the problem of land tenure, and the other three established the need for technical and financial assistance, the establishment of schools, and the distribution of personal documents (Smith 1969). In contrast to the Perené Campa congresses, the Congreso Amuesha (Amuesha Congress) was not limited to regular annual meetings. Rather, it was organized as a union. The organization was composed of a *cornesha'*, who assumed executive and representative functions; a president, who acted as coordinator; and a series of secretaries responsible for different areas of activity of the organization. The figure of the *cornesha'*, inspired by the traditional Yanesha priestly leaders, was the only position that was created in reference to the traditional political system. However, in this new context, its role no longer had the same religious connotation as had the traditional *cornesha'* role, and the range of authority was expanded to include the leadership and representation of the entire ethnic group.

Shortly after its creation, the Congreso Amuesha managed to obtain State support, mainly through SINAMOS. The presence of State officials at annual meetings, intended to facilitate the relationship between the Yanesha and the government, led to the gradual cooption of the organization. In 1977, feeling that their organization was being manipulated by State officials, the Yanesha decided to limit their role to receiving demands.

In 1974, the Ashaninka of the Pichis Valley sought to become incorporated into the Congreso Amuesha. From this date onward, meetings of indigenous representatives, under the name of Congreso de Comunidades Nativas Campa-Amuesha (Congress of Campa-Amuesha Native Communities), managed to bring about the registration and titling of most Yanesha communities and, as we will see, to encourage the registration and titling of a substantial number of communities in the Pichis Valley. Because the participation of Ashaninka communities took some energy away from the Yanesha organization and because the Ashaninka leaders aspired to form their own ethnic organization, beginning in 1978 the Congreso Campa-Amuesha was dissolved, becoming once again the Congreso Amuesha.

In 1978, the Congreso Amuesha created AgroYanesha, a committee especially devoted to improving the conditions of production in Yanesha native communities, as well as to facilitating the marketing of indigenous agricultural production. It also created the Casa Cultural Amuesha (Amuesha Cultural Center), in charge of promoting Yanesha cultural values, and the Comité de Maestros Bilingües (Bilingual Teachers' Committee), in charge of improving education in community bilingual schools.

Except for the support offered by the State through SINAMOS, the Congreso Amuesha did not have (as was the case of the Ashaninka organization in Perené) organic links with nonindigenous sectors of the population. Beginning in 1981, as a result of the new political contacts of some of its leaders and its subsequent incorporation into the leftist Confederación General Campesina del Perú (Peruvian General Peasant Confederation), the Yanesha organization modified its organizational structure, changing its name to Federación de Comunidades Nativas Yanesha (Federation of Native Yanesha Communities), or FECONAYA.

Although the political discourse of some of its leaders was modified, the changes in organizational and political dynamics were more evident in FECONAYA's external relations than in its internal organization. The federation maintained its unique function of uniting all of the Yanesha communities. In spite of the fact that the communities were scattered throughout a vast region that had been divided up by colonization, giving different sectors distinct characteristics, the Yanesha organization was accepted by all of the communities as the most adequate form of political organization for the ethnic group as a whole.

Since 1981, the Yanesha organization has negotiated with the State the objectives that the Pichis-Palcazu Special Project should have, managing to convince planners to modify the original goal of large-scale colonization, to encourage the titling of pending communities, and to create the Yanachaga National Park and the Chemellen Communal Reserve in the Palcazu Valley. In the past few years, nevertheless, the invasions of several communities in the Oxapampa zone of the Palcazu-Pachitea axis by colonists has added to the growing situation of political violence that integrally affects Yanesha communities.

Organizational Movements of the Ashaninka in Satipo

During the first six decades of this century, the history of Satipo was marked by violence practiced by the *patrones* settled in this area and on its periphery. This included raids to capture Ashaninka and Nomatsiguenga young men and women, the seizure of children by the Catholic missions of Río Negro and Puerto Ocopa, the continuous displacement of scattered families, and the abuses and physical punishment applied to indigenous peons. Although the 1947 earthquake enabled many families to escape from the *patrones,* subsequent recolonization found an indigenous population that had been dramatically affected by these processes. At that time the indigenous population was still a demographic majority in the zone, and the presence of the State was still quite fragile. Though some local indigenous leaders still supported the idea of expelling colonists by force, their attempts to arrive at a consensus were unsuccessful. The factionalism and hostilities among local groups, exacerbated by the slave raids promoted by the colonists, the desire to have access to indispensable manufactured goods, and the pressures exercised by colonists, led many indigenous families to work once more for the local *patrones*. Others, in contrast, fled to more distant, isolated areas.

Beginning in 1950, some local leaders, particularly in the Pangoa area, began to address local authorities to demand their land rights and to charge the colonists with abuses perpetrated against the indigenous population. Nevertheless, the recommendation of one of these officials to grant free land to indigenous family groups, following the formula established by the Perene Colony, was followed only very irregularly (Ortiz 1961: 497).

In the 1950s, the government named the Ashaninka leader Alberto Quin-choquer as deputy governor, with jurisdiction over the indigenous settlements of the province of Satipo to mediate the growing conflicts with the colonists and to heed demands by local leaders. This appointment put a stop to some abuses and established new mechanisms for coordination among various local leaders. At the same time, it gave some leaders of Satipo experience in dealing with the State. In spite of improved coordination among local indigenous leaders, no formal indigenous organization emerged from this experience. Thus, the representation of indigenous interests continued to be in the hands of the government-appointed indigenous deputy governor. It was through him that the indigenous peoples of Satipo established contact with nonindigenous peasant unions—first with the Huancayo branch of the Federación Nacional de Campesinos del Perú (Peruvian National Peasant Federation), and later with the Federación de Campesinos de Satipo (Satipo Peasant Federation), which was created in 1961 and represented an important segment of the local colonists (Bazán 1988). Both organizations had close ties with the Alianza Popular Revolucionaria Americana (American Popular Revolutionary Alliance), or APRA, an important social-democrat political party.

In contrast to the situation in the Perené Valley, where the strategy adopted by Ashaninka leaders was to establish an alliance between the indigenous organization and the colonist association, in Satipo a few individual leaders joined the Federación de Campesinos de Satipo under their own initiative. Two principal factors explain these differences: the degree of social disruption of the indigenous population in Satipo, and the absence of an impetus that would force the indigenous people and poor colonists to coordinate their actions in response to a common enemy. In addition, although some Ashaninka and Nomatsiguenga families had become involved in commercial agriculture, this had not yet become widespread. Thus, marketing problems were not widely shared so as to provide a common ground for Ashaninka among themselves, or between indigenous and colonist producers.

When guerrilla activity was initiated in 1965 by the Leftist Revolutionary Movement, some indigenous leaders supported them and confronted local *patrones*. Others supported the Army in repressing the guerrillas. These differences in allegiance contributed to the divisions among indigenous leaders with traditional rivalries.

When, in the early 1970s, the Perené Ashaninka began to convene congresses encouraged by SINAMOS, very few of the communities in Satipo took part, becoming affiliated instead with the government-sponsored Confederación Nacional Agraria (National Agrarian Confederation). Through local agrarian leagues, the Confederación Nacional Agraria backed the territorial claims of the

Ashaninka and proposed collective schemes for the commercialization of agricultural produce. In addition, for a brief time two of the communities in this area were affiliated with the Federación Provincial de Campesinos de Satipo (Provincial Federation of Peasants of Satipo), an organization created on the basis of the former Federación de Campesinos de Satipo and now affiliated with the leftist Confederación Campesina del Perú (Peruvian Peasant Confederation).

Only at the beginning of the 1980s did the Satipo Ashaninka form their own organization, the Federación de Comunidades Nativas Campa (Federation of Campa Native Communities), or FECONACA, under the initiative of one of the communities that had been affiliated with the Federación Provincial de Campesinos de Satipo (Bazán 1988). While the Satipo-Chanchamayo Rural Development Program was being implemented during Belaúnde's second term, FECONACA lobbied for the titling and expansion of Satipo's native communities. However, their growing affiliation with Belaúnde's regime and the naming, in 1985, of their secretary general as the incumbent political party's parliamentary candidate from the Department of Junín eroded the legitimacy of its representatives, resulting in the dissolution of FECONACA a few years later.

Throughout this period, Ashaninka and Nomatsiguenga communities from the Satipo and Pangoa valleys took part in the struggle to keep their land and to obtain public services. However, in the face of the downfall of FECONACA, they sought different organizational alternatives. Thus, encouraged by some traditional leaders and by nongovernmental organizations working in the area, some Nomatsiguenga and Ashaninka communities in the Pangoa Valley formed the Consejo Asháninca[13] y Nomatsiguenga de Pangoa (Pangoa Ashaninka and Nomatsiguenga Council). The efforts of this organization were primarily focused on conflicts with local colonists, the defense of future areas of expansion of the communities within what is considered to be their traditional territory, and the demand for public services.

The rest of the Ashaninka communities in Satipo turned progressively to CECONSEC, based in the Perené Valley, in search of support for their demands. This was possible to the extent that the expansion of commercial agriculture, the growing scarcity of land, and the lack of State services were resulting in common demands from the various communities in both areas. In 1987, CECONSEC established a chapter in the town of Satipo, expanding its training programs, its actions to defend land rights, and its commercialization schemes to include the communities in this area.

Shortly thereafter, as a result of a sharp increase in the violence against the Ashaninka population in Satipo by the Shining Path and the Army, the defense of the human rights and lives of the Ashaninka population became CECONSEC's highest priority. Because the development of violence in the valley took on particular characteristics, the communities had to adopt their own defense strategies, with their own alliances and tactics, which differed from those of the Ashaninka in the upper and central Perené Valley.

Organizational Movements of the Ashaninka of the Pichis, Ene, and Tambo Rivers

The Ashaninka movements of the Pichis, Ene, and Tambo river basins have evolved differently but share similar patterns of development, having originated in the least integrated areas of the region. Therefore, we have grouped their analyses under the same heading. In any case, the development of each movement cannot be understood without reference to the organizational dynamics of the areas we have already referred to.

A pattern common to all of these movements, which appeared at the end of the 1970s and the beginning of the 1980s, was the significant participation in their initial stages of a series of leaders associated with the Adventist and Evangelical churches. In our analysis of the process of community formation in areas of expansion, we have already noted that these communities were established under the leadership and with the support of Ashaninka families from the Perené, Satipo, and Apurímac areas who were greatly influenced by these religious denominations. The population that migrated into the Pichis, Ene, and Tambo river basins maintained close contact with their areas of origin, to the extent that some leaders returned to the Perené to participate in the initial organizing efforts in the valley. With this frame of reference and set of experiences, particularly important in the case of the Pichis Valley, years later these same leaders promoted intercommunity organizations in the valleys where they had settled. Each of these organizations had certain unique characteristics derived from their respective local contexts.

THE PICHIS VALLEY   As previously mentioned, in 1974 the Ashaninka of the Pichis Valley united with the Yanesha to form the Congress of Campa-Amuesha Native Communities. While this organization lasted, the participation of the Ashaninka was enthusiastic, to the extent that community leaders would walk for more than a week to participate in the meetings. On the basis of the Yanesha model, the Ashaninka elected a leader who was given the title of *pinkátzari* and acted as representative at the supracommunity level with authority equivalent to that of the *cornesha'*. During these years, the Ashaninka from the Pichis Valley managed to legally register 63 percent of their communities and to have 43 percent of them titled.

However, for a number of reasons—the continued predominance of the Yanesha; certain ethnic rivalries; and even the fact that in Yanesha communities leaders belonging to the Evangelical Church predominated, whereas in the Pichis the traditional leaders were predominantly Adventists—the Congress of Campa-Amuesha Native Communities dissolved in 1978.

In the early 1980s, under the direction of leaders involved in this first organizational effort, the Asociación de Comunidades Nativas Asháninca del Pichis (Pichis Ashaninka Native Communities Association), or ACONAP, was formed. This organization was encouraged by several of the Adventist ministers who originally led the organization of local native communities and who fought for the establishment of schools and reserves under Supreme Decree 03. As an organization that sought to unite all of the communities in the Pichis Valley in defense of their rights, ACONAP was a multiple-purpose organization. On the one hand, in response to the continuing expansion of cattle *haciendas,* it confronted local *patrones* and defended the local indigenous population from their abuses. Because the indigenous population that migrated into the valley in the late 1940s did not attempt to isolate itself but, instead, to develop commercial activities under improved conditions, ACONAP worked on the organization of the commercialization of annato, assisted by CECONSEC, with which it had various links. On the other hand, because of the membership of their leaders in the Adventist Church and the major importance of the church in the valley (it administered the only high school in the area, it offered opportunities for further education outside of the region, and it ran charity programs), ACONAP was a composite organization—part union, part religious organization. Thus, the language that gave legitimacy to indigenous demands and the code of ethics established by the organization were taken directly from the Old Testament. Alejandro Calderón was the figurehead of this movement.

To emphasize the indigenous character of the organization, ACONAP changed its name to Apatzahuantzi Nampitzi Ashaninka Pichis (ANAP). Under this new denomination there were no changes in the internal organization or in the platform itself. However, as the Pichis-Palcazu Special Project widened its range of action, establishing offices in Puerto Bermúdez, ANAP demanded direct participation in the project. Unlike the Yanesha organization, which managed to address a variety of demands without becoming directly involved in the executive structure of the Pichis-Palcazu Special Project, the Pichis Ashaninka requested the creation of an office of indigenous affairs, with the president of ANAP named as its coordinator. This direct coordination did not imply, however, an uncritical attitude on the part of ANAP toward the Pichis-Palcazu Special Project.

With the construction of the stretch of the Carretera Marginal that was to connect La Merced with Ciudad Constitución and Pucallpa, in the mid-1980s colonists flooded into the Pichis Valley. This generated unrest among the Ashaninka population, who believed that the presence of colonists threatened to duplicate the situation existing in the Perené Valley. At the same time, the road gave more power to traders, whose commercial activities were facilitated. In response, ANAP toughened its indigenous stance, demanding respect for the rights of the local Ashaninka.

When, in 1989, the Túpac Amaru Revolutionary Movement murdered Alejandro Calderón, accusing him of having collaborated with the Army 24 years earlier to smash one of the units of the Leftist Revolutionary Movement, the Ashaninka, outraged by the assasination of the person who was considered to be their legitimate leader, organized a politico-military movement that extended far beyond the Pichis Valley. The movement was supported by the local community members of ANAP and was organized following traditional schemes for military action. To most foreign observers the survival of this kind of military organization was a surprise, for it was thought to have been completely dismantled as a result of the "pacification" of the area, the influence of Adventism, and the establishment of union organizations. In the Pichis, the last messianic uprising in which traditional warriors were involved took place at the beginning of the 1950s (Bodley 1972).

The reaction of the members of ANAP in response not only to the assassination of Calderón but also to what they considered an affront to the political autonomy of their organization led to the death or expulsion of members of the Túpac Amaru Revolutionary Movement who had been active in the area (Benavides 1991). Although this uprising did not transform the conditions under which the indigenous population lived and worked in the valley, it reshaped the relationship between the Ashaninka and the colonists, who for a while were subjected to control by the Ashaninka army. All in all, the experience of self-defense on the part of the Ashaninka population in the Pichis Valley set the patterns for defense of all of the Ashaninka peoples in the Selva Central, contributing to a strengthening of the capacity of their organizations to respond to a new type of external aggression.

THE TAMBO VALLEY   In the Tambo Valley, indigenous organizational experiences were less impressive than in the rest of the Ashaninka territory. This was mainly because this area did not experience massive colonization. Being linked to the market economy only through logging activity, which in most cases did not affect local communities directly, the Tambo Ashaninka felt little need to organize. Extreme factionalism among traditional leaders, deepened by differences in religious affiliation, further hindered the organization of the local indigenous population.

In the early 1980s, leaders from several Ashaninka communities in the valley, led by the community of Betania, began to organize the Central Asháninca del

Río Tambo (Tambo River Ashaninka Union), or CART. The Tambo Ashaninka shaped their organization on the basis of two models. First, because the members of the leading community of Betania were Adventists and had links with the community of Nevati in the Pichis Valley, they adopted some characteristics of ACONAP, the Pichis Ashaninka organization. Second, because the leaders of CART were looking for economic options that would reduce their dependence on the local timber *patrones,* they adopted traits of CECONSEC, the Perené Ashaninka organization.

In the first years of its existence, CART tried to organize a local network for the commercialization of Ashaninka crafts and to create a market for these goods in Lima. Later, in collaboration with Lima-based nongovernmental organizations, it attempted to establish health services and to train local people, since no such services were provided by the State. It also worked to improve the quality of elementary education.

The increasing difficulties of working in the area, due both to the fact that it had become a drug-trafficking corridor and to the sporadic presence of the Shining Path beginning in the middle of the decade, led to the demise of development programs associated with CART. In time, this resulted in a reduction of its activities and of its ability to mobilize local Ashaninka people.

With the arrival of Ashaninka refugees from the Ene and lower Perené rivers, and the increasing presence of the Shining Path in the upper part of the valley, CART took a new direction in addressing the need to organize the self-defense of the local population and to attend to the problem of caring for and feeding indigenous refugee families. It was in this context that the Shining Path murdered several of the organization's leaders who were in contact with other Ashaninka organizations in the Selva Central in order to coordinate self-defense activities (Benavides 1992: 553). Thus, CART became not only more directly involved in the violent situation that affected the region but also had to redefine its platform and way of dealing with the problems of its members.

THE ENE VALLEY   The development of the Ashaninka movement in the Ene Valley took a slightly different form. As we have mentioned, the valley was one of the areas of refuge for the Ashaninka families from Satipo and from the Apurímac Valley, who were displaced from their land by Andean immigrants. The extreme heterogeneity of the local population in terms of previous experiences, kinship networks, and religious affiliations hindered the emergence of a local indigenous organization. Thus, whereas the majority of the Apurímac population belonged to the Evangelical Church, the local population was under the influence of the Catholic Church by way of the mission in Cutivireni. The absence of land-ownership problems or of serious conflicts with local *patrones,* at least until the end of the 1970s, also precluded the appearance of a supra-communal organization.

Until 1979, the Ene Valley was almost exclusively inhabited by Ashaninka. Then a wave of colonist invasions from the Apurímac area and from Ayacucho began. By 1983, colonists already constituted 47 percent of the local population (Benavides 1992: 550). These invasions cut up Ashaninka territory, leading to many land-rights confrontations between the Ashaninka and the colonists. In response, several communities united to form the Organización Campa-Ashaninka del Río Ene (Ene River Campa-Ashaninka Organization), or OCARE.

In addition to seeking help from other organizations to denounce the colonist invasions and to seek titles for communal property, OCARE developed a program for the commercialization of indigenous crafts (as had CART) and encouraged the production of cocoa and coffee to ensure a greater economic autonomy for the local indigenous families. However, following the colonist invasions, cocaine traffickers settled in the area, initially using the valley as a corridor for the transport of coca from the Apurímac Valley and later encouraging the local cultivation of coca. The weak State presence, the inexistence of other commercial economic options, and pressure from drug traffickers resulted in part of the colonist population, and later, part of the indigenous population, becoming involved in coca production. Furthermore, several local indigenous leaders became involved in the illegal sale of land to colonists and were accused of having facilitated the presence of the drug traffickers. As a result, the weak local indigenous organization lost its legitimacy, and its sphere of influence was reduced.

In 1988, the Shining Path established its first camps in the Ene Valley, which forms a natural gateway to the Ayacucho highland. However, many consider in retrospect that the invasions of colonists from Ayacucho in the early 1980s had in fact been advances of the Shining Path that were intended to disseminate its ideas among the colonist and Ashaninka populations settled in the area. In any case, part of the indigenous population in the Ene Valley formed an alliance with the Shining Path or was coerced to join the group. The armed group repeatedly attacked the Catholic mission in Cutivireni. As a result of these attacks and of the forced recruitment of young indigenous men, many families fled into Machiguenga territory in the Urubamba Valley. Others were forced to settle in encampments of the Shining Path (Benavides 1992: 550). The 1989 assassination of the leader of OCARE, Isaías Charete; the prevalent weakness of the organization; and the situation of "liberated territory" that the valley temporarily found itself in resulted in the dissolution of the Ashaninka organization in the Ene. Since then, with the help of the Ashaninka army from Satipo, the intervention of the Army, and the support of the indigenous refugee population, the area has been gradually retaken. However, at present OCARE has not regrouped. Some time will probably go by before the area becomes peaceful again and before an organization appears that can resume the defense of the Ashaninka population of the Ene and modify the terms of its relationship with the colonists and the State.

INDIGENOUS ORGANIZATIONS AND THE CHALLENGE OF INTEGRATION

The current process of economic and political integration of the region's indigenous peoples is not a result of State efforts only. In the context of territorial despoliation and expansion of the market economy, the Yanesha and the Ashaninka have developed commercial agropastoral production as a means of improving the terms for their participation in the regional economy, affirming their rights as citizens, and legitimizing their demands for land. Thus the rationale for integration as defined by the indigenous peoples of the Selva Central radically diverges from that of the State and its various brokers.

This divergence has led Amazonian indigenous organizations to be among the contemporary political phenomena most poorly understood by the country's social scientists. The indigenous organizations of the Selva Central have not escaped this lack of comprehension. On the contrary, as a consequence of their recent strategies of self-defense, their image has become even more distorted.

Some authors (Smith 1984; Benavides 1992) and the organizations themselves have discussed some of the reasons why the phenomenon of indigenous organizational movements is so poorly understood. Among them they have mentioned the hegemonic role that political parties have played in the organization of the peasant sector, the inability of political parties to accept as legitimate those organizations that are not under their direct influence, and a lack of sensitivity regarding the ethnic issue. In this final section we explore some additional elements that should allow for a better understanding of the nature and the strategies of these indigenous organizations.

One of the most frequent criticisms that is made of Amazonian indigenous organizations is that rather than being primarily unions or political organizations they are dedicated to the implementation of "development" programs (marketing cooperatives, rural training projects, and establishment of economic infrastructure and services). This argument, which has been presented primarily by some leftist nongovernmental organizations to undermine the legitimacy of these organizations in the political arena, reveals a profound lack of understanding not only of the contexts in which these organizations operate but also of the linkages between their development programs and the political strategies of the indigenous peoples.

The fact that these indigenous organizations promote development programs, a role that has traditionally been played by governmental and nongovernmental organizations, has been a response to two historical factors. First, in the areas of colonization, the State has done little to improve the marginal conditions of indigenous peoples, and when it has set up programs or made investments for this sector it has done so from an integrationist perspective, the objective of which is to make indigenous individuals "productive" and to erase the cultural traits that differentiate them. Nongovernmental organizations that act or have acted in the region have tended to develop small-scale production projects that do little to address the political and cultural needs of the indigenous peoples. Furthermore, these institutions have frequently assumed the role of brokers between the indigenous peoples and the State, or between these and international charities, using their position as a means to influence decision making within the indigenous sector. In reaction, the indigenous organizations in the region have chosen to assume directly the design and execution of development projects in an attempt to respond more effectively to their own economic needs and political objectives.

Second, when these organizations emerged, there were very few formulas through which they could acquire legal status. The formula of "indigenous or ethnic federation" was not accepted, and the State recognized only individual "native communities" as legitimate interlocutors. Available formulas either ignored the ethnic dimension, as in the case of "peasant federations," or implied a loss of autonomy, as in the case of State-sponsored "agrarian leagues." As a result, many of the new organizations opted to assume the form of marketing associations or nonprofit organizations dedicated to economic development and training.

In this context, opting for a "developmentalist" discourse has provided an ideological instrument with which, on the one hand, to demonstrate to the State that the Amazonian indigenous peoples are willing to become integrated in economic terms and that they are indeed productive, and, on the other, to obtain legal recognition for their ethnic organizations. However, this type of discourse is not simply utilitarian in nature. Because of their historical relationship with the regional and national society, nascent indigenous organizations were aware that to break into the national political arena, so as to be able to present their demands and overcome their marginalized status, a certain degree of economic integration was unavoidable. From this perspective, it is unquestionable that many indigenous organizations have been successful. Their increased participation in the regional economy has deprived State officials and colonists of one of their main arguments for ignoring indigenous claims, while compelling the State to recognize them as legitimate political interlocutors. This has been manifested, for example, in the success that indigenous organizations have had in stopping and forcing the redefinition of the objectives of the special projects that were designed under the second Belaúnde government in the 1980s.

A second criticism of Amazonian indigenous organizations is their frequent association with non-Catholic religious denominations. The fact that many early leaders were also active promoters of these religions has provoked distrust in their political message. To write off their legitimacy on the basis of this criterion reflects, however, a lack of knowledge of the history of these peoples. In effect, the first contact and experience of oppression with people of European origin occurred in the colonial era within the context of missionary expansion. Since then, local representatives of the Catholic Church have been intimately involved in the programs and plans for indigenous integration advocated by the State and have usually represented the interests of the elite groups in the region. It is not surprising, therefore, that the indigenous peoples of the Selva Central have been receptive to the messages of rival religious denominations. The same phenomenon is evident in some marginal urban and rural sectors in other parts of the country. These denominations have spread rapidly thanks to their ability to give a sense of purpose to the lives of extremely marginalized people, offer clear ethical guidelines, and create new networks of social solidarity.

In the Selva Central, in particular, the adoption of the ideologies of these religious denominations has been facilitated by their strong messianic component, shared by Yanesha and Ashaninka cultural traditions. Furthermore, the traditional political systems of these peoples were also imbued with religious aspects: in the case of the Yanesha, their political leaders were also priests, whereas Ashaninka leaders were warriors who were often associated with important shamans. The close ties between religion and politics that occurred in the initial stages of indigenous organizational movements were thus not alien to this tradition. They can also be explained by other factors: (1) church organization, based on networks and meetings of the leadership, was the first modern form of intercommunity linkage; and (2) religious leaders were more acquainted with the national culture and society. Currently this connection has weakened because new forums for the emergence and political expression of indigenous leaders have appeared. Today, the religious affiliation of indigenous leaders is a personal choice and does not necessarily represent the actions or objectives of their respective organizations.

The third kind of criticism that is leveled against Amazonian indigenous organizations is related to the actions of self-defense on the part of some of them in response to the climate of extreme violence in which they have found themselves in the last several years. After being victims of land despoliation, economic exploitation, and political subordination for several centuries, situations that were not free from major physical violence, the Yanesha and Ashaninka, as well as large sectors of the rural population in the country, were involved in a new context of violence. In the initial stages, the presence of the Shining Path and the Túpac Amaru Revolutionary Movement in the region did not directly affect the indigenous population and its organizations. Apparently these groups respected the communal rule and the autonomy of their organizations. Some Yanesha and Ashaninka joined the armed groups, won over by their promises for justice, just as people from other social sectors had done. However, since voluntary support for these groups was not as massive as expected, the armed groups began to pressure and then threaten native communities to gain their complete support. In the beginning, force was used to coerce communities to provide guides, food, or temporary lodging. Later, their tactics included forced recruitment of young people and children as well as acts of retaliation for supposed crimes involving collaboration with the Peruvian Army. The arrival of the Army in the regional arena to provide support for antiguerrilla task forces introduced new tensions in native communities. Thus, the indigenous population found itself accused by both sides in the dispute of collaboration with the enemy.

In 1989, the Túpac Amaru Revolutionary Movement murdered Alejandro Calderón, leader of the native communities grouped in ANAP. This act became the turning point that changed not only the forms of action of the indigenous organizations but also the direction of the armed conflict in the region. The organization of an independent Ashaninka army that was not related to the armed forces, and the success achieved in the expulsion of members of the Túpac Amaru Revolutionary Movement from the Pichis Valley, provided an example that began to attract the attention of indigenous organizations in other areas of the Selva Central. Gradually, small groups of communities started to organize their own self-defense committees. In some cases they had the support of the armed forces, whereas in others they formed independently. In addition, in areas that were less affected by the presence of subversive groups, many communities organized military columns with the goal of providing support to communities in more affected areas. This was the case of the Ashaninka army from the Gran Pajonal.

These communal forms of response to subversive violence did not arise only in the Selva Central. After the first failed attempts of the Army to organize committees in the Andean highlands, at the end of the 1980s local self-defense initiatives were appearing in the region based on the model of the peasant *rondas* or patrols of the northern Andes. In some cases these initiatives were coordinated by the Army. Gradually the self-defense committees of the highlands became legitimate in the eyes of the civil society. In contrast, the organization of the indigenous armies and committees of self-defense in the Selva Central generated suspicion from various fronts. For some leftist groups, the connection of some of the committees with the armed forces turned them into accomplices of the policy of indiscriminate repression favored by the State in the 1980s. For the armed forces, on the other hand, the explicit desire for autonomy of action manifested by many of the armies and indigenous self-defense committees, and the fact that indigenous antisubversive discourse was not based on the same arguments favored by the State in accordance with the doctrine of national security, meant that the loyalty of the indigenous forces with respect to the national values was suspect. Finally, for the colonists in the region, the military actions of their indigenous neighbors, even when directed against a common enemy, awoke the fear that, after driving out the subversives, they would turn their arms against the colonists to recover their ancestral lands.

The implicit ideological background that gave rise to these similar reactions on the part of such diverse sectors is the perception, which has still not been overcome, that the Amazonian indigenous peoples are not yet "civilized." For some leftist groups this would be manifested in the ease with which the armed forces are supposed to have manipulated the indigenous organizations. They doubt the political capacity of the indigenous organizations to outline their strategies independently. For the Army, the lack of civilization is reflected in the absence of a manifest adherence to national values. According to this argument, the indigenous peoples have no patriotic feelings. Finally, in the view of the colonists, this supposed lack of civilization is expressed in a latent "savageness" that could spring up again as a result of the military experience in the indigenous self-defense committees. In this sense, it is appropriate to remember that by the mid-1980s the indigenous presence had been acknowledged and incorporated into the regional identity on the basis of the assumption that their military power had been completely destroyed and that their growing economic integration was a sign of their final "domestication." The resurgence of indigenous military capability brought these assumptions into question.

The acts of self-defense undertaken by the indigenous peoples of the Selva Central show that, although their antisubversive strategy coincides, to a certain extent, with that of the government, it has not sprung from having chosen sides in the ideological debate that has pitted subversive groups against the State, but from the need to preserve their lives and their political autonomy. In this sense, the indigenous response reveals, on the one hand, an independence from the ideological baggage of both leftist and rightist groups, and, on the other, that their integration into the national society has not been passive, nor has it taken place under the conditions set forth by the State. In effect, the process of integration of the indigenous peoples of the Selva Central has not followed the "melting pot" model, where individuals become incorporated by adopting the prevailing national values while putting aside their own, but the model of "pluriethnicity," where the will to integrate does not imply an abandonment of one's identity and cultural values.

The situation of unrestrained violence since the mid-1980s has marked the beginning of a new stage of disorder for the region and its inhabitants. Although it has involved all sectors of society, because the indigenous peoples have taken the clearest stand in confronting the subversive groups they have been hit the hardest. According to reports from many colonists and indigenous people, the actions of the Shining Path against the Ashaninka communities have been especially brutal, acquiring the character of ethnic vengeance. This brutality has resulted in the leveling of entire native communities; forced displacement of residents; and hunger, sickness, and uprootedness suffered by hundreds of indigenous refugees of the war. In addition, in recent times several colonist groups have taken advantage of the chaotic situation to question the territorial rights and despoil land in native communities that had already been legally recognized. However, these conflicts have generated new forms of organization, better interaction among the indigenous populations from various areas of the region, and a new sense of ethnic pride. Furthermore, in spite of the fact that the self-defense committees have awakened fear and suspicion in various sectors, their actions have placed the indigenous peoples in a protagonistic position, allowing them to achieve new political opportunities and modifying the terms under which the struggle for integration has been traditionally defined. For the indigenous peoples of the Selva Central, a new stage has thus begun in their relationships with the national society, with all of the new challenges that this implies.

CONCLUSIONS
The Making of a Region

The long process of settling the Selva Central — starting in the early 17th century, stabilizing after 1709, interrupted in 1742, and becoming massive in the 1950s — has transformed this part of the *selva alta* into a "regional space," the characteristics of which distinguish it from other regional spaces within the Amazonian and Andean regions. The character of regional space is manifested in the consolidation of a new "ordering" based on a higher degree of internal spatial and economic articulation and in the emergence of an embryonic regional identity that transcends preexistent local and ethnic identities. The consolidation of this new ordering in the early 1970s inaugurated a new period of order. This has been short-lived, interrupted as a result of the increasing presence and activities of Shining Path and the Túpac Amaru Revolutionary Movement in the region since 1988. Nevertheless, the current situation of disorder, which arose as a result of exogenous factors but which awakens and intensifies previously existing conflicts, has not meant a change in the structural underpinnings that support the region's economy. Although it has made intrarregional communication difficult, it has not totally disrupted its internal articulation.

SPATIAL ARTICULATION

From the colonial period through the present there has been a growing process of articulation of the diverse areas that currently form the Selva Central. This has culminated in the creation of a regional space in which the city of La Merced provides the focal point for roads, immigrant population fluxes, and circulation of capital, goods, products, and technologies. The gradual configuration and current organization of this space is the result of a series of intentional and haphazard elements. Among the intentional elements we include the long-standing competition among the economic elites from the neighboring Andean cities of Huánuco, Tarma, and Jauja for the monopoly on access to the resources of the Selva Central. For a long time the competition among these cities remained unresolved, until Tarma managed to achieve a clear advantage in 1847 as a result of the opening of a road to Fort San Ramón and, later, of the opening of the Via Central del Pichis at the end of the 19th century. The rapid growth of the towns of San Ramón and La Merced, facilitated by their improved connections with consumer centers, resulted in their development into the most important economic centers in the region. State policies also contributed to this process by prioritizing the development of transportation routes into the Selva Central through Chanchamayo, instead of through Satipo or Pozuzo.

However, these intentional elements alone would not have been enough to articulate the various areas that form the Selva Central around San Ramón and La Merced. Various unintentional elements also contributed to the preeminence of this area. These include, among other things, (1) better natural conditions in Chanchamayo for the production of coffee, which became the hub of the local economy; (2) the establishment in Chanchamayo of the Peruvian Corporation, which maintained a favorable relationship with the State for many years; (3) the earthquake in 1947, which disrupted transportation between Satipo and Huancayo; and (4) the fact that the president who should have restored this connection happened to be from Tarma and was more interested in establishing the preeminence of the Lima-Tarma-La Merced-Satipo axis than other possible transportation routes connecting the Selva Central with the Andes and the coast.

Therefore, San Ramón and La Merced, with improved roads, better soils for coffee cultivation, and more concentrated capital resources and infrastructure for marketing finally consolidated their hegemony over Satipo, Pozuzo, and Oxapampa. As a result, the Chanchamayo Valley became the seat of the most powerful economic groups in the area, the most modern coffee- and fruit-producing *haciendas*, and the most important State services.

Some of the highlights that marked the gradual connection of the different areas of the Selva Central around the La Merced-San Ramón hub are (1) the construction, in 1943, of the road from La Merced to Oxapampa, which completely eliminated the option of effectively connecting this last valley with Lima by way of the Pasco highlands; (2) the construction, beginning in 1964, of the Carretera Marginal between the towns of La Merced and Satipo, which culminated in 1973 and created economic ties between these two areas, while at the same time eliminating the importance of the old Satipo-Concepción-Huancayo route; and (3) the creation, in 1971, of a branch of the Banco Agrario in La Merced, which from then on managed all of the agencies that the bank had established in the Selva Central, including that in Satipo, which until then had depended on a branch in Huancayo. The 1978 division of the former province of Tarma and the creation of Chanchamayo Province constituted the political and administrative acknowledgement of the process of internal articulation of the Selva Central, which had culminated in the early 1970s. This event did nothing more than sever the administrative ties that made Chanchamayo subordinate to Tarma and the Andean region, ties that by then had become anachronistic, insofar as the Selva Central was no longer subsidiary to the economy of the neighboring highlands and no longer depended on it.

As a consequence of this process of internal articulation, this regional space is currently formed by (1) several interconnected, well-consolidated areas of high population density and economic activity that are organized around important population centers and are primarily dedicated to coffee and fruit production (the Chanchamayo, Perené, Oxapampa, Villa Rica, and Satipo valleys); (2) peripheral areas, more recently connected with the former, that have begun to experience significant colonization processes, whose small towns barely qualify as urban centers and whose economy revolves around cattle production (the Palcazu, Pichis, and lower Perené valleys); and (3) areas of expansion that are still poorly connected with the previously mentioned areas, that are organized as economic fronts, that lack urban centers, that have a mostly indigenous population, and where the principal commercial activity is logging and, more recently, clandestine coca production (the lower Pozuzo River and the Tambo, Ene, and upper Pachitea valleys).

The first two types of areas described above are fully connected with each other and with La Merced. The third type of area, in contrast, still maintains a double linkage: that with the earliest occupied areas in the Selva Central (in politico-administrative terms and, to a lesser extent, in economic and infrastructural terms), and that with other neighboring spaces, with which they have no administrative ties but with which there is a stronger connection in terms of demographic or commercial flows. This is the case with the Ene Valley, commercially linked to the small port-town of San Francisco on the Apurímac River and to the Andean city of Ayacucho.

ECONOMIC ARTICULATION

The spatial articulation of the Selva Central has gone hand in hand with a process of economic articulation that is manifested in (1) the generalization of capitalist forms of production, distribution, and consumption; (2) the existence, with differing degrees of development, of land, labor, consumer, service, and capital markets; (3) the predominance of a highly commercial pattern of production based on the coffee-fruit-timber trinomial; (4) the regionalization of capital as a result of the spatial diversification of the economic activities carried out by local power groups; and (5) the process of economic agglomeration in the most consolidated areas.

A central characteristic of the agricultural producers of the Selva Central is the marked mercantile logic of their production and their extreme dependence on the market for the sale of their products and the acquisition of means of subsistence. The agricultural producers of the Selva Central are not peasant producers who sell a small surplus production. Rather, they are the holders of small and medium-sized lots, who, as we have seen, dedicate most of their labor and their cultivated land to commercial production. The survival of their domestic units depends entirely on their relationship with the market. This distinguishes the situation of agriculturalists in the Selva Central from that of producers in what Gonzales de Olarte (1982) has defined as "mercantile areas" and contradicts Aramburú's hypothesis (n.d.: 31) on the replication of peasant forms of production in colonization areas.

The development of market spheres has been unequal in spatial terms. Thus, for instance, in consolidated areas, where most of the "valuable land" is located and where the process of minifundization is more extreme, there is a dynamic real estate market, although in many cases the land is extremely degraded. In addition, as a result of widespread labor-intensive coffee and fruit cultivation, in these areas an extensive market for salaried labor has developed. The process of extreme minifundization leads many *minifundio* holders to sell their labor seasonally to complement the income that they obtain through commercial agriculture. This, in turn, has resulted in an increase in the proportion of local semiproletarian workers with respect to laborers coming from the neighboring highlands. Finally, because agriculture is more capital-intensive and urban centers more important, it is in these areas that we find better-developed markets for goods, services, and capital.

In contrast, in peripheral areas and areas of expansion, the real estate market is more restricted, because free public land is still relatively abundant. The labor market is also more restricted, both because of the lower density of economic activity and because the local population still maintains a significant subsistence production and has access to wildlife resources. Thus, the only incentive for selling labor is to obtain manufactured goods. Therefore, in these areas semicoercive means for recruiting and retaining labor still exist: the system of *habilitación* continues to be pervasive in spite of the increased importance of payment in cash over payment in goods. Markets for products and services are much more limited in these areas than they are in consolidated areas. Finally, markets for goods are extremely distorted in the sense that trade is generally monopolized by the owners of the biggest cattle ranches and logging companies.

The dialectical relationship between logging and agricultural activity—in which logging acts as a spearhead of the market economy and the colonization processes, whereas agriculture acts as a stabilizing factor once new areas have been incorporated—has resulted in a constant transformation of logging fronts into permanent agricultural and demographic frontiers. The constant need of the logging industry to find new sources of timber and the incessant flow of Andean migrants have fed off each other, thus becoming the motor that drives the expansion of economic frontiers in the Selva Central.

Nevertheless, most of the areas that, as a result of their altitudes and soils, are suitable for coffee production have already been occupied. Because of its location in lower altitudes, the land in peripheral areas and in areas of expansion is mostly unsuitable for this type of crop. This suggests that the dialectics between logging and the production of coffee and fruit may be reaching its maximal limit, both as a driving force for expansion and as a stabilizing factor for the agricultural frontiers in the region. If no productive alternatives are found for the peripheral areas and areas of expansion, these will continue to be dedicated primarily to cattle ranching and logging, activities that, by themselves, will generate neither economic growth nor economic consolidation. Even worse, the producers who have settled in these areas may be tempted to become involved in the cultivation and processing of coca, a process that has already taken place in some of them. Therefore, although the Selva Central may still be considered an "open" space, it may well have reached its highest degree of internal economic articulation.

One of the most important causal factors, and at the same time manifestations, of the growing economic articulation is the regionalization of capital. Until a few decades ago, the capital of local economic power groups was confined to the immediate geographic area where they were settled. In later years, because of the growth in the volume of capital and the opening of new areas as a result of the expansion of the transportation network, local economic power groups began to expand their investments, transferring capital, machinery, expertise, and technology far beyond the limits of their original areas of influence. This is especially clear in the case of the timber industry but also in the case of fruit cultivation. The commercial capital associated with the buying and selling of coffee, which is generally in the hands of export firms, circulates throughout the entire regional space. Moreover, many of the marketing cooperatives that originated as local organizations, such as the Cooperative of Villa Rica, have grown to the point that they have been able to expand their activities to other valleys.

Finally, increasing internal articulation has been expressed in a process of growing economic agglomeration in the most consolidated areas. By economic agglomeration we mean the simultaneous development of a variety of economic activities, each creating its own marketing and supply networks and giving rise to other associated activities, as well as to horizontal and vertical economic linkages. This process brings into question (at least in the Selva Central) the assumption that Amazonian economies can only survive through the constant opening and abandoning of unrelated economic fronts. As we have seen, this assumption is not valid even in the case of the timber industry, which is still active in the most consolidated areas where forest resources have become scarce. The development of small agroindustries that are associated with the most important productive and extractive activities has also contributed to this process of economic agglomeration.

The stability of the predominant pattern of production has allowed for increased economic growth with less environmental impact than other economic patterns would have caused. However, the prolonged occupation of the oldest areas (where minifundization and the overexploitation of resources are more acute) has inevitably led to obvious environmental deterioration. This is manifested in growing extensions of degraded land, the almost complete exhaustion of the most valuable forest resources, and the deintensification of land use, suggesting that these areas have reached a critical point. This brings into question the possibilities for the perpetuation of the region's economy under current technological and land-tenure conditions. If this situation is not corrected, in the near future these areas may become unproductive, reduced to the role of trading centers that depend on the opening of new fronts and the establishment of new frontiers for their existence.

IDENTITY AND IDEOLOGY

The spatial and economic articulation of the Selva Central has not been accompanied by an equivalent process of ideological articulation. In spite of the long history of colonization of the area, the most profound processes of social change are barely 50 years old. The process of construction of a regional identity is still in an embryonic state. Diversity in the ethnic, regional, and national backgrounds of its inhabitants; the differences in time of settlement in the region; and differences in position within the regional social and economic structure explain why important contradictions among different population sectors and markedly different collective identities continue to exist.

Identification with the Selva Central as a regional space is especially evident among the group of colonists who descend from European immigrants who settled in the region in the 19th century. The descendants of these "pioneers" have tended to retain a prominent place in the region's economy and in regional politics, forming the nucleus of the power groups in San Ramón, La Merced, Oxapampa, Pozuzo, Villa Rica, and Iscozacín. As a result of the geographic diversification of their activities and investments, these groups have established social and economic ties with each other, acquiring the character of an embryonic regional bourgeoisie. The core of their identity is based on their pride of being the descendants of the pioneer colonists who, from their point of view, "made" the region. This means that in social terms this group has been relatively closed. Although in recent years some local entrepreneurs have begun to extend their economic activities to Lima, this new bourgeoisie continues to be strongly rooted in the region.

The Yanesha and Ashaninka identify with this regional space on the basis of the mythical memory that ties them to their territories, their ancestral occupation of the area, and their continuous defense of their land rights. In spite of their linguistic heterogeneity and distinct historical experiences in the face of integration, the different segments of the indigenous population have experienced increased interaction as a result of their contemporaneous organizational experiences and, more recently, of their concerted actions against the violence that confronts them. On the other hand, although the improved economic, social, and political integration of the indigenous sector has led to its growing identification with regional problems, it has not resulted in the loss of ethnic identities, as many had predicted.

Conquest, in the case of the pioneer colonists, and resistance, in the case of the indigenous peoples, although opposite reference points, form the bases for their respective identification with the regional space.

In between these two groups are the migrant colonists of Andean origin. In spite of the fact that, today, this group forms the majority, it is not homogeneous either in economic terms or in terms of its identity. Andean migrants have come from different provinces and districts in the highlands, have arrived at different times, and have occupied different areas. This has meant that, in spite of the existence of a certain process of "Andinization" of the region, the profile of this group is a mosaic of microidentities. The extreme social mobility that characterizes the group accentuates these internal differences. However, economic changes resulting from their insertion into a capitalist dynamic have led to the gradual erosion of the local identities of the Andean migrants.

In spite of these opposing identities, which are often accompanied by discriminatory attitudes, there is evidence that a more generic regional culture and identity, based on elements contributed by each of these population sectors, is emerging. This is most evident in the food, music, domestic and productive technology, beliefs and traditions, and regional vocabulary. At present, in the Selva Central respect for the Andean image of Our Lord of Muruhuay coexists with that for the Yanesha and Ashaninka spirits of the forest; the horse competition of the Oxapampa German settlers coexists with the *yunza* carnival celebration of the Andean colonists; the consumption of Andean tubers coexists with that of the banana bread developed by the Pozuzo German settlers; the multi-layered skirts of the Andean indigenous women coexist with the long cotton tunics traditionally worn by Yanesha and Ashaninka men and women; and the cultivation of adapted varieties of potatoes coexists with that of indigenous peanuts and magical herbs. As a consequence, nowadays it is not unusual to see a colonist of German descent drinking the manioc beer favored by the Yanesha and Ashaninka, a Yanesha man roofing his house with wooden tiles in the style of the German settlers, or a colonist of Andean origin fishing with barbasco, a fish poison widely used by the Yanesha and Ashaninka. However, the probability that these diverse elements will coalesce to produce a true regional identity will very much depend on the development of mutual respect for the identities of the groups involved, which will occur only if current relationships of subordination and political and economic discrimination are transformed.

THE EFFECTS OF VIOLENCE ON THE PROCESS OF INTERNAL ARTICULATION

When, in 1980, President Belaúnde announced the implementation of the Pichis–Palcazu Special Project, everyone assumed that this would represent a new stage in the mass occupation of the Selva Central. The 1981 announcement of his plans to build Ciudad Constitución (conceived as the future capital of the country) at the confluence of the Pichis and Palcazu rivers was a symbolic gesture that expressed the will of the government to fully incorporate the region into the national sphere. This prompted social scientists and environmental experts to warn against the negative social and ecological impact that these projects could have and aroused the heated protest of indigenous organizations at the local and national level, who saw their rights being threatened.

Until 1985, the Pichis–Palcazu Special Project, although not very effective in achieving its original objectives, had managed to stimulate the region's economy indirectly by injecting large sums of money for the development of its activities. Productivity did not increase, nor were new sources of productive employment created. However, the entire regional space experienced a period of artificial prosperity at the cost of increased external debt. When, shortly after the rise to power of President Alan García, the sources of funding ran out and the new government established other priorities, not only did the flow of money stop but the presence of the State was seriously cut back in peripheral areas. The new

Table C.1. Terrorist Acts Reported in the Selva Central

Province	1983	1984	1985	1986	1987	1988	1989[a]	1990[b]	All 8 years
Chanchamayo	1	4	0	0	0	1	11	5	22
Satipo	1	1	1	0	1	8	6	17	35
Oxapampa	0	0	1	0	1	3	7	4	16
Selva Central	2	5	2	0	2	12	24	26	73

Sources: DESCO 1989, 1989-1990; data elaborated by the authors.

Note: These data include the violent acts of members of Shining Path and the Túpac Amaru Revolutionary Movement only.

[a]Data for September not included.

[b]Data for December not included.

roads that connected these areas with more consolidated areas did not generate the conditions necessary to achieve a sustainable economy. The debacle of the Pichis-Palcazu Special Project, whose final redoubts were in Iscozacín and Puerto Bermúdez (Palcazu and Pichis valleys, respectively), left a vacuum in the colonization fronts that were so enthusiastically promoted in 1980.

It is in this context of frustrated expectations that two new forces began to make themselves felt more and more strongly: organized bands of drug traffickers and the armed groups of the Shining Path and the Túpac Amaru Revolutionary Movement. These did not appear concurrently. The drug traffickers settled in areas of expansion, taking advantage of their isolation and the lack of other alternatives of commercial production. The presence of subversive groups was due to the strategic location of the Selva Central, which permitted them to use it as a training area, a base for attacks on targets in the highlands, and an area where the columns that were active in the Andes could retreat into. Their establishment in the region was facilitated by the vacuum left by the State after the collapse of the Pichis-Palcazu Special Project. Ciudad Constitución, which was meant to be the new capital of Peru, has become the crossroads for the nascent illegal economy of the Selva Central. After the order achieved in the early 1970s, the region entered into a new period of disorder, different from previous ones but equally disruptive.

An analysis of the number and frequency of terrorist actions reported in the region (DESCO 1989, 1989-1990) indicates that, after a few actions between 1983 and 1985, the armed groups began a period of political infiltration (Table C.1). During this two-year period, almost no armed confrontations or terrorist actions took place. Beginning in 1988, however, the number of attacks and clashes increased greatly, and permanent camps and bases were established in the Pichis,

Palcazu, and Ene valleys. From this time onward, the activity of subversive groups began to make itself felt throughout the Selva Central.

The advance of both armed groups and drug traffickers initially occurred in the poorly integrated areas of expansion that were connected with strategic highland areas: the Huánuco-Pozuzo-Mayro-Pachitea axis and the Ayachuco-Apurímac-Ene-Tambo axis. Although drug trafficking has been mainly confined to these areas, armed groups penetrated and managed to establish themselves in some peripheral areas and even in parts of the central areas of colonization: Oxapampa, Villa Rica, Pichis, Palcazu, Gran Pajonal, Perené, and Satipo. As one of the first consequences of this military strategy, the State was forced to retreat, losing its hold on some of the areas where it once played a larger role. As a second consequence, Chanchamayo, the center of the first colonization events and a required point of passage for produce from the region, was gradually fenced in.

An expression of this process was the withdrawal of the offices of the Banco Agrario from Pozuzo, Puerto Bermúdez, and Iscozacín, as well as from Villa Rica and Pampa Silva, important coffee- and fruit-producing centers, beginning in 1989. The weakening of State authority has been felt even in important consolidated areas such as Satipo. Thus, a 1989 bank report admitted that in Satipo, "the sociopolitical problems that have convulsed the coffee growing areas since 1988 have resulted in a high rate of defaulted loans" (Banco Agrario 1989). Likewise, the ability of the State to conduct other activities in rural areas, including land titling, supervision of logging operations, and agricultural extension activities, has been increasingly limited.

Aggravating the already critical situation in the Selva Central, in June 1989 the international agreement on coffee prices and export quotas was revoked. As a consequence, coffee prices immediately fell by 50 percent and have still not managed to recover. In addition, because of the state of violence and the threats that they have received, some of the most modern and efficient coffee and fruit producers in the region have abandoned their farms, either selling them or leaving them in the hands of managers. Some of those who have refused to leave or pay "revolutionay taxes" to the subversive groups have been murdered. The timber industry has also been affected as a result of the risks associated with entering areas that have no military protection. The recruitment of young people by the subversive groups has also affected the availability of labor for coffee and fruit harvests, aggravating the situation of labor scarcity. All of these elements, added to the economic crisis that has affected the country since 1988, have likewise affected the levels of productivity and volume of yield.

The murder of the Ashaninka leader Alejandro Calderón at the hands of the Túpac Amaru Revolutionary Movement worsened the climate of violence in the region. Until then, the armed groups had abstained from intervening in the affairs of the region's peasant and indigenous organizations. The death of Calderón, who had been accused of turning in a guerrilla leader of the Leftist Revolutionary Movement in 1965, touched off a violent reaction against local Túpac Amaru military columns. The Ashaninka communities of the Pichis Valley, which had, until then, been indifferent to the presence of this group in the area, reacted violently, reviving traditional forms of military organization to avenge the murder of their leader and to expel the insurrectionists from their communities. In early 1990, the Ashaninka had not only achieved this objective but had even managed to take Puerto Bermúdez and completely expel the group from the Pichis Valley (Benavides 1991).

However, indigenous military action, originally aimed at avenging the death of their leader, took on other implications for the region's nonindigenous social and power groups. For many colonists, this experience constituted a brutal reminder that the military capability of the indigenous peoples, which they believed had been obliterated since at least 1950, was still alive. If the Ashaninka were capable of driving the Túpac Amaru Revolutionary Movement out of the area, they were capable of driving out the colonists who had taken over their land only a few years earlier. The fear that the confrontations between colonists and the local indigenous population would be repeated spread like wildfire through the Selva Central. Radio stations and the local press played on the colonists' old fears with fantastic reports of poisoned arrows and enormous contingents of fierce warriors.

The Army reacted ambivalently: on the one hand, they were fearful of an indigenous uprising, which they saw as a threat to the established social and economic order, but on the other, they hoped to be able to count on the support of the indigenous population in their struggle against the subversive groups. What is certain is that the confrontation of the Ashaninka with the Túpac Amaru Revolutionary Movement, and later with the Shining Path, was not based on political differences and therefore cannot be understood either as an attack on the ideological positions of the insurrectionists nor as adherence to the military tactics and the doctrine of national security encouraged by the Army.

However, even though, from the point of view of the Ashaninka, their actions had no political objectives in a partisan sense, they certainly had strong political repercussions. The success that they achieved in their confrontations with the Túpac Amaru Revolutionary Movement and the intensification of pressures from the subversive groups motivated other indigenous and colonist settlements from Satipo, Pangoa, Perené, Gran Pajonal, and Pozuzo to organize themselves to confront them. Thus, the delicate equilibrium of forces in the Selva Central, which had maintained the civilian population at the margin of the conflict between subversive groups and armed forces, was shattered.

In the past few years, some of these groups have requested weapons from the Army, and, in other cases, the armed forces have put pressure on colonists and native communities to organize patrols to confront the insurrectionists, offering them arms and military advice. Other groups, following in the footsteps of the Pichis Ashaninka, have organized independently and operate without police or military assistance. The long-term effects of the organization of indigenous and colonists' patrols are difficult to assess. In some cases, the self-defense groups have been able to drive out rebel groups. In others, poorly organized and equipped patrols have been the target of violent reprisals from the Shining Path, resulting in entire native communities and small colonist settlements being massacred. Their survivors have had to take refuge in local towns or other valleys.

Subversive groups have managed to coopt segments of the colonist and indigenous population either voluntarily or by force. However, whenever they have encountered opposition to their objectives, they have responded by intimidating and eventually annihilating antagonistic groups. In the areas in which the indigenous population is not organized or where its organizations are extremely weak, such as in the Ene Valley, pressure from the Shining Path has forced entire communities to take refuge in remote areas, where, for lack of farm plots and as a result of scarce resources, they have had to live on the brink of starvation (Benavides 1992). In areas where there are fewer opportunities to hide, such as in the Perené Valley, indigenous families and colonists have sent their children away to avoid the possibility that they will be drafted by rebel groups.

The climate of violence that has enveloped the entire Selva Central, directly or indirectly involving all sectors of its population, has upset its internal articulation process, initiating a new period of disorder.

ORDER AND DISORDER IN THE SELVA CENTRAL

The process of occupation and integration of the Selva Central has been marked by a succession of orderings. Some of these orderings coincide with the major periods that we have identified and analyzed in relation to this process. In other cases, several orderings can be identified within the same period. By ordering we mean the socioeconomic and sociopolitical structure that develops in a certain space and time and that confers on this space a distinctive character. Because the Selva Central originated as a frontier area, the evolution of its spatial and economic articulation (both internal as well as external) is critical to the understanding of these successive orderings. In effect, each ordering is distinguished by the existence of some degree of internal articulation, as well as by the character of its external articulations. Nevertheless, this succession of orderings has not been linear in nature, such that a new ordering does not necessarily guarantee either better internal articulation or the improved integration of this area into the national sphere.

The process of incorporation of the Selva Central may, therefore, be viewed as an alternation of stages of order and disorder. However, although in terms of our definition the different orderings that have appeared may be understood more or less objectively, the notions of order and disorder are strongly influenced by subjective factors. In effect, a given ordering may be considered, by one or more sectors of the population, to be a period of order, whereas other sectors may consider it to be a period of disorder. In the Selva Central, this is the case, for example, in the ordering that emerged as a consequence of the Juan Santos Atahuallpa uprising in 1742. For the indigenous peoples, this was perceived as a period of order, whereas for the missionaries, colonial authorities, and *hacienda* owners it was a period of disorder (see Chapters 1 and 2). In contrast, the ordering that appeared as a result of the mass colonization that the region experienced in the 1940s and 1950s was perceived by the Peruvian Corporation and the other large landholders in the region as a period of disorder, whereas for Andean migrant colonists this meant the beginning of a period of order.

Because of the objectives of this work, the notions of order and disorder used here emphasize those processes that can be identified either as contributing to or blocking the process of incorporation and articulation of this space. Thus, we have considered as periods of order those phases that, in the long term, have furthered this process. However, one cannot ignore the fact that these periods of order have been very costly for some sectors of the population in the region. This is particularly true in the case of the indigenous peoples, for whom these successive stages of order have meant progressive usurpation of their land, the shrinking of their traditional territories, the breakdown of their political systems, the weakening of their networks of intraethnic solidarity, and their economic and political subordination. The indigenous sector has not been the only group, however, to bear the costs of these periods of order. The development of the *hacienda* system in the region was based on the exploitation of Andean laborers recruited coercively through the *enganche* system. These laborers were, like the Amazonian indigenous population, subject to conditions of debt peonage (Barclay 1989).

In these terms, stages of disorder are those that have worked against the process of incorporation of the Selva Central. However, the analysis of the economic history of this regional space shows that, in most of these cases, each stage of disorder has given rise to the appearance of a new ordering, characterized by better internal and external articulation. As would be expected in a frontier area, the situations of disorder have generally occurred as a result of external factors: political decisions of the central government (such as the establishment of Fort Ramón in 1847), economic phenomena (such as the rise in coffee prices on the international market at the end of the 19th century), and social phenomena (such as the spontaneous mass migration of Andean peasants since the 1940s). Each of these factors contributed to the end of a previous ordering and the emergence of new orderings. Although these maintain certain characteristic elements of the periods that preceded them, they are founded on new elements. The current stage of disorder does not escape from this type of historical law characteristic of colonized areas. In effect, although subversive groups took advantage of the existence of certain internal conflicts to reinforce their presence in the region, the current violence is not a product of these contradictions but rather a consequence of tactical and strategic considerations on the part of these groups that have little to do with the socioeconomic and sociopolitical dynamics of the Selva Central.

From this perspective, the history of the Selva Central may be seen as a series of advances and retreats. In spite of this instability, which is characteristic of areas of colonization, the integrating forces of the various agents that have acted in or around this space have had a cumulative effect over the long term. This cumulative effect is manifested in the fact that the Selva Central has become a regional space. It is precisely this character that distinguishes this space from other colonized areas of the *selva alta,* many of which, in spite of having had a long history of colonization, continue to appear as a collection of more or less dispersed and poorly interconnected economic fronts. Thus, whereas in the Selva Central the successive periods of order and disorder have resulted in a strengthening of its links with the rest of the country, in other colonization areas they constitute an expression of their weak internal and external articulation.

The violence exerted by subversive groups and bands of drug traffickers has caused the complete disarticulation of these colonization areas with respect to the national sphere. Although these spaces have not been completely transformed into "liberated territories," the presence of the State is so weak, in institutional terms, that they can only nominally be considered parts of the nation. Furthermore, although the coca economy, which develops in these areas with the support of drug traffickers and rebels alike, has a strong impact on the national economy, it completely escapes State control.

In contrast, the consensus and coordination that has developed between different sectors of the population in the Selva Central to confront the presence of subversive groups is a signal that the socioeconomic and sociopolitical structures of this space, as well as its institutional bases, are more solid and rooted than those that have developed in other areas of colonization in the *selva alta.* Equally symptomatic is the fact that the coca economy has only been able to take root in the less articulated areas of expansion; in the central and peripheral areas it has not encountered the conditions that are necessary for its development. This does not imply, however, that the current stage of disorder will not leave significant marks on the social, economic, and political profile of the region. Some of them are already visible: the destruction of colonist and indigenous settlements, the forced displacement of the population, the deterioration of the agrarian economy, the flight of capital, and the weakening of spatial and economic linkages. Others can be predicted: changes in the equilibrium of forces in the diverse sectors of the population and the economic weakening of local power groups. However, in spite of current and future changes, the Selva Central has proved to have much more resilient structures than other colonization areas in the *selva alta*. Whatever the new profile that emerges may be, it is certain that the Selva Central will retain its character as a distinct regional space.

APPENDIX
Regarding the PRONAC Information

Most of the statistical information at the district and provincial levels used in this book was compiled especially for this study on the basis of data from the Satipo-Chanchamayo Special Project, which were elaborated by the Programa Nacional de Catastro (National Land Registration Program), or PRONAC, of the Ministry of Agriculture. What follows are notes regarding the conditions under which the information was collected, the size and nature of the sample, and its representativeness.

Baseline information was collected by the Rural Land Registration Office of the Chanchamayo-Satipo Rural Development Program, as part of a program initiated in 1983 by the Pichis-Palcazu Special Project. Between 1984 and 1985, aerial photographs were taken of a total of 298,240 hectares in the provinces of Chanchamayo and Satipo. On the basis of these aerial photographs and corresponding ground controls, land units were identified, and aerotriangulation, photogrametric restitution, topographic mapping, adjustment of borders, mapping of units, and measurement of these areas was undertaken.

This land-registration program dealt with all of the agricultural units within the photographed area. Thus, the PRONAC sample is highly representative and contains fewer biases than does information from land-allocation and titling programs, which are more restricted and selective. It also reflects the diversity of legal status with respect to land tenure in the region: 25 percent of the landholders in the sample had legal titles, 67 percent did not, and 0.2 percent were tenants. The legal status of the rest was unclear.

Data collection and the elaboration of a computer database were carried out by the Rural Land Registration Office of the Chanchamayo-Satipo Rural Development Program between 1984 and 1988. To simplify interpretation, we have chosen 1988 as the date for this information. The survey was based on land-registry forms and additional forms containing information on each landholder and landholding—including area, legal status of the holding, land use, and predominant crops. Computer data were processed by the National Land Registration Program, according to instructions given by the authors.

The PRONAC data are based on a sample of 10,361 individually managed agricultural units comprising a total of 124,348 hectares (slightly less than half of the total area photographed). The sample does not include units under cooperative management, such as the Agrarian Production Cooperatives created under the 1969 agrarian reform. According to the total number of agricultural units estimated by the agrarian reform for the provinces of Chanchamayo and Satipo in 1984 (Cerrón 1985: 23), the PRONAC sample would represent approximately 57 percent of the total. More moderate estimates suggest that the PRONAC sample represents at least a third of the agricultural units in these two provinces. The size of the sample and the fact that it includes information from all of the districts that represent both provinces, except for Río Tambo (Satipo) and Vitoc (Chanchamayo), means that the PRONAC data constitute an invaluable source of information for the study of land-tenure structure in the region.

NOTES

1. Official data regarding the area cultivated in coffee are unreliable because of the methods used for their calculation. First, area estimates are based on annual yields. Given that international prices strongly influence the volume of coffee that is harvested (because of the relative weight of labor costs in the total cost of production every season), official estimates of the coffee-growing area also fluctuate greatly. Second, data are often adjusted by the Ministry of Agriculture so that cultivated area and volume of production do not exceed the levels agreed on by member countries in the International Coffee Agreement. Therefore, official estimates of the area cultivated in coffee should be interpreted as trends rather than as exact figures.

2. Estimates of coffee yields in the Selva Central are unreliable because they are based on annual yields, which vary tremendously from year to year as a function of market price and the availability of labor during the coffee harvest, rather than as a function of the actual productivity of the coffee plantations. Therefore, government agencies often produce disparate data, even for the same year. In 1982, for example, the Ministry of Agriculture estimated the mean yield for coffee producers in the region to be 0.53 metric ton per hectare, whereas the Satipo-Chanchamayo Unit of the Pichis-Palcazu Special Project put it at 0.40 metric ton per hectare.

3. It should be noted that some of the improved coffee varieties are planted without shade trees. This means that their higher yield is accompanied by accelerated soil degradation, due both to increased erosion and to the loss of nitrogen input associated with the use of pacae *(Inga feuillei)* as a shade tree.

4. Furthermore, because of these limitations on labor availability, small landholders often plant their coffee plots at relatively low densities—1,700 to 2,500 plants per hectare, as compared with 6,000 in the more technologically advanced agricultural units.

319

5. The Third National Agrarian Census took place in July 1992. Until now, only preliminary results have been published.
6. It should be noted, however, that in the estimates for the *selva alta*, only a minimal part of the area planted in coca, a perennial crop, has been registered.
7. Ordóñez (1985: 137) estimates that in 1983 in Satipo Province, pastures represented up to 36 percent of the area planted in perennial crops. This figure, which is notably higher than that resulting from the PRONAC data (see Table 5.4), is based on an area that includes the cattle-ranching district of Río Tambo, which was not included in the PRONAC sample.
8. Similar results were obtained by performing the same exercise with other groups of districts ranked according to their length of occupation.
9. Although Dourojeanni admits that, because of the demographic pressure on land in the *selva alta*, the land used for shifting agriculture and then abandoned is frequently occupied and cultivated by colonists arriving later or who have fewer resources, he does not incorporate this factor into his simulation model.
10. Data from the German Forestry Project do not always correspond with those provided by other authors. Thus, Ricse Tembladera (1987: 178) estimates that 25 percent of the cultivated area in the Selva Central has type F and X soils. In turn, Agreda (n.d.: Table 7), using information from Malleux (1975) and Dancé (1979), arrives at the conclusion that, in 1980, 74 percent of cropland and pastureland in Chanchamayo–Satipo and 88 percent of land in Oxapampa is found on class III forested hillsides, and in class I and II forests that should be protected. These two categories roughly correspond to soils suitable for forestry (F) and to soils to be protected (X) in the classification scheme used by ONERN. We believe that Ricse Tembladera's estimate is too low and Agreda's estimates are too high, which is why we prefer to use the data provided by the German Forestry Project.
11. Figure 6.1 has been obtained by superimposing two photographs (8700-167 and 8700-168) taken in August 1957. Figure 6.2 is made up of four photographs (4333, 4334, 4347, and 4348) taken in May 1977. Figure 6.3 corresponds to photograph number 353-83-A in a series of photos taken in October 1983. Comparison of aerial photographs to determine the environmental impact of colonization as well as rates of deforestation has also been undertaken by Dancé (1980), Masson Meiss (1981), González and Ruiz (1986), and Salick (n.d.).
12. It is worth noting, however, that in recent years indigenous producers have increased food-crop production, taking advantage of the availability of State-sponsored zero-interest loans for these crops, as well as of a local demand for food crops on the part of the colonist sector.
13. Asháninca is the Spanish spelling of Ashaninka.

GLOSSARY

aguardiente: unrefined liquor distilled from sugarcane

arroba: measure of weight equivalent to 25 pounds or 11.5 kilograms

capitán (pl. *capitanes*): captain; regional term referring to indigenous local headmen

chacra: agricultural plot; small landholding

chuncho: deprecatory expression applied to indigenous people meaning "savage" or "uncivilized"

condominio: legal property formula by which joint ownership over land is granted

contrata: contract with a rural laborer for a specific task

conversión (pl. *conversiones*): colonial ecclesiastic jurisdiction that comprised indigenous peoples already subjugated but in the process of conversion to Christianity; mission territories

cornesha': Yanesha traditional politico-religious leader

corregidor: colonial authority in charge of collecting tributes among already subjugated and converted indigenous peoples

corregimiento: colonial politico-administrative unit run by a *corregidor*

crianza al partir: cattle-breeding system whereby a large cattle rancher gives a small farmer a cow that is to be raised in the latter's pastureland; in time the cow is retrieved by the cattle rancher, and the offspring are divided among the associates

doctrina: colonial ecclesiastic jurisdiction that comprised indigenous peoples already subjugated and converted to Christianity

encomendero: beneficiary of an *encomienda*

encomienda: in colonial times, group of indigenous families placed under the tutelage of a conqueror as a reward for services rendered to the Crown

enganche: engagement of laborers by means of advance payments in goods or cash

fundo: medium-sized landholding

habilitación: debt-bondage or debt-peonage system

habilitado: worker engaged and outfitted by a *patrón* by means of the *habilitación* system

hacienda: large landholding

intendencia: late colonial politico-administrative unit that replaced *corregimientos*

intendente: colonial authority in charge of an *intendencia*

latifundio: large landholding

marco (pl. *marcos*): Spanish colonial silver currency

mejora: land improvement in terms of the establishment of plantations, pastures, or infrastructure

mejorero: rural laborer hired to establish and look after a coffee plantation until it begins to yield

mestizo: half-breed, of mixed blood

minifundio: small agricultural unit whose area barely suffices to ensure the livelihood of its holder and his or her family

mita: tribute in labor owed to the Inca State in pre-Hispanic times and to the Spanish Crown in colonial times

montaña: the region of tropical forest located on the eastern slopes of the Andean range between 400 and 2,500 meters above sea level; *selva alta*

obraje: wool mill

parcialidad: in colonial times, localized unit composed of indigenous extended families linked by kinship bonds and grouped around a leader

patrón (pl. *patrones*): boss, generally in reference to large landowners or timber extractors who make use of an *habilitado* labor force

purma (pl. *purmas*): formerly cultivated land left fallow, where the natural vegetation has begun to regenerate; in the land-rotation system, *purmas* are replanted after being left fallow for a specified time

quintal (pl. *quintales*): measure of weight equivalent to 46 kilograms

reducción (pl. *reducciones*): in colonial times, settlement formed by the compulsory nucleation of a subjugated indigenous population

selva alta: region of tropical forest located on the eastern slopes of the Andean range between 400 and 2,500 meters above sea level; *montaña*

selva baja: region of tropical forest located east of the Andes, at an elevation lower than 400 meters above sea level.

sol (pl. *soles*): Peruvian monetary unit in use after Independence

BIBLIOGRAPHY

Agreda, V. n.d. Las colonizaciones y la ampliación de la frontera agrícola. Photocopy.

Aguila, E. del. 1983. Proyecto Especial Pichis-Palcazu: Núcleo generador de desarrollo en la Selva Central. In *Desarrollo de la selva alta,* edited by C. Zuzunaga. Lima: Centro de Investigación Aplicada.

AIDESEP (Asociación Interétnica de Desarrollo de la Selva Peruana). 1991. Esclavitud indígena en la región Atalaya. *Amazonía Indígena* 11 (17-18): 3-13.

Alegre, J. C. 1978. Medida de la erosión hídrica en un entisol de la selva alta (San Ramón-Chanchamayo) bajo diferentes sistemas de cultivo: Resultados de las campañas agrícolas 75/76 y 76/78. Master's thesis, Universidad Nacional Agraria, Lima.

Amich, J. 1975. *Historia de las misiones del convento de Santa Rosa de Ocopa.* Lima: Editorial Milla Batres.

Aramburú, C. E. n.d. Expansión de la frontera agraria y demográfica en la selva alta peruana. In *Colonización en la amazonía,* edited by C. E. Aramburú, E. Bedoya, and J. Recharte. Lima: Centro de Investigación y Promoción Amazónica.

Aramburú, C. E., and E. Bedoya. 1987. Poblamiento y uso de los recursos en la amazonía alta: El caso del alto Huallaga. In *Desarrollo amazónico: Una perspectiva latinoamericana,* edited by C. Mora and C. E. Aramburú. Lima: Centro de Investigación y Promoción Amazónica/Instituto Andino de Estudios en Población y Desarrollo.

Arellano, M. 1983. Diagnóstico socio-económico de las comunidades nativas de las provincias Chanchamayo-Satipo. Lima: Proyecto Especial Pichis-Palcazu. Mimeographed.

Banco Agrario. 1970-1989. Memorias anuales [annual reports]. Lima.

———. 1985-1989. Relaciones de préstamos de miembros de la comunidad nativa. Agencia de Satipo. Manuscript.

————. 1989. Informe justificatorio del análisis de cartera en mora al 30/6/89. Agencia de Satipo. Manuscript.

Banco Agrícola. 1931–1950. Memorias anuales [annual reports]. Lima.

Banco Central de Reserva. 1970. *Cuentas nacionales del Perú 1960–1969*. Vol. 2 of *Anexo estadístico*. Lima.

Banco de Crédito. 1972. *Realidad, perspectivas y problemas de la selva peruana*. Mesa Redonda, Estudios Económicos. Lima.

Banco de Fomento Agropecuario. 1951–1969. Memorias anuales [annual reports]. Lima.

Barclay, F. 1980. La noción de redefinición étnica como hipótesis y perspectiva de aproximación a los grupos étnicos de la amazonía. Análisis de un caso: El grupo étnico Amuesha. Licentiate thesis, Department of Anthropology, Pontificia Universidad Católica del Perú, Lima.

————. 1989. *La Colonia del Perené: Capital inglés y economía cafetalera en la configuración de la región de Chanchamayo*. Iquitos: Centro de Estudios Teológicos de la Amazonía.

Barclay, F., R. Basurto, and F. Santos-Granero. 1977. Informe de trabajo de campo. Pontificia Universidad Católica del Perú, Lima. Manuscript.

Barclay, F., M. Rodríguez, F. Santos-Granero, and M. Valcárcel. 1991. *Amazonía 1940–1990: El extravío de una ilusión*. Lima: Centro de Investigaciones Sociológicas, Económicas, Políticas, y Antropológicas/Terra Nuova.

Barclay, F., and F. Santos-Granero. 1980. La conformación de las comunidades amuesha: La legalización de un despojo territorial. *Amazonía Peruana* 3 (5): 43–74.

————. 1991. El minifundio en la selva alta. *Debate Agrario* 11: 139–164.

Barrenechea, C. 1986. *Café: Problemática y alternativas*. Lima: Centro Peruano de Estudios Sociales.

Bataillon, M. 1976. *Estudios sobre Bartolomé de las Casas*. Barcelona: Ediciones Península.

Bazán, V. R. 1988. Mercado interno y movimientos campesinos en la provincia de Satipo (1974–1977). Paper presented at the I Seminario de Investigaciones Sociales en la Amazonía, Iquitos.

Bedoya, E. n.d. Intensificación y degradación en los sistemas agrícolas de la selva alta: El caso del Huallaga. In *Estrategias productivas y recursos naturales en la Amazonía*, edited by E. Bedoya, J. Collins, and M. Painter. Documento no. 9. Lima: Centro de Investigación y Promoción Amazónica.

————. 1991. *Las causas de la deforestación en la amazonía peruana: Un problema estructural*. Documento no. 12. Lima: Centro de Investigación y Promoción Amazónica.

Belaúnde, F. 1959. *La conquista del Perú por los peruanos*. Lima: Ediciones Tahuantinsuyo, Minerva.

Benavides, M. 1991. Autodefensa asháninca en la selva central. *Amazonía Indígena* 11 (17–18): 50–61.

————. 1992. Autodefensa asháninka, organizaciones nativas y autonomía indígena. In *Perú: El problema agrario en debate/Sepia IV*, edited by C. I. Degregori, J. Escobal, and B. Marticorena. Lima: Seminario Permanente de Investigación Agraria/Universidad Nacional de la Amazonía Peruana.

Biedma, M. (OFM). 1981. *La conquista franciscana del alto Ucayali*. Lima: Editorial Milla Batres.

Bodley, J. 1972. A transformative movement among the Campa of eastern Peru. *Anthropos* 67: 220-228.

————. 1976. Campa socio-economic adaptation. Ph.D. diss., Department of Anthropology, University of Oregon.

Brack, W., M. Suarez, A. Martel, B. Amiguero, and A. Brack. n.d. *Sistemas agrosilvopastoriles e importancia de la agroforestería en el desarrollo de la selva central.* Proyecto Peruano-Alemán / Ministerio de Agricultura / Gessellschaft für Technische Zusammenarbeit.

Burga, M. 1976. *De la encomienda a la hacienda capitalista: El valle de Jequetepeque del siglo XVI al XX.* Lima: Instituto de Estudios Peruanos.

Burga, M., and W. Reátegui. 1981. *Lanas y capital mercantil en el sur: La Casa Ricketts, 1895-1935.* Lima: Instituto de Estudios Peruanos.

Caballero, J. M., and E. Alvarez. 1980. *Aspectos cuantitativos de la Reforma Agraria (1969-1979).* Lima: Instituto de Estudios Peruanos.

CAEM (Centro de Altos Estudios Militares). 1958. Colonización y desarrollo económico de la selva central. Lima. Mimeographed.

Caja de Jauja. 1745-1752. Caxa de Jauja. Cartas-cuentas de Real Hacienda (1745-1752). Archivo General de Indias, Contaduría 1870, Seville. Manuscripts.

Caja de Pasco. 1745-1752. Caxa de Vico y Pasco. Cartas-cuentas de Real Hacienda (1745-1752). Archivo General de Indias, Contaduría 1873, Seville. Manuscripts.

Camones, M. 1986. Análisis de la economía agraria de los colonos del valle del Palcazu. Lima: Instituto Nacional de Desarrollo. Manuscript.

Capcha Rodríguez, E. R. 1986. Contribución de la industria maderera al mercado de trabajo en el ámbito del Distrito Forestal San Ramón. Licentiate thesis, Department of Forestry Engineering, Universidad Nacional del Centro, Huancayo.

Carranza, A. 1894. Geografía descriptiva y estadística industrial de Chanchamayo. *Boletín de la Sociedad Geográfica de Lima* 4.

Casanto, R. 1985. 25 años de experiencia organizativa en la sociedad asháninca del Perené. In *Balances amazónicos: Enfoques antropológicos,* edited by J. M. Arroyo and J. Gasché. Iquitos: Centro de Investigación Antropológica de la Amazonía Peruana / Universidad Nacional de la Amazonía Peruana.

————. 1986. Entrevistas: Material para la historia del movimiento organizativo en el pueblo asháninca. Iquitos: Centro de Investigación Antropológica de la Amazonía Peruana / Universidad Nacional de la Amazonía Peruana. Manuscript.

Castro de León, M. 1982. *Pre-diagnóstico del área del Proyecto Especial Satipo-Chanchamayo.* Lima: Instituto Indigenista del Perú.

Ccama, F. 1987. El uso del crédito y la asistencia técnica. In *Los hogares rurales en el Perú: Importancia y articulación con el desarrollo agrario,* edited by J. Portocarrero. Lima: Grupo de Análisis de Políticas Agrarias / Fundación Friedrich Ebert.

CDR (Centro de Desarrollo Rural) Chanchamayo. 1980. *Padrones de las plantas de aserradero 1979, 1983 y 1989.* San Ramón.

————. 1980-1989. Memorias anuales del programa de trabajo de la Oficina Agraria de San Ramón (1982-1987); Informe anual del programa de trabajo del Centro de Desarrollo Rural Chanchamayo (1988). San Ramón. Typescript.

———. 1989. Informe de la parcelación de la CAP José Carlos Mariátegui. San Ramón. Typescript.

CDR (Centro de Desarrollo Rural) Oxapampa. 1989. Registro de explotadores madereros (1967–1988). Oxapampa. Mimeographed.

CDR (Centro de Desarrollo Rural) Satipo. 1980–1989. Memorias anuales del programa de trabajo de la Oficina Agraria de Satipo (1981–1987); Informe anual del programa de trabajo del Centro de Desarrollo Rural Satipo (1988). Satipo. Typescript.

Centro de Estudios de Población y Desarrollo. 1972. *Informe demográfico del Perú*. Lima.

CECONSEC (Central de Comunidades Nativas de la Selva Central). 1981. Relación de productores de café en comunidades nativas socias de CECONSEC. La Merced. Manuscript.

———. 1988. Relaciones de productores de café en comunidades nativas socias de CECONSEC. La Merced. Manuscript.

CENCIRA (Centro de Capacitación e Investigación para la Reforma Agraria). 1974. Diagnóstico socio-económico de las cuencas de los ríos Palcazu y Pichis. Lima. Mimeographed.

Cerrón, J. 1985. Diagnóstico del desarrollo económico de la selva central, provincias de Chanchamayo y Satipo. La Merced. Mimeographed.

Chávez, M. 1989. Informe de ejecución 1983–1988: Programa de Catastro y Titulación. San Ramón: Programa de Desarrollo Rural Chanchamayo–Satipo. Typescript.

Chirif, A. 1974. Los congresos de las comunidades nativas: el inicio de la participación. *Participación* 3 (5): 46–53.

———. 1975. Ocupación territorial de la amazonía y marginación de la población nativa. *América Indígena* 35 (2): 265–295.

———. 1985. 25 años de política de desarrollo rural en la amazonía peruana y sus repercusiones en las sociedades indígenas de la región. In *Balances amazónicos: Enfoques antropológicos*, edited by J. M. Arroyo and J. Gasché. Iquitos: Centro de Investigación Antropológica de la Amazonía Peruana/Universidad Nacional de la Amazonía Peruana.

Chocano, M. 1983. Circuitos comerciales y auge minero en la sierra central a fines de la época colonial. *Allpanchis* 18 (21): 3–26.

Christensen, P. 1989. Historical roots for ecological economics: Biophysical versus allocative approaches. *Ecological Economics* 1: 17–36.

CIDA (Comisión Interamericana de Desarrollo Agrícola). 1966. *Tenencia de la tierra y desarrollo socio-económico del sector agrícola*. Lima: Comisión Interamericana de Desarrollo Agrícola, and Washington, D.C.: Unión Panamericana.

Comisión Multisectorial. 1974. Plan de desarrollo de la Selva Central. Lima. Mimeographed.

Conklin, H. 1963. *El estudio del cultivo de roza*. Estudios Monográficos, no. 11. Washington, D.C.: Unión Panamericana.

Córdoba y Salinas, D. (OFM). 1957 [1651]. *Crónica franciscana de las provincias del Perú*, edited by L. G. Canedo. Washington, D.C.: Academy of American Franciscan History.

Cotera, J. de la. 1982a. Situación actual de los aserraderos y otras plantas de transformación de la madera en Oxapampa. Oxapampa: Proyecto Especial Pichis-Palcazu. Mimeographed.

―――――. 1982b. Situación actual de los aserraderos de Villa Rica. Oxapampa: Proyecto Especial Pichis-Palcazu. Typescript.

Cotlear, D. 1979. Enganche, salarios y mercado de trabajo en la ceja de selva peruana. *Análisis* 7: 76-85.

Crist, R. 1969. *Conceptos generales sobre la colonización en la montaña peruana.* Lima: Centro de Estudios de Población y Desarrollo.

Daly, H. 1990. Elements of environmental macroeconomics. In *Ecological economics: The science and management of sustainability,* edited by R. Constanza. New York: Columbia University Press.

Dancé, J. 1979. *Evaluación de los recursos forestales del trópico peruano.* Lima: Universidad Nacional Agraria/CEPID.

―――――. 1980. Tendencias de la deforestación con fines agropecuarios en la amazonía peruana. *Revista Forestal del Perú* 10 (1): 177-184.

David, E. 1983. El transporte terrestre de madera en la selva central. Proyecto PNUD/FAO/PER/81/002-Fortalecimiento de los programas de desarrollo forestal en selva central. Documento de Trabajo no. 8. Lima. Mimeographed.

Denevan, W. 1979. Los patrones de subsistencia de los Campa del Gran Pajonal. In *Etnicidad y ecología,* edited by A. Chirif. Lima: Centro de Investigación y Promoción Amazónica.

Denevan, W., and C. Padoch, eds. 1990. *Agroforestería tradicional en la amazonía peruana.* Documento no. 11. Lima: Centro de Investigación y Promoción Amazónica.

DESCO. 1989. *Violencia política en el Perú, 1980-1988.* 2 vols. Lima: Centro de Estudios y Promoción del Desarrollo. Newsletter.

―――――. 1989-1990. *Resumen semanal: Años 12 y 13.* Lima.

Dirección de Administración. 1874. *Memoria de la Dirección de Administración, 1874.* Lima.

Dirección General de Empleo. 1982. Diagnóstico del valle del Pichis. Lima: Ministerio de Trabajo. Mimeographed.

DGFF (Dirección General de Forestal y Fauna). 1978. Plantas de aserrío, 1977. Lima: Ministerio de Agricultura. Mimeographed.

―――――. 1985. *Información del mercado forestal y de fauna silvestre, 1983-1985.* Lima: Ministerio de Agricultura.

―――――. 1987. *Anuarios estadísticos, 1980-1987.* Lima: Ministerio de Agricultura.

Dourojeanni, M. 1981a. *Estudio sobre el impacto ambiental de los proyectos de carreteras en la selva central, Perú.* Lima: Ministerio de Transportes y Comunicaciones.

―――――. 1981b. Posibilidades para un desarrollo rural más integral en el Huallaga Central y Bajo Mayo. Photocopy.

―――――. 1990. *Amazonía: ¿Qué hacer?* Iquitos: Centro de Estudios Teológicos de la Amazonía.

Eguren, F. 1987. Tenencia de la tierra. In *Los hogares rurales en el Perú: Importancia y articulación con el desarrollo agrario,* edited by J. Portocarrero. Lima: Grupo de Análisis de Políticas Agrarias/Fundación Friedrich Ebert.

Felipe-Morales, C., C. Alegre, R. Meyer, and D. Berrios. 1978. Pérdida de agua, suelo y nutrientes bajo diversos sistemas de cultivo en la localidad de San Ramón-Chanchamayo. Photocopy.

Fernández, E. 1986. *Para que nuestra historia no se pierda.* Documento no. 7. Lima: Centro de Investigación y Promoción Amazónica.

Figueroa, L., and F. Gonzales Vigil. 1979. Mapa general del complejo del café en el Perú. Lima: DESCO. Mimeographed.

Filomeno, S. 1982. Pequeños extractores de madera, tecnología y relaciones sociales de producción, Río Inuya. Bachelor of Science thesis, Universidad Nacional Agraria, Lima.

Fioravanti, E. 1974. *Latifundio y sindicalismo agrario en el Perú.* Lima: Instituto de Estudios Peruanos.

Fisher, J. 1977. *Minas y mineros en el Perú colonial 1776-1824.* Lima: Instituto de Estudios Peruanos.

Flores Galindo, A. 1977. *Arequipa y el sur andino, siglos XVIII-XX.* Lima: Editorial Horizonte.

Gasché, J., L. Trapnell, and M. Rengifo. 1987. El curriculo alternativo para la formación de maestros de educación primaria especializados en educación bilingüe intercultural y su fundamentación antropológica. Iquitos: Centro de Investigación Antropológica de la Amazonía Peruana/Universidad Nacional de la Amazonía Peruana. Mimeographed.

Gentry, A., and J. López Parodi. Deforestación e incremento de las inundaciones del alto Amazonas. *Amazonía Indígena* 4 (7):20-22.

Giordano, F. 1875. Memoria del Ing. F. Giordano sobre la excursión que practicó en compañía del Ministro Italiano a los territorios orientales de Chanchamayo. Reprinted in Larrabure i Correa, C. 1905-1909. *Colección de leyes i decretos del departamento de Loreto.* Vol. 11. Lima: Imprenta La Opinión Nacional.

Gonzales de Olarte, E. 1982. *Economías regionales del Perú.* Lima: Instituto de Estudios Peruanos.

González, M., and R. Ruiz. 1986. Deforestación de bosques tropicales en los valles de Chanchamayo y alto Perené. *Revista Forestal del Perú* 13 (2): 37-43.

Grobman, A. 1983. El desarrollo agropecuario de la selva alta del Perú. In *Desarrollo de la selva alta.* Lima: Centro de Investigación Aplicada.

Gutiérrez, J., et al. n.d. Los trabajadores eventuales en el cultivo del café: Chanchamayo y Satipo. Lima: Centro de Capacitación e Investigación para la Reforma Agraria. Mimeographed.

Hein, E., and J. R. Neale. 1954. Reporte sobre Satipo. Reprinted in Ortiz, D. 1961. *Reseña histórica de la montaña del Satipo, Pangoa, Gran Pajonal.* Lima: Editorial San Antonio.

Holshouser, J. 1972. Some aspects of economic change among the Campa of the western Montaña of central Peru as reflected in land use patterns. In *Actas y memorias,* vol. 4, edited by R. Avalos de Mattos and R. Ravines. Lima: Congreso Internacional de Americanistas.

Hopkins, R. 1987. La producción agrícola. In *Los hogares rurales en el Perú: Importancia y articulación con el desarrollo agrario,* edited by J. Portocarrero. Lima: Grupo de Análisis de Políticas Agrarias/Fundación Friedrich Ebert.

Hvalkof, S. 1986-1987. El drama actual del Gran Pajonal. *Amazonía Indígena* 6 (12): 22-35, 7 (13): 3-10.

INADE (Instituto Nacional de Desarrollo). 1984. Evaluación del desarrollo forestal en el ámbito de los proyectos especiales de selva: Análisis comparativo. Documento de Trabajo no. 4. Lima. Mimeographed.

————. 1985. Identificación de mercados para la producción agrícola de la selva central. Documento de Trabajo no. 9. Lima. Mimeographed.

————. 1988. Sistema de información geográfica de la cuenca del río Palcazu. Lima. Manuscript.

INE (Instituto Nacional de Estadística). 1986. *Encuesta nacional de hogares rurales: Resultados definitivos.* Lima.

————. 1989a. *Perú: Características geográficas a nivel distrital; Demarcación política; Principales elementos naturales y culturales.* Boletín de Estadísticas Geográficas no. 2. Lima.

————. 1989b. *Perú: Población y superficie a nivel distrital.* Boletín de Estadísticas Geográficas no. 3. Lima.

INP (Instituto Nacional de Planificación). 1980. *Datos básicos para la planificación del desarrollo de la región selva central.* Lima.

————. 1981. *Programa de desarrollo de la selva central.* Lima: Instituto Nacional de Planificación/Presidencia de la República.

INP/PNUD (Instituto Nacional de Planificación/Programa de las Naciones Unidas para el Desarrollo). 1977. Reforzamiento de centros poblados de la selva central para consolidar su poblamiento. Eje San Ramón-La Merced (Diagnóstico). Huancayo. Mimeographed.

Izaguirre, B. de. 1922-1929. *Historia de las misiones franciscanas y narración de los progresos de la geografía en el oriente del Perú.* 14 vols. Lima: Tipografía de la Penitenciería.

Johnson, A. 1974. Ethnoecology and planting practices in swidden agriculture systems. *American Ethnologist* 1.

Klaren, P. 1970. *La formación de las haciendas azucareras y los orígenes del APRA.* Lima: Instituto de Estudios Peruanos.

La Rosa, M., ed. 1969. Los pioneros: Homenaje a la ciudad de La Merced en su primer centenario de fundación. La Merced. Mimeographed.

Larrabure i Correa, C. 1905-1909. *Colección de leyes i decretos del departamento de Loreto.* 18 vols. Lima: Imprenta La Opinión Nacional.

Lehnertz, J. F. 1970. Cultural struggle on the Peruvian frontier: Campa-Franciscan confrontations, 1595-1752. Master's thesis, University of Wisconsin, Madison.

Lésevic, B. 1984. Dinámica demográfica y colonización en la selva alta peruana. In *Población y colonización en la alta amazonía peruana,* edited by C. E. Aramburú and C. Mora. Lima: Consejo Nacional de Población/Centro de Investigación y Promoción Amazónica.

Loayza, F. A. 1942. *Juan Santos el invencible: Manuscritos del año 1742 al año 1755.* Lima: Editorial D. Miranda.

Maletta, H. 1984. *Los requerimientos de mano de obra en la agricultura peruana.* Lima: Centro de Investigación de la Universidad del Pacífico.

————. 1990. El arte de contar ovejas: Intensidad del pastoreo en la ganadería altoandina. *Debate Agrario* 8.

Maletta, H., and A. Bardales. n.d. *Fuerza laboral y empleo.* Vol. 2 of *Perú: Las provincias en cifras, 1876-1981.* Lima: Asociación Multidisciplinaria de Investigación y Docencia en Población/Universidad del Pacífico.

————. n.d. *Población y migraciones.* Vol. 1 of *Perú: Las provincias en cifras, 1876-1981.* Lima: Asociación Multidisciplinaria de Investigación y Docencia en Población/Universidad del Pacífico.

Maletta, H., and K. Makhlouf. n.d. *Estructura agraria.* Vol. 3 of *Perú: Las provincias en cifras, 1876-1981.* Lima: Asociación Multidisciplinaria de Investigación y Docencia en Población/Universidad del Pacífico.

Malleux, J. 1975. *Mapa forestal del Perú; Memoria explicativa del mapa forestal.* Lima: Universidad Nacional Agraria.

————. 1981. Evaluación del potencial forestal del área de influencia del proyecto de carreteras para la Selva Central. Lima: Ministerio de Transportes y Comunicaciones. Typescript.

Manrique, M. n.d. *La Peruvian Corporation en la selva central del Perú.* Documento no. 3. Lima: Centro de Investigación y Promoción Amazónica.

Manrique, N. 1987. *Mercado interno y región: La sierra central 1820-1930.* Lima: DESCO.

Maskrey, A., J. Rojas, and T. Pinedo. 1991. *Raíces y bosques: San Martín modelo para armar.* Lima: Instituto de Tecnología Intermedia.

Masson Meiss, L. 1981. La dimensión ambiental en el proceso de deterioro de los recursos naturales de la selva peruana: El caso de la selva alta. *Boletín de Lima* 12: 44-54.

Matrícula. 1897. *Matrícula de la contribución de patentes, rústica, urbana, sobre la renta del capital movible y eclesiástica del departamento de Junín.* Edición Oficial. Lima: Imprenta Torres Aguirre.

Mayer, E. 1971. Diagnóstico social y cultural de las comunidades Campa del Río Ene-Apurímac. Lima: Pontificia Universidad Católica del Perú. Mimeographed.

Memoria Administrativa. 1888. *Memoria administrativa del Prefecto del departamento de Junín.* Tarma.

Ministerio de Agricultura. 1963-1988. Anuarios estadísticos. Lima.

————. 1976. Programa integral de desarrollo del Palcazu-Pichis. Lima. Mimeographed.

————. 1988. Listado de Propiedad Asociativa. Departamento de Junín. Lima. Typescript.

Ministerio de Educación. 1959. *Los selvícolas en marcha.* Lima.

Ministerio de Hacienda. 1910. *Matrícula de Contribuyentes 1908-1912: Provincia de Tarma, Departamento de Junín.* Lima: Talleres Tipográficos de "La Revista."

Ministerio de Industria. 1980. Estudio de la situación industrial y artesanal de la provincia de Oxapampa. Oxapampa. Mimeographed.

———. 1989. Padrón industrial de la provincia de Oxapampa, 1986 y 1989. Oxapampa. Mimeographed.

Ministerio de la Presidencia. 1989. Documento de transferencia a la Región VII Andrés Avelino Cáceres: Componente Catastro y Titulación 1982-1988. Iscozacín: Proyecto Especial Pichis-Palcazu. Manuscript.

Montoya, R. 1980. *Capitalismo y no capitalismo en el Perú: Un estudio histórico de su articulación en un eje regional.* Lima: Mosca Azul Editores.

Mori Caro, F. 1982. Evaluación de la situación agropecuaria del distrito de Villa Rica. La Merced: Proyecto Especial Pichis-Palcazu. Mimeographed.

Narby, J. 1986. El Banco Agrario y las comunidades ashánica del Pichis: Crédito promocional para productores nativos. *Amazonía Indígena* 6 (12): 14-21.

———. 1989. Vision of land: The Ashaninca and resource development in the Pichis Valley in Peru's central jungle. Ph.D. diss., Department of Anthropology, Stanford University, Stanford, Calif.

Narby, J., and S. Swenson. 1985. Poco a poco cual si fuera un tornillo: El Programa de Integración Indígena del Pichis. *Amazonia Indígena* 5 (10): 17-26.

OEA (Organización de Estados Americanos). 1961. *Integración económica y social del Perú Central.* 3 vols. Washington, D.C.: Organización de Estados Americanos/Unión Panamericana.

ONEC (Oficina Nacional de Estadística y Censos). 1970. *Anuario estadístico del Perú, 1969.* Vol. 28. Lima.

ONERN (Oficina Nacional de Evaluación de Recursos Naturales). 1963. *Evaluación e integración del potencial económico y social de la zona Perené-Satipo-Ene.* 2 vols. Lima.

———. 1970. *Inventario, evaluación e integración de los recursos naturales de la zona Villa Rica-Puerto Pachitea (Ríos Pichis y Palcazu).* Lima.

———. 1982. *Clasificación de tierras del Perú.* Lima.

ONERN/PEPP (Oficina Nacional de Evaluación de Recursos Naturales/Proyecto Especial Pichis-Palcazu). 1988. *Monitoreo medioambiental del valle del Río Pichis.* Report no. 2. Lima.

Ordóñez, L. 1985. *El valle del Ene.* Lima: Amaru Editores.

Ortiz, D. (OFM). 1961. *Reseña histórica de la montaña del Satipo, Pangoa, Gran Pajonal.* Lima: Imprenta Editorial San Antonio.

———. 1967. *Oxapampa: Visión histórica y desarrollo de la provincia de Oxapampa en el departamento de Pasco.* 2 vols. Lima: Imprenta Editorial San Antonio.

———. 1969. *Chanchamayo: Una región de la selva del Perú.* 2 vols. Lima: Imprenta y Litografía Salesiana.

———. 1978. *El Perené: Reseña histórica de una importante región de la selva peruana.* Lima: Imprenta Editorial San Antonio.

———. 1979. *Monografía del Vicariato de San Ramón.* Lima: Gráfica 30.

Page, T. 1990. Sustainability and the problem of valuation. In *Ecological economics: The* science and management of sustainability, edited by R. Constanza. New York: Columbia University Press.

PDR (Programa de Desarrollo Rural) Chanchamayo-Satipo. 1984-1987. *Parcelas linderadas: Sector Kivinaki.* San Ramón.

———. 1987. Padrón de catastro rural: Sector Kivinaki. San Ramón. Computer printout.

———. 1988. Resumen de metas. Componente 140040: Desarrollo forestal. San Ramón. Mimeographed.

PEPP (Proyecto Especial Pichis-Palcazu). 1983. Informe de avance de titulación. La Merced. Typescript.

———. 1986. Directorio de comunidades nativas de la selva central. La Merced. Mimeographed.

———. 1987. Directorio de comunidades nativas. La Merced. Mimeographed.

———. 1989. Informe de ejecución. La Merced. Typescript.

Pineda, V. 1982. *Apuntes sobre la caracterización de la provincia de Chanchamayo del departamento de Junín.* Documento de Trabajo no. 22. Lima: Programa de Desarrollo Rural Integrado.

Pino Zambrano, V. 1985. La amazonía peruana. In *Bosques tropicales húmedos: La situación mundial y la amazonía peruana,* edited by C. Caufield and V. Pino Zambrano. Cusco: Centro de Estudios Rurales Andinos Bartolomé de las Casas.

Pool, D. 1981. Agricultural potential and natural resources management of the Palcazu Valley, Peru. In *Central Selva Natural Resources Management Project,* edited by JRB Associates. Vol. 2. Lima: U.S. Agency for International Development.

PRONAC (Programa Nacional de Catastro). 1990. Cuadros consolidados del Proyecto Satipo-Chanchamayo. Lima: Ministerio de Agricultura. Computer tables.

Raimondi, A. 1879. *El Perú.* Vol. 3. Lima: Imprenta del Estado.

———. 1942. *Notas de viajes para su obra El Perú.* Vol. 1. Lima: Imprenta Torres Aguirre.

Raymond, D. 1977. Pause-café. Berne: Service Ecole Tiers Monde. Mimeographed.

Recharte, J. n.d. Prosperidad y pobreza en la agricultura de la ceja de selva: El valle de Chanchamayo. In *Colonización en la amazonía,* edited by C. E. Aramburú, E. Bedoya, and J. Recharte. Lima: Centro de Investigación y Promoción Amazónica.

Reforma Agraria. n.d. Expedientes de afectación de las haciendas de Chanchamayo. Archivo de la Dirección Nacional de Reforma Agraria. Lima. Typescript.

Renard-Casevitz, F.-M., A. C. Taylor, and T. Saignes. 1988. *Al este de los Andes.* 2 vols. Quito: Instituto Francés de Estudios Andinos/Abya-Yala.

República del Perú. n.d. *Censo nacional de población de 1940: Departamentos Huánuco y Junín.* Vol. 4. Lima.

———. 1972. *Censos nacionales de población, vivienda y agropecuario, 1961.* Lima: Instituto Nacional de Estadística y Censos.

———. 1985. *Censos nacionales VIII de población y III de vivienda, 1981.* Lima: Instituto Nacional de Estadística.

Ribeiro, D., and M. R. Wise. 1978. *Los grupos étnicos de la amazonía peruana.* Serie Comunidades y Culturas Peruanas no. 3. Lima: Instituto Lingüístico de Verano.

Ricse Tembladera, A. 1987. Desarrollo y limitaciones de la reforestación en selva central. In *Avances de la silvicultura en la amazonía peruana.* Lima: Apoyo a la Política de Desarrollo de Selva Alta.

Rivadeneira Cotera, V. H. 1986. Levantamiento situacional: Perspectiva de desarrollo agroindustrial de la selva central. Comité Multisectorial de Desarrollo de Selva Central. San Ramón: Ministerio de la Presidencia/Instituto Nacional de Desarrollo. Mimeographed.

Rizo Patrón, A. 1983. Actualidad del Plan Peru-vía. In *Desarrollo de la selva alta,* edited by C. Zuzunaga. Lima: Centro Peruano de Investigación Aplicada.

Rodríguez, D. 1990. Análisis de los procesos de cambio en las estrategias productivas de las comunidades campa de Satipo. In *Perú: El problema agrario en debate. SEPIA III,* edited by A. Chirif, N. Manrique, and B. Quijandría. Lima: Seminario Permanente de Investigación Agraria/Centro de Estudios Rurales Andinos Bartolomé de las Casas.

Rodríguez del Aguila, L. 1985. Información básica sobre la extracción forestal en Chanchamayo-Satipo. División de Forestal y Fauna, Región Agraria 16. Huancayo. Mimeographed.

Rodríguez Tena, F. 1780. Misiones apostólicas de la Santa Provincia de los doce Apóstoles de Lima del Orden de N.P. San Francisco. Vol. 2. Archivo del Convento de Santa Rosa de Ocopa. Manuscript.

Rumrrill, R., and P. de Zutter. 1976. *Los condenados de la selva.* Lima: Editorial Horizonte.

Salazar, A. 1984. Los Proyectos Especiales de Desarrollo en la selva alta. In *Población y colonización en la amazonía peruana,* edited by C. E. Aramburú and C. Mora. Lima: Consejo Nacional de Población/Centro de Investigación y Promoción Amazónica.

Salick, J. n.d. Ethnobotany of the Amuesha Palcazu Valley, Peru. New York: Institute of Economic Botany. Mimeographed.

———. 1989. Bases ecológicas de los sistemas agrícolas amuesha. *Amazonía Indígena* 9 (15): 3–16.

San Antonio, J. (OFM). 1750. *Colección de informes sobre las misiones del Colegio de Santa Rosa de Ocopa.* Madrid.

San Joseph, Fernando de (OFM). 1721. Carta a Fray Pedro Ortiz, Sonomoro, 27 de febrero. Lima 541, Archivo General de Indias, Seville. Manuscript.

San Joseph, Francisco de (OFM). 1732. Carta al Procurador General Fray Francisco Seco, Santa Rosa de Ocopa, 30 de noviembre. Lima 537, Archivo General de Indias, Seville. Manuscript.

Santa y Ortega, Alfonso. 1747. Carta del Capitán Santa y Ortega, Corregidor de Tarma, a su hermano Fray Juan de Yecla Santa, Tarma, 30 de mayo. Lima 983, Archivo General de Indias, Seville. Manuscript.

Santos-Granero, F. 1980. Vientos de un pueblo. Síntesis histórica de la etnía Amuesha, siglos XVII-XIX. Licentiate thesis, Department of Anthropology, Pontificia Universidad Católica del Perú, Lima.

———. 1985. Crónica breve de un etnocidio o la génesis del mito del "gran vacío amazónico." *Amazonía Peruana* 6 (11): 9–38.

————. 1986. Bohórquez y la conquista espúrea del Cerro de la Sal: Tres versiones y una historia. *Amazonía Peruana* 7 (13): 119-134.

————. 1987. Epidemias y sublevaciones en el desarrollo demográfico de las misiones amuesha del Cerro de la Sal, s. XVIII. *Histórica* 11 (1): 25-53.

————. 1988. Templos y herrerías: Utopía y recreación cultural en la amazonía peruana. *Boletín del Instituto Francés de Estudios Andinos* 17 (2): 1-22.

————. 1991a. Frentes económicos, espacios regionales y fronteras capitalistas en la amazonía. In *Amazonía 1940-1990. El extravío de una ilusión,* edited by F. Barclay, M. Rodríguez, F. Santos-Granero, and M. Valcárcel. Lima: Centro de Investigaciones Sociológicas, Económicas, Políticas y Antropológicas/Terra Nuova.

————. 1991b. *The power of love: The moral use of knowledge amongst the Amuesha of central Peru.* London: Athlone Press.

————. 1992. *Etnohistoria de la alta amazonía: Siglos XV-XVIII.* Quito: Abya-Yala.

Schrewe, H. 1981. La industria del aserrío en el Perú. Proyecto PNUD/FAO/PER/78/003-Mejoramiento de los sistemas de extracción y transformación forestal. Lima: U.N. Food and Agriculture Organization/Ministerio de Agricultura. Mimeographed.

Shoemaker, R. 1981. *Peasants of El Dorado: Conflict and contradiction in a Peruvian frontier settlement.* Ithaca: Cornell University Press.

Silva Santisteban, F. 1964. *Los obrajes en el virreynato del Perú.* Lima.

SINAMOS (Sistema Nacional de Movilización Social). 1975. Comunidades nativas selva central: Diagnóstico socio-económico. Lima. Mimeographed.

SIPA (Servicio Interamericano de Promoción Agrícola). 1967. Problemática agropecuaria de la región de Satipo y posibles soluciones: Informe de la Comisión Técnica sobre su visita a la zona de Satipo. Lima. Mimeographed.

Smith, R. 1969. La conferencia de líderes Amuesha. *Kiario* (Boletín del Instituto Raúl Porras Barrenechea) 1.

————. 1974. Los Amuesha: Una minoría amenazada. *Participación* 3 (5): 54-62.

————. 1976. Deliverance from chaos for a song: Preliminary discussion of Amuesha music. Ph.D. diss., Department of Anthropology, Cornell University, Ithaca, N.Y.

————. 1983. *Las comunidades nativas y el mito del gran vacío amazónico: Un análisis de la planificación para el desarrollo en el PEPP.* Lima: Asociación Interétnica de Desarrollo de la Selva Peruana.

————. 1984. A search for unity within diversity. *Cultural Survival Quarterly* 8 (4): 6-13.

Staver, C. 1981. Animal production systems in the Palcazu Valley and means for their expansion and intensification. In *Central Selva Natural Resources Management Project,* edited by JRB Associates. Vol. 2. Lima: U.S. Agency for International Development.

Swenson, S. 1986a. Producción y comercialización agrícola en las comunidades nativas del valle del Perené. La Merced: Central de Comunidades Nativas de la Selva Central. Manuscript.

————. 1986b. El impacto de la agricultura comercial en las comunidades nativas del Perené. *Amazonía Indígena* 6 (12): 3-13.

Tello, L. 1981. El mito del "gran vacío": Los valles Palcazu y Pichis. *Amazonía Indígena* 1 (3): 24-31.

Tibesar, A. S. 1950. The salt trade among the Montaña Indians of the Tarma area of eastern Peru. *Primitive Man* 23: 103-109.

————. 1952. San Antonio de Eneno: A mission in the Peruvian Montaña. *Primitive Man* 25: 23-39.

Torre, C. de la. 1985. *Estadística agraria en el Perú: Una guía para el investigador.* Lima: Fomento a las Ciencias Sociales.

Tosi, J. 1960. *Zonas de vida natural en el Perú.* San José: Instituto Interamericano de Ciencias Agrícolas.

Trujillo Mena, V. 1981. *La legislación eclesiástica en el Virreynato del Perú durante el siglo XVI.* Lima: Imprenta Editorial Lumea.

UNA (Universidad Nacional Agraria). 1982. Evaluación e inventario forestal de los recursos forestales de La Merced-Satipo. Lima: Universidad Nacional Agraria. Mimeographed.

Urrutia, J. R. 1808. Informe del Intendente Urrutia sobre las ventajas que resultan de la apertura del camino y comunicación por el Chanchamayo presentado al Virrey del Perú en 1808. Reprinted in Ortiz, D. 1978. *El Perené: Reseña histórica de una importante región de la selva peruana.* Lima: Imprenta Editorial San Antonio.

Varallanos, J. 1959. *Historia de Huánuco: De la era prehistórica a nuestros días.* Buenos Aires: Imprenta López.

Varese, S. 1973. *La sal de los cerros: Una aproximación al mundo Campa.* Lima: Editorial Retablo de Papel.

————. 1974. La selva: Viejas fronteras, nuevas alternativas. *Participación* 3 (5): 18-31.

Villagarcía, Marqués de. 1742. Carta del Virrey Villagarcía a S. Magestad, Lima, 7 de agosto. Lima 983, Archivo General de Indias, Seville. Manuscript.

————. 1744. Informe del Virrey Villagarcía a S. Magestad, Lima, 16 de agosto. Lima 983, Archivo General de Indias, Seville. Manuscript.

————. 1746. Quaderno de la Recidencia del Exmo. Señor Marquez de Villagarcía, Pieza Quinta. Escribanía 557c, Archivo General de Indias, Seville. Manuscript.

Villasante, M. 1983. Impacto del sistema de habilitación y enganche en la organización comunal y familiar de Betania, comunidad nativa Campa-Asháninca, Río Tambo. Licentiate thesis, Department of Anthropology, Pontificia Universidad Católica del Perú, Lima.

Watson, E. 1964. *Comercio y tendencias del mercado en los productos de la región de la selva peruana.* Lima: Universidad Nacional Agraria.

————. 1985. Estudio de evaluación de los Proyectos Pichis y Palcazu. Lima: Instituto Nacional de Desarrollo. Manuscript.

Watters, R. F. 1971. *La agricultura migratoria en América Latina.* Cuadernos de Fomento Forestal no. 17. Rome: Food and Agriculture Organization.

Wilson, F. 1979. Propiedad e ideología: Estudio de una oligarquía en los Andes centrales (s. XIX). *Análisis* 8-9: 36-54.

World Bank. 1982. Chanchamayo-Satipo Rural Development Project. Native Communities. Preparation Mission, April-May. Mimeographed.

—————. 1983. Draft report of the Peru Chanchamayo-Satipo Rural Development Project. Preparation Mission. Washington, D.C.: Food and Agriculture Organization/ World Bank. Mimeographed.

Zarzar, A. 1989. *Apo Capac Huayna Jesús Sacramentado: Mito, utopía y milenarismo en el pensamiento de Juan Santos Atahuallpa.* Lima: Centro Amazónico de Antropología y Aplicación Práctica.

INDEX

Page numbers followed by **t** refer to tables and those followed by *m* or *f* refer to maps or figures.

Alvarado, Velasco (president, Peru), 237
Alvarado government: agrarian reforms, 72,
77, 85; creation of SINAMOS to promote native communities, 243; promotion of native
grassroots organizations, 281, 283
Alvarez, E., 167–168, 169t
Amazonia, Peruvian, early Spanish settlements,
15–16
Amazonian region, studies of regional economic areas, 7–8
Amazon River, river connections to as way to
the Atlantic, 45, 49
ANAP (Apatzahuantzi Nampitzi Ashaninka Pichis), 291–292
Andean peoples: and Amazonian neighbors,
15; as colonists in Selva Central, 77–78, 80,
83, 96, 97t, 305, 314; as migrant labor, 49–50
annatto cultivation, 284, 291
annual crops, in the Selva Central, 188–189,
190
appropriation, as occupation of space, 12–13
Arabic coffee varieties, 111
Aramburú and Bedoya formula, of land-use intensity, 193–202, 304
armed force: use by Peruvian Corporation
against land squatters, 68; use in missionary
era as control factor, 26, 29–30
army, Ashaninka, self-defense units, 292, 294,
298
Army, Peruvian, 299; attitude towards self-defense units, 311–312; support by natives
against guerrillas, 288, 298
articulation, internal, in the Selva Central, 18–
20, 90–97, 301–306
Ashaninka (indigenous people), 15, 20–21, 28,
67, 278
    agriculture: commercial holdings, 276–
    277; as cultivators in Kivinaki zone,
    216–217, 224; effect of coffee econ-
    omy, 60–62
    contemporary organizations, 281, 282,
    283, 286; in the Ene Valley, 293–295; in
    the Pichis Valley, 290–292; in Satipo,
    287–290; in the Tambo Valley, 292–
    293; in the upper Perené Valley, 282–
    284
    enforced removal for colonist settle-
    ments, 43–44
    formation of self-defense army, 292, 294,
    298
    geographic locations, 231–232, 232t,
    233m, 241

identification with Selva Central, 307
    as labor, 51, 255–256, 260
    land distributions, 235–238, 247–248; plot
    sizes, 261–262
    reaction to Calderón's murder, 97, 291,
    292, 298, 310
    relations with Túpac Amaru Revolution-
    ary Movement, 292, 310–311
    See also indigenous peoples; Nomatsigu-
    enga
Asociación de Comunidades Nativas Asháninca
del Pichis (ACONAP), 291
Asociación de Nativos Campas del Perené
(Perené Indigenous Campa Association),
282–283
Aucayacu zone (upper Huallaga Valley), land-
use intensity, 193–194
avocado cultivation, 71, 119

Bajo Chirani community (Kivinaki zone), aver-
age family holdings, 218
Balarín family (sawmill owners), 144, 146, 147
Balarín Gustavson brothers, 146
Baldini, Carlos, 72
banana cultivation, 121
Banco Agrario, 88, 89t, 90t, 94–95, 303; with-
drawal of offices due to terrorist violence in
Selva Central, 310
Banco de Fomento Agropecuario (later Banco
Agrario), loans by, 76–77, 87–88, 92
barbasco (Lonchocarpus nicou), cultivation in
Satipo, 60, 92, 108
Barclay, Frederica, 1, 236
Bedoya, E., Aramburú and Bedoya formula,
193–202, 304
beef: marketing outlets for indigenous cattle-
men, 271, 274; yield per hectare, 192
Belaúnde government: agrarian-reform move-
ment, 77, 84; crisis effect on timber industry,
135–136; road construction, 83
Belaúnde Terry, Fernando (president, Peru), 84,
87, 245, 308
Bermúdez, Francisco Morales (president,
Peru), 134
Bermúdez government, land titles to indige-
nous peoples, 244–245
Bernard Lelong Fund, 2
berry borer (Hypothenemus hampei), effect on
coffee plants, 108, 120
Betania (Pichis Valley), as Ashaninka settlement on the Tambo River, 241
Biedma, Father Manuel, 20, 28, 30

state, the (Peru) (continued)
Central, 154, 163, 165, 171, 320n. 5; attempts
to integrate indigenous peoples, 279–280,
295–300; lands granted for missionary activities, 234; loans to coffee producers, 117; and
multiplication of *minifundios*, 179–181; promotion of annual food crops, 188; and terrorist activity in Selva Central, 310, 314. *See
also* military, republican
subsistence economy: among indigenous peoples, 232, 275, 277, 304; shift to commercial
agriculture, 193
sugarcane economy: abandonment of large-
scale production, 71; costs affecting pricing
of *aguardiente*, 42; mechanization by immigrants, 46; during the missionary era, 23–
24; replacement by coffee economy, 51–62,
189
Summer Institute of Linguistics, 239, 285
Supreme Decree 03 (1957), effect on indigenous landholdings, 85, 236–238, 285, 291
Swenson, S., 219, 263, 276

Tambo River, humid subtropical forest formation on left bank, 205
Tambo Valley: Ashaninka organizational movements, 292–293; indigenous commercial agriculture, 262; indigenous labor in logging,
255–256; native migrations to, 247
tangerines, 120
Tarma (highland city), 2, 4, 13, 302; as early
Dominican headquarters, 19; effect of Juan
Santos rebellion, 31; effect of 1879 war with
Chile, 54–55; efforts to restrict immigrant
land tenure in Chanchamayo Valley, 46; as
Inca storage center, 16; influence in road
routing, 62–63, 64–65; position to take advantage of reopening of Selva Central, 42–43; rivalry with Huánuco, 40–42
Tarma-Chanchamayo road, 91
tax revenues, on alcohol production, 54, 55
Tealdo family (venture coffee capitalists), 58
Tello, L., 207
Tello de Sotomayor, Don Fernando, 17
temples, indigenous, association with forges
during recovery period, 35
terraces, alluvial *(pampas)*, in the Selva Central,
206
territory, indigenous, recovery during 1742–
1847 period, 31–37
terrorists, 6; effect on fruit cultivation economy, 124, 125–126; effect on Selva Central's

internal articulation, 308–312, 309t; effect on
timber industry, 134, 135–136; guerrilla
movements in Selva Central, 78, 84, 94, 288.
See also Shining Path; Túpac Amaru Revolutionary Movement
textiles, importance in missionary-era economy, 20, 24, 25
timber industry, 49, 126–147; deforestation of
Kivinaki zone, 216–217; dialectical relationship with agropastural activity, 147–152, 305;
environmental impact of logging, 208–215;
as forerunner for agropastural fronts, 103–
104; intensified logging operations, results
of, 5, 133, 134, 136; production costs, 137,
139–140, 140t; sawnwood production, 127,
128–129, 130t, 136, 137t, 138–139f, 149t;
seen as nomadic activity, 135–147; terrorist
violence, 134, 135–136, 310; use of indigenous labor, 252, 255–257. *See also* road(s);
sawmills
Tingo María zone (upper Huallaga Valley),
land-use intensity, 193–194
tobacco holdings, during missionary era, 23
Tocache-Uchiza zone (upper Huallaga Valley),
land-use intensity, 193–194
tools, iron: mission towns as distribution centers, 26, 27–28; production by indigenous
peoples, 35, 36m, 37, 43–44
toro urco (Panicum pilosum), as cattle forage
crop, 273
Tosi, Joseph, 204–205
towns, in the Selva Central, 64–65, 65t
transportation: of cattle, 64, 164, 262; of coffee
to Lima, 106, 108, 114; importance in fruit
cultivation, 123, 124; means of and rural
densities, 177–178; routes through Chanchamayo, 302; sugarcane, 54; of timber products over land, 127; via airplanes, 76, 262,
283. *See also* road(s)
Tulumayo Valley, fort established, 39
Túpac Amaru, anticolonial uprising, 39
Túpac Amaru Revolutionary Movement
(Movimiento Revolucionario Túpac Amaru):
activities in Selva Central, 6, 95, 97, 126,
301; expulsion from Pichis Valley by Ashaninka, 292, 310–311; forced involvement of
indigenous peoples, 292

Ubiare (Ashaninka leader), 241
ulcumano (Podocarpus utilios), as logged tree species, 129, 131
Universalis ecclesiae (1508, papal bull), 18

Ty Q. → how to integrate specfic accounts
use the pgpU(1) for the?

Naming ....